THE STATE, INDUSTRIAL RELATIONS AND THE LABOUR MOVEMENT IN LATIN AMERICA, Volume 1

The State, Industrial Relations and the Labour Movement in Latin America

VOLUME 1

Edited by
Jean Carrière
Senior Research Associate
Centre for Latin American Research and Documentation
Amsterdam

Nigel Haworth
Senior Lecturer in Business
University of Auckland

and

Jacqueline Roddick
Research Fellow
Institute of Latin American Studies
University of Glasgow

St. Martin's Press New York

Scholarly and Reference Division,
St. Martin's Press, Inc., 175 Fifth Avenue, New York, NY 10010

First published in the United States of America in 1989

Printed in Hong Kong

Library of Congress Cataloging-in-Publication Data
The State, industrial relations, and the labour movement
in Latin America.
Bibliography: v. 1, p.
Includes index.
1. Labor and laboring classes–Latin America.
2. Trade-unions–Latin America. 3. Industry and state–
Latin America. I. Carrière, Jean, 1939– .
II. Haworth, Nigel. III. Roddick, Jacqueline.
HD8110.5.S69 1989 322'.2'098 88–31975
ISBN 0–312–02772–9 (v. 1)

Contents

Notes on the Contributors

Jean Carrière is Associate Professor of Latin American Politics at the Interuniversity Centre for Latin American Research and Documentation (CEDLA), in Amsterdam. His research focuses on popular organisations and democratisation in Central America.

Nigel Haworth is Senior Lecturer in the Department of Management Studies and Labour Relations at the University of Auckland, New Zealand. Following two years of field research among modern sector workers in the Antiplano, he has written extensively on the Peruvian labour movement. More recent research on Chile has followed. Dr. Haworth is also well known for his work on labour relations in multinational corporations in the UK.

Andrew Nickson is a lecturer in the Department of Development Administration, University of Birmingham, England. His research interests include rural colonisation, Latin American development strategies, and Paraguayan history and politics on which he has published widely.

Nico van Niekerk contributed to the chapter on the Bolivian labour movement when he was a graduate student at the Interuniversity Centre for Latin American Research and Documentation (CEDLA), in Amsterdam.

Charles Nurse obtained an M.Phil. at the Institute of Latin American Studies in Glasgow with a thesis on Ecuador. Since then he has taught in Leon in Nicaragua.

Daniel Pécaut is Director of Studies, Ecole des Hautes Etudes en Sciences Sociales, in Paris. He is the author of several works on Colombian history and politics including *L'ordre et la violence: évolution socio-politique de la Colombie entre 1930 and 1953* (Paris: Editions de l'EHESS, 1987).

Jackie Roddick is a Research Fellow at the Institute of Latin American Studies at the University of Glasgow, and co-author of *Chile, the State and Revolution* (London: Macmillan, 1977) and *Chile: The Pinochet Decade* (London: Latin American Bureau, 1983), as well as a widely used handbook – *The Dance of the Millions* – on the Latin American debt crisis (London: Latin American Bureau, 1988).

Preface

This is the first volume of what is to become a four-volume collection on labour movements and industrial relations systems in Latin America. The first three volumes are structured on a country-by-country basis, with each chapter discussing the history, structure and organisation of the labour movement in a particular country, as well as the rules governing the system of industrial relations and the role of the State in enforcing these rules. The present volume covers the five Andean countries (Chile, Peru, Bolivia, Ecuador and Colombia) as well as Paraguay. Volume II will include the three nations with the largest industrial sectors – Argentina, Brazil and Mexico – plus Uruguay and Venezuela. The Central American and Caribbean countries will form the subject of Volume III. Finally, Volume IV is designed to make connections among processes affecting the region as a whole and will contain comparative analyses of class formation, the process of proletarianisation, collective bargaining, women and labour, and the role of the State, of multinational corporations and of international labour confederations in relation to the Latin American labour movement.

It is the hope of the editors that the broad historical and geographical scope of this collection and the emphasis on structural changes and empirical reliability will ensure that it will be regarded as a useful, possibly a major reference work on the first century of workers' collective struggles in a part of the world characterised by deep economic inequalities and sharply defined class differences.

We would like to thank the Interuniversity Centre for Latin American Research and Documentation, Amsterdam, the Department of Industrial Relations of the University of Strathclyde, Glasgow, and the Institute of Latin American Studies of the University of Glasgow for their generous support. A special word of thanks is also due to Jean Monaghan, Debbie Campbell and Rita Weston for their unstinting help in typing the draft chapters. Finally, we are most grateful for the financial support provided by the Netherlands Foundation for Tropical Research for administrative and research assistance.

The editors

List of Tables

1 Introduction: Proletarianisation, Industrialisation and Patterns of Action

Jean Carrière, Nigel Haworth and Jacqueline Roddick

THE LIMITS OF PROLETARIANISATION

After the Second World War, with industrialisation proceeding in virtually all Latin America's bigger countries, and governments', workers', and academics' expectations strongly coloured by their belief that underdeveloped countries would follow the same stages of development as the industrialised West,[1] social scientists accepted without question that for Latin America, the future held an inexorable process of proletarianisation along Western lines. A 'modern' economy was seen to be establishing itself in the region's urban areas, inexorably pushing back the remnants of the 'traditional economy' of rural peasants and urban artesans. Agriculture, the dominant employer in the traditional economy, was becoming less and less important as countries urbanised and manufacturing for local consumption became more important. At some point, the dual economy which social scientists could observe throughout the region would disappear, leaving the modern capitalist sector to stand alone.

Doubts about the possibility that industrialisation would eliminate this dual economy were first raised in Latin America towards the end of the 1950s, when Fr. Vekemans at DESAL introduced the term 'marginals' to cover those in the slums and the informal economy who were not being reached by Western models of development.[2] In the debt- and depression-ridden context of the 1980s, they seem to have been confirmed. Manufacturing, the heart of the 'modern economy', has ceased to be a plausible source of future wage jobs for a growing population. Modern styles of export sector production, whether in agriculture or in mining, have become more capital-intensive and less labour-absorbing as the century has worn on. Employment in commerce and services has boomed, but at very low levels of productivity. Virtually everywhere, governments have become preoccupied with the swollen size of an urban informal sector of petty producers and traders of low productivity, and an unregulated and unregulatable 'black economy', of which they are one of the principal manifestations.

Statistics on the post-war experience confirm this picture. As Table 1.2 shows, the proportion of the Latin American labour force employed outside agriculture has risen consistently since 1950 virtually everywhere: but so too has the proportional importance of the urban 'informal sector' (here defined as the self-employed or unpaid family labour) compared to that of urban wage earners. These figures are difficult to reconcile with traditional conceptions of the process of proletarianisation. In some countries, such as Brazil, perhaps one could argue that what is happening is merely a further stage in the detachment of the rural labour force from the land and its transformation into 'free labour' for industry through an apprenticeship in self-employment and small trades. But this argument can hardly be sustained in the case of Chile and Argentina, previously at the forefront of urbanisation and industrialisation in the region. Here one could argue that we are witnessing a deproletarianisation of the urban labour force, which more recent figures suggest has intensified alongside the economic crises of the 1980s: the falling percentage of the population employed in manufacturing and the swollen numbers employed in services certainly suggest some such process. Perhaps the comparative failure of industrial development in the Southern Cone has something to do with it, compared, for instance, to Brazil's superior performance? Perhaps. Even so, for all Argentina's relative economic weakness, its working class is still proportionally larger than that of Brazil, as Table 1.1 shows.

Explanations of the growth of the urban informal sector vary from the locally contingent to the theoretically profound. In Chile and Argentina, rising numbers of artisans and small producers in the decade between 1970 and 1980 have been explained by opponents of their governments' 'free market' policies, as an aberration produced by government decisions which were simply wrong. In Peru, a professional economist at the opposite end of the political spectrum has hailed the growth of the informal sector as a victory for the free market over bureaucratically-inspired monopolies.[3] Experts from the

TABLE 1.1 *Labour Force in Selected* Sectors of Latin America as Percentage of Total Labour Force 1950–80*

	Agriculture %	*Manufacturing* %	*Commerce* %	*Services* %
ARGENTINA				
1950	27.5	24.5	13.6	22.0
1960	21.8	27.1	13.2	22.3
1970	17.9	23.5	17.6	23.6
1980	15.2	21.0	18.3	28.8
CHILE				
1950	34.8	19.0	10.3	22.0
1960	31.5	18.0	10.1	22.7
1970	24.1	15.9	11.6	27.2
1980	16.8	15.6	19.2	34.7
BRAZIL				
1950	59.9	9.4	5.5	15.7
1960	54.0	8.6	6.5	19.8
1970	44.3	11.0	7.6	22.4
1980	29.3	16.0	9.3	27.1

* Percentages do not sum to 100 due to the omission of such sectors as mining, construction, electricity and public utilities.
SOURCES: Argentina, PREALC figures: Chile, various Censuses (see Roddick, Appendix Table 3): Brazil *Anuario Estatistica 1984.*

Employment Programme for Latin America and the Caribbean (PREALC) have suggested that the comparative stability of the urban informal sector in Latin America (compared, say, with its rapid decline at a comparable stage in the economic development of the USA) can be explained by the fact that, job for job, more investment is required in the contemporary modern industrial or service sector than was the case at any similar stage in the economic evolution of the USA: conclusions very similar to the original position set out by Anibal Quijano in his own historic contribution to early theories of the 'marginals'.[4] The debate on Quijano's position has produced a handful of attempts to rebut his second conclusion, that Marx's predictions about the development of the capitalist economy as a whole have been invalidated by the emergence of this 'marginal' labour force, and many more studies pointing out the significant role played by the informal sector in local processes of capital accumulation.[5] If there is a new orthodoxy, it is one based on the wholesale rejection of traditional Marxist *and* modernisation versions of the 'dual economy'.

In the field of politics, this heterogeneous social context was

TABLE 1.2 *Traditional Rural and Urban Informal Sectors as a Percentage of the Labour Force in Latin America, 1950 and 1980*

	Non-agricultural labour as % total labour force	*Traditional rural as % labour force*	*Urban informal as % labour force*
ARGENTINA*			
1950	72.0	7.6	15.2
1980	84.9	6.8	21.4
URUGUAY			
1950	77.8	4.7	14.5
1980	82.3	8.0	19.0
VENEZUELA			
1950	51.5	22.5	16.4
1980	79.4	12.6	18.5
CHILE			
1950	62.9	8.9	22.1
1980	77.2	7.4	21.7
COSTA RICA			
1950	42.0	20.4	12.3
1980	69.5	9.8	15.3
BRAZIL			
1950	39.2	37.6	10.7
1980	68.1	18.9	16.5
PANAMA			
1950	46.7	47.0	11.8
1980	66.4	22.0	14.8
COLOMBIA			
1950	39.2	33.0	15.3
1980	64.9	18.7	22.3
MEXICO			
1950	34.5	44.0	12.9
1980	61.5	18.4	22.0
PERU			
1950	36.0	39.4	16.9
1980	57.5	31.8	19.8
ECUADOR			
1950	33.2	39.0	11.7
1980	54.2	33.4	28.6
EL SALVADOR			
1950	32.2	35.0	13.7
1980	47.5	30.1	18.9
GUATEMALA			
1950	30.6	48.7	14.0
1980	42.7	37.8	18.9
BOLIVIA			
1950	24.1	53.7	15.0
1980	41.1	50.9	23.2

* Countries are ranked in descending order according to the size of the labour force employed outside agriculture in 1980.

SOURCE: *Beyond the Crisis* (Santiago: ILO-PREALC, 1985).

faithfully reflected in early Latin American debates on populism and mass society.[6] Studies of organised labour, however, have traditionally treated it as a 'stage' of relatively primitive development which would be superseded, ultimately, by the emergence of a European-style working class organised primarily through trade unionism – even if, in the short term, this meant a relatively privileged working class co-opted by government and employers, struggling to preserve its own benefits at the cost of a larger, poorer mass of the dispossessed. Only a small number of academic studies have concerned themselves with the political implications of permanent heterogeneity for organised labour.

Of these, the outstanding attempt to pose broader questions is Martinez' and Tironi's study of the decline of the Chilean proletariat, under the first seven years of military rule. This study takes its central thesis from André Gorz's panoptic vision of European social change in *Farewell to the Proletariat* (which predicates the decline of the traditional proletariat on the emergence, not of marginal workers struggling to survive in low-productivity activities, but of a State-supported leisure class of the unemployed.[7] Some interesting work is being produced by the enthusiastic supporters of the 'new social movements', a school which draws its vitality from the desire to side-step traditional Marxist conceptions of the role of the proletariat, inspired in equal measure by the Western Left's disillusion with classical Marxism and the focus of liberation theology not on producers but on the broader category of the poor. But the significance of such studies of social movements for organised labour as such still emerges largely as a by-product of the focus on other groups. Where the new social movements enjoy a strong *de facto* alliance with organised labour we are told about it, as in Brazil, from the point of view of those who are not members of trade unions: women involved in the Movimento do Costa da Vida, members of the radical Church involved in supporting the 1978 and 1979 strike of *metalurgicos*.[8]

Detailed historical work on the political, economic and cultural relationships between organised labour and artisans, or indeed between organised labour and the world of women, remains, alas! in its infancy; though some pioneering studies of the earliest phases of working class formation have begun to point the way.[9] As for the contemporary world, studies of workers with few exceptions[10] confine themselves to the world of work or the world of the political party. Yet we know from studies of other sectors that close relationships exist. At the very minimum, 'informal sector' trader or domestic outworker and 'formal sector' factory employee or construction worker frequently meet in the same household as man and wife – as many contemporary studies of the role of women in the informal sector have shown.[11] By the same token, they often meet in the course of a single career – as young female factory workers leave to look after a family, and turn to work as laundresses or seamstresses; or as highly paid copper miners and others at the better off end of the formal sector, put their savings towards buying a truck, and become the self-employed; or as factory workers recently made redundant turn to the informal sector in order to survive.

THE LIMITS OF A 'DUAL ECONOMY' MODEL OF ORGANISED LABOUR

It may be worth reminding ourselves that the informal sector has coexisted with modern industry and modern labour movements in Latin America for as long as these have been in existence. In the Andean countries generally, of course – the specific focus of this first volume in the Macmillan series – small-scale artisan production and trade have been consistently important since the Spanish conquest: they survived the initial challenge of imported Western technology in reduced but still significant form, adapting to new circumstances and providing sources of labour, goods and opportunities, sometimes independently and sometimes as subcontractors of the new modern firms. In Peru and Bolivia, for example, they existed in the *obraje*, the basic manufacturing unit permitted by the colonial state (specific metropolitan legislation restricted local production to small-scale units servicing the local market): independence did little to transform the consequent structure. In Chile, which together with Colombia represents the most successful experience of industrialisation in this volume, firms with fewer than ten workers accounted on any available estimate for over 45 per cent of employment in manufacturing even during the apogee of large-scale industrial development during the 1950s and 1960s.[12]

PREALC studies have demonstrated that the Andean case is only a special version of a more generalised truth. Victor Tokman has highlighted the survival of an informal economy even in manufacturing as one of the peculiarities of economic development throughout the region, compared with the historical pattern of the USA.[13] Within the urban labour markets on which large-scale enterprise has drawn, the structure of labour supply and skill profiles would have been much less amenable to the demands of modern industry without a cushion of small producers: and without this sector as a safety-net, governments would have found it less easy to manage the social costs of ECLA-style policies of industrialisation, focusing as these did on the local replication of imported technologies.

The historic roots of existing labour movements in their artisan predecessors throughout the region is also very clear, as the examples of Bolivia, Chile and Colombia in this volume show. Today's modern descendants still reflect some of their trademarks: for instance, their domination by males (since the strong female artisan population in some countries was excluded from the guilds).[14] One could trace elements in the practice of industrial relations in the region to the old *mutualista* societies' preoccupation with legalism – the guilds relied on the State to fix the rates of remuneration and conditions of labour, rather than workers' independent bargaining power – a strategy which still retains a certain logic where the existence of surplus labour weakens workers' bargaining power. Perhaps today's unions have also inherited the *mutualistas*' facility at managing political alliances and securing interested allies in Congress and elsewhere.

More significantly, modern movements in Latin America have preserved the general strikes, mass demonstrations and riots which brought artisans together with miners, transport workers and those in the region's nascent industrial sector more than 50 years ago, under the influence of anarchist and anarchosyndicalist philosophies: patterns of action which recall not so much the bargaining practices of modern British or American factory workers as those of the urban crowd in London and Paris during the 18th century, so vividly described by George Rude.[15] Yet to date, efforts to explain the continuing role of these tactics in modern labour movements have been relatively disappointing. The key work remains James Payne's account of political bargaining, focused on Peru, one of the lesser industrialised countries in the region, and resolutely fixed within an evolutionary framework which specifies that these practices are primitive and will ultimately be superseded:[16] even though very similar tactics lie behind the 1969 and 1971 explosions among Argentine car workers known as the 'Cordobazo', or the rallies practiced in 1978–79 by *metalurgicos* in Brazil, both countries already well established among the world's Newly Industrialising Countries or NICs, and thus very different from the struggling and still very traditional Peru.

THE DUAL ECONOMY IN LABOUR STUDIES: THE LABOUR ARISTOCRACY THESIS

Given the fundamental differences in environment and practice between Latin America's labour movements and those of the West, it is something of a tragedy that models for the analysis of labour movements and industrial relations in Latin America should so quickly have been imported from abroad, alongside the cars and General Motors' assembly lines favoured in ECLA's industrialisation model. Imports have always been most popular, however, when they coincide with local perceptions of the labour movement; and the popularity of analyses which assumed isolation of workers in the modern sector from the rest of Latin America's poor has to be seen in a Latin American context.

Thus, the notion that industrial workers and their managers were natural allies, exported by US and European theorists of the 'end of ideology' in the 1950s, dovetailed neatly with local theories which saw the critical role in Latin America's modernisation process as being played by a rising middle class. In this version of post-Depression political history, put forward by ECLA itself in the 1950s and taken up at the time by pioneer writers on labour (such as Gino Germani), American political scientists and the influential French sociologist Touraine, the organised working class was a relatively weak force easily co-opted by the reformist rhetoric of middle class political movements.[17] The ECLA model provides one important strand in the explanation of Latin American populism, though only one; more recent studies would also stress the dependence of populist politicians on organised labour[18] (a theme which this series will take up in Volume 2).

As it happened, critics of ECLA's industrialisation strategy from the Left in the 1960s, laying the basis for the dependency school which was to form the self-perceptions of an entire generation, often adopted ECLA's scepticism about the political influence of organised labour even while they explicitly drew on classical Marxist theories to explain the failure of development in Latin America. The existence of a permanent 'structural heterogeneity', now no longer expected to give way to a predominance of employment in modern factories and offices, was seen not only as a distinguishing feature of dependent development but also as an explanation for the perceived absence of a revolutionary proletariat in countries such as Brazil. For Cardoso and Faletto, Quijano and Sunkel (though not Ruy Mauro Marini) the logic of the labour aristocracy thesis still seemed unassailable. Because modern industry in Latin America, dominated by multinationals and local monopolies, coexisted with a still impressive number of small-scale producers and a swollen, low productivity tertiary sector, it was clearly a failure: but *ipso facto*, workers as a whole were unlikely to forge a nation-wide movement for social change, and those employed in multinationals or local monopolies were likely to find the answer to their own economic problems through arrangements within the firm.[19] Furthermore, the experience of Cuba in 1959 seemed to offer an alternative political route to social change, one which was slowly taken up throughout the continent by rural guerrillas in Bolivia, and urban ones in Uruguay and Argentina, and which had a pervasive influence elsewhere on the attitudes of intellectuals and social scientists towards the relative importance of organised workers, peasants, and the unorganised working poor.

Thus, when the theory of a general 'embourgeoisement' of manufacturing workers was imported into Latin America from the West in the 1960s, it found ready takers. This was the period of di Tella *et al.*'s pioneering study of workers in Huachipato and Lota in Chile, contrasting the lifestyle and political attitudes of workers in a modern, though nationally-owned, steel factory (for whom participation in work and loyalty to the firm offered a chance of a better life) and an old-fashioned 'proletarian' coal mine (where workers and management remained at war). Di Tella's searching examination of the environment in which 'modern' and traditional' sectors lived was not, unfortunately, repeated in later studies which claimed similar findings, such as Arico's of workers in Cordoba published in 1964, and Guerrieri's of the Chilean industrial working class in 1969.[20]

As studies of the urban areas inhabited by the 'marginals' revealed that many were construction workers or employees of smaller, more traditional factories and workshops, the critique shifted from a criticism of the 'embourgeoisement' of workers in manufacturing in general towards a criticism of those sectors seen as most amenable to trade union organisation, made on behalf of workers less favoured by the existing labour market. Pastrana and Threlfall's study of an urban social movement in Chile belongs to this category,[21] as does Almeida's critical survey of the structural heterogeneity of the Brazilian working class; though by the time she was publishing, arguments deriving from the statistical nightmare of Latin American employment patterns were overlaid by others implying a distinct segregation between the labour markets of one set of workers and another, inspired by Doeringer and Piore's work on primary and secondary labour markets in the United States.[22]

The political events of the 1960s, 1970s and 1980s cast a shadow over the labour aristocracy thesis in Latin America just as the rise of a militant shop stewards' movement after 1968 did much to discourage the thesis of 'embourgeoisement'.[23] Few people were likely to credit 'labour aristocracy' status to rioting car workers in Cordoba in 1968 and 1971, or industrial workers in Chile taking over their plants under the Allende government in the early 1970s, though some such position clearly underlies Monica Threlfall's work,[24] and an essentially similar argument was widely used to explain the willingness of some copper miners to go on strike against the Allende government. On the other hand, throughout Latin America the high price paid for their militancy by shop stewards and other members of left wing movements in the military dictatorships of the 1970s in Chile, Bolivia, Brazil and Argentina has led to a renewed valuation of social peace: *concertacion*.[25] For some students of the labour movement, though not all, it is clear that the debate has shifted. The question is no longer, is organised labour militant enough? but, will its militancy disturb the very vulnerable efforts to preserve a democratic system against military intervention?

But the fluidity with which the labour aristocracy thesis has been superseded by renewed interest in worker's struggles and their political implications (however ambiguous), has had its disadvantages: not only because Latin American labour studies have generally failed to take seriously existing evidence of the interconnections between workers in the formal sector and marginals – which is clear – but even because a more sustained examination of the thesis might have taught us much more about the essential elements in the Latin American car workers' world.

Two detailed criticisms of the labour aristocracy thesis point the way. Humphrey's study of Brazilian car workers[26] shows that they hardly fit the classic model of a primary labour market: these are workers with no very special skills in their jobs, and above all, no career structure, subject to extremely high turnover, lacking any control over their working conditions and paid just that premium necessary to persuade them to put up with the intense pressure created on the assembly lines. His outline of the stresses suffered by workers within the car factories of São Paulo, in the context of a government strategy to use low wages in Brazilian industry to establish Brazil's position as a newly industrialising country, provides more than sufficient explanation for the explosive militancy of São Paulo. Jelin and Torre[27] highlight a more fundamental point. The classic model of an 'embourgeoisified' worker, one drawn in by management to share in the benefits of high productivity, presupposes at the very least an ability on the part of management and workers to reach agreement about the distribution of productivity benefits between themselves: a luxury which neither group was allowed in Argentina, where the State intervened heavily in the conditions of collective bargaining to restructure labour's price and market conditions in the search for a new 'economic strategy'. Turning back that State-backed development strategy, adopted by a military government in 1966, is what the successive explosions of the Cordobazo of 1968 and the Vibrazo of 1971 were all about.

Both studies raise questions which are as yet unanswerable. If one identifies 'corporatist' attitudes on the part of workers with a general prioritising of their sector's economic well-being and thus their own, a dangerous use of the phrase in Latin America, where corporatism has many other political meanings,[28] then, Jelin and Torre argue, corporatist action and attitudes of the kind presupposed by the labour aristocracy thesis, can only exist in a decentralised bargaining system, where the firm retains total control over the conditions of negotiation between management and labour. Argentinian collective bargaining is formally constrained within a legal framework which is, as it happens, highly centralised (as is Brazil's). Deliberate government intervention to fix wages as part of a 'low-wage' strategy for industrialisation makes matters worse.

But in a sense, arguments about the role of the existing legal framework for collective bargaining and the extent to which it centralises or decentralises power to individual firms are irrelevant to the underlying problem (however crucial a part they may play in the demands of workers attempting to hold back State intervention, such as the *metalurgicos* in Brazil). The fact that *formal* decentralisation is no guarantee of invulnerability from State interference, still less of embourgeoisement, can be readily seen in the experience of labour movements in Chile, Peru and Bolivia, reviewed in this volume. Here bargaining has been formally decentralised to plant level since the 1930s and 1940s, but problems with inflation, shifts in economic strategy and a desire to conciliate organised labour or reduce its power have all motivated constant State intervention in the bargaining process. There *are* countries with a decentralised bargaining framework where this constant destabilisation of the industrial relations system is less obvious: notably Colombia, also reviewed in this volume. But even Colombia hardly provides a satisfactory model of a functioning labour aristocracy.

The work of these few studies marks, in a sense, the dimensions of what a sustained critique of the labour aristocracy thesis might have told us: something about typical patterns of labour relations within the factory (as foreign and local management struggle with the exigencies of State policy); something about the relationships between workers and community, the sphere of 'reproduction' on which di Tella and his colleagues touched so tantalisingly, and where the equivalent debate in Africa has been so much more fruitful;[29] something about global relationships between labour and the State, and the extent to which the unpredictability of government intervention in collective bargaining is a constant in Latin American labour's historical experience. A collection such as the present one, with its focus on national experiences, is no substitute for further detailed studies of the first two dimensions: we hope it makes some contribution to the third.

There are other gaps to be filled, touching more directly on the crux of government 'unpredictability', the relationship between State policy towards labour and the evolution of capital accumulation. A crude survey of the material in the first two volumes alone would suggest that tensions here have generated predictable problems with inflation and occasional hyperinflation almost everywhere, embroiling workers in a political fight against 'stabilisation policies' which resolve inflationary problems at the cost of an immediate cut in wages. Conflicts over shifting development strategies suggest that instability may not only be built into ongoing processes of accumulation, but also into the ideas about development held by Latin American ruling classes, which at the least, have been highly susceptible to changes in economic fashion originating at the level of the world economy. Nor can one forget the role of world economic factors themselves in precipitating economic crisis within economies which are still very vulnerable: the debt crisis, whose roots arguably lie essentially in an American attempt to shore up the national economy against Japanese and German competition, has currently pushed all countries in the region but Brazil and Colombia into a crisis already longer than the Great Depression.[30]

Many of the chapters which follow contain detailed accounts of government intervention and the reaction of organised labour in one or more economic crisis. In the nature of historical and national surveys, none of them are perhaps sufficiently clear about the forces which explain the underlying predictability of instability itself, or the role which an adequate theory of labour in Latin America might give to this instability in shaping labour's reactions and institutions.[31] Meanwhile, one can only note with regret that the labour aristocracy has been displaced as an orthodoxy rather than being disproved, leaving a lingering legacy in the determination of some specialists to class trade union activists as 'instrumentalists' (in the Goldthorpe mould) on the factory floor whether or not they vote for revolutionary Marxism,[32] and whatever the likelihood that the wrong voting record for an industrial militant lead to his kidnap and murder by the agents of the State, from that same factory floor.

If a comparable critique of organised labour exists today, it centres on a concern that labour's struggle for better living standards may itself be a factor in the general instability of governments in Latin America and an invitation to military rule:[33] a Latin American rewriting of Samuel Huntington's 'praetorian society', in which the labour movement alone pressing its own particular interests, does duty for the series of interest groups – students, the middle sectors, the military themselves – on which Huntington originally blamed the emergence of dictatorships.[34] Much of this concern reflects short-term pressures on labour and those who study it to subscribe to new forms of 'social contract' in an economic crisis which has already slashed Latin America's gains in living standards to the level of 1978, and is far from over: posing the stark alternative of democracy with wage cuts, if labour controls its struggles, or military rule with wage cuts if it does not.

By paving the way for a final abandonment of the old imported evolutionary framework and returning to the difficult issue of labour's real relationship with Latin American politics, the new studies of *concertacion* may yet facilitate a deeper insight into the *modus operandi* of Latin America's labour movements in the complex world in which they live. But the degree of pressure currently faced by labour movement and intellectuals alike, to commit themselves to democracy regardless of economic disadvantage, may undermine a certain realism about the extent to which labour is as it is, because it *has* adjusted to the economics of an unstable world.

THE IMPORTANCE OF FORMATION

A better source of insights on the real relationships between organised labour and its Latin American environment may yet emerge from the debate on 'formation' which has become more popular in theoretical terms in recent years – with notable contributions by Jelin and Torre and Eugene Sofer[35] – after a revival of labour historiography by Hobart Spalding and Pablo Gonzalez Casanova[36] following two decades in which work of pioneer historians had fallen into disuse.

The point about studies of the 'formation' of a class is that formation is never finished. It covers not only the spread of wage relations and industrial organisation, and their occasional retreat, but also the forging and re-forging of working class institutions; or, to take Edward Thompson's definition, the class's self-creation out of a multitude of heterogeneous 'working classes', in the very specific context created by particular employing classes and a particular tradition of elite rule.[37] A good study of the 'formation' of a national working class thus tells us a great deal about the kind of organisation which labour has created over the years in its own defence, and thus more still, perhaps, about the areas of recurrent difficulty which have forced the building of particular institutions, as well as the extent to which historical change willy-nilly preserves some elements in working class experience even as it transforms others.

Take, for instance, the roots of Latin America's present labour organisations in artisan-based *mutualist* societies compared with those of the British or American working class in skilled workers occupying an often formally similar economic position. The important differences are not just that in Britain proletarianisation was much more comprehensive and industrialisation a much more profound social trauma, or that in the United States independent small farmers played a role that in Latin America was taken by semi-feudal landed estates. If we compare the ideologies favoured by these skilled workers, we will find that in the West, the era of revolutionary artisans and the polymorphous urban crowd is connected not with new ideologies of socialism and anarchism but with much older radical philosophies rooted in the struggle of emerging democracies against absolutist monarchs, the struggle for the universal rights of man. This is the struggle which informs Chartism in Britain, and the revolutionary triumph taken for granted by Gompers and his successors in the United States. Contrast this experience, which surely contributed a great deal towards cementing the loyalty of organised labour in both countries to bourgeois democracy, with the anarchist and anarchosyndicalist utopias dreamed by their class equivalents in Latin America a generation later, in the course of that early twentieth-century attempt to shift the dead weight of rural oligarchies and replace them with a world under the control of small producers and the *fuerzas vivas*, the forces which would shape the future.

Look again at the conditions under which the anarchists' struggle came to fruition. In not one but many Latin American countries – Bolivia, Chile, Brazil, and perhaps most notoriously, Argentina – the crucial alliance was not between labour and the middle classes (the old ECLA formulation, which Hobart Spalding's comparative work in many ways revives), but much more specifically between labour and a set of revolutionary junior officers inspired by very different ideas, drawn from Catholic organicism and contemporary experiments in Mussolini's Italy.[38] In the critical decades of the 1920s, 1930s and 1940s, the nascent union movement provided an urban crowd to legitimise these officers' attempts at a real, though limited, social revolution. In return, it secured the legal frameworks which have dominated working class life throughout most of the twentieth century: frameworks universally flawed by the overriding concern of the military to control the existing anarchist and possibly future Marxist content of labour's ideology, but still an enormous advance over the special cruelties of *laissez-faire* policies in a society with ample surplus labour.

In many Latin American countries collective bargaining was thus born of a revolution which sectors of the existing élite never accepted as legitimate. Since those heady days, much of the struggle of organised labour could be summed up as an attempt to defend the inadequate and distorted gains of that time against successive waves of counter-revolution. Chile, Bolivia, Argentina, all provide clear examples. So too, given its rather weaker working class and rather more rigid bargaining framework, does Brazil, where the tenuous right to strike accepted in populist legislation of the 1950s was completely abolished by the military government of 1964.

Chilean and Bolivian Marxism and Argentine Peronism become easier to understand in these circumstances: so too does the permanent tendency, here and elsewhere, to revert to traditions of popular mobilisation which helped secure the original bargaining framework whenever it is under threat. Correspondingly, there is not much point in the academic observation that the day-to-day concerns of Chilean or Bolivian shop stewards show few signs of revolutionary ideology, when so much of the revolutionary character of the situation comes from the hostile actions of other classes: less still in telling those involved to wait for that classic Marxist recipe for socialism, when the organised working class will constitute a majority of society at large.

Taken seriously, a study of formation is the perfect antidote to the evolutionary perspectives which postulate the Latin American working class as making one more move forward on the universal road to industrial or post-industrial society with every year that passes, while ignoring its actual history of temporary successes and often sharp reverses. In this spirit, the editors hope that the present series will represent a significant step forward towards a comparative perspective which does not assume the existence of a history or a logic of conflict in advance of the historical data.

Inevitably, in a work which synthesises so much historical experience through so many countries, some questions crucial to the labour movement will remain unanswered: above all, perhaps, the explanation for that instability in Latin America's process of capital accumulation[39] and its political forms which we have already outlined. But labour studies in Latin America have already suffered overmuch from attempts to cut through the Gordian knot of organisation-as-it-is in the search for a more logical (less creative) organisation-as-it-ought-to-be-in-theory. Different approaches may still have something to offer: Charles Bergquist's attempt to link the strong points of existing labour organisations directly to the point of national insertion in the global economy at least benefits from his own counter-vailing strengths as a sensitive analyst of labour's own institutions.[40] The test of such grand theories will nonetheless ultimately remain how well they explain the specific experience of each of Latin America's nationally organised labour movements: and in that spirit, we offer this series.

NOTES

1. See Rostow's *Stages of Economic Growth* (London: Cambridge University Press, 1960). Rostow's optimism on the likely evolution of developing countries' social structures was broadly shared by strategists of industrial development in Latin America such as the influential Raul Prebisch of the United Nations' Economic Commission for Latin America, ECLA, in spite of their rejection of the automatism of his model. Cf. Vilmar E. Faria, 'Desarrollo economico y marginalidad urbana: los cambios de perspectiva en la CEPAL', *Revista Mexicana de Sociologia*, vol. 40 (1978) no. 1.
2. Idem.

3. On Chile and Argentina, cf. R. Lagos and V. Tokman, 'Monetarism, Employment and Social Stratification', *World Development*, vol. XII (1985) no. 1. On Peru, Hernano del Soto Pilar, Instituto de Libertad y Democracia: cf. *Caretas*, Lima, *passim*.
4. See PREALC, *Dinamica del subempleo en America Latina*, Santiago (United Nations: Economic Commission for Latin America 1981) and Victor Tokman, 'Desarrollo desigual y absorcion de empleo. America Latina 1950–1980', *CEPAL Review* (Santiago: UN: ECLA, August 1981). Anibal Quijano, *Imperialismo y 'Marginalidad' en America Latina* (Lima: Mosca Azul, 1977). Cf. also, Anibal Quijano Obregon, 'The Marginal Pole of the Economy and the Marginalised Labour Force', *Economy and Society*, vol. 3, 1974.
5. Cf., for example, the debate between Quijano and James Cockcroft in *Latin American Perspectives*, Berkeley, California, vol. X, Spring and Summer 1983, nos. 2 and 3 (37/38). A very good review of the international debate on the role of the informal sector in capital accumulation is Caroline Moser's 'Informal Sector or Petty Commodity Production: Dualism or Dependence in Urban Development?', *World Development*, vol. VI (1978) 9/10.
6. See Moises' survey in *Revista Mexicana de Sociologia*, vol. XL, 1978, 'Clases populares y politica en Brasil (Notas para una revision teorica)'.
7. *Clase obrera y modelo economico: un estudio del peso y la estructura del proletariado en Chile*, 1973–80 (Santiago: SUR Documento de Trabajo, 1981).
8. Cf. Tilman Evers, 'Sintesis interpretativa del "Movimento do custo de vida", un movimiento urbano brasileno', *Revista Mexicana de Sociologia*, vol. 43 July-Sept. 1981, and N. Vink, 'Base Communities and Urban Social Movements – a case study of the Metalworkers' strike in 1980, Sao Bernardo, Brazil', in D. Slater (ed.), *New social movements and the state in Latin America* (Amsterdam: CEDLA, 1985).
9. In the case of Chile, it is worth mentioning Gabriel Salazar's pathbreaking *Labradores, Peones y Proletarios*, (Santiago: Ediciones SUR, 1985), dedicated to a detailed study of relationships among different sectors of the 'working classes', including women; and Peter De Shazo's similarly sensitive survey of the living and social conditions of workers in *Urban Workers and Labor Unions in Chile, 1902–1927* (Madison, Wisconsin: University of Wisconsin Press, 1983).
10. Peter De Shazo (1983), to his credit, is one exception. Rather better work has generally been produced on the importance of community life and community relationships for miners. See, for instance, June Nash's excellent study in Bolivia, *We Eat the Mines and the Mines Eat Us* (New York: Columbia University Press, 1979).
11. Cf. the articles by Moser and Moser and Young in *Women and the Informal Sector*, *IDS Bulletin*, vol. 12 (July 1981) 3.
12. Cf. Roddick, Appendix 2, Table 1, below. The point that the firm line drawn between 'formal' and 'informal' sectors, 'proletarian' wage-earners and the non-proletarian self-employed in many academic treatments of the subject may be much less sharp, and take in a significant

proportion of small workshops hardly smaller than artisan, is well made by Alison MacEwan Scott in 'Who are the self-employed?' in Bromley and Gerry, *Casual Work and Poverty in Third World Cities* (Chichester: Wiley, 1979).

13. Tokman, 1982, op. cit.
14. Cf. Gabriel Salazar, op. cit.
15. Rude, *The Crowd in History, A Study of Popular Disturbances in France and England* (New York: Wiley, 1964). For a restatement of the importance of a broader 'urban crowd' to union movements throughout the Third World, cf. Peter Waterman, 'Obreros, campesinos, artesanos y madres: hacia un entendimiento de las interrelaciones de la clase trabajadora en las sociedades capitalistas perifericas', *Revista Mexicana de Sociología*, vol. 43 (1981) no. 1.
16. Payne, *Labor and Politics in Peru* (New Haven, Conn.: Yale University Press, 1965).
17. *El sistema social de America Latina en la post-guerra* (Buenos Aires: ECLA, 1969). The ECLA thesis saw Latin American development as very much a product of middle class reformism, with workers being co-opted behind and used by a broader middle class movement.
18. See, for instance, J.A. Moises' study of Brazilian populism, *Greve de massa e crise politica, estudo do greve dos 300 mil em Sao Paulo* (Sao Paulo: Polis, 1978), summarised in *Latin American Perspectives* 23, Autumn 1979; or Juan Carlos Torre, 'La CGT y el 17 de Octubre de 1945', New York University Occasional Papers (May 1976) no. 22. The theoretical point is concisely summarised by Torre in 'Sindicalismo de masas y sistema politico en los paises del cono sur', Taller de Estudios Urbano Industriales (Lima, Peru: Pontifica Universidad Catolica, n.d.).
19. Cf. the classic assertion by Sunkel that consumption standards of workers in the modern sector qualify them as members of an internationalised sector, alongside the local elite, in O. Sunkel and E. Fuenzalida, 'Transnationalism and its National Consequences', in J. Villamil (ed.), *Transnational Capital and National Development* (Brighton: Harvester, 1979).

    The exception to this general scepticism is, of course, Ruy Mauro Marini, whose *Dialectica de la dependencia* identified the central axis of accumulation in Latin America as being based on the superexploitation of its labour force.
20. di Tella, Torcuato *et al.*, *Sindicato y comunidad: dos tipos de estructura sindical latinoamericana* (Buenos Aires: Instituto Torcuato di Tella, 1967); Arico, José, 'Examen de conciencia', *Pasado y presente*, Buenos Aires, vol. 1 (January-March) no. 4. Guerrieri, Adolfo, 'Consideraciones sobre los sindicatos chilenos', *Aportes* (Paris: July 1968).
21. Cf. Pastrana and Threlfall, *Pan, techo y poder* (Buenos Aires: SIAP-Planteos, 1974).
22. Maria Herminia Tavares de Almeida, 'Desarrollo capitalista y acción sindical', *Revista Mexicana de Sociologia*, vol. XL (April-June) no. 2; Doeringer and Piore, *Internal Labor Markets and Manpower Analysis* (Lexington, Mass.: D.C. Heath, 1971).
23. Cf. Colin Crouch and Alessandro Pizzorno, (eds), *The Resurgence of Class Conflict in Western Europe since 1968* (London: Macmillan, 1978).

24. Threlfall, 'Shanty-town Dwellers and People's Power' in P.J. O'Brien (ed.), *Allende's Chile* (New York: Praeger, 1976).
25. See the very clear summary which prefaces CLACSO's study, *El sindicalismo latinoamericano en los ochenta* (Santiago: 1986).
26. John Humphrey, *Capitalist Control and Workers' Struggle in the Brazilian Auto Industry* (Princeton, N.J.: Princeton University Press 1982).
27. E. Jelin and J.C. Torre, 'Los nuevos trabajadores en America Latina: una reflexion sobre la tesis de la aristocracia obrera', *Desarrollo Economico*, Buenos Aires, vol. 22 (April-June 1982) no. 85; cf. also F. Delich, *Crisis y protesta social – Cordoba 1969–1973*, Buenos Aires (Siglo XXI), 1974, and I.M. Roldan, *Sindicatos y protesta social en la Argentina (1969–1974), Un estudio de caso: el Sindicato de Luz y Fuerza de Cordoba* (Amsterdam: CEDLA, n.d.).
28. 'Corporatism', for instance, is used by US writers on Brazil to refer to the State-dominated labour relations system derived from Italian fascist philosophy, and other elements of a political system similarly dominated by the state. See K.P. Erickson, *The Brazilian Corporative State and Working Class Politics* (Berkeley: University of California Press, 1977). Philippe Schmitter, whose own work on politics laid the basis for subsequent studies in this area, distinguishes Latin American or Francoist style 'State corporatism' from the 'societal corporatism' characteristic of European societies.
29. Compare the articles by Adrian Peace and John Saul in R. Cohen and R. Sandbrook, *The Development of an African Working Class* (London: Longman, 1975).
30. On the impact of the debt crisis on Latin American standards of living and wages, see *Beyond the Crisis*, (Santiago: ILO-PREALC, 1985) and Roddick, *Dance of the Millions* (London: Latin American Bureau, 1988).
31. For a model of the relationship between political instability and organised labour's behaviour, see Payne, op. cit., and Juan Carlos Torre, 'Sindicalismo de masas y sistema politica en los paises del cono sur', op. cit. The difficulties of working with an economic model of instability even case by case and country by country, are clearly shown in Kronisch and Mericle's *Political Economy of the Latin American Motor Vehicle Industry* (Cambridge, Mass.: MIT Press, 1984), in which discussions of the global forces shaping the industry through several decades of sharp changes in company and government strategy coincide with studies of the labour movement in the industry focused essentially on the movement's own institutions and internal struggles.
32. The classic statement of this kind can be found in M. Barrera, H. Landsberger and Abel Toro, 'The Chilean labour leader: a report on his background and attitudes', *Industrial and Labor Relations Review*, vol. 17 (April 1964) no. 3, and in H. Landsberger's subsequent, 'The Labor Elite: Is it Revolutionary?', in Lipset and Solari (eds), *Elites in Latin America* (London: Oxford University Press, 1967). Compare its reformulation in F. Zapata, 'Hacia una sociología del trabajo latinoamericano', in CLACSO, *El sindicalismo latinoamericano en los ochenta* (Santiago: CLACSO, 1986).

33. Cf. the sections on 'Sindicalismo y concertación social y política' and 'Sindicalismo: política e ideologia' in CLACSO's *El sindicalismo latinoamericano en los ochenta* (Santiago: CLACSO, 1986): above all, those by Guillermo Campero and René Cortazar, 'Logicas de accion sindical en Chile' and by René Antonio Mayorga, 'La crisis del sistema democratico y la Central Obrera Boliviana' (COB).
34. Samuel Huntington, *Political Power in Changing Societies* (New Haven: Yale University Press, 1968).
35. Jelin and Torre, op. cit. and Eugene Sofer, 'Recent trends in Latin American labor historiography', *Latin American Research Review* XV (1980) no. 1. See also, Samuel Valenzuela, 'Un marco conceptual para el analisis de la formacion del movimiento laboral', in CLACSO, *El sindicalismo latinoamericano en los ochenta*, op. cit.
36. Spalding, *Organized Labor in Latin America* (New York: New York University Press, 1977). Pablo Gonzalez Casanova (ed.), *Historia del movimiento obrero en america latina*, Mexico City (Siglo XXI) 1984. Of the three volumes in this series already published, Raul Trejo Delarbe's history of the Mexican labour movement (in volume one) and Isodoro Cheresky's history of the early years of the Argentinian, are particularly good examples of the kind of study of formation advocated here. For examples of earlier works, see Victor Alba, *Politics and the Labor Movement in Latin America*, and Robert Alexander, *Organised Labor in Latin America* (New York: The Free Press, 1965).
37. *The Making of the English Working Classes* (Harmondsworth, Middlesex: Pelican, 1968).
38. A brief comparison can be found in Skidmore, 'Workers and Soldiers: Urban Labor Movements and Elite Responses in 20th Century Latin America', in V. Bernhard (ed.), *Elites, Masses and Modernization in Latin America 1850–1930* (Austin, Texas: University of Austin, 1979). Skidmore, however, is regrettably more interested in the anarchist and anarcho-syndicalist ideas of workers than in the influence of Mussolini on the soldiers. For a detailed examination of the influence of such ideas in Chile see Roddick and Haworth, 'Chile 1924 and 1979: Labour Policy and Industrial Relations through two Revolutions' (Glasgow: Institute of Latin American Studies Occasional Paper No. 42, University of Glasgow, 1984). Harding, vol. 2 (forthcoming) and *Political History of Organized Labor in Brazil*, Ph.D., Stanford, 1973 covers the impact of Mussolini's ideas on Brazil; see also Weffort, 'Origines do sindicalismo populista no Brasil: a conjuntura do apos-guerra', *Estudos CEBRAP*, 4, April-June 1973.
39. For one possible theory (and an explanation of the increased severity of such upheavals within a partially industrialised economy) see E.V.K. Fitzgerald, 'The State and the management of accumulation in the periphery', in Diana Tussie (ed.), *Latin America in the World Economy: New Perspectives* (Aldershot: Gower, 1983).
40. Charles Bergquist, 'What is being done? Some recent studies on the urban working class and organised labor in Latin America', *Latin American Research Review*, XVI (1981) no. 2, and *Labor in Latin America* (Stanford, California: Stanford University Press, 1986).

2 Peru

Nigel Haworth

It is reasonable to question whether Peru has an industrial relations (IR) system in the traditional sense.[1] Whereas most formal IR analysis follows from the existence of an empirically identifiable and relatively homogeneous pattern of collective bargaining, no such pattern may be found in Peru. Instead, there exists a fragmented, uncodified, often marginally important complex of bargaining traditions, ranging from the classically paternalistic to the 'advanced' job-regulatory. Its marginal importance may be argued to be the case on the grounds that perhaps only 30 per cent of the economically-active population are affected by something akin to formal wage bargaining, reflecting the dualism which divides the one-third of the population in the 'modern' sector from the two-thirds in the marginal or relatively-unintegrated rural contexts. Yet despite the limited numbers formally integrated into wage bargaining, and despite the relative incoherence of Peru's IR tradition, the political consequences of bargaining have been profound, particularly from the 1960s onwards. Interpreted in a variety of ways, the politics of industrial relations have reflected the complex relationship between industrialisation, proletarianisation, state formation and integration into the world economy. Hence, if the traditional concept of a system is inapplicable, that of the political economy of industrial relations is entirely appropriate. However, its very appropriateness poses a number of problems for a broad historical overview of modest length, requiring substantial compression of often crucial events and processes into manageable proportions.

In any meaningful sense, the creation of an industrial relations tradition requires large-scale and permanent growth of waged labour engaged in the extractive, manufacturing and service sectors. Hence, with a few exceptions, such as the railway industry and the guano and nitrate sector, the potential for the development of bargaining practices arises only after the 1890s in Peru. Thereafter, the opportunities grow, but at a relatively slow pace and under substantial State-imposed constraints, until the post-Second World War period – particularly the 1960s and 1970s – when the scope for growth increases. That said, even in contemporary Peru, wage bargainers bear far greater importance politically than their numbers would suggest they should, for reasons which derive from the politicised nature of union-management relations. The particular meld of economic and political inputs which define Peruvian industrial relations is matched by equally specific investment and production patterns, and a particular tradition of fragmentation in labour movement organisation, which together owe much to the post-1890s pattern of integration into the world economy. We now turn to the origins of this tradition in the period between conquest and the 1890s.

FROM CONQUEST TO STABLE INDEPENDENCE[2]

Peru emerged as a consequence of Spanish colonial expansion from the 1530s onwards. Until the 1820s, the social, political and economic organisation of the Colony was dependent upon policies imposed from Spain. Despite changing circumstances over the period, the establishment of wage-labour employment was not enthusiastically promoted for a variety of reasons. Chief amongst these were three: indigenous manufacturing was overtly discouraged, and even forcibly repressed; labour supply was based generally on a complex of forced, slave and tribute labour, particularly using the *mita* and the *encomienda*; the economic basis of the economy was skewed substantially to agricultural and extractive sectors, both of which were in turn orientated primarily to the demands of the world economy. A traditional mixture of paternalistic employer practices and naked force sufficed both to maintain labour supplies and to deal with such demands as the workforces raised.

Apart from those production sectors orientated towards either the limited local demand or the world market, a large sector of small-scale, subsistence, community-based agricultural units continued, particularly in the *Sierra*. Excluded from political power and practice, and, often, such trading channels as existed, this sector had little need for bargaining around production issues in the contemporary industrial relations sense. Their problems derived almost entirely from the various encroachments of *hacienda* owners on their traditional land holding – a threat to be countered in an overtly political manner, and often in terms of violence against violence. The continuing presence of this sector until the present day has given rise to dualist arguments which stress the exclusion of peasant agriculture from the 'modern' sector, that is, the sector in which Peruvian industrial relations has its roots.[3] However, the political ramifications of industrially-based bargaining often transcend the modern-traditional dichotomy, as perhaps the current urban actions of *Sendero Luminoso* illustrate.

The achievement of independence in the 1820s did little to transform the blockages facing the growth of generalised wage-labour based production. Two factors help to explain this: post-Independence Peru was highly unstable politically, and was only to reach a degree of political and liberal-democratic stability after the 1895 civil war; the initial economic strategies adopted within this context of political instability owed much to the *laissez-faire* tradition imported from Europe, which placed substantial obstacles in the path of industrialisation. It was clearly in the interests of many agricultural and mineral producers to maintain the traditional orientation towards the world economy, thus restricting any attempt to industrialise generally, in terms of both state policy and access to capital. Even the post-Independence state, already exhibiting the characteristics which were to make it amongst the weakest in Latin America, was never a major employer, consequently restricting a potential locus of wage-labour expansion.

In the traditional productive sectors, labour supply systems initially continued to be based on forced and tribute labour, supplemented by the use of criminals and the arrival of both slaves and indentured labour from Japan, China, Chile and elsewhere. Moreover, sugar and cotton production began to expand, as did the demand for labour in mining as the post-1890 mining take-off approached. Labour supply inelasticities became increasingly apparent in the traditional agricultural and extractive sectors, to be exacerbated by the abolition of slavery in 1854 and the ending of the supply of coolie labour in 1874. Labour recruiters responded by the generalisation of the *enganche* system, in which money forwarded to future workers had to be paid off in the form of a given period of labour in the plantation or mine. *Enganche* was to provide an adequate degree of labour flexibility in the agricultural sector well into the twentieth century, whilst transforming the labouring experience of many labourers recruited from the Sierra.

The need for *enganche* in the agricultural sector was in part a product of the post-1830 expansion of the guano and nitrate industries. Both extractive, they became growth poles in post-independence Peru which created great pressure on traditional labour supplies, highlighting the inadequacy of both extractive and agricultural labour supply practices. Their expansion heralded changes which had widespread implications. Between 1830 and 1876 there was an export-led boom, causing expansion in state activity, in the commercial and financial sectors, and, importantly, in the transport system. A limited railway network was commenced, further increasing the demand for labour in the Peruvian economy. Guano, nitrate and railway developments became the focus of a previously unattained level of wage-labour formation, coupled to the first stirrings of union activity. Although the *mutualista* tradition of the mid-late nineteenth century is often given central status in the analysis of the origins of Peruvian union formation, it is clear, following Salazar that initial stirrings of political debate and organisation became visible during the 1830–76 boom period.[4] The role of Chilean *émigré* workers, many of whom were to become resident in Peru, should also be recognised. They brought with them the anarchist, syndicalist and early socialist traditions which had already taken root in Chile, and which were later to impose definitively their mark on Peru.

The boom collapsed in 1876, and the War of the Pacific (1879–84) was a stunning blow to Peruvian society, the comprehensive defeat by Chile exaggerating both economic and political crises. Consequences of major importance followed this debacle. Political life was transformed by the 1895 Civil War, which brought into being the 'aristocratic' era of government, at least formally committed to a liberal democratic order. Party-based and committed to government by election, the 1895 victors established the political order in which the first major developments in an industrial relations system were to flower, and also provided the context for what Thorp and Bertram have seen as the rise and fall of a local development effort.

1890–1930: GROWTH, UNIONISATION AND POLITICAL ACTION

Thorp and Bertram convincingly argue that at the beginning of this period, especially in the 1890s, national capital was able to carve out a substantial role for itself across the sectoral range.[5] However, this potential basis for a national economic strategy collapsed, due primarily to a combination of unfavourable movements of relative prices in the world market, the financial power of foreign capital, and, on occasion, foreign monopoly of natural resource production.

More importantly, an initial boost to industrialisation was confounded by an export-orientated anti-protectionism, and a failure to build a pro-industrialisation lobby within the State. Instead of an autonomous economic strategy, Peru found itself enmeshed in the world market more firmly than ever by the 1920s. Simultaneously, the power of foreign capital investment was greatly increased.

The sectors which were either increasingly foreign-controlled, or orientated towards export markets, were also those in which labour supply issues were most important. In mining, 1889 saw Backus and Johnson begin the displacement of Peruvian capital in the central region; in 1901 the Cerro de Pasco Corporation entered the race, precipitating the demise of many small-scale mineral producers. This restructuring of mining – extended to the northern *sierra* by the Northern Peru Mining Company in 1921 – induced major changes in local markets for food and consumer goods, and, in the case of Cerro de Pasco, led to substantial land purchases by the firm as a result of massive pollution from the Oroya smelter. Meanwhile, the sugar industry became further concentrated in agro-industrial complexes located on the northern coast. Small and medium-sized *haciendas* were swallowed up by monopoly concerns, which came to control local commerce. *Enganche* was used to maintain labour supplies at an adequate level, though in the early years of this century a more stable, non-migratory workforce made its appearance in these agro-export concerns. Cotton production was equally export-orientated – though also catering for the local market – and was based upon a mixture of big land-holdings and sharecropping (*yanaconaje*). Foreign-owned export houses were active in this sector. Finally, the International Petroleum Company extended its production in the North, again becoming an important factor in local commerce. By the 1920s, the Peruvian economy had become a classic, enclave-dominated structure, primarily orientated towards the world market.

Sulmont argues that in this period approximately 80 per cent of the national population existed outside the 'modern' capitalist sector, remaining in the traditional rural sector and standing as a massive blockage to the formation of classical free wage labour, and, simultaneously, failing to create a 'reserve army of labour' sufficient to resolve the problems of labour supply inelasticity noted above.[6] This interpretation is borne out by Yepes' analysis of sectoral workforces.[7] He estimates that in 1916 22 466 *braceros* were working in sugar production; 9471 workers in the rice sector; and 20 514 in cotton production. In 1915, 21 480 were working in the mining sector;

through 1911 evidence suggests that 20 per cent of mineworkers were children, and that 30 per cent were under 21 years old. Arguably the profile of 1911 mining employment suggests both the weakness of the *enganche* system of labour supply, and the continuing existence of labour supply inelasticities.

Figures for manufacturing employment in this period are few and unreliable. However, some data help provide a guide to employment levels in this sector. For example, figures for 1895 give the population of Lima as 100 000, of which 16 000 had *oficios*, that is, trades. These were predominantly artisans with a small journeyman element included. Capelo, in 1895 figures quoted by Yepes, suggests total factory employment to be 7000, of which 5000 were male wage labourers and 1000 female. In 1918 Garland estimated that cotton goods workers numbered 2586, and wool workers 735, all based in Lima.[8] He suggests that only 514 cotton workers existed outside Lima in the same year, indicating the established primacy of Lima-Callao in manufacturing even at that early date. Given these figures, it is not unreasonable to hazard a figure of between 100 000 and 150 000 as the number of people engaged in regular, waged capitalist production in the whole Peruvian economy by 1918, a truly small proportion of the 4.5 million national population.

Labour movement stirrings[9]

Mention has already been made of the presence of some labour mobilisation in the period of the guano and nitrate booms after 1830. Preceding this phase of action, *gremios* had united artisans in various trades, reflecting the existence of a layer of urban, skilled craftsmen stretching back into the Colony. These *gremios* were unsuited to either the dominant, post-independence liberalism or the changing economic context as imports from industrialising Europe entered Peru. Despite violent uprisings in 1851, 1865 and 1872, a defence of traditional artisanal production was impracticable in the face of rapid economic change, and worker organisation became increasingly orientated towards new areas of occupational expansion, both in urban and rural settings, reflecting the development of a wage rather than skill-consciousness. The growing numbers of *empleados* and *obreros* borrowed the *gremio system* and its mutualist basis for their own use, establishing by the 1890s a major presence, particularly in Lima. However, its success paradoxically highlighted its own contradictions. The traditional mutualist concern with welfare issues increasingly clashed with the growing belligerence of more pronounced political traditions within mutualism. By the 1890s, anarchism, anarcho-syndicalism and nascent socialism vied for political preeminence, and the mutualist structure could not withstand the consequent pressures. Furthermore, new sectors of wage labour emerged in the 1890s – food processing, clothing, printing – as consumer industries expanded, and the mutualist tradition could not absorb either their energy or their demands. As elsewhere, mutualism was recognised as a potentially important vehicle for managerial unitarist practices – management had even fostered mutualist organisation to this end – and consequently both leaders and rank-and-file members of mutualist bodies questioned the tradition's future. Thus, despite its initial importance, mutualism was destined to fragment, leaving the field open to more radical traditions.

The major anarcho-syndicalist influence in the Peruvian labour movement stretched from the post-War of the Pacific period to the arrival of Leguía in power in 1919. It reflected the post-war expansion of wage-labour, the eclipse of mutualism, and the influence of international ideologies upon intellectuals and worker activists alike. However, the status of anarcho-syndicalism should be viewed in the context of relatively small numbers of urban-based workers, the continuing importance of enclave production in relatively remote areas of the country, and only incipient trends towards an effective organisational and ideological basis for united worker action. Not surprisingly, the libertarian traditions in anarcho-syndicalism lent a necessary flexibility to worker organisation in this period. Flexibility was a prerequisite for a number of reasons – a period of transition accompanied the decline of mutualism; ideas initially complementary to, but eventually differentiated from, anarcho-syndicalism were developing; the establishment of an industrial relations tradition increasingly based on urban production required conscious, if often contradictory, inputs from the fledgling labour movement; the class structure of the dominant groups in Peruvian society was itself facing a period of flux as challenges – given a boost by the success of the 1895 civil war – emerged to the traditional power base of the agro-export oligarchy from within its own ranks. Arguably, therefore, the anarcho-syndicalist phase is one of both consolidation and transition: consolidation of political and organisational experiences; transition to the period of populist socialist dominance after 1919.

Yepes marks the 1901 *Congreso Obrero* as the first manifestation of the presence of a powerful anarcho-syndicalist tradition in the

Peruvian labour movement. Sulmont believes that the tradition was consolidated in the 1905 adoption of the Eight-Hour Day struggle by the *Federación de Obreros Panaderos Estrella del Perú*. Undoubtedly it was this campaign, when linked to the issues of wages and conditions and safety provisions at work, which led to a rapid and impressive unity of action and reorientation towards the militant pursuit of industrial goals away from the more reflective mutualist model of action. It is interesting to note that a number of piecemeal labour-related measures were legislated in this period. For example, elementary social security provisions were enacted in 1911, in line with contemporary developments elsewhere in Latin America, as were measures relating to industrial accidents. Organisationally, anarchist workers brought together the 1913 *Federación Obrera Regional Peruana*, paralleled by similar regional and local imitations throughout Peru. The eight hour day was eventually achieved after massive mobilisation in 1918, despite waves of repression which culminated in that of the Benavides and Pardo governments (1914–19). The important participants in this movement included railway, shoe-making, bakery, textile, food processing, printing, dockyard and construction workers. All primarily urban-based, these sectors were to provide the consistent basis of union growth in the Lima-Callao region. It is also notable that the Eight Hour Day movement also counted on a degree of support from rural union organisations. Yet, in its moment of triumph, the anarcho-syndicalist tradition faced its own demise. This first major sustained campaign waged by the nascent workers' movement had permitted the growth of socialist alternatives to the libertarian-syndicalist tradition, and both Mariategui and Haya de la Torre were active in the opposition to Pardo. History overtook anarcho-syndicalism after the failure of the *Comité proabaratamiento de las subsistencias* in 1919, vanquished by Pardo's extreme repression.[10]

However, the defeat of both *Comité* and the anarcho-syndicalist tradition is merely one expression of a greater transformation of civil society in Peru. The Leguía coup of 1919 was in response to a profound crisis into which the dominant classes had plunged, provoked by internal political challenges and an increasingly dominant-foreign presence within the economy. Leguía's government between 1919 and 1930 was an attempt to resolve the crisis based on an accommodation with the international market, a restructured dominant class formation, a restructured state, and a combination of accommodation with and repression of the post-1918 victorious labour movement. When, in 1920, Leguía moved to control and repress the Labour movement using legislation and police powers, the anarcho-syndicalist tradition was incapable of organising and leading effective counter-action. Instead, the scene was set for the growth and defeat of socialist and populist alternatives within the labour movement.

The build-up to defeat[11]

The period 1919–34 is perhaps the most crucial of any for an understanding of contemporary Peruvian industrial relations. The growth of populist and socialist/communist traditions, their politicisation of the labour movement and of industrial relations, and their defeat provide the context in which the unusually unstructured nature of contemporary Peruvian industrial relations practices arise, and in which the long period between 1934 and 1968, when little coherent industrial relations development occurs, must be understood. Few Latin American economies experienced quite such a cathartic experience, and it merits detailed attention.

As noted above, Leguía's coup was in response to a crisis at both political and economic levels. Leguía's initial overtures to the labour movement were friendly and constructive, but rapidly turned to directive and repressive measures in 1920. Thereafter, labour movement organisation and action took place against a background of coherent state opposition. In this context of antipathy, two traditions came to replace anarcho-syndicalism and confront each other within the labour movement. On the one hand, the *Alianza Popular Revolucionaria Americana* (APRA), led by Victor Haya de la Torre, developed an anti-imperialist and populist programme which gained a substantial labour movement following. On the other, José Carlos Mariategui promoted the formation, firstly, of the *Partido Socialista del Peru* (PSP), later transforming itself into the *Partido Communista del Peru* (PCP), the Peruvian section of the Third International. The growth of these traditions is both confused and complex. Haya de la Torre and Mariategui worked together until 1923, when Haya was deported. Thereafter, a well-documented split developed, passing through the formal creation of APRA in 1924, growing divisions between Haya and Mariategui, and the effects particularly of the 1927 Leguía repression, to the 1928 establishment of APRA's Peruvian party, the *Partido Nacionalista Libertador Peruano* and the 1928 formation of the PSP, and its final metamorphosis into the PCP in 1930.[12]

The development of these contending traditions imposed a heavy cost upon the labour movement. Moves towards the creation of a national union body took place against a background of state repression and internal political wrangling, exacerbated by the formal split announced in 1928. Moves, promoted particularly by Mariategui-inspired intervention, towards the formation of a *Confederación General de Trabajadores del Peru* (CGTP) commenced in 1929, and a first plenary session was held in 1930. The impetus behind the formation of the CGTP grouped together textile, railway, printing, transport, food processing and rural-based organisations. Martinez de la Torre, quoted by Sulmont, gives an idea of the size of union membership in these sectors. Thus, for example, the textile federation brought together 3435 workers; Printing 860; transport 3000 plus; railway 2000; dockworkers 2600; food processing 360. Simultaneously, miners' organisations in the Central *Sierra* met in a Regional Congress which maintained links with the Lima-based CGTP. Regional involvement included activity in Arequipa, the sugar producing regions of the North, and the cotton-producing regions south of the capital. Although claiming a following of 50 000 workers, the CGTP faced internal discord as some elements of the membership were disenchanted by the PCP-CGTP link, and others were explicitly linked to APRA – especially in the textile and food-processing sectors, and, of course, in the established centre of APRA support in the 'solid North'. Consequently, by 1930, the political traditions of the labour movement were in disarray, as were the organisational forms the movement had adopted.

THE TURNING POINT IN PERUVIAN INDUSTRIAL RELATIONS: 1930–34

There was to be no opportunity for these problems to resolve themselves over time. Leguía was toppled in 1930 by a military coup led by Sanchez Cerro, provoking a period of great political turmoil and repression. The important events of this period are amongst the most traumatic in all the Peruvian labour movement's history. Sanchez Cerro opted for an overtly fascist approach to government, after initially toying with a more liberal populism. The CGTP was banned in late 1930 during a great repression of worker militancy. However, APRA was to suffer most in this period. Haya pushed Sanchez Cerro very closely in the elections of 1931, and violence erupted in the wake of vote-rigging accusations. Draconian emergency legislation was passed in 1931, and the violence culminated in the notorious 1932 Trujillo massacre of *Apristas* following an abortive military adventure by APRA. Despite a limited liberalisation in 1933–34 – following the assassination of Sanchez Cerro – APRA was driven into an underground existence from 1934 to 1944 – the so-called period of the Catacombs.

The consequences of the political and military defeat of APRA were enormous. Not only was the major political organisation representing workers and sections of the emergent middle classes crushed and made ineffective for ten years, but trade union activities in and out of the CGTP associated with APRA were fatally wounded. The context in which other workers' parties could prosper was destroyed, illustrated by the decline of the PCP, which was reduced to a marginal political status. The dominant classes, and the economic order grounded in the agro-export sector, would be unchallenged and would have to contend only with their internal concerns and the control of state power for the same period. Equally, the space for a detailed codification of industrial relations practices was lost, with major consequences up to the present day.

The importance of this lost space may not be immediately apparent. Yet, unlike Argentina, Brazil, Mexico, Chile and elsewhere, Peru has never provided a coherent labour code in which bargaining takes place between employer and employee. Rather, the system adopted, such as it is, is a piecemeal collection of legislation, often contradictory and ambiguous in its content, and lacking the comprehensive provisions which historically reigned elsewhere. The comparison with the Chilean example is most apposite.[13] Between 1924 and 1931 Chile enacted the series of legislative measures which formed the basis of the Labour Code which reigned until the 1970 overthrow of Allende. The origins of the Chilean Labour Code lay in an accommodation stuck between State, Capital and Labour, an accommodation resting on a series of *quid pro quos*. The need for the accommodation stemmed from the economic and political crises which dogged Chile post-1918: the slump hit Chile earlier than the rest of Latin America; worker mobilisation and politicisation were threatening, the dominant classes were at odds with one another about both their relative configuration and state policy. The resolution of these crises – the accommodation – was elegant: capital received substantial investment benefits and enhanced protection from the ravages of the world market; labour received a structured bargaining system plus an advanced package of social security and welfare benefits; the state presided over a civil society functioning around the accommodation and therefore less likely to resort to open violence in pursuit of class interests. In this sense, the crucial component of the accommodation was the incorporation of unions and labour into a strictly-patrolled bargaining process based on conciliation, incorporation into consensual bargaining practices, and reliance on state mediation.

Most Latin American countries adopted such a pattern in one form or another in the 1920s, 1930s and 1940s. The pattern of the accommodation varied from case to case as circumstances differed, but, universally, codified bargaining practices were used to defuse, divert or defeat worker mobilisation by incorporating it into a legal framework.

Peru never adopted this model. The combination of factors which gave rise to its adoption elsewhere did not materialise in the crucial period of crisis between 1930 and 1934. If we take each of the three elements of the accommodation, labour was weak, fragmented, and defeated by 1934. It no longer threatened the existing order, hence the need for an accommodation did not arise. Capital was disunited, but the agro-export sectors still dominated, whilst the basis of an industrial bourgeoisie was insufficiently strong to challenge the dominant groups. Again, the need or demand for an accommodation was not forthcoming. Finally, the defeat of effective opposition left little challenge to the existing state structure. There was no need to seek *quid pro quos* within an accommodative framework, a situation which was to continue until the 1960s. The governments of Benavides, Prado, Bustamante, Odria and Belaundé each in their own way reinforced the piecemeal basis of Peruvian industrial relations, emphasising the failure to provide a codified structure in the early 1930s.

DEPRESSION, DEFEAT AND RESURGENCE: 1930–48

The period between 1930 and 1942 may have witnessed the exclusion of effective worker organisation from political and bargaining recognition, but it also provided the context for an increased economic autonomy in Peru, consequent upon the effects of the international downturn upon the linkages binding together national economic activity and the world economy. 1930–42 saw increased state economic intervention, import substitution, exchange and import controls, and legislative support for local manufacturing enterprise. However, for Thorp and Bertram, it is not the trend towards increased economic autonomy which is remarkable, but the poor performance of Peru in its attempt to take advantage of international market dislocation. They point to limited economic diversification, limited displacement of dominant, foreign-owned export firms, and a state strategy which foundered on ineffective protection controls, rapid inflation, and a chronic balance of payments problem. The reasons for this poor performance are linked in particular to the weakness of support for an industrialisation model. Groups capable of promoting industrialisation were fragmented and unable to exert the social and political force needed to impose such a policy.

The continuing domination of the economy by the agro-extractive sectors, supported by a high level of export product diversity, perpetuated both the obstruction of internal market formation and an anti-industrialisation tradition amongst state policy-makers. Consequently, manufacturing development was limited, providing few opportunities for a dramatic increase in free labour employment in urban centres. The export-orientated enclaves remained the key centres in which wage labour was concentrated, but there the effects of the international downturn resulted in a drop in labour recruitment, increased unemployment and declining wages. Mining employment suffered a sharp slump in the early 1930s, followed by a recovery in the late 1930s and early 1940s. Cotton employment fluctuated similarly, as it began to lose its importance in the export economy. Rice and sugar employment fluctuated to a much less marked extent over the same period. Factory-based wage labour increased from 21 000 in 1925 to 34 000 (1930), 43 000 (1935), 65 000 (1940) to 88 000 in 1945. However large this increase may appear though, it must be compared with the continuing high level of non-factory artisanal production throughout the same period – 298 000, 308 000, 325 000, 331 000 and 320 000 for the same years. Clearly, a renovation of the organisations of the labour movement after the defeats of the early 1930s was not going to be forced by the sheer weight of newly-proletarianised workers in the 1930–48 period.

The experiences of both APRA and the PCP in this period were unhappy. Both faced the consequences of defeat – repression, fragmentation of organisation and debate, logistical problems associated with clandestine activity and so on. The PCP, smaller and weaker at the onset of the repression, was particularly badly hit as its limited resources were stretched beyond capacity. Suffice it to say that the PCP only regained its cohesion in the 1960s. APRA, though in many ways subject to greater attack, was able to maintain a presence in community, factory and *hacienda*, and could count on continuing tacit support from a relatively wide base in the population. Politically, however, at least until the early 1940s, this was a period of quiescence within the formal organisations of the labour movement, exacerbated by the consequences of the world crisis. Despite this, it was a period in which labour legislation was developed. Two issues are generally raised, both introduced during the Benavides government (1933–39). Although implacably opposed to APRA, Benavides was committed to a wide range of 'modernising' policies. Thus, apart from the creation of a compulsory social security system for workers in 1936, further measures relating to labour contracts, the working day, health and safety and so on were enacted. Similarly, a *Dirección de Trabajo* with specific responsibilities for labour issues was established between 1935 and 1936. Though the measures were often limited, and open to accusations of window-dressing, they constituted the most comprehensive programme of industrial relations-related measures yet introduced in Peru, far surpassing those of the pre-1919 period. However, they again illustrate the piecemeal and contingent basis of labour legislation, evolving haphazardly out of perceived requirements at the time, rather than from a coherent long-term strategy. The mid-1930s measures were undoubtedly informed by circumstances elsewhere in Latin America, and, as elsewhere, corporatist thinking was active in Peru, particularly in the pro-fascist *Union Revolucionaria*. But corporatism and fascism failed to dominate, staying on the margins of the centrist and pragmatic Benavides government.

The year of opportunity: 1943

1943 opened the next phase in the political and organisational development of the labour movement. The economic context is again important. As noted above, the impact of the Second World War was to promote growth and expansion in the Peruvian economy as the consequences of the Depression abated. Employment levels had by and large recovered themselves after the decline in the early 1930s. The improvement took place across all sectors, and reflected a degree of diversification, particularly in such manufacturing sectors as textiles, where small-scale, independent production grew, and in a variety of consumer and intermediate goods — shoes, clothing, chemicals and engineering, for example.

An increase in unionisation followed this recovery, opening the way for the competition between APRA and the PCP to grow again. Under the 1936 legislation unions could seek formal registration, and the Prado government, despite a profound antipathy to the growth of industrial conflict towards the end of 1945, was prepared to recognise formally the spate of new unions. Figures for the period 1940–1944 show that 118 unions were recognised, compared with a meagre 33 between 1936 and 1939. In turn, the 1940–44 figure should be compared with that for 1945–47, when 264 unions were recognised under the Bustamante government. The areas in which pre-1944 unionisation particularly grew were food processing, including brewing, leather working, transport, commerce, and a variety of service sectors.

The major consequence of union growth and activity was the creation of the *Confederación de Trabajadores del Perú* (CTP) in 1944. The continuing importance of Lima-Callao for union action is borne out by the make-up of the CTP. Textile workers, mainly based in Lima, were to the fore, as were many of the same sectors which had created the CGTP in 1929–30. Perhaps the biggest difference between the CGTP and the CTP was the greater importance of service workers in the latter, and the presence of numbers of white-collar workers. Formed in the context of increasingly bitter conflicts about the cost of living – then a major issue, as, according to Sulmont, it had risen 83 per cent between 1939 and 1945 – the CTP was a key actor in the September 1944 general strike in Lima. The attempt to generalise the Lima action to a national level created a difficult situation as APRA political leaders bargained with the Prado government, whilst APRA union leaders went ahead with militant action. The outcome was the marginalisation of the PCP from the process, as by 1945 APRA domination of the CTP was absolute, and PCP militants made little headway in their attempt to create an alternative focus of organisation.

The formation of the CTP, and the growth of active union militancy after the years of defeat in the 1930s, are crucial factors in Peru's labour movement history. Despite their small numbers – in 1940 *obreros* and *empleados* were only 14 per cent of the economically active population of 434 000 – workers, centralised in Lima-Callao, had once again become a major political force, both through their involvement with party organisations – especially with APRA –

and through their capacity to take to the streets. The strike weapon became once again a major factor in determining the outcome of political crises. Hence in many ways Payne's view of the politicised nature of bargaining can be understood given the experience of the mid-1940s.[14] However, unlike most cases in Latin America, the Peruvian union-party tradition was still fragile in terms of political power and resilience. The consolidation of the populist and communist traditions had been impossible in the late 1920s and early 1930s, and the ensuing period of repression had undermined many of the effects of that earlier growth period. The new-found freedom of post-1943 Peru could not be taken for granted, and a tremendous degree of consolidation would be needed to establish firmly the basis for political and economic action. Unfortunately for the labour movement, time was not to permit such a consolidation.

The rise and fall of Bustamante: 1945–48

In 1945, the *Frente Democratico Nacional* came to power, with the Benavides-supported Bustamante y Rivero as President. Bustamante's government counted on the support of APRA, and presented itself as a continuation of the centrism and progressive traditions of the Benavides period. However, under Bustamante, APRA was allowed to return to legality in 1945, and there was a significant relaxation in the constraints on overt political action. One obvious aspect of this relaxation was the boost to unionisation, which developed apace across all sectors of employment. Miners, petrol workers, sugar workers, white collar sectors, peasants – all threw up new and important organisations. Simultaneously, the bargaining process became more general as officially-recognised unions sought to establish mechanisms for negotiation. As this process extended, the need for training, advice and legal support for negotiations became more apparent, and the appropriate infrastructure began to develop. This again marks the mid-1940s as a qualitatively new phase in Peruvian industrial relations, in which the possibility of a systematic consolidation of bargaining practices at plant and sectoral levels arose. Certainly, wage levels increased markedly in the 1945–47 period as unions bargained to their advantage, but as crisis re-emerged, the situation deteriorated in 1948, with the gains of the earlier period threatened.

The years 1947 and 1948 saw the agro-export sectors increasing their attack on Bustamante's centrism, and, as they saw it, his unnecessary and economically-demanding accommodation with APRA and the new wave of unions. The 1948 General Strike, supported by the Left and APRA rank-and-files, only served to sharpen tensions, and Bustamante initiated a distancing movement away from APRA support in an attempt to safeguard his government. However, as confrontations increased in 1948, pressures on Bustamante grew alarmingly, and culminated in the coup of October 1948, heralding the *ochenia* of Odría.

A return to the wilderness: 1948–68

The fall of Bustamante, and the vicious oppression unleashed on union and opposition groups by Odría, stopped short the process of consolidation and development allowed in the years between 1943 and 1947/48. The economic background against which this reverse for the labour movement took place constituted what has been described as the 'era of total integration' into the world market. The basis of this integration was substantial foreign investment across all productive sectors, which permitted – bar a short hiccup in 1953/54 – general growth until the late 1950s, whereupon a declining export performance, limited internal market development and the continuing weakness of a national 'industrial bourgeoisie' provoked the crisis of 1968. The employment profile consequent upon this integration exhibits important changes. There was a substantial fall-off in agricultural employment in the waged sector between 1950 and 1972 – from 58.8 per cent to 42.0 per cent. Mining, always relatively minor in employment terms also showed a decline – from 2.2 per cent to 1.4 per cent. Manufacturing rose from 13 per cent in 1950 to 14.5 per cent in 1970, but was to fall away again to 12.8 per cent in 1972. Construction, commerce and general services also increased their importance in waged employment, and the conclusion may be drawn that the period after 1950 saw a relative increase in the importance of urban-based employment against the relative decline in rural waged employment, much as might also be borne out by the evidence of major urbanisation from the late 1940s onwards. However, despite these relative movements, of the economically-active population of 3 926 700 in 1968, only 541 800 (14 per cent) were in manufacturing, and of this figure, only 288 900 were factory-employed blue collar workers, and 51 200 white collar workers; and this of a population of approximately 13 000 000.

Three governments held power in the period between 1948 and

TABLE 2.1 *Sectoral Composition of the Labour Force in Peru, 1950, 1961, 1970 and 1972 (%)*

	1950	*1961*[a]	*1961*[a]	*1970*	*1972*
Agriculture	58.8	52.8	49.8	44.5	42.0
Mining	2.2	2.2	2.2	1.9	1.4
Manufacturing	13.0	13.5	13.2	14.5	12.8
Factory	–	–	4.5	5.4	–
Artisan	–	–	8.7	9.1	–
Construction	2.7	3.4	3.3	3.0	4.2
Commerce	6.6	8.6	8.9	10.9	10.5
Electricity	0.2	0.3			
Transport	2.7	3.1			
Banking	0.4	0.6	18.9	21.3	23.9
Government	4.0	5.5			
Other services	9.3	10.1			
Not specified	–	–	2.6	2.2	4.2
Aspirants	–	–	1.1	1.1	–

[a]Estimates of the Central Reserve Bank and Ministry of Labour respectively.
SOURCE: for 1950, 1961 and 1970, Rosemary Thorp and Geoffrey Bertram, Peru 1890–1977; *Growth and Policy in an Open Economy* (London: Macmillan, 1978) p.259; for 1972, Denis Sulmont, *Historia del Movimiento Obrero en el Peru* (Lima: Ediciones Tarea, 1977).

1968. Between 1948 and 1956 the *Ochenia* of Odría re-established the pattern of either repression or restriction of the labour movement coupled to overtly pro-international investment strategies, especially in mining. Yet the Odría government faced a growing contradiction between the importance of developing manufacturing sectors – engineering, chemicals – and services – banking, teaching – and the claims of their workforces for bargaining rights, union recognition and representation, and freedom of action. Hence, the *Ochenia* attempted to balance a programme of incorporation of certain worker organisations into a popular political base against an overt repression of APRA-based unions, APRA itself and the incipient Left. The CTP was banned, its leaders murdered, and extreme emergency legislation was promulgated (1949) which introduced draconian measures to maintain public order. At the same time, in 1949 the first Ministry of Labour was set up, providing a framework for collective bargaining procedures and conciliation mechanisms. Social security provision for *empleados* was extended and formalised. Profit-sharing schemes were put on statute, but never allowed to function effectively. Wage increases, processed through the government, reflected the expansion of key economic sectors, linking productivity and rewards directly.

As the early 1950s passed, opposition to Odría increased from two directions. On the one hand, general discontent arose in 1950, 1952, 1955 and 1956, and popular risings, particularly in Arequipa, united communities, unions and parties against the regime. On the other, unions themselves faced increasing manipulation from pro-government union leaders. Sulmont describes the variety of methods used in detail, pointing in particular to the parallel organisations established, attempts to subvert the CTP, and even attempts to establish a Peronist-style union tradition. However, despite such schemes, independent union organisation continued, with sugar workers, textile workers and the Arequipa unions taking leading roles in anti-Odría mobilisations. In the event, a united popular opposition, including the new centrist, modernising *Acción Popular* and *Partido Democrato Crisiano* parties, precipitated elections in 1956, in which Prado, supported by APRA and representing a *Coalición Nacional*, won. Henceforward, APRA chose to accommodate itself with the party in power rather than take on a militant oppositional role, and space appeared for the Left and radical *Apristas* to develop alternative opposition programmes for the community in general and the union movement in particular.

Prado's government (1956–61) maintained the openness to international investment, sought to increase the rate of industrialisation by means of the Industrial Promotion Law (1959), and looked to construct a consensual, democratic middle way with the support of APRA and the growing centrist tradition. However, just as Odría faced economic crisis in 1953/54, so Prado was confronted by downturn in 1958/59 and thereafter, which gave rise to a significant popular mobilisation in which unions and the labour movement played a key role. Perhaps the crucial political characteristic of the 1956–62 period was the *Convivencia Democratica* which bound APRA and Prado together. A consequence of this alliance was the legalisation of CTP activity and the return of important union leaders from exile. Space for union growth expanded, particularly in the service sector. Key unions grew in engineering, mining, education and general manufacturing. For example, 1957 saw the establishment of the *Federación de Metalurgicos del Peru*, 1959 the *Federación Nacional de Mineros, Metalurgicos y Similares* and the *Federación Nacional de Educadores*. By 1964, teachers achieved full union rights following extended campaigns for better conditions and against state provisions prohibiting state-sector unionisation.

Yepez and Bernedo point to three measures enacted in this period which bolster union growth.[15] In March 1957 legislation was enacted which made employers responsible for the costs of travel by union officials if such travel was at the behest of state authorities. More importantly, in April 1957 measures were introduced which provided legal protection for union activists against arbitrary dismissal by the employer. This was a crucial protective measure, especially for unions in their early days of formation when they and their leaders were at their most vulnerable. Reflecting the nature of the *convivencia*, this same legislation recognised the CTP as the sole force in the national union structure. This recognition was broadly in line with the reality of union organisation in the period. As pointed out above, the CTP and APRA emerged out of the 1940s as the only coherent, national locus of political power outside the oligarchy. The *convivencia* explicitly captured this reality, yet, paradoxically, provided a stick with which APRA could be beaten at a later date. For, as APRA and the CTP received the state imprimature, the PCP tradition lay fragmented, weak but stirring. It would not forget easily APRA's willingness to co-operate with Prado's commitment to world market integration and an expanding, often externally-controlled productive base. Finally, in the same legislative tradition, it was established that plant-based unions should consist of 20 or more workers, union federations of five or more plant-based unions and confederations of ten federations or more. The significance of this structure is great. Its enactment brought Peruvian labour legislation into line with ILO recommendations pertaining to union recognition. Thus, on a piecemeal basis, another element of a mature IR system was put in place. It has continued to the present day and defines the organisational lines of battle for political control of Peru's labour movement. It simultaneously defines the levels of action which give Peru's labour movement many of its unique characteristics. If plant-level and confederation organisation have their own clear parameters in which power struggles operate that is, the local and the national, the intermediate federation level permits an added dimension to intervene and complicate union activity. Federations will tend to operate at sectoral/or regional levels and offer an important context for pluralist and conflictual representation to develop. In a sense, the tradition which controls the dominant federation structure in the region or the sector dominates the local and the national. Political interventions into the labour movement have not been slow to recognise this consequence of Prado's legislation.

A further point arises from this last disposition. Although groups of workers numbering 19 or less do have some union rights guaranteed in law, their status is less well established than those covered by the Prado legislation. In an economy where 44 per cent of manufacturing units employ less than ten workers it is clear that the cut-off point of 20 is likely to weaken union power generally and create a layer of relatively unprotected wage labourers. In practice, workers in small units have been able to ally themselves via federation-links with more powerful union forces, but is has also been noted that big unions may be less than willing to use their muscle in support of their smaller colleagues.

In 1958 economic crisis precipitated a general social unheaval. In particular, industrial disputes grew in number as Prado attempted to implement International Monetary Fund IMF restrictive policies. Regional and sectoral union mobilisations in Lima, Cuzco and Chimbote, and in steel production, clothing manufacture, construction and education challenged government policy and exacerbated discussions in the CTP. PCP activity took on significant proportions in the Arequipa and Cuzco regions and in construction and service sectors, whilst Christian Democracy threw up an alternative opposition around the *Movimiento Sindical Cristiano del Peru* (MOSCIP). Inevitably, clashes followed this tendency to fragmentation, and pluralist unionism was apparent in the proliferation of conflicting parallel organisations at sectoral and regional levels. However, one crucial body emerged which in changing form was to play a leading role in the eventual decline of CTP hegemony in the labour movement – the 1962 *Comité de Reorganisación y Unificación Sindical de la CTP*. Although initially grouping together a variety of anti-CTP and APRA tendencies, this committee also included PCP supporters and was eventually to give rise in the mid-1960s to demands for an alternative to the CTP to be established.

One aspect of the anti-CTP/APRA tradition deserves more detailed discussion at this juncture. This opposition was not simply the burgeoning PCP, now in full recovery after the defeats of the 1930s and 1940s. It was also the incipient 'New Left', an amalgam of Maoist, Trotskyite and Castroite traditions given life in the late 1950s and early 1960s, particularly by the Cuban revolution. This set in motion the double action of labour movement politics which continues today. The first action was PCP versus APRA, the second the

'New Left' against the PCP and APRA. Obviously each action produced a reaction, and it is this constant motion, played out in terms of organisational power and political consciousness which gives texture to labour movement politics from the early 1960s to the present day. If the 'New Left' could not hope to rival the PCP in terms of numbers and organisational breadth, it has been able to maintain a tenacious presence within the union movement. A thorn in the side of the post-1968 CGTP, and a constant critic of the electoral politics of the post-Morales Bermudez era, the ideological impact of the 'New Left' should not be underestimated.

In June 1962, presidential elections gave APRA a very narrow edge over Belaunde's *Acción Popular* (a centrist reformist party established in 1956) and the persistent Odria. In the ensuing constitutional crisis, claims and counter claims of fraudulent electoral practices proliferated and the Armed Forces intervened in the form of a *junta* presided over by General Perez Godoy. Belaunde was pronounced victor in rearranged elections held in June of the following year and the five-year period of *Belaundismo* followed. Government policy in the period aspired to modernise Peru's economy and society in line with parallel modernisation projects in train in Chile and elsewhere. Unfortunately a two-fold pressure ensured the failure of the project. On the one hand the economy, never healthy, moved into ever-deeper crisis such that economic difficulties became a major spur to military intervention in 1968. On the other hand, different sectors of the community threw up organised opposition to government policies. In particular, organised urban labour proved an ever more militant threat to stable government, a mobilisation paralleled by unprecedented rural militancy throughout the country.

The inability of CTP action to deter military intervention in 1962 served to strengthen the hand of the *Comité de Reorganisacion*. Major disputes involving metal workers, bankworkers and other sections of the manufacturing labour force provided a focus for anti-APRA feeling within the labour movement and gave the *Comité* an opportunity to enhance its status within an increasingly political worker constituency. However, the *Comité* proved incapable of translating its opposition into effective control of the CTP and by 1964–65 APRA had reasserted its power within the *central*. However, Belaunde's attention was elsewhere, coping with the guerrilla threat which came and went between 1963 and 1966. A military fiasco, the move into rural guerrilla warfare by the 'New Left' was to educate its next generation about the need to build links with urban labour and the union movement. Inevitably, the rural struggle polarised the government camp between those in favour of faster reform and those wanting the impose a harsher solution to unrest. Into this growing division intervened the economic crisis of 1967 and its consequent humiliating devaluation. Thereafter, burgeoning crisis dominated Belaunde's government and resulted in the October 1968 military coup, led by General Juan Velasco Alvaredo.

In 1965 it was finally accepted by many activists that attempts to reform the CTP from within were futile. The PCP moved to create the *Comité de Reforma y Unificación Sindical* (CRUS) which rapidly attracted support from unions across the sectoral spectrum. By 1967 CRUS was confident enough to recreate the CGTP at a famous Callao congress. Although the CTP maintained a power base in certain sectors (sugar, textiles, printing, finance and some services), it was the CGTP which became the key union body in the post-1968 period. The eclipse of the CTP was due to three major factors. Firstly, the CTP became over-identified with APRA's political machinations which increasingly reflected a cynical search for political power and an instrumental view of CTP action. Secondly, the CTP was held by increasing numbers of workers to be ineffective in the defence of wages and conditions as the economic crisis of the late 1960s developed. Thirdly, the rhetorical and organisational militancy of CRUS and the CGTP reflected the material demands of many workers. It should be clearly understood that the growth of the CGTP did not imply a homogeneous commitment to PCP politics by union members. Affiliation to the CGTP was based on a more complex set of perceptions of organisational efficacy, ensuring material benefits, political orientation and established union traditions, Rank-and-file attitudes to the CGTP were to remain as big a headache for the CGTP as those same attitudes had meant for the CTP.

The growth of rural unionisation

It is appropriate at this juncture to discuss the impact of rural unionisation. Rural unions grew in a disjointed manner throughout the post-Second World War period. The underlying impetus to this growth was a tendency towards the increased commercialisation of agricultural production in line with the post-war modernisation process, and a related expansion of waged labour in rural production. The extent of these changes should not be exaggerated. Large sectors of the *Sierra* continued to be dominated by traditional land tenure patterns which were resilient in the face of increasing commercial pressure. The rural sector became the site of a wide range of changes in the organisation of production and an equally wide range of struggles between landowner and wage-labourer, peasant and *hacendado*, merchant and peasant and so on. The possibility of rural union organisation arose in only a fraction of the contexts which spread through the post-war rural economy.

Two organisations symbolise the expansion of rural organisation – the *Federación Nacional de Campesinos del Peru* (FENCAP) and the *Confederación Campesina del Peru* (CCP). Each reflects a different trajectory in the creation of rural workers' organisations. FENCAP, created in 1960, derived principally from APRA-led initiatives, particularly amongst the sugar workers of the Trujillo region. APRA's base in the 'Solid North', established since the 1920s, gave ready access to the permanent and migrant labour in the substantial sugar estates which dominated the region. Throughout the 1950s, clashes had become more frequent on the estates with the APRA-led *Federación de Trabajadores Azucareros* building on its experience since the Bustamante era. Inevitably, FENCAP became the centre of clashes between APRA and the PCP, but in its early days APRA came to dominate its actions. More importantly, FENCAP's growth illustrates the role of large-scale waged labour employing capitalist enterprises in the development of rural labour organisation. This sector was to play a major part in the implementation of the Military's agrarian reform policies after 1968.

The CCP was formed in 1962 as a PCP-led alternative to FENCAP. Lacking the firm base of FENCAP in the 'Solid North', the CCP was unable to consolidate its role to the same extent. The Agrarian Reform of 1964 and anti-guerrilla tactics had particularly detrimental effects on CCP organisation, particularly in its *Sierra* bases in the Cuzco region. One aspect of CCP action merits particular comment. As a peasant organisation, the CCP illustrated the problem of applying urban-style organisational traditions to a rural setting. Unions are not necessarily appropriate organisations in which to gather together peasant producers, who may have only marginal links with wage labour and who are not engaged in bargaining with employers or their equivalents. Consequently, although the term 'rural union' was used, it should not be presumed that such organisations displayed the same characteristics as the unions involved in the CTP or CGTP. Nor should contacts between unions in the two settings be presumed, and it is the case up to the present day that urban-rural union links are patchy – good in the case of sugar workers, for example, but not in the case of many groups of peasant producers in the Sierra. Despite these provisos, between 1936 and 1975 599 rural unions were permitted to register by the State, compared with 1803 in the manufacturing sector; although the former is a much smaller figure, nonetheless reveals the desire to create appropriate representative bodies on the part of the rural workforce.

Revolution, resurgence and retreat: 1968–80[16]

The military government led by Velasco took power in October 1968 in the midst of economic crisis and growing popular unrest. The re-establishment of the PCP as a major oppositional force, and its domination of the newly-reconstructed CGTP, loomed as a further challenge rooted in the labour movement. It is therefore not surprising that the radical-nationalist stance taken by the new government should have startled observers. The period 1968–75 saw an attempt to wrest and consolidate a degree of autonomy from the world market, a strategy at odds with that adopted since 1948. Central to the Velasco strategy for autonomy were policies designed to transform the production relations in both industry and agriculture. To this end, industrial participation and self-management were introduced into the industrial sector, whilst co-operative ventures of various sorts were commenced in agriculture. However, the military's policies confronted a major contradiction. The purpose of this transformation of production relationships and institutions was the modernisation and industrialisation of the national economy such that, on the one hand, industrial production might be expanded and made more productive, and, on the other, that agriculture might be modernised, capitalised and made increasingly market-orientated. Yet the success of such a modernisation programme rested on the maintenance of economic and political stability, a stability still fundamentally determined by Peru's linkages into the world economy via cash-crop and mineral exports and international debt commitments. Such stability was not forthcoming, and, combined with internal problems of policy and faction-fighting, led to the undermining of the radical policies post-1975.

The Velasco government introduced a number of new elements into labour law. For example, minimum wage legislation was laid down in 1972. However, two major innovations were particularly important: the 1970 law guaranteeing *estabilidad laboral*, and the new approach adopted on the issue of union recognition. Though excluding many workers, including state employees, the security of employment legislation was a breakthrough for labour, and provoked substantial opposition from employers. Legal frameworks for dismissal were laid down, including access to courts and forms of compensation. Though it was open to abuse and managerial avoidance, no similar legislation had been enacted previously in Peruvian labour relations history. Turning to the union recognition policy, post-1968 saw a dramatic increase in formally-recognised unions, reflecting an upsurge in plant-level organisation. Perhaps surprisingly, the government displayed little immediate concern about this development in the 1968–75 period, despite the importance of radical, often highly-critical, inputs to union formation. Undoubtedly, some of the more radically-minded ministers viewed labour organisation with equanimity, but as 1975 approached explicit criticisms of 'unco-operative' union activities became more frequent.

However rhetorically-radical appeared the ideological approach of the 1968–75 period, there was no attempt made to codify the industrial relations system in any formal sense. For the Velasco government, the answer for problems of labour-capital conflict lay not in a codified, patrolled collective bargaining structure, but in an apparently far more radical reconstruction of production relations. The framework chosen by Velasco's team rested on a complex of worker participation and self-management, a 'third way' between Capitalism and Communism which rests on a number of participative traditions, particularly that of Yugoslavia. The *Comunidad Laboral*, effecting industrial, telecommunications, fishing and ministry sectors, consisted of a complex of capital- and profit-sharing schemes designed to create a unitary level between workers and managers. Some 288 000 workers in 4000 plants and enterprises were effected by the *Comunidad Laboral*, with a variety of consequences: in general, management power in the firm was little affected; the benefits of both capital- and profit-sharing schemes were very uneven, and, on the whole, not dramatically valuable in income terms for workers; consensual management-labour relations were not implanted; many firms which should have been reformed never implemented the *comunidad*; the *comunidad* often allied itself with the plant unions against management; the period between 1970 and 1977 – when the *comunidad* was effectively disarmed – provided too short a time for the experiment to take root effectively; the failures of the *comunidad* provided a rallying point for critics of the government of all political persuasions. In industrial relations terms, these consequences signified the failure of the government's approach to the coherent restructuring of labour-capital relations. Unitary, participative processes foundered on the rocks of employer opposition, political turmoil, and the commitment by many workers to a militant offensive against state and capital.

The self-management sector – *Propriedad Social* – manifested equivalent problems. Designed as a self-financing, self-reproducing system of *empresas autogestionarias*, and benefitting from extensive inputs from international experts in the self-management field, *Propriedad Social* never came to dominate the industrial sector as originally proposed. The number of functioning units was minimal, though grandiose plans consistently looked to bigger and better things, and problems of training, finance, project choice, and worker involvement dogged the experiment. By the time that retrenchment set in in 1975, this ambitious scheme was still primarily a strategy on paper, and rapidly resolved itself into a rump of the original proposals. Again, in industrial relations terms, the expectations raised by the scheme failed to materialise in practice, and it was rapidly overtaken by more traditional, conflictual relationships between labour and capital.

A third strand, supporting the *Comunidad Laboral* and *Propriedad Social*, was designed to underpin the 1968–75 alternative to traditional labour relations. This consisted of the attempted incorporation of large numbers of workers into the ideological approach of the 'First-Phase'. Perhaps two vehicles illustrate this strand most clearly: the *Sistema Nacional de Apoyo a la Movilizacion Social* (SINAMOS), and the *Central de Trabajadores de la Revolución Peruana* (CTRP). SINAMOS was established in 1971 as the mobilising agent of support for the government. Nationally active, it intervened particularly – through its *Area Laboral* – in industrial relations issues, and sought, firstly, to promote the ideologies and practices necessary to foster the *comunidad* and *Propriedad Social*; secondly, to defend the importance of ideology against technocratic views emanating particularly from the Ministry of Industry and Tourism; thirdly, to oppose militant criticism of the government from either APRA or the Left; fourthly, to intervene politically in workplace and community in order to influence and direct people's actions. Perhaps SINAMOS' biggest failure was its attempt to control and direct the *Comunidad Laboral*. In the murk of complex political in-fighting, the first national congress of the *Confederación Nacional de Comunidades Industriales* (CONACI) took place in 1973, with the key issue being the degree of autonomy CONACI would have from the State and SINAMOS. The outcome of the conflict was a victory for the Left, which won a degree of autonomy for CONACI which was at odds with SINAMOS' functions, and boded ill for the effective construction of unitary industrial relations. By 1974 SINAMOS was in decline as a force, and its effective demise rapidly followed. State-inspired incorporation had apparently failed.

The creation of the CTRP in 1972 was an explicit attempt to incorporate large sections of the labour force into a pro-government union *central*, in the process hopefully creating an effective counterweight to the growth of the CGTP. Again the strategy went awry. The threat to the CGTP was not from the CTRP, but from the Left. The CTRP was never able to establish an effective base within the industrial workforce, and a variety of ruses were required to massage its membership figures to a reasonable size. The government had also unleashed a tiger in the CTRP. Many of its members were strongly committed to the radical policies of the 'First Phase', and when, after 1975, many of these policies were downgraded or dismissed, increasingly large sections of the CTRP moved into opposition against the 1975–80 Morales Bermudez 'Second Phase'. Thus, not only had the CTRP failed to incorporate the labour movement; it had also harboured a source of future militant opposition to the government.

The period between 1968 and 1975 was, therefore, a watershed in Peruvian industrial relations history. Rejecting a traditional collective bargaining approach, the government attempted to provide a coherent participative framework for labour relations based on the general incorporation of workers into co-operative processes. This was undoubtedly the first attempt in Peruvian history to provide a framework on this scale, and it failed. The failure was due, in broad terms, to three factors. Firstly, there is a question-mark hanging over the likelihood of such proposals ever being effective, especially given the constraints imposed by the Peruvian situation in the world market. Secondly, the economic stability required to nurture such ambitious proposals was by 1973 greatly threatened. Velasco's overthrow in 1975 may be put down to the combination of failing policies, internal opposition within the government, and, crucially, the declining economic fortunes of Peru, which placed the country at the mercy of World Bank deflationary policies. Thirdly, the labour movement, having gained political and organisational confidence in the 1960s, was in no mood to be 'incorporated'.

The agrarian reform of 1969 introduced a variety of participative mechanisms into the rural sector, which faced problems peculiar to itself. A two-tier system of collective agricultural production was designed to function parallel to the continuing peasant sector. Co-operative organisation in the established centres of capitalist, export-orientated sugar production on the coast gave rise to problems of participation and productivity, whilst, primarily in the Sierra, SAIS (*Sociedades Agrarias de Interes Social*) grouped together peasant and community based production. Both models of collective production gave rise to problems, but those of the sugar industry took on a particular importance. Sugar was not only a major export, upon which many government hopes rested; it was also a heavily-unionised, militant and, often, APRA-linked sector, which was neither easily incorporated into the government's model, nor slow to challenge perceived threats to its status and organisation. At no stage between 1969 and 1975 were either of the problems – productivity, worker organisation – resolved by the military government, and they continue to the present day.

The labour movement: 1968–80[17]

The qualitative transformation in the fortunes of the labour movement during the 1960s and 1970s is demonstrated by both figures for unionisation and the strike record over the period.

The organisational focus provided by CGTP after 1967 gave the PCP the central role in union politics, displacing decisively the status of APRA. However, the defining feature of the 1968–76 period was the challenge which emerged from the Left to the position of the CGTP. This challenge – fragmented, often transient, rank-and-file based – sought to capitalise on the organisational gains made in the late 1960s, and to take advantage of relative freedom of action provided by the 'First Phase'. To understand the challenge, the position of the CGTP and PCP *vis-à-vis* the Velasco government requires explanation. Between 1968 and 1971 the PCP/CGTP offered critical support to the government, based upon a relatively positive appreciation of the nationalist and radical aspect of Velasco's policies. After 1971, and on to 1978, the PCP/CGTP was increasingly under attack from the State, yet maintained active support for the government policies. Thereafter, as the repudiation of the 'First Phase' gained ground under Morales Bermudez, the PCP/CGTP moved into a combined position of defence of the 'First Phase', and attack on the repudiation. However, despite gains made in the

TABLE 2.2 *Peru: Patterns of Trade Union Recognition*

(a) Recognition by period

	All Unions	Industrial sector
Unions recognised before 1968	2152	776
Unions recognised 1968–75	2020	931
Total	4172	1707

(b) Unions recognised 1969–74 by sector

	Number of Unions
Agriculture	172
Mining	88
Manufacturing	776
Construction	28
Energy	7
Commerce	250
Transport	88
Services	177
Total	1586

(c) Unions recognised 1974–1984

Year	Number of unions recognised
1974	344
1975	234
1976	126
1977	30
1978	54
1979	28
1980	61
1981	60
1982	42
1983	22
1984	6

SOURCES: (a) Alan Angell 'Peruvian Labour and the Military Government since 1968' (Institute of Latin American Studies, Working Paper No. 3, 1980) p. 9, citing B. Stephens, 'The Politics of Workers' Participation: the Peruvian Approach in Comparative Perspective' (Yale University PhD thesis, 1977); (b) Denis Sulmont, 'El Desarrollo de la Clase Obrera en el Peru' (Lima: Pontificia Universidad Catolica, Departamento de Ciencias Sociales, mimeo, 1974); (c) Adapted from Yepez and Bernedo (1986) p. 25.

1968–73 period, the average worker thereafter felt the impact of economic crisis as wages failed to keep pace with inflation and austerity policies began to coincide with more overtly anti-union moves. In this context, continuing PCP/CGTP support for the government provoked strongly-critical reactions within the labour movement. In 1974 these reactions gave rise to the formation of the *Comité de Coordinación y Unificación Sindical Clasista* (CCUSC) a leftist amalgamation of political activists and unionists, opposed to the government and to the 'collaborationist' policies of the CGTP/PCP. Though CCUSC was always numerically weak and was in decline by 1976, it reflected the growth of important radical alternatives to the PCP, and a greater complexity within the political life of the labour movement.

Four sections of workers were particularly important in the challenge to the PCP/CGTP. Miners clashed with the government throughout the early 1970s, leading to the bulk of their representation leaving the CGTP. CENTROMIN miners, with others, were represented at the founding conference of CCUSC. Secondly, teachers, organised in the Leftist-influenced *Sindicato Unico de Trabajadores de la Educación el Peru* (SUTEP), were mobilised in opposition to the government's educational reforms, and on the issues of salaries and conditions. Thirdly, anti-PCP/CGTP activity was present in the traditional sectors of urban employment, with the metalworkers organisation (FETIMP) exemplifying the Leftist challenge. Finally, state-sector workers – for example, in CENTROMIN, SIDERPERU (steel), PESCAPERU (fishing) – reacted to the less-supportive treatment they received in comparison to private-sector employees, and were active in terms of organisational initiatives and strikes.

Women in the industrial workforce

At this point it is appropriate to shed limited light on the role of women in both production and the union movement, Scott has produced a pioneering contribution to the elucidation of this question, and, using Lima-based data, opens the way for a more general assessment of women's waged work in Peru.[18]

The benchmark for analysis of women's activity in waged work is their participation rate and its changing level since the 1940 census. It is generally accepted that in certain sectors (textiles, for example — see Chaplin's 1967 essay) women's participation in formal, waged work has declined substantially. The usual explanation for this decline, in part supported by Scott's argument, is that work benefits peculiar to women, and consequent labour market 'stickiness', led employers to substitute male for female labour. Scott, however, offers a more detailed analysis of participation rates which notes that the general participation rate fell from 40 per cent in 1940 to 33 per cent in 1972, and the women's rate fell from 26 per cent to 22 per cent in the same period. As a result, the proportion of women in Lima's labour force remained stable at around 28 per cent. Scott's data on the distribution of employment by economic sector and by sex indicates a move by women out of manufacturing and into commerce and services, paralleled by a most dramatic increase in women's employment in white collar positions. As Scott says:

> The rise in female white collar labour has been truly spectacular; it represented half the net increase in total female employment and its rate of growth was two and a half times that of the total female labour force . . . . . . The rise in women's salaried labour has taken place in every sector: within the manufacturing sector its share rose from 9% to 29%, in commerce from 35% to 40%, and in services from 20% to 43%. By far the highest proportion of white collar women were concentrated in the services sector (57%) and the majority of them were employed by the State.

Scott's analysis leads her to conclude that in certain kinds of enterprise women would continue to be employed despite the perceived costs of conforming to state maternity benefits and similar provisions. However, in absolute terms neither the growth of industrial white collar opportunities nor the stable growth of petty manufacturing have made up for the fall in the incidence of female waged work. This adverse effect arose despite evidence suggesting that in educational and training terms women were 'appropriate' for waged factory work. Scott concludes that:

> the segregation of labour markets by gender, which cuts across sectoral and educational divisions, requires a . . . . . complex set of explanations. Women's position in Lima was primarily influenced by changes in the rates of growth of 'women's jobs' . . .

Although the 'complex set of explanations' subsequently offered are convincing, it is interesting to speculate (in the absence of detailed studies) about the consequences of the changes described above for women's role in the labour movement. Firstly, despite the fall in numbers employed, certain industrial sectors – textiles, footwear, chemicals – still employ large numbers of women. Union power in these sectors is at least partly dependent upon the integration of women into union organisation. However, many major sectors of manufacturing still predominantly employ males and the role of women in those sectors' unions will be concomitantly less. In areas where state employment has expanded, the consequent expansion of women's employment opportunities gives rise to a new potential for women's involvement in labour movement action. The expansion of the teaching profession, its unionisation and its politicisation (particularly by the actions of the *Sindicato Unico de Trabajadores de la Educacion Peruana* – SUTEP) is one of a number of cases in which women can be seen to be very active in organisational and activist roles.

Secondly, the expansion of white collar opportunities for women indicates the growth of female membership of *empleado* rather than *obrero* union bodies, where white collar unionisation is permitted at all. Risking charges of over-generalisation, it is arguably the case that Peruvian *empleado* organisations are generally less politically orientated and more unitarist in tone and action than *obrero* bodies. Where this is the case, it is likely that white collar employment opportunities will not lead to any great politicisation or union consciousness amongst women.

A third factor may reinforce the effects of the second. The traditional roles attributed to women by a particularly 'macho' society, linked to the continuing involvement of women in 'appropriate' paid and unpaid domestic labour, reinforces the image of women as beyond the organisational limits of the traditional union movement. Against this, however, it may be argued that the importance of the workplace-community bond in the urban setting leads to industrial issues taking on a wider social function rather than a simple economistic narrrowness. If this is the case, and there is some evidence particularly from the 1970s to show it to be so, then the politicised role of women may find its central expression beyond the narrow confines of union membership.

Morales Bermudez and the second phase

Mid-1976 saw the policy of reversing the Velasco tradition in full swing. The Morales Bermudez government watered down many of the 'First Phase' reforms, particularly relating to the *Comunidad Laboral* and security of employment provisions. Devaluation of the currency, rapid increases in the prices of consumer goods, declining real wages (down 21 per cent in real terms in 1977 and 18 per cent in 1978 and an IMF-sponsored 'stabilisation' strategy set the scene for the often-violent confrontations between the State and the labour movement which led up to the democratisation of 1980. The central confrontation was the first all-out general strike organised in Peru since 1919, when in July 1977, the CGTP, sectors of the CTRP and other union bodies won concessions over prices and wages, an end to the existing State of Emergency, and an acceleration of the democratisation process. This success was paralleled by electoral success for the Left in the Constituent Assembly elections of 1978, when it won an unprecedented figure of 30 per cent of the total vote. Supporting these two central successes were successful general strike calls in February, April and May 1978, and protracted disputes with teachers and miners during 1979.

TABLE 2.3 *Peru: Strike Figures, 1968–84*

Year	*Strikes*	*Workers Involved*	*Hours/Person Lost*
		(000)	
1968	364	107.8	3.4
1969	372	91.5	3.9
1970	345	111.0	5.8
1971	377	161.4	10.9
1972	409	130.6	6.3
1973	788	416.3	15.7
1974	570	362.7	13.4
1975	779	617.1	20.3
1976	440	258.1	6.8
1977	234	406.5	6.5
1978	364	1398.4	36.1
1979	637	841.1	13.4
1980	739	481.5	17.9
1981	871	856.9	20.0
1982	809	548.8	22.5
1983	843	785.0	20.0
1984	247	452.0	8.0

SOURCE: Adapted from Yepez and Bernedo (1986) p.35.

The Constituent Assembly elections precipitated dramatic political reconciliations. Two leftist electoral fronts were formed in 1978. FOCEP united Trotskyists, pro-Albanians and some independent leftists whilst the UDP consisted primarily of Vanguardia Revolucionaria, the PCR, much of the MIR and further small splinter elements. The PCP stood aloof from these 'ultra-leftist' forces and entered the electoral process on its own platform. Belaunde's *Accion Popular* initially moved to put up candidates, then decided to boycott the whole proceeding. In the end, the elections took place against a background of a general strike call in May 1978, numerous clashes, deportations and arrests. APRA was the largest single party with 35.3 per cent of the vote, the right-of-centre PPC received 24 per cent in Accion Popular's absence, but the surprising result was the combined vote for the Left which reached the impressive figure of 30 per cent.

By any reckoning this was a remarkable electoral achievement by the Left, yet this obscures three basic issues. Firstly, APRA, though apparently vanquished in the labour movement in the late 1960s, clearly won the 1978 Constituent Assembly elections, anticipating their eventual victory in the 1985 elections. Secondly, electoral unity and coherent general strike activity in the late 1970s obscured the continuing fragmentation of both Left parties and union organisations. Sectarianism and division remained an ever-present threat to consolidated labour movement action. Thirdly, despite the level of activity achieved in the late 1970s, it had not necessarily gained the economic rewards expected. Recent analysis (Parodi 1986) suggests that a degree of disillusionment with union action was being generated amongst the rank-and-file consequent upon the perception that returns to militancy were not forthcoming. To this may be added the results of management strategy which moved to dismiss large numbers of union organisers and militants. This arguably further qualified the union successes of the late 1970s. However, the late 1970s witnessed the highwater mark of the successes built on since the 1960s. Five years of a Belaunde presidency were to qualify this success.

The elections in 1980 for the new democratic government were dominated by crises in both APRA and the leftist alliances. The death of Haya de la Torre in 1979 led to internal squabbling in APRA, not resolved until Alan Garcia was declared leader in 1982. On the Left, the ARI political front (the UDP, Patria Roja plus others) foundered rapidly as did a PCP, PSR and FOCEP alliance. Meanwhile, Belaunde and *Acción Popular* stepped into the electoral scene to such an effect that they gained a clear victory with 45 per cent of the poll. Broadly, neither APRA nor the Left did well, and Belaunde appeared to have acquired a clear mandate for his policies.

Democratisation, recession and reaction: 1980–85[19]

The return to democratic government in 1980 was ominously overshadowed by economic difficulties, despite a temporary upsurge in 1980 and 1981. The year 1983 saw a 13.2 per cent decline in per capita gross output, whilst the index of manufacturing production had declined from a 1981 high of 124 to 100, equivalent to the level achieved in 1973. Employment suffered in equal measure. Unemployment generally reached 9 per cent in Lima, but, perhaps more importantly, underemployment rose dramatically, from 26 per cent in 1980 to 45 per cent in 1983. At the national level, underemployment reached 57.1 per cent in 1983 and seemed unlikely to reverse its upward momentum. Average incomes were similarly affected, falling in Lima by 15 per cent in 1983 and a further 20 per cent in 1984. Clearly, recession was to be a defining factor in the development of union responses to democratisation.

TABLE 2.4 *Peru: Gross Domestic Product by Sector, 1986–90*

		(%)			
	1986	*1987*	*1988*	*1989*	*1990*
Agriculture	11.4	11.3	11.1	11.1	11.0
Fishing	0.8	0.9	0.9	1.0	1.0
Mining	11.4	11.1	10.9	10.7	10.4
Manufacturing	22.9	23.3	23.7	23.8	24.1
Commerce	18.0	17.9	17.7	17.7	17.6
Electricity-Water	1.2	1.2	1.2	1.2	1.2
Financial Services	8.6	8.9	9.2	9.2	9.5
Government Services	7.8	7.5	7.5	7.4	7.2
Others	12.6	12.5	12.2	12.0	11.2
INP-EPC					

SOURCE: Medium-Term, Plan, INP, LIMA, 1986.

Belaunde's economic policy was predicated on a free market strategy imported from the USA by Prime Minister Ulloa and his economic aides – known collectively as 'the Dynamo'. Stressing the importance of the private sector, competition and international comparative advantage, Ulloa sought to transform radically the Peruvian economic structure, in particular by attacking the state sector, which by 1980 accounted for more than a third of national production. Unfortunately, much as happened in Chile under the 'Chicago Boys', the import boom unleashed by policies promoting competition – especially the reduction of import tariffs and quotas – decimated national industrial production, with manufacturing output falling by more than 20 per cent between 1981 and 1983. Traditionally important industries such as textiles and leather goods suffered drastically, as did vehicle assembly and general engineering. The financial sector fell on hard times as the recession grew in 1983. Droughts and other natural disasters complicated an already fraught picture. The fall of Ulloa in late 1982 did little to alleviate the growing crisis, and Peru was forced into the arms of the IMF again, albeit unwillingly.

Acción Popular and labour relations[20]

Belaunde's *Acción Popular* government came to power ostensibly promoting an orthodox commitment to collective bargaining on the part of both employees and the State. However, the union's enthusiastic response to this policy provoked problems for state policy. Unions threw themselves into bargaining with all the gusto of a labour movement which had seen a steady fall in its purchasing power since 1973. Adjustments were sought not merely for the effects of the previous year's price increases, but for the decline in wage levels over the previous decade. A dramatic growth in strike activity paralleled this tabling of demands, the number of strikes doubling between 1979 and 1981. Both the PCP/CGTP and the radical left were active in promoting this explosion of bargaining and pressure, though with different emphases in their respective policies. The PCP/CGTP sought to consolidate the power of the CGTP in the new democratic era, consequently attempting to distance itself from both state and radical left, and seeking to maintain its union base whilst simultaneously entering the newly-freed political area in constitutional fashion. In practice this watered down the influence of the radical left within the union sector, primarily because unions were more immediately concerned with the improvement of wages and conditions. Consequently, it has been argued that democratisation led to a disarticulation of union demands and organisation from the Left's involvement in constitutional democratic politics – economism asserting itself within the union sector in the early days of post-military government. Clearly, the unity of political and union interests fostered during the Morales Bermudez period in particular still manifested the traditional fragility of Peruvian labour movement development.

In the short run, the expansion of collective bargaining in the early years of Belaunde's government brought substantial gains for waged labour. The steady decline in real incomes was halted and a modest resurgence in the value of the wage was set in train by 1982. Parodi argues that the distribution of gains was not uniform, and reinforces a view held by others that the differential density of unionisation has been a crucial factor in the determination of returns to bargaining. Hence, well-unionised, highly-experienced workers – for example mining, manufacturing, banking – received increases in the 4–10 per cent range whilst many groups of *empleados* lost between 13 and 21 per cent. A further consequence of the inequity in returns was union differentiation, primarily between those which perceived themselves as self-reliant and logistically capable of achieving gains through their own efforts, and the weaker unions dependent on a united front of solidarity action for success. As was seen in the heyday of the Industrial Community in the 1970s, powerful unions were often unwilling to put their status and power behind the claims made by smaller, weaker unions. In turn, this has implications for the '*clasista*' interpretation of union development in the late 1960s and 1970s. A continuing organisational self-interest on the part of bigger unions indicates that left-wing belief in union action transcending sectional interests was at least compromised, or, taking a harsher view, misguided. Economistic fragmentation of union efforts was a continuing reality in the early 1980s.

Sectional self-interest was also indirectly promoted by state policy on incomes. Operating under constraints imposed by the International Monetary Fund, Belaunde's government applied an indirect incomes policy designed to reduce wage pressure on inflation. Given that bigger, more powerful unions could expect to use militant action as a means of breaking government norms, it was inevitable that weaker workforces would be more likely to conform to government norms. Simply, less powerful unions could not use militancy to break either employers or the State, and could not expect to receive the support of the powerful unions to effect a successful campaign.

Further evidence of sectional fragmentation appeared when the question of redundancy in restructuring emerged as recession took hold. Once again the thorny problem of part-time and contract labour reared its head. The lack of a coherent, general policy for bargaining, and the establishment of self-interest as a major driving force in the bargaining process in 1980–82, led to a willingness to sacrifice workers who did not enjoy the protection of *Estabilidad Laboral* in order to defend those with such protection. Segmented labour market theory would point to this as a likely outcome of restructuring. However, it again cuts across the perception of a newly cohesive, political working class which was prepared to fight for the conditions of all workers regardless of individual status.

Parodi is led to argue that union action in the second Belaunde period lost much of its collective power as workers increasingly came to adopt an individualistic view of the world. Individualism was not simply a product of union weakness and fragmentation, but was also a consequence of conscious management strategy designed to weaken the sense of a collective worker identity. He provides evidence of this in terms of a decline in the participation rates in union meetings, falling union subscriptions and a difficulty in filling union posts of responsibility. Furthermore, he argues, 1983 saw a 64 per cent drop in man-hours lost through strikes, and a further drop of 24 per cent in 1984. Finally, Parodi presents evidence that in a relatively large number of cases in the 1983–84 period, workers employing collective bargaining techniques have fared worse than those without the benefits of the traditional bargaining structures.

Parodi's analysis is perhaps over-bleak in its prognosis. His legitimate emphasis on the fragmentation of the union movement in the face of economic crisis is understandable and follows in the footsteps of other analysis. However, many of the phenomena noted above are not peculiar to the mid-1980s. As discussed above, worker adherence to unions has always been subject to contradictory pressures, particularly the clash between the individualist instrumental and the collective 'clasista' perspectives. Equally, evidence based on 27 cases of the failings of collective bargaining methods is at best simply indicative rather than conclusive. The decrease in strike incidence is more telling, but a two-year data series again leaves much open to question. A more balanced interpretation might reflect on the cyclical nature of labour organisation in Peru, which suggests that economic crisis, a return to democracy and a fragmented political leadership disorientated the labour movement in the short period between 1982 and 1984. Against the image of disorientation might be raised the spectre of miners engaged in consistent anti-state action, albeit under adverse conditions, the continuing militancy of numbers of state-sector employees, the organisation of six national strikes between

1981 and 1984, continuing regional union militancy, and maintenance of effective union federation and confederation structures. Certainly, the post-1985 period, under the presidency of APRA's Alan Garcia, has seen a consistent level of union activity around both economic and political issues.

During the 1980–85 period, greater fluidity emerged in the structure of Peruvian unions and their political affiliations. The CGTP instigated general strike action in March and September 1983, and in March 1984. In all three cases independent unions supported the call to action; in the first and the last case support was also forthcoming from the CTP, CNT and the CTRP. A willingness to undertake joint union action was paralleled by an erosion of the strictly sectional traditions of *central* organisation. Hence, the inclusion of SUTEP and the miners' union in the CGTP reduced the impact of the PCP's political leadership and promised an increasingly pluralistic framework for decision-making. The CTP also began to look outward rather than in, as the crisis over APRA's leadership was resolved and as APRA itself called for a more open aspect in the CTP's presentation. Political action also became more extrovert as the defeats of 1980 were considered. The IU brought together most of the leading Left groups around a common electoral programme in late 1980, and in the 1983 municipal elections the IU gained 29 per cent of the vote, compared with the newly-united Apra's 33 per cent. *Accion Popular* won a mere 17 per cent.

However, unions had to confront the piecemeal attempt by the Belaunde government to restructure labour legislation, particularly that left over from the military regime of 1968–80. During the period 1980–85 legislation was introduced which threatened the rights of state employees to bargain collectively, imposed a Tripartite Commission on employment relations in order to create a Peruvian 'social contract', imposed a new strike law, attacked the *Comunidad Industrial*, rendered more insecure social security provision and reduced statutory impositions on newly-established firms. Much of this legislative thrust was in line with commitments made to the International Monetary Fund, and with the Belaunde government's free market policies. 'Flexibility' in labour relations was one specific requirement which the government sought to meet, and many of the piecemeal legislative changes were designed to fulfil this requirement. Equally important in the search for flexibility was the attempt to reduce the State's role in 'directing' the course of labour relations in Peru. In practice, the fall of Belaunde and the election of APRA's Garcia halted this process, but the new APRA government was faced with a legislative structure governing labour relations which was an unfortunate hybrid of the practices introduced in 1968–80 and 1980–85. It remains to be seen whether Garcia's government will attempt to rationalise this structure, or replace it with a new integrated structure. Either strategy brings with it major problems with both unions and management and the decision about policy directions cannot be easily delayed as APRA's election will raise high hopes on the labour movement's part.

CONCLUSIONS

Perhaps the most apposite point on which to conclude concerns the future of Peruvian industrial relations. As an industrial relations tradition, it is irrevocably politicised, much as argued by James Payne in the 1960s. The future of plant, federation and confederation union organisation is enmeshed with that of political parties and alliances, and so it has been since the early stirrings of anarcho-syndicalism and union activity at the turn of the century. Peruvian industrial relations, left unstructured, will consequently always transcend the simple demands of economism. However, one theme raised throughout this argument has been the unstructured, uncodified nature of employer-employee relationships. Even today, after Belaunde's piecemeal attempts to reconstruct the labour relations model in terms of free market criteria, his efforts have simply made more convoluted an already complex system. As under Belaunde, the future focus of labour relations developments initiated by the state should be the institutionalisation of the labour relations system in the hope that this will achieve and maintain a disjuncture between political parties and union organisations.

Such an achievement might well benefit both employers and the State. It is not so obvious that it would serve unions and their members so well. Despite Payne's injunctions, the intimacy between party and union, and the parallel relationship between community and workplace, which currently denotes Peruvian labour relationships, reflects the complex and often contradictory interests of resident and worker, union organisation and community body. The erosion of this intimacy would be to the advantage of state and employer; it would strike at the heart of the greatest strength the Peruvian labour movement possesses – its consciousness and its traditions which together, despite political defeat, fragmentation and repression, are its historically-established common bond.

NOTES

1. The classic statement of the systems approach in industrial relations is found in Dunlop (1958). Payne (1965) implicitly adopts this approach in his interpretation of the Peruvian IR tradition, and suggests reforms which might bring this tradition in line with the Dunlopian model. Haworth (1987a and b) discusses Payne's analysis in detail.
2. A more detailed historical account of the proletarianisation process in Peru may be found in Haworth (1984).
3. Perhaps the most articulate application of the dualist model to the political economy of Peru is that provided by Fitzgerald (1979).
4. See Salazar (1985) where also an account of the role of Chilean workers in Peru may be found.
5. Thorp and Bertram (1978) stands as the most readable and comprehensive economic history of Peru over the last century. It is an essential source of reference for students of the Peruvian economy.
6. Sulmont (1975, 1978, 1982) are classic accounts of the growth of the Peruvian labour movement, supplemented by numerous other publications. As in the case of Thorp and Bertram (1978), Sulmont's work is required reading for those interested in the Peruvian labour movement. Sulmont's work contains very useful bibliographies for those wishing to study Peruvian labour relations in greater depth.
7. See Yepes (1972) which offers not only insights into labour movement formation during the last century but also provides a respected interpretation of Peruvian economic development in the nineteenth century.
8. Garland (1905) is an oft-quoted analysis of industrial formation at the turn of the century. It is generally thought to be more accurate about the Lima-Callao data but less accurate about provincial material, which is clearly underrepresented in his account.
9. Blanchard (1975) is an excellent starting point for a study of the labour movement in the opening decades of this century. His bibliography is most useful.
10. The outcome of the struggles of the 1918–19 period, particularly as it affected the strength of the anarcho-syndicalist tradition, remains one of the most interesting and least understood eras in labour movement formation. This period, and the years between 1929–34 and 1943–48, are the crucial periods of labour movement formation which require more detailed historical interpretation.
11. Haworth (1987a and b) offer a basic interpretation of the failure to create a Chilean-style accommodation in Peru. However, this interpretation requires substantial research for it to be confirmed unequivocally.
12. For discussions of the nature of APRA see, for example, Alexander (1973), Klaren (1973), Kantor (1966), Villanueva (1977), North (1972).

On Mariategui and the growth of the PSP/PCP the literature is much thinner. Unlike the case of APRA, one must still turn to Mariategui's own writings for the best understanding of his perspective. Bazan (1970), Choy *et al.* (1970) may also be of some use.

13. For a more detailed discussion of the 'accommodation' argument, see Roddick and Haworth (1983).
14. Again, Haworth (1987a and b) provide a more detailed account of Payne's central thesis and its problems.
15. Yepez and Bernedo (1986) also provides an interesting account of contemporary unionisation in Peru.
16. The best source material on the period 1968–80 is found in Booth and Sorj (1983), Lowenthal (1975), Chaplin (1976), Fitzgerald (1979), Philip (1978) and Stepan (1978). These texts also offer extended bibliographies – particularly the Booth and Sorj collection.
17. Haworth (1983) offers an interpretation of labour movement activity in the 1968–79 period which complements that of Angell (1980).
18. See Scott (1986) for an extended analysis briefly outlined here.
19. Reid (1985) is by far the most accessible source of information and analysis about the post-1980 period, though it is both short and necessarily descriptive at times. Ballon *et al.* (1986) is a more analytical collection which complements Reid's work well.
20. Parodi's article, found in Ballon *et al.* (1986) raises many questions the answers to which must remain unclear for some time. However, the piece is in interesting contrast to the more overtly 'political' argument found in Sulmont (1982).

BIBLIOGRAPHY

ALBA, V. (1968), *Politics and the Labor Movement in Latin America* (Stanford: Stanford University Press).

ALBERT, B. (1976), 'An Essay on the Peruvian Sugar Industry' (University of East Anglia, Norwich).

ALBERT, B. (1982), 'The Labour Force on Peru's Sugar Plantation 1820–1930: A Survey'. Mimeo.

ALBERTI G., SANTISTEVAN J. and PASARA, L. (1977), *Estado y Clase: La Communidad Industrial en el Peru* (Lima: Instituto de Estudios Peruanos).

ALEXANDER, R.J. (1973), 'Aprismo: The Ideas and Doctrines of Victor Raul Haya de la Torre' (Kent State University Press).

ANGELL, A. (1980), 'Peruvian Labour and the Military Government since 1968' (University of London, Institute of Latin American Studies Working Paper no. 3).

ASTIZ, C.A. (1969), *Pressure Groups and Power Elites in Peruvian Politics* (Ithaca: Cornell University Press).

BALLON, E. *et al.* (1986), 'Movimientos Sociales y Crisis: El Caso Peruano' (DESCO, Lima).

BAZAN, A. (1970), 'Biografia de J C Mariategui' (2nd ed., Lima).
BELAUNDE, F. (1959), *La Conquista del Peru por los Peruanos*, 2nd ed. (Lima: eds 'Tawantinsuyu').
BLANCHARD, P. (1975), *The Peruvian Working Class Movement 1883–1919* (PhD: University of London).
BOOTH, D. and SORJ, B. (1983), *Military Reformism and Social Classes: The Peruvian Experience 1968–80* (London: Macmillan).
BOURRICAUD, F. (1970), *Power and Society in Contemporary Peru*. (New York: Praeger).
CABIESES, H. (1976), *Comunidad Laboral y Capitalismo: Alcances y Limites* (Lima: DESCO).
CHAPLIN, D. (1967), *The Peruvian Industrial Labor Force* (Princeton: Princeton University Press).
CHAPLIN, D. (1976), *Peruvian Nationalism: A Corporatist Revolution* (New Brunswick, N.J.: Transaction Books).
CHOY, E. *et al.* (1970), *Lenin y Mariategui* (Lima: Ediciones Amauta).
COTLER, J. (1968), 'The Mechanics of Internal Domination and Social Change in Peru', *Studies in Comparative International Development*, vol. 3, no. 12.
COTLER, J. (1970–71), 'Political Crisis and Military Populism in Peru', *Studies in Comparative International Development*, vol. 6, no. 5.
COTLER, J. (1975), 'The New Mode of Political Domination in Peru', in Lowenthal (see below).
De WIND, J. (1979), 'From Peasants to Miners: The Background to Strikes in the Mines of Peru' in Cohen, R. *et al.* (1979) *Peasants and Proletarians* (London: Hutchinson).
DUNLOP, J. (1958), *Industrial Relations Systems* (New York; Henry Holt).
FAVRE, H. (1977), The Dynamics of Indian Peasant Society and Migration to Coastal Plantations in Central Peru in *Land and Labour in Latin America*, K. Duncan and I. Rutledge (eds) (Cambridge: Cambridge University Press).
FERNER, A. (1977), *The Industrial Bourgeoisie in the Peruvian Development Model*. DPhil, University of Sussex.
FIGUEROA, A. (1975), 'La Redistribucion del Ingreso y de la Propiedad en el Peru, 1968–73, in Richard Webb and Adolfo Figueroa, *Distribucion del Ingreso en el Peru* (Lima: Instituto de Estudios Peruanos).
FITZGERALD, E.V.K. (1976), *The State and Economic Development: Peru since 1968* (Cambridge: Cambridge University Press, Department of Applied Economics Occasional Paper no. 49).
FITZGERALD, E.V.K. (1979), *The Political Economy of Peru 1956–78. Economic Development and the Restructuring of Capital* (Cambridge University Press).
FLORES, A. and PLAZA, O. (1975), *Haciendas y Plantaciones en el Peru* (Lima:).
FLORES, A. (1976), *Arequipa y el Sur Andino* (Lima: CISEPA).
GARCIA-SAYAN, D. (1974), 'La Comunidad Industrial y las Concepciones Doctrinarias del Gobierno', in Pasara *et al.* (see below).
GARLAND, A.C. (1905), Resena Industrial del Peru (Lima: Imprenta La Industria).

GONZALES, M. (1978), *Cayalti: the formation of a rural proletariat on a Peruvian Sugar Cane Plantation 1875–1933* (PhD, University of California, Berkeley).

HAWORTH, N. (1982), *The Industrial Community in Arequipa: the failure of two unitarisms* (PhD, University of Liverpool).

HAWORTH, N. (1983), 'Conflict or Incorporation: the dilemma of the Peruvian Working Class 1968–80' in Booth and Sorj, op. cit.

HAWORTH, N. (1983), 'The Peruvian Working Class 1968–1979' in Booth and Sorj, op. cit.

HAWORTH, N. (1984), 'Proletarianisation in the World Order: the case of Peru' in Munslow, B. and Finch, H. (1984), *Proletarianisation in the World Economy* (London: Croom Helm).

HAWORTH, N. (1987a), 'Reordering Disorder: Problems in the Analysis of Peruvian Industrial Relations' (Centre for Latin American Studies, University of Liverpool).

HAWORTH, N. (1987b), 'Labour and Politics in Peru Revisited'. Monograph (Department of Industrial Relations, University of Strathclyde).

HILLIKER, G. (1971), *The Politics of Reform in Peru: The Aprista and Other Mass Parties of Latin America* (Baltimore: Johns Hopkins Press).

KANTOR, H. (1966), *The Ideology and Programme of the Peruvian Aprista Movement* (New York: Octagon Books).

KLAREN, P. (1973), *Modernisation, Dislocation and Aprismo: Origins of the Peruvian Aprista Party 1870–1932* (Austin: University of Texas Press).

KNIGHT, P. (1975), 'New Forms of Economic Organization in Peru: Toward Workers' Self-Management', in Lowenthal (see below).

KRUIJT, D. and VELLINGA, M. (1977), *Labour Relations and Multinational Corporations: The Cerro de Pasco Corporation in Peru 1902–1947* (Utrecht:).

LAITE, J. (1981), *Industrial Development and Migrant Labour* (Manchester: Manchester University Press).

LOWENTHAL, A. (1975), *The Peruvian Experiment: Continuity and Change under Military Rule* (Princeton: Princeton University Press).

NORTH, L. (1973), *The Origins and Development of the Peruvian Aprista Party* (PhD: University of California, Berkeley).

PASARA, L., SANTISTEVAN, J., BUSTAMANTE, A. and GARCIA-SAYAN, D. (1974), *Dinámica de la Comunidad Industrial* (Lima: DESCO).

PARODI, J. (1986), 'La Desmovilización del Sindicalismo Industrial Peruano em el Segundo Belaundismo' in Ballon, op cit.

PAYNE, J. (1965), *Labor and Politics in Peru* (New Haven: Yale University Press).

PEASE, H., VERME, O. (1974), *Peru 1968–73: Cronológia Politica*, vol. 1 (Lima: DESCO).

PHILIP, G. (1978), *The Rise and Fall of the Peruvian Military Radicals* London: (Athlone Press).

QUIJANO, A. (1971), *Nationalism and Capitalism in Peru* (New York: Monthly Review Press).

QUIJANO, A. (1975), 'La "Segunda Fase" de la "Revolución Peruana" y la Lucha de Clases', *Sociedad y Politica*, no. 5 (Nov.).

QUIJANO, A. (1977), 'Las Nuevas Condiciones de la Lucha de Clases en el Peru', *Sociedad y Politica*, no. 7 (May).
REID, M. (1985), *Peru: Paths to Poverty* (London: Latin American Bureau).
RODDICK, J. and HAWORTH, N. (1983), *Chile 1924 and 1979: Labour Policy and Industrial Relations through Two Revolutions* (University of Glasgow: Institute of Latin American Studies monograph series).
SANTISTEVAN, J. (1977), 'El Estado y los Comuneros Industriales', in Alberti *et al.*, op. cit.
SALAZAR, G.C. (1985), *Labradores Peones y Proletarios* (Santiago: Ediciones Sur).
SCOTT, A. (1986), 'Women and Industrialisation: Examining the "Female Marginalisation" Thesis', *Journal of Development Studies*, July.
SCOTT, C. (1976), Peasant, Proletarianisation and the Articulation of Modes of Production. *Journal of Peasant Studies*, vol. 3, No. 3.
STEPAN, A. (1978), *The State and Society: Peru in Comparative Perspective* (Princeton: Princeton University Press).
STEPHENS, E. (1977), *The Politics of Workers' participation: The Peruvian Approach in Comparative Perspective* (PhD, Yale University).
SULMONT, D. (1972), 'Dinámica Actual del Movimiento Obrero Peruano' (Lima: Pontificia Universidad Catolica, Departamento de Ciencias Sociales, mimeo).
SULMONT, D. (1974), 'El Desarrollo de la Clase Obrero en el Peru' (Lima: Pontificia Universidad Catolica, Departamento de Ciencias Sociales, mimeo).
SULMONT, D. (1975), *El Movimiento Obrero en el Peru 1900–1965* (Lima: Pontificia Universidad Catolica).
SULMONT, D. (1977), *Historia del Movimiento Obrero en el Peru* (Lima: Ediciones Tarea).
SULMONT, D. (1982), *Historia del Movimiento Obrero Peruano* (1890–1980) (Lima: Ediciones Tarea).
TAYLOR, L. (1979), *Main Trends in Agrarian Capitalist Development: Cajamarca 1880–1976* (PhD, University of Liverpool).
THORP, R. and BERTRAM, G. (1978), *Peru 1890–1977: Growth and Policy in an Open Economy* (London: Macmillan).
VILLANUEVA, V. (1977), 'The Petty-bourgeois Ideology of APRA', *Latin American Perspectives*, vol. 4, no. 3.
WACHTAL, N. (1977), *The Vision of the Vanquished* (Brighton: Harvester).
YEPEZ de CASTILLO, I. and BERNEDO, A.J. (1986), *La Sindicalizacim en el Peru* (Lima: Fundacion Friedrich Ebert/Pontificia Universidad Catolica).
YEPEZ, E. (1972), *Peru 1820–1920: un Siglo de Desarrollo Capitalista* (Lima: IEP).

3 Paraguay

Andrew Nickson

ORIGINS OF THE PARAGUAYAN TRADE UNION MOVEMENT

The origins of the Paraguayan trade union movement can be traced to the mutual aid societies founded in Asunción in the period following the War of the Triple Alliance (1865–70). Established initially by foreign residents, these groups later came to include skilled Paraguayan artisans. By 1887 there were 11 such societies with 1384 members, many of whom were self-employed. It is significant that the same year there were still only an estimated 1700 paid employees in Asunción.

In 1880 the first mutual aid society organised by Paraguayan workers was founded. Called the *Sociedad Santa Cruz*, it refused membership 'to those not belonging to the working-class and the people'. Two years later another Paraguayan mutual aid society, *Los Artesanos del Paraguay*, was formed by the initiative of a group of printworkers. Unlike its predecessors, membership of this society was not restricted to the working-class, who soon ceased to control its leadership. The first anniversary celebration of the society was even attended by the then President of the Republic, Bernardino Caballero.

Dissatisfied by the philanthropic orientation of *Los Artesanos* and prompted by the wish to campaign against the sale of votes, which was prevalent at the time, printworkers broke away in 1885 to form the *Sociedad Cosmopolitana de Socorros Mutuos 'Verdaderos Artesanos'*, replacing the former's motto of 'Union and Work' by that of 'Progress and Work'. In addition to the establishment of a mutual fund and savings and loan department, the new society set up a library and evening classes. This group of printworkers was the vanguard of Paraguay's nascent trade union movement and also published the first trade union paper, *El Artesano*, which ran to 31 issues during 1885–86. Moreover, on 14 May 1886 they founded the *Sociedad Tipografica del Paraguay*, the first trade union in the country, with 28 founder members. At this time there were still only four small printing houses in Asunción. The new union was inspired by reformist ideology, one of its objectives being to 'seek perpetual harmony between workers and owners of printworks and newspapers'.

The effect of the Baring Crisis and the Argentine economic depression of 1890–94 was soon transmitted to Paraguay through reduced demand for Paraguayan exports. The rapid depreciation of the local currency over this period, coupled with a rise in the public sector deficit as a result of mismanagement, led to inflation and a steep decline in real incomes for workers. At the same time, the burgeoning labour movement in Argentina encouraged a new militancy among Paraguayan workers as well as the introduction of anarchism into the trade union movement.

In March 1889 and again in November 1891, workers on the Central Railway, which had only recently been sold by the State to British investors and which was being extended from Paraguari to Sapucai, went on strike in protest at non-payment of salaries. In June 1892 carpentry workers obtained a 25 per cent pay increase agreed to by 23 employers, while the following year saw the formation of a telegraphic workers' union and the specific demand for an eight-hour day raised for the first time at a meeting of 200 bricklayers.

The publication of an inflammatory anarchist manifesto in *La Democracia* on 21 May 1892, which was signed by a group calling itself 'The Sons of the Chaco', provoked much controversy and was dramatic evidence of the growth of anarchist ideology within the trade union movement. Earlier in the same month a strike meeting of bakers had been broken up by the police after an anarchist pamphlet was read out. Some measure of the extent to which foreign influence nurtured anarchist power in the trade union movement is attested to by the fact that half of the 22 arrested at the meeting were foreigners – four Argentinians, three Spaniards, two Italians, one Frenchman and one Bolivian. Anarchism was increasingly seen as a threat by the *laissez-faire* liberal post-war political élite, who encouraged alternative trade union structures of a more reformist nature such as the *Sociedad Obrera Cosmopolitana*, set up by skilled artisans in July 1893. The President of the Liberal Party himself, Cecilio Baez, promoted trade union organisations along the lines of the mutual aid societies – the *Asociación General de Trabajo* (1897) and the *Centro General de Obreros*. All of these initiatives failed because they were considered too reformist by trade union members preoccupied with the decline in real wages and who were increasingly influenced by the radical ideas of anarchism. In November 1897 demands for better pay and working conditions led to a successful strike by 160 bakers and in September 1901 carpentry workers became the first trade union to obtain an eight-hour day following a one week strike. Under the influence of two Spanish militants, José Serrano, an anarchist, and Juan Rovira, a Catalan socialist, the *Sociedad de Carpinteros* became the first radical trade union in Paraguay.

THE LIBERAL ERA

The 1904 'revolution' (by which the Liberal Party replaced the Colorado Party) had important repercussions for the growth and nature of the trade union movement. There was widespread dissatisfaction with the corrupt administration of a succession of Colorado governments since the end of the Triple Alliance War, and the revolt undoubtedly had a measure of popular support. In 1902 peasants at Agaguigo in the Department of Concepción had resisted eviction and in June 1904 strikes by tramway drivers and dockers in Asunción precipitated the political crisis. Popular disillusionment with the 1904 'revolution' would, in turn, provide the impulse for the creation of the first national trade union structures.

The 1904 'revolution' ushered in a period of *laissez-faire* liberalism with strong influence from Argentina. The enormous forest reserves of the Paraguayan Chaco began to supply the timber needs of the rapidly growing Argentine railway network. More than 20 Argentinian *quebracho* companies and log-mills were set up along the west bank of the River Paraguay, most of which were to collapse after the Argentine railway boom ended. The increase in foreign investment rapidly expanded the size of the working-class and the vanguard of the trade union movement soon passed from the artisans of Asunción's cottage industries to the new industrial workers in the tannin, logging, yerba, sugar and transport sectors, which were mainly under Argentine ownership.

The labour movement prior to 1904 had reflected the weak development of the capitalist mode of production which had been introduced since the end of the Triple Alliance War. Trade unions were unstable and confined exclusively to Asuncion. All of the 17 strikes recorded between 1892 and 1906 were spontaneous reactions in defence of real wages due to constant devaluations.

The refusal of employers to honour the 1901 agreement led to a protracted struggle culminating in a victorious strike by 300 carpenters from 9–22 October 1905, as a result of which they obtained a guaranteed eight-hour day and a 20 per cent wage increase. Elated by the successful strike, the anarchist vanguard within the *Sociedad de Carpinteros* contacted two other unions, the printworkers and the tin-smiths, and together they set up the first national trade union organisation, the *Federación Obrera Regional Paraguaya* (FORP), on 22 April 1906. Its paper, *El Despertar*, controlled by the anarchist tendency in the carpenters' union, appeared on 1 May 1906, the first time that May Day had been celebrated in Paraguay. Two foreign anarchists – Rafael Barret (Spaniard) and Pedro Gori (Italian) provided strong intellectual support for the establishment of the FORP.

On 15 May 1906, Paraguayan Independence Day, workers marched to the Presidential Palace where Cecilio Baez, in his address to them revealed the Liberal hierarchy's fear of anarchism which had earlier prompted his ill-fated attempts to establish reformist trade union bodies.

> I do not regard you, the workers, as the enemies of capital, nor as the disturbers of the peace, but as humble solicitors of justice. In the same way, I do not consider capitalists, in general, to be the oppressors of your organisations. The supposed conflict between capital and labour affirmed by some, does not exist. You come to the National Palace to demonstrate your joy on the anniversary of our glorious Independence and to express with your noble conduct that your guide is not the red rag of anarchism but that same tri-colour flag which our predecessors adopted as the emblem of the Republic.[1]

The FORP remained firmly under anarchist control and as such refused to align itself with any political party. However, growing social discontent, fanned by the repression following a military rebellion in 1908, gave birth to a minority within the trade union movement who argued in favour of greater emphasis on political campaigning. In 1913 this tendency, under impulse from the printworkers, broke away from the FORP to set up a rival organisation, the *Unión Gremial*, under the leadership of Rufino Recalde Milesi. This new organisation attracted 12 unions and published its own paper, *Voz del Pueblo*. In 1915 the same tendency formed the *Partido Obrero* which changed its name to *Partido Socialista Revolucionario (PSR)* in 1918.

The First World War increased the international demand for

Paraguayan tannin, cotton and *mate* on the world market, thus providing a spur to the growth of the labour movement. In 1916 a reactivated FORP changed its name to the *Centro Obrero Regional del Paraguay* (CORP) whose first secretary-general was Ignacio Ñũnez Soler. It launched a weekly paper, *El Combate*, later renamed *Renovacion*, under the editorship of Juan Deilla. In the same year the CORP backed a successful strike by railwaymen during which its leaders were jailed. For the first time university and secondary school students demonstrated their support for strikers in the streets. Regional affiliates of the CORP were established in interior towns such as Concepcion, Villarrica and Encarnación. The first piece of labour legislation, prohibiting Sunday work, was introduced by Law No. 242 of 6 June 1917.

Both the CORP and the *Unión Gremial* devoted resources to cultural activities such as the performing of plays with a social

TABLE 3.1 *Labour Legislation in Paraguay*

6 June 1917	Law 242 granting Sunday holiday.
6 August 1931	Law 1218 regulating the hiring of workers in the Alto Parana.
24 October 1936	Decree 5952 prohibiting payment in the form of tokens.
9 December 1937	Decree 2448 regulating child allowances and maternity benefits.
6 January 1938	Decree 3544 regulating length of workday.
29 June 1942	Decree 13 294 protecting Paraguayan nationality in industry and commerce.
8 February 1943	Decree 16 875 prohibiting the employment of children under 12.
13 April 1943	Decree 17 071 establishes Social Security System.
2 October 1943	Decree 620 establishing a minimum wage.
2 January 1947	Decree 211 granting Saturday afternoon holiday.
22 December 1951	Decree 17 307 regulating payment of annual bonus (*aguinaldo*).
4 May 1957	Decree 417 establishing new norms for payment of *aguinaldo*.
22 December 1951	Decree 8608 establishing paid annual leave.
31 August 1961	Law 729 establishing a Labour Code.
27 December 1974	Law 506 revising articles in Labour Code referring to employment of minors and to paid annual leave.
14 March 1977	Decree 29 765 creating a Department of Occupational Hygiene and Safety in the Ministry of Labour.

message at the national theatre. A young journalist and supporter of the *Union Gremial*, Leopoldo Ramos Gimenez became an outspoken critic of the treatment meted out to the estimated 50 000 *mensu*, or yerba collectors employed by companies in the Alto Parana. In July 1916 he was wounded in an assassination attempt and in 1923 his play, *La Inquisición del Oro* about labour conditions in the yerba areas was performed by the *Unión Gremial's* theatre group, '*Juventud*'.

As a result of the increase in foreign trade during the First World War, the maritime workers became the principal nucleus of organised labour in Paraguay. In 1915 seamen and dockworkers joined together in the *Federación Naval*, which during 1919–20 conducted a bitter strike lasting 14 months against the Mihanovich shipping company in conjunction with Argentinian and Uruguayan seamen. This led to a split which gave birth to the *Liga Obrera Maritima del Paraguay* (LOMP).

Despite the pointer of the 1913 division in the trade union movement, it was not until the late 1920s that the anarcho-syndicalist hegemony over organised labour was effectively challenged by socialist ideology. The reactivation of the Argentinian economy after 1923, the pole around which the Paraguayan economy continued to turn, made it possible for Liberal President Eligio Ayala to place the country's finances on a sounder basis, and relations improved between his government and the major opposition Colorado Party. The socialist tendency identified with the PSR took advantage of the unusual political *détente* during Ayala's term of office to create the *Unión Obrera del Paraguay* (UOP) in 1927. Its main strength lay in its affiliated seamen's and printworker unions. Its newspaper, *El Socialista*, later changed its name to *Peber*. In 1927 the UOP organised railway workers into a new union, the *Asociación Ferroviaria* and led strike action in the foreign-owned meat-packing plants at San Antonio and Zeballos-Cve.

The replacement of Eligio Ayala as President by another Liberal, José P. Guggiari in 1928, marked a turning point in Paraguayan history. The deepening ideological divisions within the Liberal Party which the Guggiari administration tried to paper over, and the emergence of socialist movements all reflected the delayed political expression of a working-class consciousness which was finally challenging decades of liberal hegemony.

As the threat of war with Bolivia emerged in 1928, the UOP voiced its opposition to the war-mongering in communiqués to the Second and Third Internationals. Both the UOP and CORP sent delegates to a peace conference held in Montevideo in 1928 at the initiative of the Third International. In the same year, the UOP decided to affiliate to the Fifth Congress of the International Trade Union Confederation to be held in Moscow in 1930. Franasco Gaora, Recalde Milesi and Villalba were designated as delegates.

A dramatic indication of the heightened social conflict was the tense situation in the tannin ports of Alto Paraguay. On 4 July 1927 12 died when troops were used to quell a strike at the Puerto Pinasco tannin factory owned by the US company, International Products Corporation (IPC), in which the workers were demanding an eight-hour day and the freedom to unionise.

In 1928 the *Liga Nacional Independiente* (LNI) was founded as a political club by university intellectuals who advocated social and economic reforms. The LNI would later exercise a strong influence on the *febrerista* movement. On 19 February 1928 a group of workers and intellectuals founded the *Partido Comunista Paraguayo* (PCP), although this initial group soon disintegrated. Meanwhile revolutionary anarchists were carrying out a series of violent actions, culminating in the attack led by Obdulio Barthe on the border town of Encarnación which was declared a 'revolutionary commune' for a day on 20 February 1931.

The nadir of the Liberal Party was reached on 23 October 1931 when troops killed 11 and wounded 29 when they fired on students protesting against the policy of appeasement toward Bolivian aggression in the disputed Chaco region. In the days that followed, Asunción was occupied by troops and many trade union leaders were deported.

The outbreak of war with Bolivia in 1932 symbolised the final demise of anarchism as a major force within the trade union movement. The Communist Party was revived in 1933 with the incorporation into membership of former anarchists such as Obdulio Barthe who had been converted to Marxism during his exile in Argentina. The PCP refused to support the war effort, denouncing the conflict as one fomented by competing imperialist oil interests. In 1935 the PCP reorganised the seamen's union LOMP and the trade union at the British-owned Liebigs meat-packing factory at Zeballos-Cue.

THE FEBRERISTA REVOLUTION

Following victory over Bolivia in the Chaco war, dissatisfaction with the weak negotiating position of the Liberal government at the Chaco

Peace Conference led to a military revolt on 17 February 1936, which was widely supported by war veterans. The new government, known as the *Febreristas* and headed by war hero Colonel Rafael Franco, announced a programme of populist reforms, including measures favourable to the labour movement, such as the gradual introduction of an eight-hour day, the prohibition of payment for work in the form of tokens, obligatory medical attention in factories and a major wage increase.

The awakening of popular aspirations by *febrerista* rhetoric fuelled labour militancy, and led to mounting strikes and street clashes between police and demonstrators. Radical orators even urged workers to take direct control of the government. On 5 March 1936 a group of trade union leaders sent a letter to President Franco declaring their support for his 'popular government' and including an eight-point list of demands, as follows:

(1) Eight-hour workday throughout the country.
(2) Wage and salary increase to match the cost of living, and a reduction in food prices and house rents.
(3) Implementation of labour legislation which had been approved at the International Labour Conference in Santiago, Chile, with the support of the Paraguayan delegation. Regulation of night work, piece-work, child labour, female labour and accident compensation.
(4) Annulling of all laws and decrees restricting trade union freedom to organise; guarantees from the authorities in rural areas.
(5) A foreign policy based on the desire for peace.
(6) Protection and assistance (in the form of credit, subsidies, lower taxes) for national firms against competition from Trusts or large companies, thereby resulting in higher wages and lower consumer prices.
(7) Intervention by the Government in the financial management of foreign companies which were threatening to close their factories.
(8) Freedom for the worker Caballero. Arrest and trial of police officials Troche, Villalba, Santuchi, Marcos Rodriguez, and so on, accused of torturing trade union militants, such as Miguel Martin, Jara and Riquelme during the previous regime.

The letter also called for the convening of a *Confederación Nacional de Trabajadores* (CNT) to create a single trade union body in

Paraguay after 30 years of division. An inaugural conference was subsequently held on 13 March 1936 attended by 37 trade unions, at which Francisco Gaona was elected secretary-general.

The *Febreristas* established the first National Labour Department, *Departmento Nacional de Trabajo* (DNT), by Decree No. 2303 of 24 June 1936 and the first labour code which was drafted by Interior Minister, German Soler. The DNT, which functioned as part of the Ministry of the Interior, was charged with the enforcement of the labour code, arbitration in labour disputes, inspection of working conditions and the promotion of co-operatives. Trade unions were required to register with the DNT which was also authorised to 'study, revise and approve the statutes of these organisations'. The legal basis was thus established for government control of trade unions in subsequent decades.

The labour code itself was mildly progressive. Its activities were aimed at the gradual application of the eight-hour day with Sundays free, the right to unionise and to demand a just wage, paid annual holidays and payment to be made in the national currency. This last point related to the still prevalent practice among the tannin factories and yerba companies of paying their isolated workers with tokens which could only be exchanged at company stores. Although the requirement of government recognition before they could legally bargain or strike restricted the freedom of action of trade unions, in the short term this corporativist system enhanced their bargaining power with employers. By August 1936 Interior Minister Soler could report that the DNT had already settled 17 strikes and that 73 new trade unions had been formed with a combined membership of 7320.

However, the widespread and heterogeneous support for the *febreristas* soon evaporated as President Franco first purged his Cabinet of fascist sympathisers and then imprisoned communist and other trade union leaders. The CNT headquarters were attacked by the army on 1 October 1936 while the Council of Delegates was in session; 61 trade unionists were arrested and imprisoned for three months and the CNT was closed for four months. Liberal rule was restored by a military coup on 13 August 1937. Despite this, the toleration of increased social protest witnessed during the short-lived *Febrerista* government continued under the new government of Felix Paiva. CNT headquarters were invaded and closed down for a second time on 7 September 1937. Nevertheless, the CNT gave critical support to the new liberal government in order to secure the release of trade union leaders Barthe, Pujol and Alcaraz. They were members of the PCP, which continued to strengthen its position within the trade union movement through the CNT. An indication of the continued pressure for labour reform was the promulgation of Law No. 3544 of 6 January 1938 which introduced the eight-hour day and reduced it to six hours in the case of unhealthy work. Payment of overtime was fixed at time-and-a-half rates, with night work and work on holidays and Sundays at double the usual rates.

From 28 May–1 June 1939 the first Congress of Paraguayan workers was held, attended by 95 delegates from 39 of the 48 affiliated trade unions. The Congress was obliged to change the name of the organisation from the CNT to the *Confederación de Trabajadores del Paraguay* (CTP) because of an executive decree prohibiting the use of the word 'national' in the name of any non-governmental body. Francisco Gaona, a *febrerista* then in exile was appointed secretary-general, with a communist, Adolfo Yegros of the shoe-makers union, as interim secretary-general, since Gaona had been refused permission to return. On 1 May 1940 the CTP organised a march to the Presidential Palace where they were received by the newly elected Liberal President José Felix Estigarribia and his Ministers. They delivered a statement demanding solutions to a series of workers' grievances, of which the most pressing was the lack of effective legal protection for trade union activity. Shortly before his accidental death in September 1940, Estigarribia visited the four largest tannin factories in the far north of Paraguay where newly-recognised trade unions were protesting working and living conditions. This hitherto unprecedented visit by a President of the Republic to these company towns was expressly for the purpose of 'personally informing himself about working conditions', and was a reflection of official concern over social unrest throughout the tannin ports. This protest was led by trade unions which had been granted recognition for the first time under the *Febrerista* government.

THE MORINIGO DICTATORSHIP

The corporativist ideology which inspired the dictatorship of President Higinio Morinigo (1940–48) produced the first moves towards the direct incorporation of the trade union movement by the State: a goal which would later be realised under President Stroessner. On 9 January 1941, under pressure from its communist leadership, the CTP declared an indefinite strike in support of seamen protesting the abandonment by the Port authorities of their earlier promise to hire only union members. The strike collapsed since only the strong seamen's union, LOMP, was able to sustain it for more than a few days. By decree DL4545, Morinigo suspended all trade union activity for a year and arrested more than two hundred union activists who were confined to a remote detention camp at Pena Hermosa on the River Paraguay. The CTP soon disappeared under the repression, to be replaced by a clandestine Committee for the Defence of Trade Unions, *Comite de Defensa Sindical* (CDS), in which the PCP and *febreristas* vied for leadership. By a series of strikes in August and December 1941, which reflected the resilience of the trade union movement, the CDS forced Morinigo to recognise the legal rights of trade unions.

In an attempt to take the wind out the CDS sails, and in line with his corporativist philosophy, Morinigo was responsible for the first major labour legislation in Paraguay. Minimum wages were established for the first time by DL 620 of 2 October 1943 and social insurance legislation covering sickness, maternity and old age was introduced by DL No. 17 071 of 13 April 1943. A Social Security agency *Instituto de Prevision Social* (IPS) was set up on 1 February 1944 to operate the scheme. Benefits were to be financed by a tripartite weekly contribution, as follows: insured employee 3 per cent of wage, employer 6 per cent and the State 1.5 per cent. Industrial accident insurance was financed solely by an employers' contribution at the rate of 4 per cent of the total wage bill.

Opposition to a proposed DL 1217 of November 1943 establishing rigid control over trade unions, together with suspicions regarding the use to which IPS funds would be put, led to a general strike by the CDS on 15 February 1944 and subsequently to the arrest of several hundred trade unionists. Most of the detainees were sent to prison camps in the Chaco and a list of 103 of the prisoners was published in August 1945 by a Uruguayan journalist who investigated their conditions. His findings revealed the following breakdown by sector: railwaymen (23), seamen (20), plumbers (9), bakers (9), brewery workers (8), students (7) and others (27).[2]

Despite repression, the strike was successful in forcing Morinigo to shelve the proposed decree. A fortified trade union body emerged in the shape of the new Workers' Council of Paraguay, *Consejo Obrero del Paraguay* (COP) which henceforth replaced the CDS. At first the powerful COP operated in semi-clandestine form but soon obtained legal recognition as the Morinigo dictatorship crumbled. The COP was firmly under the control of the PCP, which provided its first secretary-general, the construction workers' leader, Timoteo Ojeda.

As a result of the Allied victory in 1945, there was a gradual relaxation of military rule and Morinigo was obliged by growing domestic and international pressure to exclude Nazi sympathisers from his government. Following a series of public demonstrations in favour of democratisation, a coalition government was formed under the nominal leadership of Morinigo which included colorados and *febreristas*. This brief six-month interregnum was a period of intense political activity as all parties vied for political support. The PCP was legalised for the first time in its history and its membership grew to 10 000 compared to less than 1000 a decade before. As members of the PCP headed some 30 unions it strengthened its control of the COP. On 1 May 1946 the COP held an open-air rally in the national football stadium, attended by 20 000. As a counter to this growing Marxist influence within the labour movement, the fascist *guionista* faction of the Colorado Party, which had collaborated with Morinigo, launched its own trade union body, the *Organización Republicana Obrera* (ORO). In 1945 the Colorados made their first inroad into the trade union movement when *guionista* leader, Enrique Volta Gaona, was appointed as legal advisor to the LOMP.

Growing *guionista* influence within the government was demonstrated by the official response to a number of major labour conflicts. In July 1946 the DNT ordered compensation of only 15 days' pay for 700 workers laid off without regard to length of service by the British meat-packing company Liebigs. By decree No. 16 534 of 18 November 1946 the State assumed formal control over conflicts between employers and workers, thereby legitimising a situation which had existed *de facto* throughout the Presidency of Morinigo. In response to a strike at the Friedmann sugar refinery in November 1946, the DNT refused to recognise the trade union involved and ordered an end to the strike. In December 1946 it declared illegal a strike by workers at the San Antonio meat-packing plant of the US company, IPC, because 'the channels for negotiation' had not been exhausted. Subsequently the DNT upheld the decision of the company to hire strike-breakers.

In March 1947 the uneasy peace dissolved into a military revolt, following the arrest of a number of *febrerista* and communist leaders. This soon developed into a civil war between the Colorado Party, which mobilised a peasant militia, known as the *py nandi* and an uneasy alliance of *febreristas*, liberals and communists.

The victory of the Colorado Party in the civil war enormously strengthened its role in the trade union movement during the coming years. In August 1948 a Ministry of Justice and Labour was created which centralised aspects of labour control previously divided between DNT and Ministry of the Interior. Many trade union activists had been killed in the fighting, especially those from the tannin factories in the north, and many more, including two previous secretary-generals of the COP, Timoteo Ojeda and Antonio Gamarra, were among the 2000 political prisoners detained in squalid conditions in Asunción. Thousands more had fled to Argentina to escape the vengeance wrought throughout the countryside by marauding bands of *py nandi*. Under the leadership of *guionista* Enrique Volta Gaona, the ORO began to impose affiliation to the Colorado Party as a precondition for trade union membership. Large numbers of peasants from the *py nandi* thereafter joined the ranks of the urban proletariat, replacing workers who had either been killed or exiled during the war, or simply sacked for not belonging to the Colorado Party.

RISING LABOUR MILITANCY

The renewed militancy of the labour movement so soon after the reverses suffered during and after the civil war was fuelled by a period of hyper-inflation and consequent steep declines in real wages experienced from 1950 onwards. This inflationary spiral was the by-product of an intense struggle for power between the military and *democraticos* within the Colorado Party. In a bid to reconcile competing interests, a series of short-lived Presidents resorted to massive increases in the money supply in order to finance a rapidly growing public sector borrowing requirement.

In response to the rapid increase in the cost of living, the trade union leadership came under increasing pressure from below to defend the workers' living standards. In March 1950, under its secretary-general, Florentin Lopez, ORO won a 40 per cent wage increase. However, at the second national labour congress in 1951 the ORO was replaced by the new Paraguayan Confederation of Workers, *Confederación Paraguaya de Trabajadores* (CPT). This decision reflected the desire to regain international respectability by the moderate *democratico* tendency which was now challenging the *guionistas* within the ruling Colorado Party.

The economic situation of the working class deteriorated sharply after 1951. Between July 1951 and September 1953, while the minimum wage rose by 165 per cent, the official cost of living index rose by 321 per cent. The British Consul at the time wrote, 'During 1951 food alone has shown an increase of over 50 per cent. There is no doubt about the degree of inflation and despite substantial wage increases the purchasing power of wages has not been maintained'.[3]

As the labour movement began to recover its strength under the Presidency of *democratico* Federico Chaves, the CPT also became less sectarian. Some 119 trade unions participated in the third national labour congress in 1953 with 64 unions from Asuncion and 55 from the interior. At the Congress non-Colorado trade unionists began to regain positions inside the CPT. The Catholic Workers Organisation, JOC, which boasted 20 delegates at the Congress saw five of its members elected to the executive committee of the CPT. The Congress also decided to affiliate to the US-backed regional trade organisation, ORIT, marking a set-back for the Peronist lobby within the CPT.

THE STROESSNER DICTATORSHIP

In May 1954 General Alfredo Stroessner seized power in a military coup. Shortly afterwards his main rival for power, the populist and pro-Peronist Colorado leader Epifanio Mendez Fleitas was ousted as head of the Central Bank, from where he had engineered a policy of moderate opposition to the International Monetary Fund (IMF). His successors Gustavo Storm and Cesar Romeo Acosta, who replaced Storm shortly afterwards, introduced an IMF stabilisation plan, involving a strict wage freeze, liberalisation of exchange controls and a reduction in public subsidies. The sudden drop in real incomes for urban wage-earners which this brought about led to a new militancy inside the CPT, with supporters of both Mendez Fleitas and non-Colorados increasing their strength.

The first industrial census in 1955 revealed the continuation of a very low level of industrialisation in Paraguay when compared to other Latin American countries. The vast majority of the 2732 establishments covered by the census were artisanal, occupying mainly self–employed persons. Out of a total employment of 34 449 in the industrial sector, no more than 20 048 were classified as salaried workers, with the following distribution by age, sex and geographical location:

TABLE 3.2 *Paraguay: Distribution of Salaried Workers, 1955*

	MALE	*FEMALE*	*TOTAL*
Total salaried workers	16 801	3 247	20 048
Over 18	15 889	3 058	18 947
Under 18	912	189	1 101
In Asuncion	6 169	2 092	8 261
Over 18	5 686	1 975	7 661
Under 18	483	117	600
Elsewhere	10 632	1 155	11 787
Over 18	10 203	1 083	11 286
Under 18	429	72	501

SOURCE Censo Industrial, 1955

The low level of industrialisation revealed by the industrial census confirmed the lack of structural change in the Paraguayan economy during the previous decades – itself a reflection of the general economic stagnation of the country. An economic study in 1953, referring to the period 1926–50, noted that 'there were no significant changes in the sectoral composition of GNP in Paraguay. The share of manufacturing and commerce remained constant. The per capita output of manufactured goods fell, constituting a unique case within the general experience of Latin America'.[4] Manufacturing remained confined to the processing of primary products for export without any import substitution programme to provide domestic stimulus to industrial growth.

THE GENERAL STRIKE

In 1956 the CPT demanded a 29 per cent increase in the minimum wage, from ₲ 121.00 to ₲ 156.52. This demand was endorsed by the fifth national labour congress in August 1957, by which time supporters of Mendez Fleitas had a clear majority within the executive committee of the CPT. Strike activity escalated as the CPT intensified its demand for an increase in the minimum wage in response to the effects of the IMF stabilisation plan. Strikes took place at the IPC meat-packing plant and in the State Electricity Corporation, ANDE. At the same time the tannin industry faced a crisis with the closure of two major plants as Puerto Sastre and Puerto Guarani, involving the dismissal of 2000 workers. In addition to demanding compensation for the dismissed workers, the CPT supported a bitter struggle against harsh working conditions at the largest tannin port of Puerto Pinasco, also owned by IPC.

In pursuit of its repeated demand for an increase in the minimum wage, the CPT proposed and obtained the establishment of a tripartite 'Commission for the study of a basic salary and price control', composed of representatives from the CPT, the employers' organisation, FEPRINCO, and the government, with technical collaboration from the Central Bank, Ministry of Health and FAO officials. The CPT presented a memorandum to the Commission, which based its demand for an increase in the minimum wage on the cost of living index of the Central Bank, even though the latter used a weighting system devised in 1938. This index suggested a minimum daily requirement per family of ₲ 211, equivalent to a daily wage of ₲ 253 (assuming a 30-day month and a five-day week). Nevertheless, the CPT continued to limit their demand to ₲ 156, an increase of only 29 per cent, and unchanged since originally put forward in July 1956.

The growing political dimension to the conflict over the minimum wage was illustrated by the 1958 May Day speech by CPT secretary-general Vicente Cortesi Scappini. The speech called for the repeal of all repressive legislation, the ending of the state of siege and for freedom of organisation, speech and of the press. On 1 July the Council of Delegates of the CPT reiterated its call for an increase in the minimum wage.

On 15 August, Stroessner was re-elected President for a five-year term in an election in which he was the only candidate. In a calculated move on 14 August the CPT had circulated its member unions with a call for a general strike on 27 August if the 29 per cent wage demand was not met. This initial one-day stoppage was to be followed by an escalating series of stoppages from 3 September if the demand had still not been met.

Negotiations proved to no avail. On 24 August over 1000 workers attended a meeting at CPT headquarters when 20 delegates described their fruitless discussions with government officials during the previous week. The following day the *Junta de Gobierno* of the ruling Colorado Party offered a wage increase of 5 percent, threatening that its rejection by Colorado Party union members would mean their expulsion from the party. This offer was rejected immediately and unanimously by a mass meeting at CPT headquarters. On the eve of the general strike Stroessner called 15 CPT leaders to a meeting at which he angrily rejected the demand for a 29 per cent increase in the minimum wage. The outcome of the meeting was immediately reported back to a 2000-strong meeting at CPT headquarters at which 102 out of 127 affiliated unions were represented. The decision to strike with the effect from midnight of 26 August was total.

The government countered the strike threat with a co-ordinated and pre-emptive move. With ample prior notice of the strike, an anti-strike squad had already been set up under General Avila, composed of special units from the police, army and navy. On 12 August police arrested the communist leader Antonio Maidana, who had been directing support for the strike. Together with PCP militants Rojas and Alcorta, arrested in January and November 1958 respectively, Maidana would spend the next 20 years in jail.

Within hours of the beginning of the strike the anti-strike squad invaded the CPT headquarters, arrested 18 trade union leaders and removed the CPT archives. In a co-ordinated move, the headquarters of most leading trade unions were also taken over. By administrative decree No. 229 of the DNT, the CPT and all its affiliated unions were declared 'intervened'. By day-break some 200 trade union activists had been detained, most of them in their homes. Following several days of physical assault in the Police Investigations department they were confined to remote villages in the forests of the Alto Parana.

The initial one day strike was successful. Asunción came to a virtual standstill and rail and river transport was stopped throughout the country. However, with the leadership of the CPT removed at one fell swoop, the direction of the strike soon deteriorated, despite the formation of a clandestine emergency committee to replace the arrested leadership, which operated from a Church basement. On 30 August over 700 seamen attended a strike meeting in the headquarters of the LOMP. Police attacked the headquarters using tear-gas and the strikers were forced to take refuge in a nearby school belonging to the Salesian order. On 2 September Vicente Cortesi, secretary-general of the CPT and a Parliamentary Deputy, was duped into signing an agreement to call off the strike on the understanding that all detainees would be released, sacked workers would be reinstated and that the intervention of the CPT would end. However, after signing the agreement Cortesi was himself arrested and sent to confinement. The vacating of a Church after a week-long sit-in by several hundred trade unionists and their families marked the final collapse of the general strike and at the same time a severe setback to the trade union movement, which was not to recover for 20 years.

THE NEW ORDER

From 7–8 March 1959 a national congress of the CPT was held to institutionalise the new leadership. It was now dominated by political appointees from within the *stronista* faction of the Colorado Party, many of whose trade union credentials were tenuous. The new secretary-general was a former police-chief of San Bernardino, Rodolfo Echeverria, who appeared as a leader of the bus-drivers' union. Enrique Volta Gaona, former head of ORO and a leading organiser in crushing the general strike, became legal advisor to the CPT.

The government played a cat and mouse game with the remaining independent trade union activists who had survived the general strike unscathed. Responding to the growing opposition within the Colorado Party to the authoritarian rule of the *stronistas*, and in order to redress the poor international image of the CPT, non-Colorado trade unionists were offered posts on the executive committee. Five members of the Christian Democrat trade union organisation *Movimiento Sindical Paraguayo* (MSP) and two *febreristas* joined the committee – the first sign that Colorado party hegemony within the CPT had been loosened. However, the pact was short-lived and the independents soon resigned in protest at the continued *stronista* control over the CPT. The international image of the CPT suffered another setback when the US-backed inter-american trade union body, ORIT decided to recognise the CPT-in-exile, which was founded in Montevideo on 13 April 1959 by the majority of the leadership of the CPT who had fled there following the defeat of the general strike.

Popular support for the regime had been narrowed by the 1958 general strike and by the purging of the *democratico* faction within the Colorado party when Parliament was closed in May 1959. During the next few years there were several unsuccessful attempts to overthrow Stroessner by force. In December 1959 and April 1960 the *14 de Mayo* movement of liberals and *febreristas* launched guerrilla invasions from Argentina. In June and December 1960 the FULNA movement, under the direction of the PCP, launched further unsuccessful invasions.

Repression directed against opponents of the regime working legally inside Paraguay was intensified in response to these invasions attempts, thereby gradually eliminating the last vestiges of independence within the trade union movement. Nevertheless, overt opposition was still evident as late as 1961 when the CPT organised a May Day rally in support of the government. The Minister of Labour,

Juan Ramon Chaves, was greeted by catcalls and was unable to deliver his speech. Hostility from the crowd eventually forced him and Raimundo Pizurno, secretary-general of the CPT, to abandon the platform. The rally was then turned into a popular tribune during which a succession of trade union activists denounced the economic policy of the regime, although several of those who spoke from the platform were subsequently arrested.

In August 1961 a comprehensive labour code was enacted for the first time, the effect of which was to institutionalise the dependent relationship of the trade union movement to the State under the Stroessner regime. Only officially recognised unions were permitted and strikes by public sector employees were prohibited. The DNT of the Ministry of Justice and Labour was reorganised for more efficient surveillance of trade union activity.

THE BLEAK YEARS

Following the *stronista* takeover of the CPT, the elimination of the vestiges of clandestine opposition within the trade union movement and the destruction of the urban apparatus of the PCP in 1963, the labour movement experienced a decade of tight political control (1964–74). Trade union membership stagnated and strikes became virtually unknown. The minimum wage was held constant for seven years (1964–70) and even official figures show that the real value of the minimum wage fell by 23 per cent between 1964 and 1977 (Table 3.3).

The lack of trade union militancy throughout this period was partly the result of harsh repression of union dissidents, together with the hermetic control which the State exercised over the CPT. Three governmental bodies were involved – the Ministry of Justice and Labour, the *Junta de Gobierno* of the Colorado Party and the Police Investigations Department. The Ministry of Justice and Labour, headed since 1968 by former *guionista* Saul Gonzalez, continued to use its power to grant or deny legal recognition to trade unions according to political considerations. The Ministry granted recognition to many fictitious unions, especially in the maritime sector, in order to ensure continued control by *stronista* appointees within the CPT hierarchy. As a result the CPT functioned as an appendage of the Ministry, from which it received an annual grant and under whose heading it appeared in the Asunción telephone directory. Corruption

TABLE 3.3 *Paraguay: Minimum Wage Rates in Current and Constant Terms, 1964–85*

	Minimum Wage Rate (current value) (guaranis)*	*Consumer Price Index (base year, 1964)*	*Index of Real Value of minimum wage (1964 = 100)*
1964	6 992	100.0	100.0
1965	6 992	103.8	96.3
1966	6 992	106.8	93.6
1967	6 992	108.3	92.3
1968	6 992	109.0	91.7
1969	6 922	111.5	89.7
1970	6 992	110.5	90.5
1971	7 718	116.0	95.2
1972	7 718	126.7	87.1
1973	9 750	142.0	98.2
1974	11 700	178.9	93.5
1975	11 700	190.9	87.7
1976	11 700	199.4	83.9
1977	11 700	218.1	76.7
1978	13 470	232.1	83.0
1979	17 820	310.3	82.1
1980	23 610	385.4	87.6
1981	27 150	427.5	90.8
1982	27 150	460.9	84.2
1983	29 910	522.8	81.8
1984	39 556	663.8	85.2
1985	43 512	713.7	87.2

SOURCE: Bolétin Estadistico del Banco Central, Dirección General del Trabajo, Ministerio de Justicia y Trabajo.

* Before deductions of compulsory 10 per cent employee contribution to IPS social security scheme.

was rife within the Ministry and officials were renowned for their failure to investigate union complaints of non-compliance by employers with the Labour Code and non-payment of statutory contributions by employers to the Social Security agency, IPS.

The labour affairs section of the *Junta de Gobierno* exercised the authority of the Colorado Party through the trade union movement, ensuring that the leadership of individual unions did not fall into the hands of non-Colorados. The CPT leadership remained firmly under the control of political appointees of the Stroessner regime who vigorously supported his re-election every five years and who annually declared him to be 'Paraguay's number one worker'. This accommodation of the CPT leadership was facilitated by provision for trade union representatives as highly paid members of the board of directors of parastatal bodies such as the IPS, ANDE, CORPOSANA and the *Banco Nacional de Trabajadores* (BNT). The Junta also controlled trade unions through its party branches, known as *seccionales*, whose role was both to care for the welfare of party members and to organise surveillance of non-party members at the local level. It was not rare to find the same person as both President of the local *seccional* and secretary-general of the local union branch, and union meetings were often held in *seccionales*. As there are 25 *seccionales* in Asunción, city workers commonly referred to the CPT as the '26th *seccional*'.

Physical repression of opponents to *stronista* rule within the trade union movement was exercised by the labour section of the Police Investigations Department. Police officials regularly attended union election meetings at the behest of the CPT leadership. In the event of a serious challenge to the authority of CPT-backed candidates, election meetings were broken up by the police. The imprisonment without trial and torture of trade unionists became a regular feature of the political scene.

However, part of the explanation for the low level of trade union militancy must also be sought in the lack of structural transformation of the Paraguayan economy. There was almost total stagnation in the industrial development of Paraguay throughout the 1960s and early 1970s. The National Accounts data published by the Central Bank show that the share of manufacturing remained stationary at only 15 per cent of GDP between 1964 and 1976. The 1976 industrial census showed a total industrial employment of 35 724, barely above the figure of 34 499 shown by the previous census in 1956. Of this total, only 19 761 were classed as salaried employees. There were only 28 factories employing more than one hundred workers, with a combined employment of 6317. Half of these factories were in Asuncion, where they employed a total workforce of 2668.

During the 1960s, in contrast to almost all other Latin American countries which were undergoing a process of industrialisation based on the model of import-substitution, the *stronista* development strategy emphasised *crecimiento hacia afuera*, export-led growth. This strategy involved minimal protection for domestic industry, whose growth problems were compounded by the small size of the domestic market, high freight costs for imported inputs and most importantly of all, the ill effects of the extensive smuggling of a wide range of consumer goods from neighbouring countries.

In addition to the stagnation of light industry, there was an overall decline in the numbers employed in agricultural processing, which had hitherto been the mainstay of large-scale industrial employment. A collapse in foreign demand led to the demise of meat-packing and tannin extraction with the loss of 10 000 jobs by the mid-1970s. These two industries had formerly constituted the vanguard of the trade union movement. Nor was there much evidence of net growth in public sector industrial activity to compensate for these job losses. On the contrary, the gradual decline of the State Railway Company and the winding up of the State Meat Corporation, COPACAR, only served to worsen the overall job loss. Data from the Social Security agency, IPS, support the view that industrial employment stagnated throughout the 1960s. The number of industrial workers insured under the scheme fell from 26 000 in 1958 to a low of 18 000 in 1964, rising again slightly to 20 000 by 1969.

THE CATHOLIC TRADE UNION MOVEMENT

The Catholic Young Workers' Organisation, *Juventud Obrera Catolica* (JOC), was founded in Paraguay in 1941 and by 1946 two of its leaders, Efigenio Fernandez and Inocencio T. Franco, were members of the council of delegates of the COP. The anti-communist ideology of the JOC in the immediate post-war period facilitated relations with the guionista trade union body, ORO. The JOC held its first national congress in 1948 and by 1955 had 20 official delegates at the third national congress of the CPT. In 1957 the trade union department of the JOC was converted into a separate *Movimiento Sindical Paraguayo* (MSP) as an agitation and training organisation for Catholic trade unionists, especially in rural areas where the institutional support of the Catholic Church was strongest.

Following the failed rapproachement of the MSP with the new leadership of the CPT after the general strike of 1958 and the resignation of five MSP activists from the executive committee of the CPT in 1960, the Christian trade union movement decided to establish its own trade union organisation. The *Central Cristiana de Trabajadores* (CCT) was founded in 1963, three years after the foundation of the Christian Democrat Party. Although operating within the law, the CCT has always been denied official recognition by the Ministry of Justice and Labour. It has operated in a *de facto* manner with no guarantees against harsh repression to which it has been continually subjected.

THE PEASANT LEAGUE MOVEMENT

The absence of a strong trade union movement in the rural areas of Paraguay reflects the low level of agricultural development. The highly unequal system of land tenure created by the land sales at the end of the Triple Alliance War remained largely unaltered until the mid-1970s. However, landless labour was not a characteristic feature of the rural population. This was partly due to the fact that large-scale migration from rural areas to Argentina acted as a 'safety valve' throughout the twentieth century. It was also due to the colonisation programme introduced in the early 1960s by the Stroessner regime which alleviated pressure for land reform in the central zone near Asuncion. As a result of this colonisation programme, Paraguay was the only country in Latin America to register an increase in the share of the total population living in rural areas – to 67 per cent by the mid-1970s. The effect of both international and internal migration was to lessen the objective conditions for social conflict in the rural areas. The development of a rural proletariat was also precluded by the virtual absence of capitalist forms of agricultural production until the mid-1970s. Extensive forms of cattle-ranching absorbed relatively few workers. Sugar and tobacco, traditional cash crops, were produced almost exclusively by small peasant producers and plantations were noticeably absent from the agricultural scene.

Beginning in the early 1960s, a peasant co-operative movement arose which came to be known as the *Ligas Agrarias Cristianas,* (LAC). It represented the first signs of independent political action by the Paraguayan peasantry which had hitherto been bound by ties of traditional loyalty to one or other of the two major political parties established in the aftermath of the Triple Alliance War.

The inspiration for the LAC came from two similar and competing sources within the Catholic Church. With the institutional support of the Latin American Christian Democrat trade union organisation, CLAT, to which it is affiliated, the Christian Democrat trade union body, CCT, had been active since the early 1960s in the formation of peasant co-operatives. In January 1968 it organised the inaugural congress of its *Federación Cristiana Campesina,* (FCC) with 500 peasant delegates. A more radical peasant movement also emerged, during the 1960s, inspired by progressive Jesuit and Franciscan priests and layworkers. Loosely grouped together in the *Federación Nacional de Ligas Agrarias Cristianas,* (FENALAC), this organisation emphasised the autonomy of grass-roots based communities, *communidades de base*, and the role of popular education in the process of social change.

By the end of the decade the LAC boasted a national membership of 10 000, more or less equally divided between the FCC and FENALAC, and organised in a network of regional leagues, *ligas*, throughout the country. The rapid growth of the LAC began to sap the traditional support which large numbers of the peasantry gave to the ruling Colorado Party. This political threat was the major reason for a sharp deterioration in relations between the Stroessner regime and the Catholic Church from 1969. Mounting repression followed against the LACs – torture and imprisonment of peasant leaders, destruction of Christian communities, deportation of progressive clergy and a media campaign denouncing communist infiltration in the Catholic Church. In turn this repression led to a questioning by LAC members of the non-violent approach which had inspired them since their formation, together with a renewed interest in the radical ideas associated with the theology of liberation. Faced with a common external threat, an attempt was made to unite the two strands of the LAC movement. In August 1971 a new unitary organisation, the *Coordinación Nacional de Bases Campesinas Cristianas* (KOGA) was formed to which all FENALAC bases were affiliated as were several FCC bases and various independent groups of more recent formation.

The repression of the peasant movement reached a peak in April-May 1976. The government accused the *ligas* of involvement in an embryonic peasant-student guerrilla movement, the *Organisacion Primero de Marzo* (OPM). Almost all *ligas* became inoperative as over 2000 peasant members of the LAC were arrested in a series of raids throughout the country, as well as a hundred students in Asuncion. Twenty peasant leaders and four students were killed in the repression, and several hundred people were detained for over 12 months.

In December 1977 at Ypacarai the CCT organised a private meeting of peasant leaders from the LAC movement who had survived the 1976 repression, to which both FENALAC and FCC delegates were invited. The meeting was invaded by police, who arrested 19 including several CLAT officials. Several of those detained were severely tortured. For the first time since the 1958 General Strike, the CPT expressed its concern to the government about the fate of the imprisoned activists, and the AFL-CIO sent a delegation to Paraguay to enquire on their behalf.

THE MOVEMENT FOR REFORM

Beginning in the mid-1970s a reform group, known as the *aperturistas*, developed within the trade union movement. Its emergence can be attributed to a combination of factors. Firstly, the construction of the largest hydro-electric project in the world at Itaipu on the border with Brazil, and the associated influx of Brazilian colonists into eastern Paraguay, triggered off an economic boom. The average growth rate during 1976–80 was over 9 per cent a year. Although trade union activity was strictly prohibited at Itaipu, where a maximum of 13 500 Paraguayans were employed in 1978, the associated foreign investment boom led to a substantial rise in trade union membership, especially in the construction sector, which grew at an annual rate of 26 per cent between 1975 and 1978.

Secondly, the economic boom led to an unaccustomed bout of inflation, following a decade of low price rises. Real wages fell as wage increases failed to keep pace with the rise in prices (see Table 3.2). Article 257 of the Labour Code provided for revision of the minimum wage if the cost of living increased by more than 10 per cent. However, the Central Bank cost of living index devised in 1964 had became unrepresentative, given the considerable change in the structure of consumption of working-class households over the intervening period. The Central Bank had been long criticised for under-estimating the real increase in the cost of living in order not to exceed the 10 per cent threshold, and so justify non-revision of the minimum wage. However, since 1974, when even the Central Bank index regularly reported annual inflation rates above 10 per cent, there were long delays in increasing the minimum wage.

Thirdly, foreign influence was important. The US trade union body, AFL-CIO, began to operate in Paraguay through its training affiliate, the *Instituto para el desarrollo del sindicalismo libre* (IDSL) which openly pressed for reform of the trade union movement towards the non-political ideology characteristic of its parent body. In this respect it soon conflicted with the *stronista* policy of firm party control over the CPT. Since its establishment in Asuncion in 1971, over 8000 workers from 103 trade unions participated in training courses organised by IDSL and some hundred trade union leaders were sent to the USA on AFL-CIO scholarships. The training courses often served as the basis for the creation of new unions, as in the case of the retail-workers' *Sindicato de Empleados y Obreros del Comercio* (SEOC).

In November 1979 the CPT withdrew from the International Confederation of Free Trade Unions (ICFTU) and from its Latin American affiliate, ORIT, to avoid its own expulsion on the grounds of political subservience. Shortly afterwards, an internal power struggle led to a change in the leadership of the CPT. In an attempt to counter growing international criticism, the new secretary-general, Dr Modesto Ali, manager of the State Railway Company, promised a more independent position with regard to the government. The AFL-CIO successfully pressed Ali to allow the journalists' union, SPP, to hold their inaugural congress at the CPT headquarters despite the refusal of the Minister of Justice and Labour to grant legal recognition to the union. Its secretary-general, Alcibiades Gonzalez Delvalle, was detained on several occasions in 1978 and 1979.

The first attempt at an organised reform movement within the CPT since the 1958 General Strike surfaced in 1979 with the appearance of the 'Group of Nine', which included the following unions: *Sindicato de Trabajadores de Paraguay Refrescos* (SITRAPAR), *Sindicato Nacional de Trabajadores de la Construccion* (SINATRAC), *Sindicato de Empleados y Obreros del Comercio* (SEOC), *Sindicato Nacional de Obreros Metalurgicos y Afines* (SINOMA), *Sindicato de Periodistas del Paraguay* (SPP), *Federacion de Trabajadores Bancarios del Paraguay* (FETRABAN), and *Sindicato de Obreros Graficos del Paraguay*. The Group exerted pressure on the CPT leadership to defend real wages and to ensure compliance with aspects of the 1961 Labour Code which had fallen into abeyance since its introduction. Foremost among these were demands for security from dismissal for union activists (*fuero sindical*) and the introduction of collective bargaining, (*contratos colectivos*.) The group planned to revitalise the CPT by resurrecting the broadly-based and representative council of delegates which had not met since 1958. Although bitterly opposed by the *continuistas* within the CPT hierarchy, the Council of Delegates was eventually convened in February 1980, thanks to support given to the Group of Nine by Dr Modesto Ali. Many delegates from the 85 unions represented openly criticised the CPT leadership and pressed for greater independence from government interference in union affairs.

In response to the threat to their entrenched positions, the *continuistas* circulated an anonymous report to the Ministry of Justice and Labour denouncing infiltration by opposition political parties in the trade union movement through the Group of Nine. As a result, the Group's broadsheet, *Trabajo*, was forced to close after only four issues following threats from the Ministry of Interior. The printworkers and construction workers' unions gradually distanced themselves from the Group and attempts to reconvene the Council of Delegates were thwarted by the *continuistas*.

The conflict between reform and reaction within the CPT now shifted to the impending 14th National Labour Congress. Reform elements were determined to oust the existing deputy leader of the CPT, Sotero Ledesma, a diehard union bureaucrat who personified the *continuista* faction. Ledesma had led the LOMP ever since the 1958 general strike. Although the LOMP was once the most militant trade union federation in Paraguay, most of its affiliated unions were now little more than groups of independent canoe-owners. Meanwhile the bulk of Paraguayan maritime workers remained outside the LOMP, since unions are prohibited for workers in the State merchant navy and the State Ports Authority, ANAP.

The reform movement proposed the re-election of Dr Modesto Ali as secretary-general, but with *aperturista*, Julian Acuna of the bakers' union as deputy leader instead of Ledesma. In response Ledesma announced his own candidature for the post of secretary-general with another *continuista*, Rogelio Coronel, as deputy leader. However, the unique prospect of an open contest for the leadership of the CPT failed to materialise. Days before the opening of the Congress in March 1981, the Minister of Justice and Labour, Saul Gonzalez, put pressure on Ali to withdraw his candidature. In a vivid display of the ideology of *stronismo*, Gonzalez declared to the press that his intervention did not constitute outside interference, since the government had the right and obligation to ensure harmony within the CPT. The way was then left open for Ledesma to reaffirm *stronista* control over the Paraguayan labour movement. Ten of the 19 members of the newly elected executive committee of the CPT represented so-called maritime unions. Days after the Congress ended, in a belated recognition that 'the Government of Paraguay does not recognise a separation of party and the trade union movement', the AFL-CIO announced the closure of their affiliate, IDSL, in Paraguay, thus completing the international isolation of the CPT.

Following the victory of the *continuistas* in the CPT Congress, a number of trade union activists identified with the reform movement were sacked. The most publicised case was that of the local subsidiary of Coca Cola, *Paraguay Refrescos*, whose trade union, SITRAPAR, was a leading member of the Group of Ten. Between January-August 1982 the company sacked 200 employees under the pretext of resiting the factory outside Asuncion. During the period armed police accompanied foremen on their rounds inside the plant to discourage protest strikes. The operation culminated in the dismissal of seven leaders of SITRAPAR. In response 17 unions formed the *Movimiento de Solidaridad Sindical* in support of SITRAPAR. In mid-September they launched an effective consumer boycott against Coca Cola by means of press advertising and leafletting in the streets. Within weeks Coca Cola sales fell by more than half. On 6 October the company backed down and agreed to reinstate the sacked workers. It was the first victory by the independent trade union movement in Paraguay for several decades.

The reform movement inside the CPT had risen during a period of very rapid economic growth in the 1970s but evaporated with the recession in the early 1980s. The construction of Itaipu, the expansion of the agricultural frontier in the eastern border region (EBR) and the associated real estate boom in Asuncion all contributed to a rapid increase in the demand for labour. This produced a temporary labour shortage which undoubtedly strengthened the bargaining power of organised labour. From 1977 to 1981 real incomes of working-class households rose as (1) increases in the minimum wage kept pace with inflation, (2) many workers received increases higher than the officially decreed minimum due to labour shortages, especially in the construction sector, and (3) participation rates increased due to labour shortages.

However, the completion of the Itaipu project in 1981 and the closure of the agricultural frontier produced a sudden end to this economic boom, leading to negative growth rates of –1.0 per cent and –3.0 per cent in 1982 and 1983 respectively. The recession hit the construction sector hardest, resulting in widespread lay-offs of building workers. The changed economic situation weakened the reform movement and enabled *stronista* diehards to reassert their authority inside the hierarchy of the CPT. As a result, trade union pressure for upward revision of the minimum wage was weakened, despite a continued high rate of inflation. This led to a drop in real incomes of workers, which, compounded by a growth in open unemployment in urban areas (officially recorded at 8 per cent in 1983), led to reduced real incomes of working class households during 1981–84.

CONCLUSION

By comparison with its counterparts in other Latin American countries, the failure of the labour movement in Paraguay to promote progressive social change can be explained by its small size and the limits to its freedom of action imposed by the long-lived Stroessner regime. After a decade of rapid economic growth (1972–81) the industrial sector still contributed only 17 per cent of GDP in 1984 and employed only 132 000, equivalent to 13 per cent of the workforce. Manufacturing remains largely small scale and geared to the processing of primary products. There are still very few large factories and in 1982 some 72 per cent of the industrial labour force were employed in establishments of less than 20 workers. The government's rejection of import-substituting industrialisation and its unyielding support for the economic interests of agriculturally-based exporters has reinforced an official policy of minimising real wage costs. This is designed to maintain the international competitiveness of primary product exports which are saddled with high freight costs due to Paraguay's geographical location. The construction of the Itaipu hydroelectric project and the rapid expansion of cash crop production in the 1970s failed to provide the catalyst for a process of industrialisation in Paraguay. The government gave scant attention to the possibilities of domestic utilisation of the enormous electricity production of Itaipu. Accordingly, the bulk of the Paraguayan power share will be exported to Brazil. In the absence of any policy of reafforestation, the booming saw-mill industry collapsed with the elimination of the forest cover of the EBR at the end of the 1970s. Similarly the industrial processing of edible oils did not develop despite the dramatic increase in the production of soya and cotton, which are exported in unprocessed form.

There are currently 153 trade unions affiliated to the CPT with the nominal representation of some 80 000 members. At least another 30 000 workers in public sector enterprises are denied trade union rights. In practice fewer than 20 unions are strong and active. These represent workers in textiles, construction, metal working, road transport, retailing, banking, catering, printing and journalism, in addition to three maritime unions. Very few unions have maintained complete independence from State control. The bank workers union federation, FETRABAN, was virtually the only case until it was recently joined by the journalists' union, SSP and shop-workers' union, SEOC. Most active unions, while seeking a greater and more independent role for organised labour, nevertheless, still operate within the ideological constraints of *stronismo*. The majority of fictitious unions, especially in the maritime sector, serve the exclusive purpose of ensuring State control over the organised working-class. They fulfil important functions as mechanisms by which unrepresentative but politically obedient trade union 'leaders' have been able to maintain a stranglehold over the CPT during the post-1958 period, thereby neutralising workers' demands.

The regime of President Stroessner remains firmly committed to the furtherance of an economic structure dependent on the export of primary products, with a low level of industrialisation. While these structural conditions prevail, the prospects for the growth and influence of the Paraguayan labour movement must remain limited.

Abbreviations

ANDE	Administración Nacional de Electridad.
BNT	Banco Nacional de Trabajadores.
CCT	Central Cristiana de Trabajadores.
CDS	Comité de Defensa Sindical.
CLAT	Central Latinamericana de Trabajadores.
CNT	Confederación Nacional de Trabajadores.
COP	Consejo Obrero del Paraguay.
CORP	Centro Obrero Regional del Paraguay.
CORPOSANA	Corporación de Sanamiento Ambiental.
CPT	Confederación Paraguaya de Trabajadores.
CTP	Confederación de Trabajadores del Paraguay.
DNT	Departmento Nacional de Trabajo.
EBR	Eastern Border Region.
FCC	Federación Cristiana Campesina.
FENALAC	Federación Nacional de Ligas Agrarias Cristianas.
FEPRINCO	Federación Paraguaya de Industria y Comercio.
FETRABAN	Federación de Trabajadores Bancarios del Paraguay.
FORP	Federación Obrera Regional Paraguaya.
FULNA	Frente Unido de Liberación Nacional.
IDSL	Instituto para el Desarrollo del Sindicalismo Libre.
IPC	International Products Corporation.
IPS	Instituto de Previsión Social.
JOC	Juventud Obrera Catolica.
LAC	Ligas Agrarias Cristianas.
LNI	Liga Nacional Independiente.
LOMP	Liga de Obreros Maritimos del Paraguay.
MSP	Movimiento Sindical Paraguayao.
OPM	Organizacion Primero de Marzo.
ORIT	Organizacion Interamerica de Trabajadores.
ORO	Organizacion Republicana Obrera.
PCP	Partido Comunista Paraguayo.

SEOC	Sindicato de Empleados y Obreros del Comercio.
SINATRAC	Sindicato Nacional de Trabajadores de la Construcción.
SITRAPAR	Sindicato de Trabajadores de Paraguay Refrescos.
SPP	Sindicato de Periodistas del Paraguay.
UOP	Unión Obrera del Paraguay.

NOTES

1. Quoted in Gaona, F., *Introducción a la historia gremial y social del Paraguay* (Buenos Aires: 1967).
2. Borche, C., *Campos de concentración en America* (Montevideo: 1945).
3. HMSO, *Economic and commercial conditions in Paraguay* (London: 1952).
4. Taboada, Edgar, *El Desarrollo economico del Paraguay* (Sàntiago, Chile: CEPAL, 1953).

BIBLIOGRAPHY

Acosta, Dr Cesar R., Social Legislation in Paraguay, ILO Review vol. L, July-December 1944, pp. 40–6.

Barret, Rafael, 'Lo que son los Yerbales', in Proyección, (ed.), *El Terror Argentina* (Buenos Aires: 1971).

Borche, Carlos, *Campos de concentración en America* (Mision en Paraguay) (Montevideo: 1945).

Chartrain, Francisco, 'El Mundo del Trabajo en el Paraguay entre 1870–1936' in *Revista Paraguay de Sociología*, no. 27 May-August 1973.

Diaz de Arce, Omar, 'Contemporary Paraguay', in *Tricontinental*, No. 3, 52 (Havana, Cuba: 1977).

Gaona, Francisco, Introducción a la historia gremial y social del Paraguay, vol. 1, Arandu (ed.), (Buenos Aires: 1967).

HMSO, *Economic and Commercial Conditions in Paraguay*, Overseas Economic Surveys (London: 1952).

ILO, *Situacion y Perspectivas del Empleo en Paraguay* (Santiago, Chile: PREALC, 1975).

Lewis, Paul H., *The Politics of Exile* (University of North Carolina Press: 1968).

Ministerio de Industria y Comercio, *Paraguay: Primer Censo Industrial* (Asuncion: 1958).

Ministerio de Industria y Comercio, *Censos Economicos – 1963* (Asunción: 1966).

Miranda, Anibal, *Apuntes sobre el desarrollo Paraguayo, 1940–73* (University Catolica, Asunción: 1980).

Montaldo, Dr Francisco A., *La Nutrición en el Paraguay* (Buenos Aires: Imp. Oeste, 1955).

Montaldo, Dr Francisco A., *La situación alimentaria de la población ante el*

problema del desarrollo economico-social del pais (Asunción: 1962).
PCP, *Relatorio sobre la actividad enemiga de Oscar Creydt*, ed. Adelante (1967).
Perez Echeguren, José A., *Relieve y Categoría de la Revolución Paraguaya* (Asunción: Imp. Nacional, 1940).
Republica del Paraguay, *Codigos del Trabajo y Procesal del trabajo*, ed. Comuneros (Asunción: 1980).
Soler Núnez, Ignacio, *Evocaciones de un sindicalista revolucionario* (Asunción: 1980).
US Department of Commerce, Investment in Paraguay (US Government Printing Office: 1954).

4 Ecuador

Charles Nurse

LABOUR AND THE STATE UNDER THE COLONY

The origins of the Ecuadorian labour movement and the industrial relations context in which it exists have much in common with other regional experiences of the Spanish conquest. During the colonial period – the mid-sixteenth century until the early nineteenth – the territory corresponding roughly to the present-day Republic of Ecuador was administered by the *Audiencia* of Quito – a collective body which exercised a broad range of political, administrative and judicial tasks on behalf of the Spanish crown.[1] Since the territory was soon found to lack significant mineral wealth, the indigenous population, located largely in the *sierra*, became the most important economic resource – both as a source of labour and of tribute. As elsewhere, one of the main methods of appropriating Indian labour was through the *encomienda* system, although this gave neither title to land nor the right to extract labour from the indigenous population, but merely obliged the title holder to protect the Indians, to provide them with religious training and to give military assistance to the King. In addition to the *encomienda* (abolished in 1720), three other methods were used in the *Audiencia* to extract forced labour. Under the system known as *repartimiento de indios* (distribution of Indians), the authorities arranged for a certain number of Indians to be taken to the cities to be employed by certain prominent colonists in agricultural work, mining or in personal service – work for which officially they were to be paid. A second form of forced labour was provided by the *mita*, under which a fifth of the Indians between the ages of 18 and 50 were assigned, on an annual rotating basis, to work in the mines or in agriculture. In addition to these, black slavery was practised in some areas of the *Audiencia*.

The sparse gold and silver deposits in the *Audiencia* were soon exhausted, including the two most important deposits in the provinces of El Oro and Cotopaxi. In the absence of significant mineral resources the economy of the *Audiencia* was predominantly agrarian. The most important area was the sierra where cereals were cultivated and sheep raised. There was, however, a small manufacturing sector which grew up, especially in the seventeenth century. Since Spanish producers were unable to meet colonial demand, textile manufacture flourished in the favourable conditions provided by abundant raw materials and low labour costs. By 1681 there were about 200 *obrajes* (workshops) employing some 28 000 workers. At the same time Guayaquil had become the major shipyard on the Pacific coast of South America.[2]

These industries were, however, to decline in the eighteenth century. As the Bourbons permitted freer trade in the colonies, Ecuadorean textiles went into decline. Shipbuilding also declined, although, in fact, the port of Guayaquil prospered as a result of the increase in trade, especially of cocoa. During the colonial period the main labour organisation was the artisans guild, based on the system of guilds organised in early sixteenth-century Spain. The first guilds were formed soon after the conquest – as early as 1537 the *Cabildo* (town council) of Quito issued an order regulating the prices charged by the iron-workers guild.[3] The *Cabildo*, composed mainly of the owners of *encomiendas* and mines, closely regulated the guilds, being particularly concerned with price regulation but also supervising the granting of qualifications and the condition of workshops. These guilds were, in effect, an organ of the state and their leaders were nominated by the *Cabildo*. Under a regulation of the *Cabildo* issued on 9 January 1598 all guilds were to have an *alcalde* (master) and a *veedor* (inspector), who would be chosen by the *Cabildo*. The tasks of these officials were to ensure a fair distribution of work, to maintain the quality of goods and to ensure that the prices determined by the *Cabildo* were maintained.[4]

This guild system was limited to the types of occupations in which whites worked; occupations which were filled largely by Indians, such as mining, agriculture, construction and transport, were excluded from the system. Moreover, in an attempt to maintain price-levels, Indians were excluded from the activities controlled by guilds by the guild members themselves.[5]

One notable feature was the involvement of the Church in labour matters during the colonial period. The guilds themselves developed into *hermandades* (religious brotherhoods), each of them with a patron saint. In the early seventeenth century Padre A. de Solis encouraged the establishment of a series of these brotherhoods to provide mutual aid, assistance for the needy and religious instruction.[6]

THE AFTERMATH OF INDEPENDENCE

Independence and the removal of colonial restrictions on trade did not noticeably alter the Ecuadorean economy and society. The removal of trading restrictions encouraged the growth of an agro-export trade in the coastal region, but on the other hand cheap imports of manufactured goods hit such domestic manufacture as existed, especially textiles. Overall, however, integration into the world economy was slight until the end of the nineteenth century when Ecuador became, for a short time, the world's leading cocoa producer. The cocoa boom brought important changes in the hitherto sparsely-populated Guayas Basin, including the growth of a class of planters and exporters. The increasing wealth and strength of these coastal elements and the weakness of the traditional landowning élite of the *sierra* resulted in the overthrow of the latter in the Revolution of 1895.

Backed by the planters and exporters, the Radical Liberal Party, which took power, presided over the dramatic expansion of cocoa. As the coastal economy boomed, the population of Guayaquil grew rapidly and migration from the *sierra* occurred. Although the legal restrictions on the movement of the *campesinos* of the *sierra* were eased in order to supply the needs of the great coastal plantations, the Radical Liberal Party was content to leave the social structure of the *sierra* unaltered and the position of the large landowners of the region unchallenged. Moreover, in the coastal economy itself, little diversification occurred, either within the agricultural sector or into manufacturing. Much of the revenue from the export of cocoa went to shore up the political position of the Radical Liberal leaders, while a large proportion of the profits was spent on luxury imports.[7]

The damage inflicted on the coastal economy by the world economic crises of the 1920s and 1930s was exacerbated by the devastation of the cocoa plantations by disease and by the growth of competition from Brazilian and African cocoa. With the collapse of the cocoa boom came the abandonment of many of the spectacular public works projects undertaken in the years of plenty. Also abandoned were many of the plantations themselves, with the owners acquiescing in their takeover by the former plantation workers at low rents or rent-free.

The pattern of mono-export boom followed by collapse was to be repeated after 1945 with the so-called 'era of the banana'. At a time when the Central American banana plantations had been hit by the onslaught of diseases, President Galo Plaza Lasso made use of his close relationship with the United Fruit Company to promote banana production in Ecuador. By the mid-1950s Ecuador had become the world's leading banana producer. Not only was the crop grown on many of the former cocoa plantations, but, in addition, extensive new areas of the coastal region were opened up for production by a large road-building programme. The general rise in world commodity prices during the decade following the end of the Second World War also gave a stimulus to the production of other crops such as coffee and, once again, cocoa. The collapse of this second boom occurred partly as a result of the recovery of the Central American banana plantations and the spread of diseases to the Ecuadorean plantations. The situation was accentuated by the development of new strains of bananas in other producing countries and by the fall in world commodity prices from the mid-1950s.

As a result of this new crisis the 1960s saw Ecuadorean governments facing worsening balance of payments problems and a recurring shortage of revenues. The late 1960s, however, also witnessed an increased interest in the potential of the oil resources of the *Oriente* – the Ecuadorean part of the Amazonian jungle. The completion of a 500-kilometre pipeline from the oilfields to the coast near Esmeraldas in 1972 and the country's admission as a member of the Organisation of Petroleum Exporting Countries (OPEC) in the following year seemed to many to mark the onset of a new era for the Ecuadorean economy.

THE SIERRA VERSUS THE COAST

One effect of the boom-slump pattern of the Ecuadorean economy was to increase the differences between the coastal region and the *sierra*. In the *sierra*, walled off behind the natural barrier of the Andes, with poor communications and a totally different climate, social relationships remained largely unaffected by developments on the coast. The descendants of the Spanish *conquistadores* continued to dominate the economic and social life of the *sierra* and it was not until after the end of the banana boom that the first tentative steps were taken towards agrarian reform. The 1964 Agrarian Reform Law did, finally see the abolition of a number of forms of tenure left over from the colonial period. Chief among these was *huasipungo* – a system of sharecropping – and the fate of the peasants freed from *huasipungo* is a useful comment on the 1964 law. In spite of their new legal status as owners of smallholdings, the conditions of these *campesinos* has improved little. Not only did they receive the worst land and have to pay compensation to the landowners for it, but, in addition, they found themselves having to pay for a number of 'services' – including water, the use of access roads and pasture land and the collection of firewood. In these circumstances it is hardly surprising that many *campesinos* are now as tied to the landowners by their debts, by their dependence for such services and by their need for employment as they were before the 1964 Act, which has served to substitute one system of domination for another.[8]

Meanwhile the effects of the cocoa and banana periods and the ensuing slumps on the rural social structure of the coast have been profound. Not only did the cocoa economy of the early twentieth century lead to migration from the *sierra*, but, moreover, the shortage of labour during that period improved the bargaining position of the rural labour force.[9] One effect of this has been the greater independence of the coastal *campesino*, who is less subject to the domination of the large landowners than is his counterpart in the *sierra*. One manifestation of this difference can be observed in the much higher percentage of wage-earners on the coast than in the *sierra*. By the early 1960s it was estimated that some 52 per cent of agricultural workers on the coast were wage-earning — a much higher figure than in the *sierra*.[10]

With the decline of the coastal plantations in the 1920s large areas were occupied by the former plantation workers who 'squatted' on the land until the upturn in the coastal economy in the late 1940s. Under the more favourable market conditions of the post-war years, plantation owners began to drive the *campesinos* from the land they were squatting on and the level of social conflict on the coast rose rapidly.

Another consequence of the pattern of the coastal economy during the twentieth century has been to multiply the differences among the coastal *campesinos*. The coastal rural sector labour force is engaged in a wide variety of circumstances with the result that the economic and social structure of the region has come to resemble what has been described as:

> Successive agricultural frontiers, the oldest of which retain traditional qualities that we cannot observe in the more recent.[11]

Although during the nineteenth century the disease-ridden coastal region was largely uninhabited, by the early 1970s the population of the coast had overtaken that of the *sierra* as a result of migration and a significant reduction in the mortality rate on the coast.[12] Related to the fluctuating fortunes of the coastal economy has been not only the pattern of migration from the *sierra* but also the rapid growth of the coastal towns, especially Guayaquil. Following the collapse of the cocoa economy, many former plantation workers moved to Guayaquil and the surrounding towns in search of work. They were followed in the 1950s by *campesinos* driven from the land they had previously rented or squatted on by landowners who wished to cultivate bananas, coffee and cocoa. When market conditions deteriorated in the late 1950s and early 1960s many of the wage labourers employed on the plantations were dismissed and followed the former tenants to the urban areas.[13] A further twist to this movement was applied in the late 1960s as landowners in the rice-growing areas of the Guayas Basin shifted into cattle-breeding, often in an attempt to pre-empt trouble from increasingly recalcitrant tenants.[14]

The towns and cities of the *sierra* have also witnessed an influx of migrants, particularly since the abolition of the traditional forms of tenure by the 1964 Agrarian Reform Law. By the early 1970s, as a result of migration, Quito, with a population of over 600 000, and Guayaquil, with an estimated 800 000 inhabitants, far outstripped other centres in size and importance.

INDUSTRIALISATION AND LABOUR MOVEMENT FORMATION

While there was little diversification into industry during the periods of the cocoa economy and the banana economy, most manufacturing was on a small scale. Apart from the textile industry, established in Quito at the end of the nineteenth century, manufacturing in the early years of this century was carried out almost entirely in artisan's workshops. It was not until the 1930s that further growth of manufacturing industry occurred with the establishment of food-processing plants, drinks industries and cigarette factories in and around Guayaquil. As late as 1950 there was little other manufacturing industry. The food, drinks and tobacco industries between them accounted for 45 per cent of industrial capital and 31 per cent of the industrial labour force. A further 21 per cent of total industrial capital was invested in the textile industry which employed 31 per cent of the total industrial labour force.[15]

It was in Guayaquil and – to a lesser extent – in Quito that early organisational activity among the artisans occurred at the end of the last century. In the capital the *Sociedad Artistica e Industrial de Pichincha* was founded in 1892 by some 200 artisans, artists and industrialists, with the aim of liberating workers and artisans 'from certain oppressions' to which they were being subjected and 'to encourage the arts'. The Society included the following guilds – music, painting, sculpture, tailoring, silverwork, carpentry, hair-dressing, metalwork, saddle-making, armoury and hat-making.[16]

Two years later the *Circulo Católico de Obreros* was established. Meanwhile in Guayaquil a number of organisations were founded at roughly the same time, among them the *Sociedad de Tipografos del Guayas* (1884) and the *Unión de Panaderos* (1898).

From such beginnings the years of the cocoa boom saw a significant increase in activity, leading to the convening of the first National Congress of Ecuadorean Workers in Quito in 1909. The Congress established the Ecuadorean Union of Workers, the aims of which included the encouragement of organisations of workers and the calling of a workers' congress every two years.[17] In spite of the latter aim, no further congress was held until 1920. These years also witnessed sporadic outbreaks of strikes, particularly among workers employed in building and running the railway lines being constructed at the time. With the onset of the economic crises of the post-war years and the problems of the cocoa economy, a further upsurge in activity occurred, especially among the miners of Portovelo, the electricity workers, sugar workers, municipal employees and, once again, the railway workers.[18] The culmination of this militancy came with the general strike of November 1922 in Guayaquil, which was brutally suppressed by troops.[19]

Early labour legislation

While governments in general showed extreme hostility to these early labour movements, some attempts were made to introduce labour legislation. In 1916 a decree introduced an eight-hour working day and made holidays on Sundays and *fiestas* obligatory. It also introduced a 30-day period of notice of dismissal and laid down wage-scales for overtime work.[20] Following the 'July Revolution' of 1925, the new military junta established a Ministry of Social Welfare and

Labour and in 1928 an array of labour legislation was introduced, dealing with individual work contracts, dismissal, responsibility for accidents at work and their prevention, length of working day and female and child labour. Article 151 of the new constitution of 1929 included provisions for the regulation of industrial relations and guaranteed the right of association and the right to strike.[21] Nine years later a further step along the road to legal recognition of organised labour was taken with the drafting of the first labour code.[22]

Two points need to be made about this process. Although much of this legislation was in part a response to pressure from labour and from intellectuals sympathetic to it, much of the motivation for such legal recognition came from the desire of governments to 'tame' the early labour movement and to channel its activities.[23] Secondly, of course, much of this legislation existed on paper only and has never been properly enforced, even if that were possible given the low standards of living.

The labour movement coalesces

Organisationally the labour movement in Ecuador began to take on something of its present-day form between 1938 and 1944. The establishment in September 1938 of the *Confederación Ecuatoriana de Obreros Catolicos* (CEDOC) was, according to its founders, part of an attempt to stem the 'communist advance' in the labour movement.[24] Two months earlier at a Congress held in Ambato an attempt had been made by the Ecuadorean Communist Party (PCE) and the Ecuadorean Socialist Party (PSE) to set up a national labour organisation but it was not until 1944 with the foundation of the *Confederación de Trabajadores del Ecuador* (CTE) that the attempt met with success.

Although the foundation of CEDOC and of the CTE stimulated the establishment of new labour organisations, membership of the labour movement remained low. The CTE was the more influential of the competing confederations and by 1950 had won representation on the Consultative Committee of the Ministry of Labour and Social Welfare. Widely regarded as a 'communist' organisation at the time, the CTE was, in fact, led by figures from the Socialist Party, successive secretaries-general from 1946 to 1963 being members of the PSE. The CTE's claims to a membership of 60 000 in 125 affiliated organisations in February 1952 sound, however, grossly inflated in view of most estimates made in later years.[25] Although the CTE was active among the *campesinos* of the coast through the *Federación Ecuatoriana de Indios*, most of the confederation's support came from the manual workers in and around Guayaquil.

Throughout the 1940s and 1950s CEDOC was strongly influenced by the Catholic Church and the latter's political ally, the Conservative Party, and it was from the *sierra*, where these two bodies were most influential, that CEDOC drew most of its membership. This membership was very limited – one estimate in the early 1960s put total membership at 6000 – and overwhelmingly drawn from among the artisans.[26]

In an attempt to weaken the influence of the 'communist' CTE, moves were made in the early 1960s to establish a rival confederation with United States backing. These culminated in the foundation of the *Confederacion Ecuatoriana de Organizaciones Sindicales Libres* (CEOSL) in Quito in May 1962. The new confederation was immediately affiliated to the ICFTU and to the latter's inter-American arm, ORIT. Support also came from the *Instituto de Educación Sindicalista Ecuatoriana*, which was set up in 1962 as the local wing of AIFLD as part of the Alliance for Progress. AIFLD has claimed that its courses for trade unionists were attended by over 23 000 workers in Ecuador between 1962 and 1975.[27]

During its early years CEOSL was a small organisation, even by Ecuadorean standards, centred mainly on Guayas and drawing its limited membership chiefly from tertiary-sector workers and artisans.[28] CEOSL benefitted from the policies of the 1963–66 military junta, which suppressed both the CTE and the PCE and arrested leaders of both bodies. The junta's relations with CEOSL and CEDOC were less clear-cut. Although the latter maintained a critical posture, it was not banned and its activities were permitted to continue. CEOSL, which carefully avoided attacking the junta, was able to benefit from the attacks on the other sections of the labour movement.[29]

Although it continued to work underground, the CTE was weakened, particularly with the departure from its ranks of two of the most important affiliates, the Ecuadorean Federation of Professional Drivers (FCPE) and the National Federation of Oil Workers (FNTP).[30] The problems of the CTE were further increased by the playing-out of a series of divisions and disputes in the Ecuadorean left during the 1960s, prominent among which was the fracture of the PSE and the establishment of the Ecuadorean Revolutionary Socialist Party.

THE CONTEMPORARY LABOUR MOVEMENT

The exploitation of Ecuadorean oil reserves from the Amazonian jungle and the country's admission to the ranks of OPEC may not have brought about the kind of changes envisaged in optimistic predictions of the early 1970s, but the effect of the oil boom on social and economic conditions in the country has been considerable.

One consequence has been an increase in foreign interest, not only in the oil industry but also in manufacturing. Until 1960 there was, in fact, little foreign capital in Ecuadorean industry, the domestic market being considered too small to warrant such interest. Although foreign investment in the economy increased from 29.7 million dollars in 1961 to 78.9 millions in 1968,[31] it was the exploitation of oil and the marketing opportunities promised by the development of the Andean Pact which were to lead to a significant increase in foreign investment. By 1975 of an estimated 134 foreign-owned enterprises in Ecuador, 110 had been established since 1967.[32]

The growth of modern industry, both Ecuadorean and foreign-owned, has centred, not surprisingly, on Quito and Guayaquil, thus further increasing the importance of these two cities in the national economy. By 1973 the provinces of Pichincha and Guayas (which include Quito and Guayaquil respectively) contained 76 per cent of all manufacturing establishments and accounted for over 80 per cent of manufacturing production. Such modern industry has also tended to be concentrated in the already-established sectors of food processing and, to a lesser extent, textiles. By 1973 the largely Guayaquil-based food processing and drinks industries accounted for 30 per cent of manufacturing establishments, 31 per cent of total manufacturing production and provided employment for some 19 000 workers.[33]

Such modern industry, whether in foreign or Ecuadorean hands, contrasts markedly with the more traditional industrial sector, being relatively large scale and capital intensive and requiring a small, highly-skilled labour force. This is most noticeable in the oil and oil-related industries, where much of the labour force is recruited from non-Ecuadoreans.

The growth of the urban labour market

With population growth occurring at an annual rate of 3.4 per cent throughout the 1960s and 1970s, the Economically Active Population (EAP) has been increasing by 50 per cent per decade. In contrast, new industries are estimated by the Economic Institute of the University of Guayaquil to provide fewer than 2700 new jobs a year.[34] High rates of rural-urban migration have continued since the early 1960s, particularly to Quito and Guayaquil, but also to coastal centres such as Machala, Manta, Milagro and Portoviejo. Between 1974 and 1982 some 600 000 Ecuadorean *campesinos* migrated to the cities.[35] The consequences, common throughout the 'Third World', have been increasing underemployment, increased employment in marginal tertiary-sector activities and a growing gap between the mass of the labour force and the small group of relatively skilled and relatively well-paid workers in the modern sector of the urban economy.

Official statistics on employment – such as the 1975 figure for urban unemployment of five per cent – are meaningless, given their political sensitivity and the need for those who might be considered unemployed to make a living somehow or other. Underemployment is notoriously difficult to quantify but some indication of its extent is provided by figures produced by the *Centro de Analisis Demografico* for 1968, which put the level of male underemployment in urban areas at 28 per cent.[36]

Although the extent to which the tertiary sector acts as a sponge to soak up workers unable to find employment elsewhere is difficult to ascertain, official figures for 1974 indicated that some 32 per cent of the EAP were employed in 'commerce' or 'services' or were unclassified. This pattern was not limited to Quito and Guayaquil but was common throughout the urban areas.[37]

The trends in wages and prices

The flooding of the urban labour market by migrants from the impoverished rural areas has helped depress income levels of unskilled workers while, at the same time, the skilled nature of much employment in the 'modern' sector has created a demand for skilled labour which at least maintains the wage levels of most groups of such workers well above those of the mass of the labour force. The result, as Griffin has pointed out, is the consolidation of two 'non-competing' sectors in the urban labour force.[38]

Although official figures on such matters as prices must be treated with scepticism, it is clear that one side-effect of the oil bonanza of the 1970s has been to help stimulate inflation. During most of the 1960s inflation was a relatively minor problem – official sources indicate that the cost of living index rose at about 5 per cent per annum for most of the decade. This situation altered dramatically in the early 1970s with the official general price index rising by over 20 per cent in 1974, before declining to hover around the 10–15 per cent level from 1975 to 1981.[39] The food and drinks price index, which more closely reflects the spending priorities of the poorest groups in Ecuadorean society, recorded an even greater increase, especially in 1974 and 1975.[40]

Such figures as are available on income seem to indicate that income-levels in the manufacturing sector kept pace with increases in the food and drinks index during the 1970s.[41] The usefulness of such figures is limited, however, as they refer to a minority of the labour force and group together both the 'modern' and more traditional manufacturing sectors. Figures on incomes for the non-industrial labour force are more difficult to obtain and are of little value in view of the type of non-wage earning employment common in the primary and tertiary sectors. Most indicators, however, point to a drop in the level of real incomes of the bulk of the labour force during the 1960s and 1970s. One estimate put the drop in real incomes between 1972 and 1974 at 28.5 per cent.[42] Although there were fairly frequent increases in the officially-regulated minimum wage in the 1970s,[43] the minimum wage remained below half the average wage in manufacturing industry. In May 1983 the Economic Institute of the University of Guayaquil estimated that a family of five needed a monthly income of 11 000 sucres to meet their basic needs. At that time the official minimum wage was 5600 sucres a month. Moreover, the minimum wage is so widely ignored as to be meaningless and it has been estimated that over half of the EAP earns less than this minimum.[44]

The indications are that living standards, already among the lowest in the Western Hemisphere, deteriorated in the 1960s and 1970s. Between 1963 and 1969 the average daily consumption *per capita* varied between 1830 and 2210 calories.[45] In spite of the appalling conditions that characterise the shanty-towns of Guayaquil, it is in the rural areas that living conditions are worst. Rural overcrowding is particularly severe in the *sierra* and is increasing with the high birth rate. In 1975 it was estimated that over 1 850 000 people existed on 1 236 000 hectares of land in the *sierra* – an average of 150 per square kilometre.[46] *Per capita* production of agricultural goods is, at best, stagnant – in the 1960s it dropped by 0.6 per cent and, despite a good harvest in 1970, the decline accelerated in the early 1970s with *per capita* production dropping by 1.7 per cent in 1971, 2.6 per cent in 1972 and 2.8 per cent in 1973.[47]

Against this background even the modest proposals put forward in the Agrarian Reform Law of 1964 have been emasculated. Since the fall of the military junta in 1966 the body set up to administer the reform – the *Instituto Ecuatoriano de Reforma Agraria y Colonización* (IERAC) has been starved of funds and forced to concentrate on 'colonisation' – the opening up of uninhabited parts of the country – rather than redistribution. During its first 13 years of existence IERAC handed over more than five times as much land through colonisation as through redistribution.[48]

If the oil revenues have not led to an improvement in the living standards of the Ecuadorean masses, they have had the effect of increasing the ability of the state to intervene in the economy and in society and of increasing the 'potential scale of government bureaucracy and paternalism'.[49] One aspect of this has been an expansion in public sector employment, which was already occurring under the government of Velasco Ibarra (1968–72) and which served the function of helping to maintain the President's shaky hold over the disparate forces which had brought him to power.[50]

The increase in unionisation

The increase in the size of the public sector – by 1974 the public sector labour force was 150 000 – has been accompanied by increasing organisation among the public sector labour force. The *Confederación Nacional de Servidores Publicos*, founded in 1968, claims that some 85 per cent of all public servants are affiliated to it.[51] Although this is undoubtedly an exaggeration, the unionisation of public sector workers has contributed to the noticeable growth in the labour movement which has occurred since the overthrow of the 1963–66 military junta.

Some indication of the scale of this growth is provided by an analysis published in 1974 which indicated that almost as many labour organisations were set up in Ecuador between 1967 and 1973 as had been established over the previous 40 years.[52] Although any statistics on labour organisations in Ecuador and on their membership have to be treated with caution, this expansion in the labour movement appears to be due to increasing unionisation of workers in primary, secondary and tertiary sectors of the economy.[53]

The development of unionisation among the *campesinos* is in part related to the various attempts at agrarian reform since 1964 and the frustrations surrounding these. In the Guayas Basin further impetus was provided by the droughts of the late 1960s and the increasing tension between landowners and tenants and squatters. Of the three *centrales* (or confederations) the one most active among the *campesinos* has been CEDOC, the *campesino* wing of which, known as the *Federación Nacional de Organizaciones Campesinas* (FENOC), grew in membership and importance in the early 1970s. Organisation of the *campesinos* has tended to be concentrated in the provinces of Pichincha and Guayas, reflecting in part the influence of the labour movement in the nearby urban centres of Quito and Guayaquil. Another factor in this is the greater commercialisation of agriculture in areas near these urban markets, one indication of which is the relatively high proportion of the primary sector labour force in these two provinces which is wage-earning.[54]

Accurate figures on the size of the labour movement and on the strength of the three *centrales* do not exist but some information does emerge from a number of surveys carried out in the late 1960s and early 1970s, the most detailed of these being the INEFOS survey of 1976.[55] It is clear that since the early 1960s the domination over the labour movement by the CTE has declined, as the membership of both CEDOC and CEOSL has increased. The INEFOS study also reveals clearly the small size of most labour organisations in Ecuador. On the basis of the INEFOS figures, it is apparent that fewer than one in eight of the EAP is organised. Moreover, fully half of those organised are members of independent organisations not affiliated to one of the *centrales*. Another aspect of this is that, especially outside Pichincha and Guayas, the average labour organisation has a very low membership. In Bolivar province, for example, 49 labour organisations have a combined membership of 1668. In most of the 15 provinces none of the *centrales* can boast a total membership of 2000.

The problem of union fragmentation

One of the causes of this fragmentation of the labour movement in Ecuador is to be found in the Labour Code, which distinguishes between factory committees (*Comites de Empresa*), with powers to negotiate with the management and to call strikes, and the union

(*Sindicato*), which is accorded powers over such matters as professional training and education.[56] These two organisations may – and often do – exist side by side in a workplace, raising the possibility of conflict, especially when one is controlled by the employer or when they are controlled by groups from different political parties.

More important, however, is the fact that labour organisation in Ecuador is plant-based, partly as a consequence of political hostility and problems of communication. Organisations do exist at both national and provincial levels – apart from the *centrales*, which have provincial affiliates, there are occupational federations, which claim to speak for all the workers in a particular industry. Just as many organisations are not affiliated to one of the *centrales*; many plant organisations are not affiliated to one of the occupational federations and even when such affiliation has occurred, it may be of little significance.

That affiliation to occupational federations and to the *centrales* is so unattractive is hardly surprising. Many of these national organisations straddle the divide between 'modern' and more traditional sectors. Relatively privileged groups of workers have little to gain from affiliation. A further factor is the fragmented nature of ownership of sectors of the economy. In the textile industry, for example, in 1973, 12 000 workers were employed in 139 factories – figures which did not include many textile-workers employed in small workshops and legally classified as artisans.[57] With few large enterprises and few state-run industries, such occupational federations as exist generally exercise little influence or power. Two exceptions to this are the drivers' federation (FCPE) and the teachers' federation (*Unión Nacional de Educadores* or UNE).

On drivers and teachers

The drivers are probably the most powerful groups of workers in Ecuador, although their position as owners of buses and taxis makes many of them more akin to self-employed businessmen. The power of the drivers' national federation is partly based on its operation of what is, in effect, a closed shop by means of its control over the training institutes, which enables it to limit the numbers of drivers.[58] Another aspect of the federation's power is through its role as a negotiator with the government on behalf of the drivers. Public transport in Ecuador is mainly operated by small co-operatives owning a few taxis or buses. Licences to operate particular routes are issued by the government, which also regulates the level of fares. As a result of the political sensitivity of the issue, municipal bus fares were not increased between 1959 and 1978. However, while rejecting the drivers' demands for higher fares due to fears of violence and demonstrations,[59] particularly in Quito and Guayaquil, successive governments have been forced to find other ways of placating the drivers and avoiding strike action which would cripple the two major urban areas and the rest of the country. As a result petrol prices have been kept low, the government in effect subsidising all motorists,[60] and the drivers have been exempted from the normal high duties levied on imports of vehicles and vehicle spares. When, in October 1982, the government withdrew part of the subsidy on petrol, as part of a package imposed by the IMF in 1980, the resulting 100 per cent increase in the price of petrol brought the drivers out on strike, which ended only when the government acceded to their main demand and allowed an increase in fares.[61]

The power of the teachers is, not surprisingly, by no means as great as that of the drivers, as was indicated by the way the military government dealt with a national teachers strike in May-June 1977, decreeing the teachers' union dissolved, arresting and dismissing many teachers.[62] In 1983, when the teachers' union called a national strike in support of demands for an increase in the minimum wage for teachers from 5000 to 8000 sucres, it attempted to put moral pressure on the government by means of hunger strikes.[63] However, the fact that the teachers' union was able to call and sustain a national strike makes it a notable exception to the plant-based unionism common in Ecuador. One way in which the teachers differ from most other groups is that their employer is the government and negotiations are thus focused at the national level rather than at plant level. The situation of the drivers is similar in that they too have to deal with the government over fares and related matters. It is, moreover, noticeable, that the drivers, as the most powerful labour group in Ecuador, are not affiliated to one of the *centrales*, having disaffiliated from the CTE in 1966.[64] The strength of the drivers, based on their bargaining position, is such that affiliation to one of the *centrales* would appear to offer them little advantage.

Towards a greater unity?

Although rivalry between the *centrales* is keen, there have been moves to increase the co-operation between them since the late

1960s. Faced with the hostility towards agrarian reform of the civilian governments which succeeded the 1963–66 military junta, the CTE and CEDOC established a *Frente Unido para la Reforma Agraria* in 1967. In 1971 the same two *centrales* combined with several non-affiliated organisations in the *Frente Unico de Trabajadores* to oppose the policies of the Velasco Ibarra government. The one-day general strike called in June 1971 was the first joint stoppage organised by the CTE and CEDOC.[65] Such joint action was extended during the 1972–77 military governments. In August 1974 all three *centrales* issued a joint manifesto. Often referred to at the time as the 'Nine Points', this demanded changes in the Labour Code, a substantial increase in the minimum wage, an 'effective' agrarian reform and a wide-ranging programme of nationalisation, with the state taking control of all aspects of the oil industry, foreign trade, the electricity industry and the distribution of basic essentials.[66] A series of joint demonstrations were organised in support of the 'Nine Points', including one-day general strikes in November 1975 and May 1977. Following the return to civilian government in 1979, the *centrales* organised the *Frente Unitario de Trabajadores* (FUT) to press their case. This called a one-day general strike in December 1981 and a 48-hour stoppage in September 1982 in support of a series of demands including a 7000 sucre a month minimum wage indexed against inflation. Other demands included a freeze on bus fares, water rates and other public service charges, the nationalisation of public transport, state control of the marketing of bananas, coffee and cocoa, job security for five years and the full application of agrarian reform.[67]

Following the government's announcement of a cut in subsidies on a whole series of products in October 1982 – which caused petrol to double in price and the price of wheat to increase by 45 per cent – the FUT called an indefinite strike from 8 November to force the repeal of these measures. This was, in fact, postponed, largely due to the divisions in the FUT which had already surfaced during the strike action of September 1982.[68]

While the *centrales* have been engaged in joint action, one of the proclaimed objectives of which was claimed to be the establishment of a joint labour confederation, the internal divisions of the *centrales* themselves have become increasingly apparent. At its sixth national congress, held in Manta, in October 1974, CEOSL split into two factions, one led by the secretary-general, Luis Villacres Arandi, and the other by the president of the organisation's Pichincha branch,

José Chavez Chavez. In the ensuing recriminations Chavez accused Villacres of being a tool of the CIA, Villacres responding with accusations that Chavez was a 'communist infiltrator'. The Chavez wing, which enjoyed the support of the majority of the organisations affiliated to the *central*, continued to work with the CTE and CEDOC in support of the 'Nine Points'. This was roundly condemned as further evidence of communist infiltration by Villacres, whose support was reduced to a rump based on the province of Guayas. Villacres's accusations were not taken seriously by the virulently anti-communist ORIT which recognised both factions and attempted to stay out of the dispute.[69]

In the early 1970s tensions also built up in CEDOC, coming to a head in May 1976. The dispute which erupted in that month left Jorge Cuisana Valencia, elected president of the *central* in April 1975, at the head of a rump which adopted the name 'The Workers' CEDOC' (*CEDOC de los Trabajadores*). Emilio Velasco Ortiz, secretary-general before May 1976, became president of a more radical CEDOC, which enjoys the support of most of the organisations affiliated to CEDOC before May 1976, including the numerically important *campesino* organisation, FENOC.[70] In the battle of words that followed, the Cuisana faction accused their rivals of being communists and of being 'a miniscule group of pseudo-labour leaders, inspired and directed by intellectuals and students'.[71] The reply of Velasco and of the new leadership of the majority faction of CEDOC that their rivals were in league with the CIA was given greater credibility by the accusations levelled against leaders of 'The Workers' CEDOC' such as Isabelle Robelino Bolle by Philip Agee.[72]

Behind the rhetoric employed, significant differences of outlook do exist between the two groups. Most of the leaders of 'The Workers' CEDOC', including Dr Robelino herself, emerged in prominent positions within CEDOC in the early 1960s, when the *central* moved away from its earlier identification with the Conservative Party and the Catholic Church and became identified with the forces of Christian Democracy. A prominent figure in the development of Christian Democracy in Ecuador was Oswaldo Hurtado, academic, founder-member and President of the Christian Democrat party, who was to become President of Ecuador in 1981.[73] Also important was Emilio Maspero, secretary-general of CLAT, whose attacks on the 'communism' of Emilio Velasco Ortiz and his supporters has matched those of Jorge Cuisana Valencia and Dr Robelino.[74]

The new leaders of CEDOC, notably Velasco and Alberto Pilalot Vera, were elected to the Executive of the *central* in 1975, having worked their way up very rapidly through FENOC, the *campesino* wing of CEDOC, which grew so rapidly in membership in the late 1960s and early 1970s. Unlike Robelino and Hurtado, authors and intellectuals, Velasco and Pilalot are from working backgrounds and became involved in the affairs of FENOC during the battles over agrarian reform on the coast during the late 1960s.[75]

Rank-and file attitudes

The interest of the rank and file in such disputes is probably limited. Several observers have commented on the lack of any significant relationship between a worker's affiliation to a *central* and his level of class-consciousness:

> Frequently the revolutionary ideology is only accepted by the upper leadership and not by the rank-and-file of the union . . . in this there appears to be no difference between the workers affiliated to the C.T.E., to C.E.D.O.C. and to C.E.O.S.L.[76]

That this should be the case is hardly surprising if we consider the plant-based nature of Ecuadorean unionism and the lack of importance of the *centrales* to the average affiliated member. Moreover, since most labour disputes appear to centre on immediate, material issues – job security, better working conditions, increased pay and the payment of benefits and bonuses[77] – rather than long-term, national issues, the task of the more politically-motivated leadership in attempting to increase the class-consciousness of their members is difficult indeed.

This is not to say, however, that Ecuadorean workers are not militant and do not take action, but rather that they will only do so when their own interests are threatened. In the words of Oswaldo Hurtado:

> Workers tend to have recourse to the union structure, the petition process and strikes only as a means of securing the recognition and rights and interests of group members, not as political tools.[78]

Mobilising beyond the workplace

Although the *centrales* have attempted to back up their demands by calling general strikes, the effectiveness of such tactics must be open to doubt, since only about 8 per cent of the work force are unionised and this minority generally take action only in defence of their interests. Much more effective than strike action (with the exception of stoppages by the drivers) have been demonstrations and riots, which usually involve the unorganised labour force of the urban areas. Such demonstrations are not confined to the major cities but are becoming increasingly common in the provincial capitals as a means of attempting to bring pressure on the government to deal with local grievances.[79]

It is the threat of such violence, rather than the opposition of organised labour, that has deterred governments from raising urban bus fares. Widespread violence, such as occurred in December 1975 and in October 1982, give ammunition to critics of the government, and whether the latter is civilian or military, may lead to the intervention of the armed forces. This is, naturally, part of the strategy of the demonstrators but in periods of civilian rule it may produce divided loyalties, for it may be felt unwise to demonstrate against a civilian government if the end result is military intervention. It is noticeable that in September 1982 CEDOC and FENOC opposed the call by the FUT for a 48-hour general strike on the grounds that it would 'destabilise the government' of Christian Democrat Oswaldo Hurtado and that it was not 'furthering class interests'.[80]

State and unions

The years following the overthrow of the 1963–66 military junta witnessed an upsurge in the level of militancy, particularly in the rural areas of the coastal region. Following the *autogolpe* of President Velasco Ibarra in June 1970,[81] however, the labour movement found its freedom of action increasingly restricted by a series of reforms to the Labour Code. Decree 054, issued in July 1970, extended the list of groups of workers whose right to take industrial action was prohibited or severely restricted. Decree 1305, issued in 1972, further extended this restriction to include workers in services such as electricity, water, sanitation, social security, telephones and telecommunications and those who 'take part in the production, sale or distribution of those food stuffs which are most essential, when this occurs by means of public entities'.[82]

Another decree of January 1974 (Decree 064) made collective agreements legally binding, the interpretation of this being left in the hands of Ministry of Labour officials.[83] This measure attracted particular hostility from the labour movement, being used, in practice, to declare illegal any strike of importance or of a politically embarrassing nature. Moreover, since the Labour Code made it clear that sympathy strikes were only legal where the original strike was legal, and since the government could dissolve any labour organisation for contravening Article 416 of the Labour Code, which, in effect, prohibits intervention 'in acts of party politics',[84] it is clear that the labour movement had little room to manoeuvre.

Under the military junta which overthrew General Rodriguez Lara in January 1976, relations between labour and the government worsened. In October 1976, when the *centrales* were planning a one-day stoppage in support of the 'Nine Points' manifesto, the Ministro de Gobierno, Colonel Bolivar Jarrin Canahuelas, issued a thinly-veiled threat that:

> the labour leaders know that, in promoting an illegal movement, they will suffer the consequences.[85]

Similar warnings were sounded on the eve of the one-day stoppage in May 1977. That such warnings were not without substance was indicated on a number of occasions. In May 1977 vigorous action was taken against striking members of the teachers' national federation. In October 1977 police were ordered in to deal with striking workers at the AZTRA sugar mill and at least 25 sugar workers were killed.[86]

Relations between labour and the government were not, however, as uniformly hostile as this might suggest. The so-called National Revolutionary Government established by General Guillermo Rodriguez Lara in February 1972 gained considerable support from the CTE for its much-vaunted 'nationalist' stance against the American oil companies. Moreover, the Rodriguez Lara government set up channels for communication with the labour movement. In March 1974 the government established a National Wages Council (*Consejo Nacional de Salarios*) and a series of Sector Commissions (*Comisiones Sectoriales*). The latter, composed of representatives of employers and employees in different sectors of the economy were given the task of fixing and revising wages. The influence of the labour representatives on such bodies is, however, severely limited. Only one of the six members of the National Wages Council represented the labour movement and the role of the Council was defined as being strictly advisory.[87]

In 1981, following the return to civilian rule, the government altered the minimum wage system, abolishing the general minimum wage levels and creating 81 Wage Commissions, one for each sector of the economy.[88] Each Wage Commission made up of representatives of the government, employers and employees, has the task of considering and setting minimum wage levels. One of the effects of this is to introduce greater variation into the legal minimum wage, as some groups of workers are able to bargain more effectively than others.

CONCLUSION

It is probable that the influence of the Ecuadorean government over the labour movement increased during the 1970s and early 1980s. This is in part related to the increased role of the state in Ecuador since the early 1960s as governments have paid increasing attention to social and economic matters. The government's ability to play this larger role has been enhanced by the availability of oil revenues since the early 1970s. This increased influence is probably most noticeable, in the case of the labour movement, in the rural sector. During the 1970s all of the *centrales* paid greater attention to the rural sector labour force. Although the effects of agrarian reform policies have been severely limited, the prolonged process of agrarian reform has facilitated the growth of state influence over the *campesino* movement. As it is the organs of the State which allocate the land and which extend credit to the co-operatives which receive this land, the *campesino* organisations become increasingly dependent on the State. This has been stressed by Redclift:

> as the agrarian reform has taken shape each *campesin* movement has become tied to the various components of the state bureaucracy . . . active participation in the process through which land is transferred and agricultural credit obtained has served to neutralise the more politically radical peasant organisations.[89]

Such influence is not, however, restricted to the rural sector. The provisions of the Labour Code bring the Ministry of Labour and Social Welfare into the heart of industrial relations and allow the Ministry scope for discrimination between more radical and more 'amenable' sections of the labour movement. Indeed, one of the explanations of the political divisions within and between the *centrales* lies in this increased dependency of labour on government agencies.

NOTES

1. The best introductory work on Ecuador is O. Hurtado, *Political Power in Ecuador* (University of New Mexico Press, 1980). For the colonial period see Chapters 1–3. See also J.L. Phelan, *The Kingdom of Quito in the Seventeenth Century* (University of Wisconsin Press, 1967).
2. Phelan, op. cit., pp. 69–70.
3. I. Robelino Bolle, *El Sindicalismo en El Ecuador* (Quito: INEDES, 1976) p. 34.
4. Ibid., pp. 35–9. O. Hurtado and J. Herudek, *La Organización Popular en El Ecuador* (Quito: INEDES, 1974) pp. 59–60.
5. Robelino, op. cit., pp. 40–1.
6. Ibid., pp. 42–3.
7. For a stimulating account of the Ecuadorean cocoa economy and its collapse see L.J. Weinemann, *Ecuador and Cacao: Domestic Responses to the Boom-Collapse Mono-Export Cycle* (University of California: PhD. thesis, 1970).
8. O. Hurtado, *Dos Mundos Superpuestos* (Quito: INEDES, 1975) pp. 57–9.
9. M. Reclift, *Agrarian Reform and Peasant Mobilisation on the Guayas Coast* (London: Athlone, 1978) pp. 19–20.
10. Ibid., p. 44.
11. Ibid., p. 39, citing the report of the Comite Inter-Americana de Desarollo Agricola, *Tenencia de la Terra y Desarrollo Socio-Economico del Sector Agricola*, Ecuador (Washington DC).
12. In 1973 the mortality rate in the coastal provinces was 7.7 per thousand, while the rate for the sierra was 12.0 per thousand. Instituto Nacional de Estadistica, *Serie Estadistica 1968–1973*, p. 35 (henceforth referred to as *Serie 1968–1973*).
13. Hurtado, *Dos Mundos Superpuestos*, pp. 134–40. On migration in Ecuador see R.S. Landmann, *Politics and Population in Ecuador: The Impact of Internal Migration on Political Attitudes and Behaviour* (University of North Carolina: PhD. thesis, 1968).
14. Redclift, op. cit., pp. 75–7.
15. Hurtado, *Dos Mundos Superpuestos*, pp. 87–9.
16. Robelino, op. cit., p. 71.
17. Ibid., p. 74. A good summary in English of the main developments in the labour movement during these years is contained in A. Middleton, 'Division and Cohesion in the Working Class, Artisans and Wage Labourers in Ecuador', *Journal of Latin American Studies*, vol. 14 (May 1982) no. 1, pp. 171–94.
18. Robelino, op. cit., pp. 71–9.
19. This massacre has gained the status of legend in the history of organised labour in Ecuador. In the words of Reyes: 'The masses were rounded up and the soldiers carried out a horrifying slaughter in the streets, in the squares and inside houses and shops . . . Later during the night, numerous lorries and wagons collected the corpses and threw them into the river'. O.E. Reyes, *Breve Historia General del Ecuador*, vol. II, p. 257. See also Robelino, op. cit., pp. 79–82.

20. Robelino, op. cit., p. 87.
21. Ibid., pp. 87–8.
22. Ibid., pp. 96–8.
23. See, for example the comments of Antonio Ortiz Mera, made at the time, quoted in Robelino, op. cit., pp. 97–8. See also Hurtado, *Political Power in Ecuador*, pp. 228–33.
24. Hurtado and Herudek, op. cit., p. 69.
25. L. Linke, *Ecuador: Country of Contrasts* (London: 1960) p. 69. The same number is given by Agee for 1960, P. Agee, *Inside the Company* (Harmondsworth: Penguin, 1974). p. 112. On the early years of the CTE see P. Saad, *La C.T.E. y su Papel Historico* (Guayaquil: Editorial Claridad, 1968).
26. Robelino, op. cit., pp. 104–7. Saad, op. cit., pp. 37–8.
27. According to a report to the US Congress in 1973, about 7 per cent of total US technical aid to Ecuador was directed towards the promotion of 'free trade unions'.
28. Of 136 organisations represented at the inaugural congress in 1962, 51 were from Guayas and 24 from Pichincha. Fewer than ten were organisations of factory-workers and support from *campesinos* was negligible. Robelino, op. cit., p. 132.
29. For Agee's view of relations between CEOSL and the Junta, see Agee, op.cit., pp. 300–01.
30. See below.
31. R. Baez, 'Hacia un Subdesarrollo "moderno"' in L. Mejia *et al.*, *Ecuador: Pasado y presente* (Quito: Universidad Central, 1975). pp. 249–71.
32. Redclift, op. cit., p. 14.
33. *Serie 1968–73*, pp. 90, 103–4.
34. *Latinamerica Press*, vol. XV (6 October 1983 no. 36).
35. Ibid.
36. 'Sublempleo – Disfraz de Crecimiento', Nueva, no. 16 (February 1975) p. 24, quoting figures from the Centro de Analisis Demografico.
37. *Serie 1968–73*, pp. 47, 49, 111.
38. Griffin has calculated that, if the income of an Ecuadorean *campesino* is taken as 100, that of a worker in the 'informal urban sector' is 159, that of a landowner is 1036 and that of someone in the 'modern urban sector' is 1563. K. Griffin, *Land Concentration and Rural Poverty* (London: Oxford University Press, 1976) p. 198.
39. See Appendix I.
40. See Appendix II.
41. See Appendix III.
42. 'Salarios e Inflación', *Nueva*, no. 29 (May 1976) p. 23, quoting figures from the Instituto de Investigaciones Sociales of the Universidad Central in Quito. See also G. Abad, 'Los Efectos Sociales de la Industrialización', *Nueva Sociedad*, nos. 19/20 (July-Aug./Sept.-Oct. 1977) pp. 106–20.
43. See Appendix IV.
44. *Latin American Economic Report*, vol. IV (27 February 1976) no. 9, p. 36.

45. S. Weil, *Area Handbook for Ecuador* (Washington DC, 1973) pp. 126–7. According to Gibson in 1971, the average Ecuadorean diet was some 50 per cent deficient in animal protein, 34 per cent deficient in calory intake and 34 per cent deficient in some fats. C.R. Gibson, *Foreign Trade in the Economic Development of Small Nations: the Case of Ecuador* (New York: Praeger, 1971) p. 40.
46. Redclift, op. cit., p. 33.
47. Griffin, op. cit., pp. 177–8.
48. Between 1964 and the end of 1976, 1 521 296 hectares of land were distributed in colonisation schemes and 358 352 hectares redistributed. *Latin American Economic Report*, vol. IV (15 July 1976) no. 27, p. 107.
49. R. Bromley, *Development and Planning in Ecuador* (London: Latin American Publications, 1977) p. 64.
50. On the nature of Velasco Ibarra's appeal see A. Cueva, *El Proceso de Dominación Politica en el Ecuador* (Mexico City: Editorial Diogenes, 1974).
51. Robelino, op. cit., p. 142.
52. Hurtado and Herudek, op. cit., p. 86.
53. CEDOC has also been active in attempting to recruit women workers. In 1980 a CEDOC affiliate, the *Union de Mujeres Trabajadores*, held its first Congress and proclaimed as its main aim the recruitment of *campesino* women in the labour movement. On *campesino* women in Ecuador see A. Bronstein, *The Triple Struggle* (London: War on Want, 1982).
54. According to one estimate 50 per cent of the primary sector labour force in Pichincha province is wage earning compared with 20 per cent in the province of Chimborazo and 16 per cent in the province of Loja. *Latin American Economic Report*, vol. VI, no. 16 (28 April 1978) pp. 125–6.
55. The *Instituto Ecuadoriano de Formación Social* (INEFOS) is funded by CEDOC. For details of the INEFOS survey of the labour movement see Robelino, op. cit., Appendix.
56. *Codigo de Trabajo, 1976*, esp. Art. 429–430.
57. *Serie 1968–73*, pp. 103–04.
58. Robelino, op. cit., p. 76.
59. The decision by the Rodriguez Lara government to allow a rise in municipal bus fares in December 1975 helped to spark off a series of disturbances in Quito and Guayaquil which culminated in the replacement of General Rodriguez Lara by a three-man military junta.
60. In January 1980 the price of petrol was 5 sucres ($0.20) per gallon.
61. See *Latin American Weekly Report*, nos. 41–3 (22 October-5 November 1982).
62. *El Comercio*, 16 May-19 June 1977.
63. In June 1983 UNE claimed that 1000 of its members were on hunger strike. *Latin American Weekly Report*, no. 23 (17 June 1983).
64. For Agee's view of the importance of securing the disaffiliation of the drivers from CTE see Agee, op. cit., p. 306.
65. Robelino, op. cit., p. 112.
66. *Unidad Sindical*, no. 203 (Jan.-Feb. 1976) p. 16.
67. *Latin American Weekly Report*, no. 36 (17 September 1982).
68. *Latin American Weekly Report*, nos. 38–43 (I October-5 November 1982).

69. Neither were these claims taken seriously by the US Labour Attaché, Mr Wilson, in an interview with the author in August 1976.
70. 'C.E.D.O.C.: División Para La Unidad Obrera', *Nueva*, no. 30 (June 1976) pp. 7–10.
71. *El Comercio*, 21 May 1976.
72. Agee 'named' Dr Isabel Robelino Bolle, a labour lawyer and a key figure in CEDOC from the early 1970s (as well as a writer on the labour movement) as a 'labour agent' of the CIA. Agee, op. cit., p. 620.
73. Hurtado was elected Vice-President to Jaime Roldos in 1979 and assumed the Presidency in May 1981 on the death of Roldos in a plane crash.
74. Maspero is alleged – by his opponents – to have sent an 'agent', Eduardo Garcia, to Quito in April 1976 to try to rally support for Cuisana, See *Latin America*, vol. X (11 July 1976) no. 28, p. 219. See also *C.E.D.O.C. 1938–1976*, (Quito: CEDOC, 1976), esp. p. 32. For Maspero's views on the new leadership of CEDOC see, for example, *Informativo C.L.A.T.*, vol. X (October 1977) no. 18, p. 4.
75. On Alberto Pilalot Vera, for example, see the comments of J.F. Uggen, *Peasant Mobilisation in Ecuador* (University of Miami: PhD thesis, 1975) pp. 164–73, 253.
76. Hurtado and Herudel, op. cit., p. 91. See also A. Bernal, *Trabajadores Organización Popular y Conciencia de Clase en el Ecuador* (Quito: INEDES, 1973).
77. According to unpublished figures from the *Ministerio de Trabajo y Bienestar Social*, over 60 per cent of disputes in 1975 were concerned with these issues.
78. Hurtado, *Political Power in Ecuador*, p. 238.
79. For example, in November 1981 the province of Tungurahua was paralysed by an indefinite stoppage, called in protest at the government's refusal to provide 300 million sucres for water and drainage projects. *Latin American Weekly Report*, no. 47 (27 November 1981).
80. *Latin American Weekly Report*, no. 38 (1 October 1982).
81. On 22 June 1970 President Velasco Ibarra dissolved Congress and assumed dictatorial powers.
82. *Codigo del Trabajo, 1976*, Art. 437. See also 'Decretos Anti-Obreros', *Nueva*, no. 29 (November 1976) pp. 34–9.
83. Ibid., pp. 34–9.
84. *Codigo del Trabajo, 1976*, Art. 416.
85. *El Comercio*, 14 October 1976.
86. *Latin American Political Report*, vol. XI, (28 October 1977) no. 42, p. 329. Other reports put the number killed as high as 120.
87. *Codigo del Trabajo, 1976*, Decreto 2532.
88. For details see ECLA, *Economic Survey of Latin America*, 1981, pp. 386–7.
89. Redclift, op. cit., pp. 116–17.

APPENDICES

Appendix I

4.AI Consumer Price Changes, Quito, 1951–81

Year	*% Increase*
1951	5.4
1952	3.0
1953	–
1954	3.0
1955	2.0
1956	–4.9
1957	1.0
1958	1.0
1959	–
1960	7.0
1961	3.8
1962	2.8
1963	6.3
1964	3.4
1965	3.3
1966	4.0
1967	3.8
1968	4.4
1969	6.3
1970	5.3
1971	8.4
1972	7.8
1973	12.9
1974	23.4
1975	15.3
1976	10.7
1977	13.0
1978	11.9
1979	10.3
1980	13.0
1981	16.4

SOURCE: *Boletín* of the *Banco Central* of Ecuador.

Appendix II

4.AII Food and Drink Price Index, Quito, 1967–79

Year	*Index*	*% Increase*
1967	114.0	5.1
1968	118.7	4.1
1969	130.5	9.9
1970	134.8	3.3
1971	143.6	6.5
1972	159.5	11.1
1973	191.8	20.3
1974	253.9	32.4
1975	301.2	18.6
1976	335.4	11.4
1977	381.5	13.7
1978	420.7	10.3
1979	462.6	10.0

SOURCE: *Yearbook of Labour Statistics* (ILO).

Appendix III

4.AIII Income in the Manufacturing Sector, 1965–77

Year	*Sucres Per Week*	*Index*	*% Increase*
1965	184	100.0	–
1966	193	104.9	4.9
1967	206	112.0	6.8
1968	226	122.8	9.6
1969	274	148.9	21.3
1970	293	159.2	6.9
1971	331	179.9	13.0
1972	391	212.5	18.1
1973	440	239.1	12.5
1974	545	296.2	23.9
1975	672	365.2	23.3
1976	812	441.3	20.8
1977	921	500.5	13.4

SOURCE: *Yearbook of Labour Statistics* (ILO).

Appendix IV

4.AIV Minimum Wage in Ecuador, 1971–81
(Sucres per month)

Year	General Workers	Agricultural Workers (Sierra)	Agricultural Workers (Coast)	Domestic Servants	Artisans
1971	750				
1974	1000	600	750	450	700
1975	1250	750	900	550	850
1976	1500	960	1080	660	1140
1977	1500	960	1080	660	1140
1978	1500	960	1080	660	1140
1979	2000	1350	1500	900	1550
1980	4000	2500	3000	1500	2800

SOURCE: ECLA *Economic Survey of Latin America*, 1980, 1981.

BIBLIOGRAPHY

ABAD, G., 'Los efectos sociales de la industrialización', *Nueva Sociedad*, Nos. 19/20, Jul/Aug. and Sept/Oct. 1977.

BERNAL, A., *Trabajadores, Organización Popular y Conciencia de Clase en el Ecuador* (Quito: INEDES, 1973).

BROMLEY, R., *Development and Planning in Ecuador* (London: Latin American Publications, 1977).

BRONSTEIN, A., *The Triple Struggle* (London: War on Want, 1982).

Hurtado, O., *La organización Popular en el Ecuador* (Quito: INEDES, 1974).

HURTADO, O., *Dos mundos Superpuestos* (Quito: INEDES, 1975).

HURTADO, O., *Political Power in Ecuador* (Albuquerque, New Mexico: University of New Mexico Press, 1980).

MIDDLETON, A., 'Division and Cohesion in the Working Class, Artisans and Wage Labourers in Ecuador', *Journal of Latin American Studies*, Vol. 14, No. 1, May 1982.

REDCLIFT, M., *Agrarian Reform and Peasant Mobilisation on the Guayas Coast* (London: Athlone, 1978).

ROBELINO, I.B., *El sindicalismo en el Ecuador* (Quito: INEDES, 1974).

SAAD, P., *La C.T.E. y su Papel Historico* (Guayaquil: Editorial Claridad, 1968).

5 Bolivia

Jacqueline Roddick and
Nico van Niekerk

THE BOLIVIAN LABOUR MOVEMENT: INTRODUCTION

Although Bolivia is still predominantly an agricultural country (Table 5.1), one of the poorest in Latin America, and the conditions and living standards of its workers are among the lowest in the continent,[1] the weight of organised labour in Bolivian politics has had few parallels elsewhere. During the first half of this century labour played a key role in struggles against the tin oligarchy, finally displaced from power following the mass insurrection of 1952. When a continent-wide cycle of military dictatorships invaded Bolivia in the 1960s, the parties of Opposition rallied to the COB (*Central Obrera Boliviana*) and organised labour became the centre of resistance to military rule.

In the face of periodic violent defeats, the Bolivian working class has demonstrated an enormous capacity to organise clandestinely, pressure governments into restoring a legal freedom of movement for its organisations, and recover the political initiative. The explanation of this extraordinary vitality has to be sought in the emergence of a unique pattern of mass participation which propelled Bolivian unions (particularly in the mines) far beyond their traditionally limited role in collective bargaining – under circumstances in which real economic gains have had to be defended against the declining resources of the tin industry (Bolivia's principal export), over-supplied international markets, a weak local State readily accessible to foreign pressures, and a local market for manufactured goods too small to make industrialisation a viable strategy, given the continued weight of subsistence agriculture.[2]

In Bolivia, commentators agree, parties do not provide the key to union behaviour: the union absorbs the party. Parties are badly fragmented and on the whole short-lived, though the traditions of the MNR-led Revolution of 1952 have had a long life and so have those political figures and union leaders associated with it – Paz Estenssoro, Hernán Siles Zuazo, Juan Lechín. The central importance of unions in politics has reflected the solidity and remarkable durability of

TABLE 5.1 *Structure of the Bolivian Labour Force by Sector 1950–76 (%)*

	1950	*1965+*	*1976*
TOTAL	100	100	100
AGRICULTURE*	72.1	65.7	46.1
EXTRACTIVE INDUSTRIES**	3.2	3.7	4.0
MANUFACTURING	8.1[@]	7.8	9.6
CONSTRUCTION	——	2.2	5.4
TRANSPORT AND COMMUNICATIONS	1.5	3.4	3.7
COMMERCE	4.2	6.0	7.1
SERVICES	10.9	10.9	18.8

+ estimate
* includes rural artisans before 1976.
** mining and petroleum
@ includes urban artisans, construction

SOURCES: Census data for 1950 and 1976 (no Census was taken between these dates): estimated data for 1965 in Klein (1969).

working-class organisational traditions in this world of persistent political upheaval – traditions formed before the 1952 Revolution, tested by the victorious MNR's attempts to bring labour under political control, and baptised with fire in the succession of military coups which followed.

THE EMERGENCE OF ORGANISED LABOUR AND INITIAL REACTIONS BY THE STATE

In its day, Bolivia was a strategic outpost of the international economy, the major source of the Spanish empire's supplies of silver: Potosí, where the silver was mined, was one of the largest cities in the Americas, with 160 000 inhabitants, and the area covered by the present State then had a population as large as neighbouring Argentina. Once Bolivia achieved independence, silver mining disappeared as a viable export with the Spanish technology and imported mercury which had made it possible. It took the new State 40 years to reconstruct a mining industry with the help of foreign (Chilean and British) capital, and thus reinvent its old role as an exporter of minerals to world markets.

When the world market for silver declined with the introduction of the gold standard, the local élite found an answer to declining export revenues in a new mineral, tin. By 1920, three families dominated the local tin industry, one of the tin barons – Patiño – was en route to a new status as multinational capital, and the *rosca* or 'mining super-state' controlled the nation's political life. That control lasted until 1952.

The prehistory of the labour movement is thus marked first of all by the social patterns of a long-term decline, for before Potosí, Bolivia was also a centre of the Inca empire. Labour's early organisation coincided with the defensive efforts of a regionally-dispersed urban artisanate, with long historical roots, weakened by the post-colonial impact of manufactures, impoverished, but still powerful enough to play an occasional role in élite politics even during the nineteenth century.[3]

Since then the critical chapters of labour history have been written largely by workers linked to the export economy: railway workers at first, followed by those in the mines, whose potential economic leverage is illustrated by the fact that tin accounted for 57 per cent of the country's total exports even in 1977, in the heyday of diversification.[4] Nevertheless, it took years to build a stable organisation in the isolated, company-dominated and initially, easily-repressed mining camps: the *Federación Sindical de Trabajadores Mineros de Bolivia* (FSTMB) was not finally formed until 1944, when favourable political conditions coincided with a boom in tin production during the Second World War.

The urban movement thus dictated the conditions under which Bolivia's labour institutions were first formed. Early labour organisations were formed by transport workers and State employees, but earlier still, by small craftsmen – 'ruined artisans' as Whitehead once called them, who not only formed their own mutual benefit societies, but spread out across the southern cone looking for work, bringing back new anarcho-syndicalist and socialist ideas from Chile and Argentina, and spreading these in turn not only in the towns but also into the mines.[5] Artisans were still a critically important part of the urban milieu in 1952, the basis for the MNR's *grupos de honor* – alongside the predominantly female street traders who first came to prominence in the anarcho-syndicalist *Federación Obrera Feminina* and were later themselves organised by the MNR.[6]

In social terms, the old artisan community was defined by its racial characteristics: *cholos*, people of mixed blood sandwiched between a small white landowning élite and a rural Indian majority, itself

TABLE 5.2 *Urbanisation in Bolivia, 1900–50*

	1900	*1950*	*Increase (%)*
TOTAL POPULATION	1 766 451	3 091 031	70.9
La Paz	71 860	267 000	271.5
Cochabamba	21 900	80 795	268.9
Oruro	15 900	62 975	296.0
Potosi	20 900	43 579	108.9
Sucre	20 900	40 128	92.0
Santa Cruz	18 300	42 746	133.5

SOURCE: Klein, *Parties and Political Change in Bolivia* (1969).

divided between self-governing *comunidades* and the near-feudal conditions of life of *colonos* on the expanding estates of a white landlord class. Urbanisation increased dramatically during the nineteenth century as rural conditions deteriorated and more Indians took refuge in the towns (Table 5.2).

As Laurence Whitehead has shown, politicians were already aware of labour's potential importance as a source of votes in a tiny electorate and perhaps also as a source of mobilisable support for the alternative tactic, in a highly corrupt democracy, of organising a coup.[7] By the beginning of the twentieth century, 'cholos' in general and artisan societies had established clear links with the Liberal Party. A decade later, these were on the wane, and the urban working class, disillusioned with Liberal failures to look after its interests, was a critically important source of support for the new Republicans. Organised labour was beginning to have an impact on national life: in early 1920, railway workers (closely in touch with their Chilean colleagues) called the first national industry-wide strike when conservatives threatened the deputy they regarded as their parliamentary representative. The Republican coup of 1920, which itself followed hard on the heels of a strike of State telegraph workers, brought immediate benefits in the form of a legalised right to strike, and in 1921 a duly elected Republican government amplified these initial laws, establishing a legal framework for arbitration between employers and workers and the first timid steps towards health and accident compensation.[8] In 1922, the first national general strike was organised in solidarity with taxi drivers, whose hours had been legally restricted, perhaps because they were suspected of transporting arms for a coup.

Though urban workers arguably gained some benefits from these laws, not always enforced (even if the bargaining rights of State telegraph workers, like those of railway workers, were recognised by the State), they offered no easy solution to those in the mines, and the repressive experiences of this period played their part in the formation of unions here with a profoundly radical tradition and a strong preference for armed organisations of self-defence. The flimsiness of the new legal framework was fully revealed in 1923, when, after the election of a supposedly sympathetic local Deputy, miners in Uncio organised a 4000-member local union and called a strike. The government sent troops into the mining camp in support of Patiño's interests, not for the first time, and the massacre which followed not only set the tone for miners' future relations with the State but became an anniversary to remember for Bolivia's still inchoate left-wing community, whose activists had been deeply involved in the organisational drive, and more important, confirmed the radicalism of a future stronghold of the Left, the Siglo XX-Catavi complex.[9]

1932–52: THE EMERGENCE OF PLANT UNIONISM AND THE DOMINANCE OF THE MINES

The Great Depression caused a profound impact on Bolivia as on other contemporary Latin American societies, as thousands of Bolivians returned from the Chilean nitrate mines to swell the ranks of Bolivia's own unemployed. But its local impact on labour was overshadowed by the much greater national trauma of the Chaco War, fought with Paraguay over disputed territory rich in oil resources, and, at least in popular memory, essentially to defend the interests of Standard Oil against those of Royal Dutch Shell.[10] The War cost Bolivia 215 000 square kilometres of land and perhaps 80 000 lives, stimulating a ferment of demands for political reform in the urban areas, and a new nationalism which was ultimately to culminate in the founding of the MNR (*Movimiento Nacionalista Republicano*) in 1941. More important, it brought a generation of young nationalist officers into Bolivian politics as social reformers in their own right: these 'military socialists' drew their ideas on labour less from socialist sources than from Mussolini, but they nonetheless laid down the framework of labour legislation for the future labour movement, under Colonel Toro and General Busch (1936–39) and Major Villarroel (1943–46).

The first 'military socialist' coup followed a wave of strikes triggered by post-War inflation, which drew in miners in Corocoro and female tobacco workers in La Paz, re-established the vigour of Bolivia's old local labour federations (badly damaged by the impact of forced exile on pacifist objectors to the War), and culminated in an indefinite general strike called by printing workers, who took over the streets of La Paz for six days. Workers' grievances focused on wages, but they nonetheless provided the pretext for the 1936 coup.

Toro's accession as President gave Bolivia its first Minister of Labour, the syndicalist leader of the printworkers. A new law making unionisation obligatory was promulgated (supposedly a step towards 'functional democracy'; in which unions and other corporate interests would be organised into a new political system). In 1937, under President Busch, Bolivia was given its first Labour Code. The code acknowledged the right to strike and required conflicts between employers and workers to be submitted to arbitration. It also established workers' rights to form craft or professional unions with a minimum of 20 members, or industrial or plant unions limited to a single enterprise, provided these had the support of 50 per cent of the firm's workers. Only one industrial union could be formed in a plant, thus providing labour with a democratic focus for union and political debates which would serve members well over the next half-century.[11] Opposition from the *rosca*, however, delayed the code's final promulgation until 1942.

Bolivia's small and much fragmented Left – socialist, anarcho-syndicalist, communist and increasingly also nationalist – essentially co-operated with the 'military socialist' programme, recognising perhaps that the armed forces were too weak to impose a purge of political forces they might dislike. The obligatory unionisation law thus provided cover for the first real unionisation drive, and under its auspices, Bolivia's first trade union confederation was formed, the CSTB (*Confederación Sindical de Bolivia*), founded in 1937, a federation of all active political tendencies which itself accepted a ban on its own participation in politics. The CSTB survived until pro-communist groups attempted to commit it explicitly to the Moscow-oriented *Partido Izquierdo Revolucionario* (PIR), founded in 1940, when it formally split in the face of opposition from some local Marxist groups as well as the anarcho-syndicalists.

These were years of intense conflict with the essentially right-wing government which took power after Busch's death, when the fledgling PIR did equally well in recruiting labour support. Labour pressure continued to win concessions from the factions disputing possession of the government, though the costs were high. A general strike of railway workers, printers, some white-collar organisations and miners called in 1941 won some concessions, but at the cost of seeing its leaders imprisoned on an island in Lake Titicaca. In 1942 tensions in the mines culminated in a strike which the government first attempted to avert by promulgating the Busch Labour Code, and then finally to suppress with troops. The outcome was a massacre of 400 people at Catavi, the Siglo XX ore concentration plant. The MNR's parliamentary protests caused miners' political loyalties to swing behind it, at the cost of the PIR: and after the 1952 Revolution, the MNR took the name of Maria Barzola, Catavi's first victim, to grace its own organisation of female shock troops in the urban areas.[12]

In 1943 Major Villarroel, another 'military socialist', took power with MNR support. The new regime consolidated trade union rights by establishing their officers' immunity from dismissal and requiring employers to deduct dues at source. Yearly bonuses for workers were established as a form of participation in company profits, and companies with more than 80 workers were required to provide houses and medical services. The first steps were taken to eliminate *pongueaje* and other servile 'obligations' in agriculture,[13] and women for the first time were given a vote, if only in local elections. Both sets of reforms were to be completed by the 1952 Revolution, strengthening the MNR's popularity with peasants, who represented the overwhelming majority of Bolivia's people, and women of the popular as well as the educated classes.

Urban workers sympathetic to the MNR took advantage of the new regime to establish national confederations for the first time, notably flour mill workers and those in manufacturing. But the government was not so well disposed to other sectors of the labour movement, teachers' strikes in particular being suppressed. The PIR continued to retain much urban support which was swelled by a failed assassination attempt on its leader, José Antonio Arze, and the execution of leading opposition figures involved in an abortive revolt in Oruro, a traditionally militant town. In June and July a teachers' strike provided the opportunity for a mass urban uprising against the government, supported by the PIR and the USA, and Villarroel was lynched by an urban mob.[14]

The mines were inclined, with some hesitation, to side with Villarroel. In 1944, Bolivia's scattered mining camps had taken advantage of the government's sympathy to found the FSTMB (*Federación*

Sindical de Trabajadores Mineros de Bolivia), whose first Congress issued Villarroel a public invitation to participate, and was as publicly disowned by the urban and artisan-dominated CSTB. Juan Lechín, recently appointed by the government as sub-prefect for the Siglo XX-Catavi district and already famous for a confrontation with mine management, was elected General Secretary. To all intents and purposes, the MNR and the government seemed to control the mines, whose sympathy with Villarroel was perhaps more marked because war-time demand had led to an increase in employment and a 30 per cent wage rise.[15]

Within three years, however, the economic situation had deteriorated, as the USA sold its accumulated stocks of tin on world markets and pre-empted any price increase. Due to its own quarrels with Villarroel, the MNR was effectively banned; and Lechín and the FSTMB had developed transitory ties with the Trotskyist POR.[16] The immediate outcome of this new influence was the Thesis of Pulacayo, adopted before Villarroel's fall by an extraordinary Congress of the FSTMB, calling for direct working class leadership of the revolution and committing the union to working class independence of any capitalist government or multi-class political party. In 1947, the POR and the FSTMB together formed an electoral front which won seven seats in parliament, the first tentative step towards an independent political role for the union, and a clear marker of its formal detachment from the MNR, whatever the movement's rank and file popularity. The fluidity of labour's political alliances was already marked, as was its unwillingness to tie itself to any single political faction.

Nonetheless, the FSTMB had already taken advantage of its existing political contacts to displace the PIR-dominated, artisan-centred CSTB from the centre of the Bolivian labour movement. In 1946, miners, flour mill workers, factory workers and printworkers came together to form the *Central Obrera Nacional*. The commitment of the PIR to a post-Villarroel government of retrenchment, and its open participation in the so-called 'white massacre' of 1947 in which 5000 mining activists were dismissed, marked the end of its hegemony within the urban as well as the mining labour movement, as urban and mining labour movements together organised a series of insurrectional strikes, backed by armed working-class militias, which cemented their own union federations as functioning bodies, and in 1952 finally secured a transfer of State power to the MNR.[17]

UNIONS, POLITICS AND INDUSTRIAL RELATIONS BEYOND 1952

By 1952, not only the legal framework constraining union structures and industrial relations, but also the local culture of the labour movement and some of its most characteristic demands, were already clearly evident, and would remain constant over 30 years of democracy and dictatorship.

A questionnaire survey of trade unionists in 1968, during the Barrientos dictatorship, found surprisingly high percentages aware of key figures in the news. It also found workers surprisingly literate – 302 out of 313 surveyed – in a country where, at the time, 33 per cent of the adult population as a whole could not read and write: a necessary qualification perhaps, for reading the party and union pamphlets which even under conditions of dictatorship continued to be produced (in the case of the badly repressed FSTMB, with the help of local university students) and hand-distributed throughout the mines.[18]

For miners and factory workers – critical elements in the new labour movement – government economic policies were of immediate personal interest: to factory workers, because they were dependent on government tariffs to limit imported manufactured goods, and more generally to extend the 'modernisation' of the country and thus their markets, and to miners, for the much more depressing reason that declining reserves of tin, their principal product, and an over-supplied international market, made the nationalisation of the local industry their only hope in a desperate search for reasonable wages and working conditions which has lasted throughout the modern era.[19]

These real economic interests in the country's management have given a cutting edge to Bolivian labour's demand for 'participation' perhaps sharper than anywhere else in the world, the more so because the economic record of post-Revolutionary governments has been so poor. Labour's single most vital achievement during the 1952 Revolution was to be the nationalisation of Bolivia's mines, which gave the country some control over the revenues of its principal export product. But even this real gain immediately became the site of a new battleground between the urban and technocratic interests of the MNR and the miners, as the MNR used tin revenues to bolster a newly developing oil industry while it systematically neglected investment in new equipment for traditional mines or even in open-

TABLE 5.3 *Political Awareness of Bolivian Trade Unionists, 1968 (%)*

	Oil Workers	*Factory Workers*	*Miners*
Vice-president's name	83	84	81
Commander-in-chief of armed forces (General Ovando)	78	76	79
Ex-Minister of Defence who sold Che Guevara's diary to Castro	67	85	71
Author of latest coup attempt (Gral Vázquez)	49	48	39
Gulf Oil	87	50	35
Provisions of new government agreement with Gulf Oil, ceding national oil reserves	37	17	14
German/Ovando responsibility for new tin smelter	26	28	23
Triangular Plan (standing international agreement for modernising mines)	14	16	36

SOURCE: Magill, *Labour Unions and Political Socialization* (1974) p. 91.

ing up new deposits,[20] and as urban white-collar workers were brought in to the new State corporation COMIBOL to benefit from party patronage and ensure party control over the mines, at privileged salaries and with privileged conditions. For the miners, the institution of *control obrero* in COMIBOL, which gave them limited rights to co-management from the outset, was a badly needed and insufficiently powerful weapon against the corruption of a new middle management which still lacked any real commitment to bettering their salaries and conditions, and, worse, the productive base itself. Lost in 1963, its reinstatement and expansion under the military government of Torres in 1971 was one of labour's principal gains during that brief sally towards generalised workers' power. Lost again during the Banzer dictatorship and the years of military rule which followed, it was demanded and reinstated under the civilian government of Hernán Siles Zuazo in 1983, with the result that finally, in 1984 – in perhaps the most desperate economic crisis in Bolivia's history – miners achieved a limited investment in new mining sites;[21] though the achievement was of short duration.

For Bolivia's miners at least, then, the ability to influence the State has been vital to preserving their economic interests. Conversely, loss of influence over the State brought with it the threat of a return to appalling poverty, malnutrition, and a shortened life-span: or worse, as governments threatened by the determined resistance of the FSTMB have resorted to massacres to reassert their own control over the mines.

Yet, just because national politics is so vital to workers' ordinary interests, and the experience of seeing these betrayed by national political forces of one kind and another has been so common across the successive economic crises of Bolivian history, working class shifts in loyalty have often been rapid. Teachers, whose strike triggered the uprising of 'democratic' but conservative forces in 1946 (justifiably in terms of Villarroel's treatment of their previous struggles, as well as his attempt to assassinate the leader of the PIR, which they currently supported) could participate with equal determination in the uprising against the 'sexenio' and the PIR, four years later. The mines themselves, where the PIR's organisational drive was making some headway in 1940, were strongholds of the MNR three years later, of the POR as Villarroel's regime began to enter into further conflicts with the MNR and organised labour, and of the MNR again after Villarroel's overthrow and as the Revolution of 1952 drew closer. The Thesis of Pulcayo was Trotskyist in inspiration, but it is surely more important as the expression of a well-earned distrust of government and politicians which was to remain vital to the preservation of working-class interests in the post-Revolutionary world, which made little permanent impact on the grim poverty of the mining camps or on the average miner's nine-year working life.

Labour's early shift towards a political life based on the union rather than a single party is thus understandable. As Llobet Tabolara observes of the early 'military socialist' era,

> the majority of attempts to form a party appeared to be precarious and weak, close to repeated failure, while one could observe a growing reinforcement, an ever more solid sense of permanency, about the unions . . . The masses received their education through the union, which did not make it any less passionate; and what is still more important, this education was woven through and through with politics . . .[22]

But if it was of vital importance to workers that parties should subordinate themselves to the union, and a more cautious view of

TABLE 5.4 *Voting Patterns in the Mining Camps, National Elections of 1956*

	Siglo XX	*Huanuni*	*Colquiri*	*San Jose*
MNR	4179	4967	2362	2437
Communist	130	2	10	68
POR	68	2	–	3
Falangist*	38	24	57	116
Null and Blank	85	95	151	45

* right-wing

SOURCE: Whitehead, *mimeo* (1976)

workers' interests than might be associated with any single political project, governments – military, civilian, revolutionary and conservative – self-evidently have had an interest in the reverse. And here lies a second paradox. For as Llobet says, it was the years of 'military socialism' which first taught workers the utility of an armed political alliance with other groups to secure power over the State. Yet it was also 'military socialism' which in spite of its own corporatist instincts, confirmed the characteristic national pattern of an ultra-democratic syndicalism: providing unions with an institutional framework which favoured mass assemblies in which all the existing parties, however fragmentary, could compete with one another for the ears of a rank and file not fundamentally committed to any party's politics, and simultaneously setting strict limits on the ability of any national union bureaucracy to assert over-all control.

Mass assemblies in the mining camps, the democratic control of camp delegations to federal bodies, the independence of strike committees from national organisations and the ease with which union bodies could remove leaders with which they disagreed (legally, local unions elected their leaderships once a year[23]) would allow a tiny party such as the POR to preserve a tradition of independent organisation within the FSTMB, even when the post-revolutionary wave of enthusiasm for the MNR reduced its real presence to a handful of activists in Siglo XX (Table 5.4). Equally significantly, they helped turn the union into a centre of working class life in the camps: protector of basis economic interests, focus for mass participation in national politics, organiser of local militias, cultural centre, even occasionally the arbitrator in family conflicts. After the 1952 Revolution, the FSTMB was not to be immune from strains between a national 'bureaucracy' and rank and file militancy, and the very complexities of national politics would reinforce the attraction for rank and file workers of individual leaders with a known record and the experience necessary to find urban allies at not too high a price, giving some trade union officers – like Lechín himself, executive secretary of the FSTMB from 1952 to 1985 – a phenomenally long career at the head of their organisations.[24] But the premium which both union traditions and the legal framework within which they were constructed set on local democracy, would do much to keep any pressures towards a 'bureaucratisation' of the miners' union under control,[25] and may also explain the extraordinary vitality of union organisation within the camps, even under military occupation, from 1964 to 1983.

Little has been written on the urban labour movement compared with the detailed studies of union life in the mines, but it is nonetheless clear that factory workers and teachers, like miners, had very little difficulty in asserting rank and file control over the politics of their national union organisations when economic pressures dictated.

THE FAILURE OF CO-OPTION AND ITS IMMEDIATE CONSEQUENCES: 1952–64

The MNR in control

In April 1952 armed workers' militias destroyed the Bolivian army, and the new MNR government with Paz Estenssoro as its President was initially totally dependent on their support, a fact of life reflected in the presence of five trade unionists as government Ministers, *co-gobierno*. Some observers have seen this period as carrying within it the seeds of dual power, limited only by the hegemony of the MNR's essentially nationalist and petty bourgeois ideology within the labour movement itself.[26] In practice, the critical puzzle of these years is perhaps not why Bolivia's union assemblies, constantly debating the progress of the Revolution, did not become soviets, but why the MNR itself failed in a battle strongly supported by its American advisors to gain the kind of control over the labour movement exercised elsewhere by the equally nationalist, equally revolutionary Mexican PRI.

The immediate outcome of the Revolution was a brief period of almost unanimous working-class support for the MNR, reflected in the mining camps (Table 5.4) and elsewhere, as it substantially displaced other parties. Factories, oil workers, office clerks, urban teachers, rural teachers, artisans, bank workers, printers, rubber workers, sanitation men, communications workers, bakers, journalists, were all identified as strong party supporters by the new government.[27] Within days of the takeover, Lechín, now Minister of Mines, and Butron, General Secretary of the Factory Workers, now Minister of Labour – both firm supporters of the MNR – presided over the inaugural sessions of a new national labour confederation, the *Central Obrera Boliviana* (COB). Factory workers, railwaymen, bank workers, private sectors employees, construction workers and peasants each sent two delegates. Old union organisations linked to the CSTB disappeared, and new federations were created.[28]

American observers credited the MNR with virtually total domination of the labour movement throughout the 1950s. In fact, the situation was a little more complex. Whatever their sympathies, the majority of workers were organised independently through the unions and the COB, with no direct links between them and the party apparatus. The COB's support in turn was translated in practice as the operation of a semi-independent left-wing of the MNR. The POR maintained an active presence in the COB during its first year and in local assemblies in the mines thereafter, although from 1953 onwards the new government subjected its activists to a degree of real persecution.[29] So, on a broader scale, did the new Communist Party, which MNR activists initially found to be a convenient ally in their early drive against the POR. Both parties were virtually eliminated from the COB Congress of 1954, as popular support for the MNR swept all before it, but their traditional access to union assemblies at local level remained more difficult to eliminate, and these in turn retained their original patterns of a democratic election of local officers.[30]

Where the MNR boasted independent party factions within the labour movement, these were thus usually 'relabelled segments of the national labour unions'.[31] The party's *comandos especiales*, centrally organised and carefully sited so as to maintain a party control over crucial mining or railway centres, recruited their membership essentially from white-collar, managerial and technical staff. Control over the armed militias was similarly divided, with some attached to specific work-places under COB and local union discipline, while others were party organisations, such as the *grupos de honor* dominated by artisans in the urban areas and surface workers in the mines. The subsequent reputation of non-union militias under the MNR's Control Politico, as agents of political repression and petty gangsterism, would play an important role in labour's willingness to see them disbanded and a regular army restored in the late 1950s, one of the conditions of continued American financial assistance to the new regime.[32]

The power of the COB during the Revolution's early years secured outright nationalisation of the tin mines, contemplated in the Thesis of Pulacayo but not, originally, in the programme of the MNR. However, this step gained the government only marginal extra power over the local economy, and its own white-collar cadre proved less than adept as managers and technicians. Over the FSTMB's protests, compensation was paid to the *rosca*, thus adding to the new State corporation Comibol's financial worries. Control of smelting remained outside the country, dominated by Patiño's own UK facilities and a US government-owned smelter in Texas. Tin prices were not to rise to the level of the early war years again until after 1964, and Comibol made no significant advances even in marketing its minerals, let alone in developing new mines. The new regime concentrated on siphoning off tin revenues to finance investment in a new State oil industry.

Nationalisation under these conditions gained the miners short-lived benefits, which had to be shared with a growing sector of white-collar surface workers recruited into COMIBOL from the ranks of the MNR's urban supporters (Table 5.5). As inflation became a major national problem, miners' relative wages, rising during the Second World War, seem to have fallen in real values[33] (see Table 5.6) though this deterioration in purchasing power was compensated for by a rise in the price subsidy on essential goods in the company store or *pulpería*, leaving miners to augment their salaries by selling scarce goods in the urban black market. More real gains were made in employment, where those fired during the previous 'white massacre' were rehired, those with damaged lungs being taken on as surface workers;[34] and perhaps in housing, where the appallingly crowded housing conditions allowed by the *rosca* were brought up to a standard of decency comparable to a Glasgow tenement or Lancashire mill town during the Industrial Revolution.[35]

There were other gains: the automatic check-off of union dues had been established in 1944, and payment of union officers may initially have strengthened the MNR's political control,[36] but the institutionalisation of *control obrero*, originally established in a union drive to

TABLE 5.5 *Tin Prices, Production Levels, Total Employment and Comparative Face and Surface Manning Levels 1944–68*

Year	*Tin Output (1000 tons)*	*Market Price (US$ per lb)*	*Employment**	*Face (%)*	*Other (%)*
1944	39.3@	$0.61	n.a.	n.a.	n.a.
1948	37.8@	$0.94	24 200	n.a.	n.a.
1951	28.4	$1.26	24 000	55.0	45.0
1952	27.3	$1.17	29 000	48.9	51.1
1953	26.0	$0.93	30 000	46.8	53.2
1954	25.8	$0.88	32 800	44.3	55.7
1955	23.5	$0.90	34 200	36.9	63.1
1956	23.0	$0.98	35 700	32.1	67.9
1957	21.6	$0.91	32 100	33.7	66.3
1958	17.4	$0.94	27 900	31.8	68.2
1959	15.8	$0.98	27 200	32.0	68.0
1960	15.2	$0.97	27 400	32.8	67.2
1961	14.8	$1.17	26 400	30.2	69.8
1962	15.3	$1.08	25 500	28.8	70.2
1963	15.4	$1.16	24 000	36.8	63.2
1964	17.7	$1.53	23 800	37.1	62.9
1965	16.5	$1.70	24 600	n.a.	n.a.
1966	18.4	$1.59	n.a.	n.a.	n.a.
1967	18.6	$1.49	22 700	n.a.	n.a.
1968	18.6	$1.40	n.a.	n.a.	n.a.

* to the nearest 1000
@ export figure
n.a. not available

SOURCE: R.S. Thorn (1971).

limit white-collar corruption, gave local officers some resources with which to defend workers' social conditions, even if it failed to reverse COMIBOL's declining technical efficiency or change appalling working conditions within the mines. Local union assemblies took full advantage of the possibilities, often by deliberately choosing a representative who was not a member of the MNR.[37]

The MNR attempt to divide labour: cities vs. mines

The era of easy union gains quickly came to an end, however, as economic crisis began to limit the government's room for manoeuvre, and the bureaucracy and corruption inherent in the MNR's style of administration became a serious drain on the country's capacity for

TABLE 5.6 *Miners' Daily Wages and Subsidies, 1950 and 1955* (current bolivianos converted into US$ at free market rates*)

	1950	*1955*
WAGE PAYMENTS		
Basic Wage	108.59	528.85
Family allowance	——	75.58
Bonus (13th month) @	8.84	65.39
Bonus	8.07	——
ALL WAGE PAYMENTS	125.50	669.82
AS % TOTAL BILL	80.2%	21.2%
DOLLAR EQUIVALENT	$ 2.09	$ 0.24
INDIRECT SUBSIDIES		
Calculated company store losses	5.46	2094.51
Hospital and medicines	6.88	106.48
Schools	3.23	54.31
Recreational services	0.96	5.92
Housing (rent)	——	2.37
TOTAL INDIRECT SUBSIDIES	16.53	2263.59
AS % TOTAL BILL	10.6%	71.5%
DOLLAR EQUIVALENT	$ 0.28	$ 0.79
INSURANCE		
Social insurance	10.61	55.23
Redundancy reserve	3.83	117.10
TOTAL INSURANCE	14.44	172.33
AS % TOTAL BILL	9.2%	5.4%
DOLLAR EQUIVALENT	$ 0.24	$ 0.06
ALL INCOME AND SUBSIDIES	156.47	3165.74
FREE MARKET EXCHANGE RATE PER US$	60.00	2849.67
income as $ equivalent	$ 2.61	$ 1.11

* The official exchange rate, 60 bolivianos to the dollar in 1952, was raised to 190 to the dollar in 1953 and frozen; between 1952 and 1955 the consumer price index rose from 100 to 814.

SOURCE: Iriarte, *Galerias de muerte* (1972), quoting Ford, Bacon and Davis Report.

growth. 'By 1960', comments a sympathetic American, 'the huge and unwieldy MNR was one of the major drains on the nation's meager resources'.[38] The costs of nationalisation and calculated risk of investment in oil were being financed, not by declining tin revenues, but by inflation at the cost of urban consumers. Agrarian reform – one of the

TABLE 5.7 *Strikes, 1956–61*

YEAR	*NO. OF STRIKES*	*NO. OF WORKERS*
1956	220	60 000
1957	310	90 000
1958	1570	147 000
1959	1272	40 000
1960	336	18 000

SOURCE: Thorn (1971), using Ministry of Labour data.

major gains of the revolution – was restricting food supplies to the towns, creating much-resented urban queues.

In these circumstances, the FSTMB became a convenient scapegoat for the government's own shortcomings. The availability of cheap food at the *pulpería* and the fact that miners were to be found reselling it in urban markets could be presented, not as a failure on the government's part to organise appropriate cash wages, but as miners themselves exploiting the urban consumer. *Control obrero*, the miners' attempt to control bureaucratic waste within COMIBOL, took the blame for all COMIBOL's manifest ills.

The crucial alliance between the mines and urban trade unions thus came under strain at precisely the point at which the government itself was being tempted to solve its economic problems by a systematic attack on workers' living standards. By 1956, the MNR's desperate search for US financial and food aid, as well as co-operation in marketing its tin, had entangled the party irredeemably with American priorities. One result was the introduction of an 'economic stabilisation' programme, a typical US conservative solution to the problem of inflation, which included the phasing out of State subsidies on consumption, government acceptance of a specific commitment to free enterprise and foreign investment – and itself made a specific and highly influential attack on the miners.[39]

The costs of this stabilisation policy were borne in the end by both the mines and manufacturing. Manufacturing output fell by 30 per cent in a year, and employment declined from a peak of 25 400 in 1956 ('artificially inflated by labor pressure') to 16 300 by 1960.[40] Table 5.7 shows the similar decline in COMIBOL's payroll, though as white collar supporters of the MNR defended their own positions the proportion of those working underground hardly changed at all.

The initiative for a campaign against the government's new proposals came from the rank and file of the FSTMB via their 1957 national congress (over which the MNR had no control, although by now it had some leverage over the national executive) and a POR-inspired resolution calling for the end of *co-gobierno* and a general strike. The call was approved by a similar COB Congress in June, by 260 votes out of 439, but divisions within the movement were fostered by the PCB's decision to back the government against possible threats of a right-wing coup, and by the successful efforts of Paz Estenssoro's successor as President, Hernán Siles Zuazo, to back the stabilisation programme with a personal hunger strike and mobilise the support or urban workers against 'privileged' miners. At the congress, railway, construction and oil workers supported Siles, and in the days before the strike, bank employees, teachers, factory workers and finally the majority of the mining camps themselves one after another withdrew.[41]

This temporary government victory set the stage for an attempt by the MNR to isolate the FSTMB's independent militants permanently, as Siles consolidated his support within the COB by organising urban workers and those mines controlled by the MNR's *comandos especiales* into a *Bloque Reestructurador*, supervised and financed by the Minister of the Interior. Railway, construction and oil workers, truck and taxi drivers, the print, bank clerks, and telegraph and postal workers all joined the new Bloque. The majority of mines, school teachers, municipal and sanitation workers, artisans, bakers, and forestry workers supported Lechín and formed an alternative *Bloque Revolucionario* representing essentially the MNR's own left-wing. Manufacturing workers refused to be aligned. The result was a temporary victory for party control over the COB, leaving Lechín as a powerless figurehead. But the new coalition was badly damaged by a scandal in May 1957, when Siles used his base among textile workers to try to rig elections for the leadership of the factory workers' federation, damage which was hardly compensated for by his subsequent appointment of the union's leader, Ayora, to the Ministry of Labour.[42]

The *Bloque Reestructurador* finally collapsed in January 1959, when rank and file factory workers voted out their entire union leadership and replaced them with militant Lechinistas, denouncing Ayora as a traitor to the working-class. Whatever the position of its executive, rank and file militants within the mines were quick to capitalise on this shift in urban sympathy towards them. In February, the FSTMB called a strike which was marked by considerable tensions between the camps and the union's national executive, whose security in control of the union increasingly depended on the new private mines; but which nonetheless achieved a 20 per cent rise in wages and the preservation of subsidies on a core of essential foodstuffs – and, perhaps more important, cemented a new relationship between militants in the miners' strike committee and increasingly dissatisfied workers in the urban areas, railway workers and teachers as well as factory workers.[43]

The collapse of the *Bloque Reestructurador* marked the end of the MNR's drive to assert real party control over organised labour, although Lechín's personal loyalty to the party was temporarily resecured by offering him the role of Vice-Presidential candidate in the 1960 elections, in which Paz Estenssoro stood as the MNR's Presidential candidate. Once elected, however, Paz was more concerned to conciliate the US government than the FSTMB. In 1961 the government was offered American and other international aid to finance a modernisation of COMIBOL, on condition that it put an end to *control obrero*, dismiss 20 per cent of the workforce and secure 'total government control over the union process',[44] an interesting indication of US determination to curb the FSTMB's independent militancy. The MNR government accepted, and used the excuse of an 18-day strike centred on Siglo XX to justify the arrest of 18 local union officials as a pre-emptive demonstration of force. Among those arrested were three members of the FSTMB executive who owed their political loyalties to the PCB. A hastily-organised local housewives' committee organised protest demonstrations in La Paz, in the face of violent counter-protests by the MNR's female *barzolas*: with the support of factory, construction and municipal workers, they staged a hunger strike which secured the release of the prisoners.[45] The existence of an effective alliance between urban activists and those in the mines was once again in evidence. Nevertheless, in the subsequent FSTMB Congress, the national leadership headed by Lechín continued to support the Plan.

The new 'Triangular Plan' required 8000 redundancies. A government lockout at Siglo XX early in 1963, triggered by its failure to dismiss more than a quarter of this number, led to a strike which spread throughout the mines and lasted 100 days. The strike failed to stop the Triangular Plan, but it did succeed in finally severing the movement's lingering loyalties to the MNR. Lechín set up an independent force called the PRIN (*Partido Revolucionario de la Izquierda*

Nacional) to safeguard his own position.[46] Attempts by the American Embassy to organise another, rival, pro-government labour movement in 1963 and 1964 came to nothing. Discontent in the mines was now running hand in hand with that in the urban areas, with repeated strikes by school teachers and other urban workers (Table 5.7), the taking prisoner of American technical advisors as hostages at Catavi in December 1963 (among them the US labour attaché) and permanent anti-government demonstrations.[47] The exhaustion of the national movement as a political force was patent, soon to be made official by the imposition of a military dictatorship which would resolve the problems created by the MNR's loss of popular support by attempting to seal off all channels of popular expression, as the army, reorganised and modernised with American aid, provided its own authoritarian solution to the crisis.

The years of military rule: 1964–82

Eighteen years of military rule followed the 1964 coup, 18 years during which the military repeatedly tried to impose a new union structure on organised labour, replacing the local plant unions, assemblies, and national delegate congresses which had proved in the past to be the backbone of labour's political independence, with a centrally-organised union movement whose officers were military appointees (Table 5.10). Just as repeatedly, brutal repression failed to make the new institutions work: these 18 years show a history of semi-clandestine union organisation, flagged with illegal congresses, general strikes, and intermittent massacres, which provide their own witness to the stubborn ability of the miners in particular to reorganise under repressive conditions, in spite of the armed forces' success in imposing wage cuts so vicious that by 1965, serious problems of malnutrition had re-appeared in the mining camps.[48]

Eighteen brutal years passed, as the armed forces' own techniques of control through violence, learned in part at US army schools, became more sophisticated with the help of Brazilian, Argentinian and Chilean imports; 18 extremely grim years for labour, punctuated in 1969–71 by a dying flare of military nationalism which recalled the years of Busch and Villarroel, and witnessed a new national experiment in workers' control which, this time, did take on certain of the characteristics of a soviet.

During this period, the country's economic structure changed. Tin prices briefly rose to their highest post-war level under General

TABLE 5.8 *The Years of Military Rule, 1964–82*

Date/Takeover		*Government*	*President*
* Nov.	1964	Military	Gnrls Barrientos/Ovando
@ July	1965	Elected military	General Barrientos
* Sept.	1969	Military	General Ovando
* Oct.	1970	Military	General Torres
* Aug.	1971	Military	General Banzer
* Nov.	1974	Autogolpe	
@* June.	1978	Military	General Pereda
* Nov.	1978	Military	General Padilla
@ July	1979	'Elected' civilian	Guevara Arce
* Nov.	1979	Military	Colonel Natusch
o Dec.	1979	Civilian appointee	Gueiler
* July	1980	Military	General Garcia Meza
* Aug.	1981	Military	General Torrelio
* July	1982	Military	General Vildoso
@o Oct.	1982	Civilian elected July 1980	Siles Zuazo

@ election
* military coup
@* fraudulent election
o* other

SOURCES: Dunkerley (1980, 1984).

Barrientos (1964–69), the benefits going to the armed forces and urban centres rather than the mines. They rose again, though less than oil prices, during the commodity boom of the mid-1970's, giving General Banzer's regime (1971–78) a wholly undeserved reputation for good economic management, in spite of the continuation of policies of underinvestment and over-exploitation which had previously plagued COMIBOL, now applied to the State oil company YPFB. Urban and regional prosperity was simultaneously swelled by burgeoning foreign debt and a growing illegal trade in cocaine. Oil and cocaine in turn, added to the benefits of a boom in prices of local agricultural exports, helped together to shift the economic axis of the country out of La Paz and towards Santa Cruz, with a long right-wing tradition untroubled by militant unions. Santa Cruz thus provided the backbone of the *Banzerato*, in alliance with nearby Brazil: while cocaine, in turn, strengthened the position of those sectors of the military supporting García Meza in 1980.

TABLE 5.9 *The Bolivian Labour Force, 1976* (1000 workers)

	Total	*Wage Labour@*	*Self-Employed+*	*Employers*
TOTAL	1501.4	573.0	856.9	14.0
%	100.0	100.0	100.0	100.0
Agriculture	693.0	85.5	600.5	4.5
%	46.1	14.9	70.1	32.1
Mining and Oil	60.6	54.8	4.8	0.8
%	4.0	9.6	0.5	5.7
Manufacturing	145.4	60.4	81.5	2.5
%	9.6	10.5	9.5	17.9
Construction	82.4	58.4	22.6	.8
%	5.4	10.2	2.6	5.7
Commerce	106.9	17.4	87.1	2.1
%	7.1	3.0	10.2	15.0
Transport and Communications	56.0	36.2	18.2	0.8
	3.7	6.3	2.1	5.7
Finance	12.9	9.6	2.8	0.3
%	0.8	2.2	1.1	2.1
Services	281.9	242.7	35.0	1.8
%	18.8	42.3	0.4	12.8

* because of the elimination of 'other', 'unspecified', and 'looking for first job', totals may not sum, and percentages may sum to less than 100 per cent.
@ includes *obreros* (blue-collar) and *empleados* (white-collar).
+ includes unpaid family workers.

SOURCE: National Statistics Institute, 1976 Census of Population and Housing.

These changes had little apparent impact on the structure of the labour force (Table 5.9), encouraging if anything the persistence of traditional employment patterns in spite of a commoditisation of peasant agriculture which rendered the peasantry more vulnerable to changing urban prices, and encouraged a definite upswing in peasant unrest from 1974 onwards. In 1976 57 per cent of Bolivia's labour force was self-employed or unpaid family labour, 56 per cent even of the labour force in manufacturing, one indication of the continuing importance of urban and rural artisans.

Matched with the undeniably conservative role of the peasantry in the 1950s and 1960s, when their caciques provided first the MNR and then Barrientos with a sure base, these economic trends might have been expected to weaken the power of organised labour – the more

TABLE 5.10 *Military Labour Policy and Union Resistance, 1964–82*

President/Date	*Congress and Strikes*	*Government Labour Policy*
1964 BARRIENTOS		Military occupation of mines; miners' militias destroyed; existing COMIBOL officers all sacked; COB, FSTMB abolished; only government-controlled union organisations allowed; no past holder of political office to hold union post.
May 1965	General strike (failed)	
Sept. 1965	clandestine FSTMB Congress	
June 1967	clandestine FSTMB Congress	Massacre of miners 'Night of San Juan'
June 1967	14-day strike of Siglo XX	
1969 OVANDO		Legalisation of COB; restoration union rights.
Apr. 1970	FSTMB Congress	
May 1970	COB Congress	
Oct. 1970	General strike against junta coup	
1970 TORRES		
June 1971	'Asamblea Popular' and local *asambleas*; workers' takeover of press, and so on.	Offer of *co-gobierno* (refused); miners' pay back to 1965 levels; co-management in State oil co.
1971 BANZER		COB outlawed; repression, exile of union leaders, torture institutionalised.
1972	Clandestine union elections in strongest mines	
1973	Clandestine FSTMB elects national leadership	

TABLE 5.10 *continued*

President/Date	*Congress and Strikes*	*Government Labour Policy*
Jan 1974	General Strike of La Paz factories, banks, mines, peasant demonstrations	'Massacre of the Valley' of Cochabamba peasants.
Nov. 1974		'*Autogolpe*': all existing union officers replaced by government appointees, strikes prohibited, meetings controlled by martial law.
Jan. 1975	Siglo XX-Catavi strike against military destruction of radio stations	
May 1976	FSTMB Congress	Arrest of FSTMB executive.
June 1976	Strike of mines, factories	Military occupy mines; 950 miners dismissed.
Jan. 1978	Mass hunger strike (mines, urban areas; 1000 strikers)	Concession of full trade union liberties though military still in mines.
1978 PEREDA		Miners' wages increased 35%
May 1978	FSTMB Congress	
July 1978	FSTMB threaten protest strike over electoral fraud	
1978 PADILLA		Break-up of government (pro-Banzer) peasant union and recognition of independent peasant unions; prosecution of 1600 official government union officers for US$ 3 million fraud; but troops remain in mining areas.
May 1979	COB Congress	

TABLE 5.10 *continued*

President/Date	*Congress and Strikes*	*Government Labour Policy*
1979 GUEVARA ARCE		
1979 NATUSCH	General strike: mines, peasants blockade roads.	Offer of *co-gobierno* refused by COB: leading to 'Massacre of All Saints' in which COB offices blown up, 200 died, 125 'disappeared'.
1979 GUEILER		
Dec. 1979	COB demonstration against new economic programme; peasants blockade roads. Rise in strike levels.	
1980 GARCÍA MEZA	Strike of miners supported by peasants	Murder of three union, political leaders at meeting in COB; use of stadium for arrests, assassinations; attack on mines, mass murders at Caracoles and Viloco mining towns. Union officers replaced with 1000 government appointees; introduction of Argentine-style paramilitary squads.
Jan. 1981	Successive 48-hour general strikes in urban areas, mines	Assassination of MIR leaders
July 1981	General strike of major mines, large factories, cut off of supplies of petrol, food to La Paz.	
1981 TORRELIO	Strike in Huanuni for restoration of union rights.	Military occupy mine.

TABLE 5.10 *continued*

President/Date	*Congress and Strikes*	*Government Labour Policy*
Nov. 1981	Solidarity stoppages in other mines, factories, hunger strikes of 1000 people.	Legalisation plant unions, COB, promised 'within the year'.
Feb./Mar. 1982	48-hour general strikes against economic programme.	
Sept. 1982	COB demo of 100 000 – call for general strike.	

SOURCE: Dunkerley (1980, 1984).

so as oil workers had always represented a relatively conservative force within the labour movement.[49] In fact, the early years of this gradual 'traditionalisation' of Bolivia witnessed a substantial victory for organised labour, as one military effort after another failed to suppress independent trade unionism (Table 5.10). Again and again, the FSTMB demonstrated its ability to survive direct repression and preserve its cohesion in the face of a disastrous collapse in living standards (dramatically increasing malnutrition), and in spite of a substantial expansion of the private sector in mining.[50] After 1974, the peasantry themselves moved from conservatism to militancy, depriving the military of their once-secure electoral base. Labour remained a rallying point for opposition to increasingly brutal dictatorships, 'the only site of anything approaching democracy in modern Bolivia'.[51]

Barrientos

When Generals Barrientos and Ovando took power in 1964, both distinguished members of the MNR's own military cell, the prevailing disorientation among party and union leaders was so great that both the PCB and Lechin's PRIN originally supported the coup. However, the military were constrained by their alliance with Washington, which was demanding a freeze on salaries and social benefits: by early 1965, the 'May system',[52] the first military attempt to introduce a new

TABLE 5.11 *Cuts in Employment and Wages at Comibol, January-April and July-December 1965*

	January-April		*July-December*	
	No./employed	*Wages*	*No./employed*	*Wages*
Faceworkers (manual)	8529	Bs.867	8076	Bs.527
Faceworkers (employee)	623	1221	554	1086
Millworkers (manual)	2586	589	2551	486
Millworkers (employee)	575	970	498	662
Surface workers (manual)	4531	514	4711	452
Surface workers (employee)	4587	862	4074	690
TOTAL	21 431		20 464	
AVERAGE WAGE		Bs.770		Bs.407

SOURCE: DUNKERLEY (1984), p. 126.

system of labour control, was in operation; the COB was abolished, Lechin deported, and a wave of arrests eliminated left-wing politicians and labour activists alike.

A general strike, hastily called by an *ad hoc* committee of miners, factory and construction workers, teachers and *gastronomicos* already alarmed at Lechín's failure to defend eroding union rights, failed badly. Milluni and Siglo XX, one private mine and one COMIBOL, were bombed from the air, and hundreds of activists lost their jobs.

Attempts by POR militants such as César Lora and Isaac Camacho and PCB militants such as Federico Escóbar to set up clandestine unions in the mines had some success, though all three were to lose their lives within the first three years of military rule: with the aid of university students, a clandestine FSTMB Congress was even organised. But although these initiatives were successful in preserving a tradition of 'free unionism' in the face of clumsy government attempts to create an 'official unionism' (based on *empleados* within the mines, like the *comandos especiales* of the MNR), they provided no protection against the collapse of wages and social security benefits detailed in Table 5.11. Nor could clandestine unions prevent Barrientos from mobilising sufficient support among the peasantry to win a reasonably fair election for the Presidency in 1966.

The initial shock of military occupation of the mines had hardly been digested, however, when a second shock sent ripples through the Bolivian State itself. In 1967, with ambiguous and half-hearted support from the PCB, Che Guevara chose Bolivia as the site for an ill-considered effort to establish a foco at the heart of the South American continent. His presence inspired a certain recuperation of spirits in the mines, reaching a climax with a new FSTMB congress called at Siglo XX in late June. On the Night of San Juan, in the middle of the combined traditional and union festivities, the government attacked the camp, killing 87 people, including women and children. The massacre and subsequent arrests failed to forestall mass protest demonstrations, or a two-week strike in Siglo XX: but these in turn failed to prevent a new wave of dismissals.[53]

Generals Ovando and Torres

If Che's arrival only briefly raised labour spirits, the campaign against him and his subsequent murder, organised by CIA agents 'reinforcing' the local military establishment, paradoxically triggered a new wave of nationalist sentiment among officers deeply troubled by the speed with which Barrientos had opened up Bolivia's mineral resources to foreign exploitation.[54] In April 1969 Barrientos died in a helicopter crash, and General Ovando – already identified with a more nationalist policy, after his successful negotiation of a contract for COMIBOL's first smelting plant with a German firm – took power in a new coup, restoring trade union rights in a deliberate attempt to secure popular support, and nationalised the US-owned Gulf Oil company.

The new government, modelled on the Velasco regime in nearby Peru, represented only a faction of the armed forces and was inherently unstable. After several unsuccessful coups, a triumvirate of conservative officers was installed by Ovando's rivals, only to be overthrown by a general strike of the labour movement in October 1970, in effective support for another progressive military bid for power, that of General Torres. The FSTMB's Congress, called in April before Ovando's final fall from grace, but still reeling under the impact of disillusion with the MNR, had passed a resolution demanding that the labour movement preserve its independence from any and all governments, particularly military ones. This position was ratified at the COB's subsequent Fourth Congress in May, but the COB also elected to create a *Comando Politico* providing collective leadership for the delicate political balancing act which lay ahead. On the *Comando*, representatives of the COB were joined by others from individual unions and the leading parties of the left, including the POR and the PCB.

Torres offered the COB the possibility of several government ministries, but after an eight-hour debate, in which the PCB and a faction of the old PRIN were defeated, the labour movement refused the offer, although it continued to support Torres against coups, defeating Banzer's first attempt in January 1971 with a general strike. The extent of working-class mobilisation during this period (which saw several urban firms taken over) forced the government to make further concessions, and even give tacit support to the *Asamblea Popular* called in June 1971 by the *Comando Politico*, a deliberating council composed largely of union representatives, with a few from the political parties, dominated by manual workers, with token peasant representation corresponding to that on the CB itself.

Among the Assembly's achievements were the drafting of a new scheme of *control obrero*, bringing the miners' closer to majority control of COMIBOL. Some writers have seen it as a revolutionary parliament and others as a soviet, though it lasted only ten days and wasted much time on debating procedure. Certainly business and American interests alike viewed its appearance, and the prospect of a second session, as revolutionary, concentrating their energies on the successful August coup. In August, however, the *Asamblea's* Military Commission failed to persuade Torres to distribute arms to the labour movement and thus it could do little to protect the government against Banzer, in spite of a final general strike; the toll for its resistance was 300 deaths and perhaps 1000 wounded during two days of fighting.[55]

The Banzerato

Banzer's was to prove incomparably the most successful attempt to establish a stable system of military rule. Externally, the coup had the support of governments in the USA and Brazil: internally, it was supported not only by the military establishment but also by the new export bourgeoisie encouraged after 1955 by the MNR's own American-inspired policies of promoting private enterprise, which Banzer was once again to put into practice – the new private mining sector and agro-industrial interests around Santa Cruz. This powerful support, which brought the *Confederación de Empresas Privadas de Bolivia* into the government (together initially with a faction of the MNR under Paz Estenssoro),[56] was cemented by the temporary but convenient commodity boom of the mid-1970s, and towards the end of the 1970s, by the growing traffic in cocaine. Using funds robbed from COMIBOL and YPFB, and by increasing the foreign debt (which shot up from US $ 500 million to US $ 3100 million by the end of 1978) the government also gathered around it circles of personal supporters, an 'economic interest' all its own.[57] In spite of a US–sponsored attempt to 'destabilise' Torres along lines similar to those already being practised in Chile, Banzer had no union support outside the self-employed transport workers of La Paz, and little among the peasantry either.

The cost of this rarified élite authoritarianism to labour was very high. At least 200 opponents of the government were killed, 15 000 jailed 'for offences against the state' and 19 000 forced into political exile between 1971 and 1977, as Banzer institutionalised a Chilean-style secret police.[58] The COB's own data show a decline of 36.3 per cent in the purchasing power of wages and salaries in 1978 as compared to 1971, and the proportion of national income going to wages and salaries declined from 47 per cent to 31 per cent, although broader social trends may have influenced this pattern as well as wage cuts.[59]

But these policies were not to be imposed without labour resistance. The devaluation of the peso in October 1972, one of the government's first economic measures, raised enough pressure from the battered unions to force the government to concede a 'patriotic bonus' at Christmas.[60] The labour movement, already reorganising in the mines, was inspired to attempt to reorganise the COB by means of an 'Interunion Pact' which the government forestalled with a wave of arrests. Nonetheless, in November 1973, the FSTMB succeeded in organising its Fifteenth Congress, re-electing its exiled leaders, Lechin, Escobar and Reyes (PCB), and reasserting its own loyalty to the COB. A second economic package in January 1974, which attempted to eliminate State subsidies on basic consumer goods, triggered massive protests: a 36-hour strike by La Paz factory workers turned into a successful national general strike in manufacturing, joined by the mines and banks, and swelling such a massive mobilisation of peasants in the Cochabamba valley that the government felt it necessary to send in the troops. The resulting 'Massacre of the Valley' led to the deaths of between 80 and 200 peasants, and effectively killed any future possibilities of a military-peasant alliance. The government was now fighting opposition on two fronts, a labour movement successfully regrouping in spite of repression, while among the hitherto tractable peasants, independent organisations resistant to government control were beginning to make some headway for the first time.[61]

Banzer responded with an attempt to replace the existing free union movement with one organised by 'co-ordinators' under official control. This second military experiment in substitute unionism was introduced after the 'autogolpe' of 1974, when the President shed Paz Estenssoro and the MNR as supporters, and declared all existing political parties 'in recess' in a deliberate imitation of the nearby Chilean regime.[62] Much like Barrientos' similar initiative, it quickly came to grief on the ability of face-workers to sustain a clandestine organisation underground, and their possession of sufficient economic leverage to force the COMIBOL management to negotiate with genuine representatives. This time, if anything, the reaction within the mines was smoother than in 1964, and the impact of arrests less decisive. A confrontation emerged very quickly, in January 1975, when a military attempt to remove miner-controlled radio stations in Siglo XX and Catavi triggered a protest strike which forced the return of some of the transmitters, including that of the Canadian Oblate fathers, themselves increasingly converted from simple anti-communism to a spirited defence of trade unionism by the appalling conditions in the camp.

In the early years of military rule, the geographical isolation of the miners and their difficulties in contacting the urban labour movement had taken their toll of resistance. The real success of miners' initiatives always depended on the ability of factory workers and students based in the cities to organise their own opposition to the military. However, urban workers also recovered fairly quickly from the 'autogolpe', with a successful strike by workers at the Bata-owned Manaco shoe factory in Cochabamba in 1976, and the miners, organised locally in rank and file committees, decided to launch their own offensive. At a barely clandestine Sixteenth National Congress of the FSTMB held at Corocoro in May, they denounced the government's wage policies, its repression of union and political organisations, and the handing of mining and oil resources over to foreign firms, and gave the regime 30 days to increase salaries by 110 per cent.

On 8 June this upsurge of labour militancy suddenly received an additional boost when news of Torre's assassination in exile in Argentina reached the country, sparking off mass protests in the urban areas. The government reacted by re-occupying the mines with a force of 2000 soldiers, and arresting the FSTMB's entire executive, deporting 52 of its union leaders to Chile. In Siglo XX, miners organised a mass meeting in the mouth of the mine and demanded the withdrawal of troops from all mining camps, freedom for their detained leaders, the devolution of their radio transmitters, and a wage increase. Other COMIBOL mines joined Siglo XX on strike, while factory workers and students organised solidarity movements elsewhere. The strike lasted a month, in spite of a government siege of the mines, with miners and their families hiding underground, the camps deprived of electricity, and even food and water having to be smuggled in at night. Its final defeat depressed local levels of political and union activity, miners' wages and conditions, and the national struggle against the regime alike.[63]

The final popular offensive against the regime was nonetheless not far off, hastened by the post-1976 collapse of commodity prices on world markets, which affected not only the country's revenues from tin and oil, but also exports of sugar and cotton to which regional agriculturalists in Santa Cruz were deeply committed. As the economy's over-all rate of growth declined and its foreign debt passed the US $3000 million mark, parties of the traditional right joined the opposition to Banzer, and divisions began to appear within the armed forces. Worse still, the election of Jimmy Carter as President of the USA, determined to clean up his government's record on human rights, spelled the end of the military regime's principal external prop. Banzer began to retreat, offering elections in July 1978, and carefully nominating his own military candidate, Pereda.

The final death-throes of this alternative institutional order were triggered by the December 1978 hunger strike of four wives of prominent FSTMB leaders: Angelica Flores, Luzmill Pimentel, Aurora Villarroel and Nelly Paniagua – all demanding a real, not token, amnesty in a bid to free their husbands from jail and exile. This quickly became a mass movement, with more than 1000 hunger strikers throughout the country, supported by the Church, the middle class, and other sectors. Faced with simultaneous external and internal pressure against his dictatorship, Banzer finally restored formal trade union liberties (although the troops were left in control of the mines), and slowly began to disassociate himself from Pereda, recognising the inevitability of a return to civilian control.

The long and conflictive road to democracy: 1978–82

Commonly and ironically known as 'the democratic opening', the next four years saw seven Presidents follow in quick succession, five of them from the armed forces and none actually elected; while on three separate occasions the electorate gave a clear majority to Presidential candidate Hernan Siles Zuazo of the old MNR and his new coalition, the *Union Democratica y Popular*.

For virtually a decade, the COB was to be torn between labour's political role as a rallying point for the return of a fragile democratic system which had to be preserved against new threats of coups, and its role as the defender of working-class economic interests, as it faced the collapse of tin prices, temporary famine, and pressures from abroad for the payment of Bolivia's foreign debts: a deterioration in the local economy which inevitably brought with it serious conflicts between unions and civilian governments. Tensions between organised labour and democratic regimes became acute with the return of relatively stable democracy under Siles Zuazo (1982–85) and Paz Estenssoro (1985–). But they first appeared much earlier, in December 1979, when bank workers, teachers, construction sites, road works and mills came out on strike against the IMF-backed economic programme of the short-lived Gueiler government, though without the COB's formal blessing or the participation of the miners. Over the decade, they took the overt form of an intense internal debate between different party factions, as the Bolivian Communist Party and other members of the UDP coalition first of all failed at successive FSTMB and COB congresses to secure a formal declaration of adhesion for Siles Zuazo, before and after his advent to power in October 1982; and then, after the failure of an attempted *rapprochement* between government and labour in 1983, saw the COB's own executive taken over by independents, anti-government nationalists and Trotskyists as labour moved increasingly towards the position of opposition to the existing civilian government which it would formally assume in March 1985.

Labour thus preserved a formal political independence throughout this transition to democracy, one which perhaps hardly mattered in the years 1978–82 as it led the struggle against military intervention. The unification of social forces around the COB during these years was made much easier by the consolidation of a representative union of peasants independent of any form of military or government control, the CSTUB (*Confederación Sindical Unica de Trabajadores Campesinos de Bolivia*). The appearance of the CSTUB formalised the emergence of the Bolivian peasantry as a social force in its own right, laying to rest forever the ghost of MNR and military attempts to turn the sector into a secure and unquestioning base for the government in power, and thus perhaps also spelling the death-knell for any possible 'populist' solution to the instability of Bolivia's political institutions. A formal alliance between workers and peasants as independent forces was cemented just before the CSTUB's founding Congress, when in May 1979 its two principal components joined the COB at its own fifth Congress (though not without a fractious debate which saw the departure of the Maoists, hitherto in control of the COB's purely token peasant representation, two seats on an executive committee of 34.[64]

Successive military efforts to flout the electoral verdict, coups, and increasingly savage repression were the principal triggers for strike activity during 1978–82. The peak of coherent union organisation behind the drive for democracy was reached in the November 1979 general strike against an attempted coup by Colonel Natusch, when the COB in alliance with the CSTUCB paralysed the entire country, urban and rural, in a succession of strikes at 24-hour intervals. The outcome of this united effort was the installation of an interim civilian regime under the presidency of Lidia Gueiler (once leader of the MNR's women's organisation), and an economic crisis, as tin production fell to levels not seen since 1965 and a run on the peso forced closure of the banks. Gueiler's stabilisation programme (which increased prices of petrol, gas and kerosene by 120 per cent, and devalued the peso, thus eroding working-class purchasing power) resulted in the emergence of open tension between labour and government and thus weakened the COB's ability to act as a guarantee of democratic institutionality. The COB called a demonstration in La Paz in December, which attracted crowds of 50 000 and subsequently a one-day token general strike: but this formal organisation of opposition to the measures was insufficient in the eyes of the organised peasants, who imposed blockades on major roads, and sectors of the union movement who called independent strikes the following spring. By May the COB and the Gueiler government had reached a formal agreement on minimum wages and compensation for inflation, at the cost of alienation of the employers federation, the Private Enterprise Federation.

However, the agreement was countermanded virtually immediately by a new coup, as General García Meza attempted to reimpose the institutional regime of which Banzer had dreamed – this time with unprecedented savagery. After its own internal disputes during the Gueiler era, the COB's traditional ability to field an alliance of urban workers, miners and for the past decade, organised peasants, now collapsed, and the mines were left to stand virtually alone in a heroic and futile resistance which lasted two weeks, at the cost of the most appalling massacres yet in their history, with 900 dead, 'disappeared', wounded or taken off as prisoners in the single mining town of Caracoles alone.[65]

Fortunately for labour, García Meza was unlucky in his external alliances – the Reagan administration in the USA, elected in 1980, proved distinctly cool to a military regime notoriously connected with cocaine – and unlucky too in facing an increasingly desperate economic crisis. In January 1981 he followed Lidia Gueiler's example in attempting to impose a programme of cuts in State expenditure: this time, urban labour and the mines acted in harmony to impose successive 48-hour stoppages, and the tide of united working-class protest rose again. In July 1981 miners in Huanuni came out on strike for the restoration of trade union rights; in August mines and factories went on strike, joining sections of the military themselves in open rebellion against the regime. García was replaced by a less intractable supporter of Banzer's philosophy through an internal military coup.

His successor, General Torrelio, came to office with the intention of maintaining military controls over the labour movement, including those of the secret police. However, Bolivia's economic crisis was worsening, with exports shrinking in the face of world recession and inflation increasing rapidly. The military were no longer capable of imposing political control. Between November 1981 and February 1982, the labour movement successfully forced the final demolition of military trade unionism in a series of strikes which originated once again in Huanuni, but by mid-December had spread to industry, gathering another thousand hunger strikers in an echo of the mobilisation which had forced Banzer's withdrawal two years before. Torrelio promised a restitution of independent plant unions within three months, and the legalisation of the COB within the year, thus writing the final chapter to Barrientos' original attempt to demolish the institutional framework set in place by military nationalists in the 1940s which, over 30 years, had consistently secured labour's independence from government control.

However, while the armed forces' decision to hand over the Presidency to Siles Zuazo in October 1982 was welcomed by the labour movement (triggered as it was by a COB-convened protest march on 17 September, which attracted 100 000 people, and the threat of a new indefinite general strike), for labour it marked the end of its role as the centre of national opposition to arbitrary rule and the beginning of a period of acute divisions, as the leaders of the

COB sought to protect democratic governments without jettisoning the interests of workers themselves. Siles Zuazo's inauguration brought with it the worst drought in the Altiplano in living memory. Inflation spiralled out of control, reaching levels of 200 per cent in 1982, 700 per cent in 1983 and 1600 per cent in 1978. By 1984, real wages for the economy as a whole had dropped by a staggering 65 per cent. By 1985, on Inter-American Development Bank figures, exports had fallen to 68 per cent of their 1980 value. Siles Zuazo's effective dependence on COB support to counter-balance the military initially set obstacles to the adoption of a straight-forward IMF programme of adjustment; however, it could not resolve the economic straightjacket imposed by drastically declining export revenues and the consequent inability of the country to import needed parts and equipment, reflected in strike calls by both miners and oil workers for the government to supply their industries with additional foreign exchange.

Conflicts with the UDP initially took the form of a demand for 'co-management' in COMIBOL and other State agencies, pressed forward by the COB in a search for alternatives to equally urgent wage demands, which threatened to destabilise the new democratic regime. The FSTMB supported the demand. Torres' concession to the FSTMB of parity control over COMIBOL's board of management was remembered now not with nostalgia, but as a step which could and should be bettered, and the miners wanted majority control. But workers' control was a matter of principle, it also had a practical side: the miners were not likely to forget that Siles Zuazo's original administration had continued the original MNR policy of packing COMIBOL's higher echelons with its supporters, while neglecting investment in the mines in favour of oil. With tin prices depressed in world markets, the local cost of producing tin had begun to outstrip its export value, and the need for new investment to revitalise the mining economy had become ever more urgent. Without workers' control, the FSTMB was afraid that COMIBOL would be broken up and sold to private, perhaps foreign, capital.[66]

In April 1983 the miners seized effective control of seven mines and six processing plants to pre-empt a strike by white-collar workers and technicians which they regarded as irresponsible and claimed was a threat to the new government's position. The FSTMB occupied the headquarters of COMIBOL. Grudgingly, Siles Zuazo conceded the union majority representation on the board, after a half-hearted attempt to secure independent representation for technicians. In

November 1983 the FSTMB finally took over, stressing that its involvement represented a real risk and a sacrifice on the union's part for the nation: 'if the company goes under, the country will go with it.' Sadly, the truth was now rather different, as the oil industry's contribution to Bolivia's foreign exchange outstripped that of tin by a factor of four.[67] The FSTMB's 'victory' lasted only until the 1985 election of Paz Estenssoro.

Faced with mass workers' demonstrations in La Paz in early 1983, Siles Zuazo briefly sought to revive the MNR's old strategy of *co-gobierno*. But his government was under pressure from the IMF and foreign bankers to introduce a more conventional solution to the economic crisis, devaluing the peso and cutting State expenditure, a radically different policy from the COB's suggestions; repudiation of the foreign debt and the IMF, majority workers' control in State enterprises, the peasants to control emergency programmes in agriculture through the CSTUCB. Government and labour were both increasingly ill-representative of the real economy and increasingly powerless in the face of economic disaster, as centres of prosperity shifted eastward towards Beni and Santa Cruz, foci of the cocaine trade, and the new industry of gold-panning in the Amazon region, a haven for small prospectors and smugglers which provided employment for perhaps 100 000 economic refugees from central Bolivia, but did nothing in the short term to add to the State's own resources.[68]

By August 1983 it seemed that the UDP had opted for an IMF-style solution, in the hope of getting further funding from abroad. By late September, with inflation over the previous two years at 1000 per cent, the government faced a spontaneous strike wave culminating in an unofficial nation-wide general strike. Among the strikers were miners led by Huanuni, demanding urgent food supplies and the replacement of local equipment: the protest spread to half Bolivia's total mining force. At the time, miners' families in Catavi were receiving only 1 kg. of meat a month, out of a supposed monthly ration of 55 kg.; and they were living off a total food supply of 20 small bread rolls a day.[69]

Hoping to retain some credibility with its rank and file while simultaneously avoiding any action which might provoke a coup, the COB itself called a 48-hour general strike in December. But in the face of the government's programme of devaluation and expenditure cuts – which threatened to triple the cost of bread and bus tickets – internal tensions were increasingly pulling the labour movement apart. In May 1984 the COB called another 72-hour protest strike. Pressworkers (printers and journalists) refused to join it on the grounds that it was acutely dangerous given the fragility of the democratic regime. Bank workers staged an independent sit-in in the Central Bank, being thrown out by police on the government's orders, to the COB's protests. Factory workers led by the Trotskyist POR pressed ahead with their own demands for an indefinite strike (in spite of Lechin's resignation from the COB in protest) while oil workers and railway workers ignored the strike call entirely to set up private negotiations for a better individual agreement with the government.

The 'kidnapping' of President Siles Zuazo by paramilitary forces led the COB briefly to suspend its campaign against declining wages and stage an official mass demonstration in support of the government, threatening a general strike if the government were overthrown.[70] But this *rapprochement* was brief, given a deterioration of salary levels which was unprecedented in the labour movement's history. In June, the COB called another official general strike, which won some concessions from the government. However, the trials of the previous six months had lost supporters of the UDP within the COB, notably the Bolivian Communist Party, their electoral base. In the May 1984 Congress of the FSTMB, the miners elected a general-secretary representing 'independents' with no ties to the government, Victor Lopez. In September, at the COB's Sixth Congress, opposition forces took control of the executive.[71] The COB continued to press its own economic programme on the government.

A two-day general strike called in November lasted nine days in all, with miners, teachers and local provincial state employees continuing on strike after the COB, recognising waning urban support and increasingly bitter conflicts with the middle-class, had called the action off. The defeat of this strike allowed the government to implement its full stabilisation programme, devaluing the peso by 78 per cent, raising fares and basic food stuffs by 450 per cent, and satisfying Bolivia's external creditors if not the UDP's local supporters.[72] The impracticality of these measures led to their quickly being discarded; nonetheless, the defeat's effect on the labour movement, rapidly succumbing to a collapse of the local economy, which made even its most dramatic pressures on government useless, was little short of catastrophic. In December, right-wing supporters of ex-President Banzer won the elections in Huanuni, an event which, given Huanuni's record of tenacious opposition to military rule, can only be seen as an index of complete desperation. In January 1985 miners from San José occupied the main square in Oruro and set off dynamite explosions in an effort to secure payment of their monthly wages. In February a 24-hour general strike paralysed all activities except emergency services, as the COP pressed for payment of a 200 per cent wage increase to factory workers, ordered by the government in November but boycotted by the employers. The inflation rate in 1984 had reached a total of 2117 per cent.

As the country edged towards complete economic collapse, democratic obligations began to take second place in the labour movement's mind to the urgent search for a regime which would offer an acceptable economic solution; and the COB, failing to organise its own distribution system on a sufficiently large scale to feed those in need, turned to thoughts of insurrection on the one hand and on the other, to the possibility of promoting a 'progressive' military coup to prevent the return of Banzer.[73] But the COB's own real powers were on the wane. A further indefinite strike in late March, lasting 16 days, was strongly supported by miners and other State workers whose salary sources were in doubt, but not the relatively protected oil workers, nor transport workers, nor yet the peasantry. Its failure led to calls for a reassessment of the COB's own internal structure, to bring its executive closer into line with the changing economic structure of the Bolivian labour force, at a minimum upgrading the representation of the peasantry on its executive committee.

The Siles Zuazo government resigned and called elections in July 1985. The victor was not Banzer, but Paz Estenssoro, that other veteran of the original MNR. Within the year, President Paz had taken steps to demolish the power base of the FSTMB, closing down unprofitable mines, selling off those with some years of life left in them to the private sector, and turning over those of marginal profitability to the miners themselves to be run as co-operatives. A protest march on La Paz by miners was successfully surrounded by troops and dispersed before reaching the city. With the collapse of tin prices and the exhaustion of the original tin deposits worked by the *rosca*, the era when the FSTMB could provide the core of the Bolivian labour movement was clearly coming to an end.

The years of democratic rule have thus presented the COB with a threat to its very survival of a kind never seriously posed by those of military rule. At stake is not only the structure of the old labour movement – its reliance on the miners to provide a redoubt of union organisation around which other workers could mobilise, one capable of surviving under the worst conditions of repression and economic hardship – but also perhaps its most basic patterns of organisation, centred on the union and its mass assemblies, as the economic position of the State itself weakens and the great bulk of the Bolivian economy slides back into the patterns of a rural subsistence economy, artisan production, smuggling and drug trafficking more typical of the pre-1900 era. At the time of writing, it is impossible to predict how far this pattern of disintegration will go.

NOTES

1. GNP was officially US $505 in 1983, lower than that of any other Latin American country except Haiti (US$310): comparable figures for other countries studied in this volume are Colombia (US$1033), Ecuador (US$1141) Peru (US$959), Chile (US$1602), Paraguay (US$1271). Inter-American Development Bank, *Economic and Social Progress in Latin America*, 1984, p. 420.
2. Fox (1970) says of the problem of declining tin resources:

   'In 1938, the average tin content of ore coming from the large mines was 3%: in 1950, it had fallen to 1.87%: in 1964, it was only 0.82%. The working out of higher grade deposits, accelerated by the demands of the Second World War and by the policy of the big three tin barons in gutting their mines before nationalisation, has had several repercussions.'

   On the issue of the small size of local markets, Zondag (1966) cites local business estimates that in 1950, only 40 per cent of the Bolivian population consumed manufactured goods, though by 1960 the proportion had risen to 47 per cent.
3. Notably during the dictatorship of the caudillo Belzu (1848–55) and the Liberal Revolution of 1899. See Lora (1977).
4. Thoburn (1981) p. 46: Bolivia's exports of fuels and minerals together accounted for 79 per cent. Comparable figures for other tin exports (tin as percentage of all exports) are Malaysia (11 per cent), Thailand (7 per cent) and Indonesia (2 per cent).
5. Whitehead (1976) provides the best account of the early social composition of the mines, citing the following report of Patino's Jefe de Trabajo at Uncia on the breakdown of his labour force:

plasterers, smiths, tailors, and shoemakers	15 per cent
carpenters	15 per cent
mechanics	10 per cent
miners	10 per cent
peasants	35 per cent

Gamarra, organiser of the first Siglo XX union, was a carpenter turned miner, later to be a leader of the woodworkers' union (Lora, 1977); Domitila Barrios de Chungara's father was a tailor turned miner and political activists (Barrios, 1978).

Magill (1974) asked factory workers, miners and oil workers whether they or their fathers had been peasants, in a survey covering 313 individuals in 1968. Of factory workers, only 15 per cent had been peasants themselves at some time, and only 31 per cent were the sons of peasants. The percentages of miners with a peasant background was higher, but still quite low: 23 per cent and 47 per cent respectively. It was slightly higher for oil workers. It would therefore seem a mistake to overemphasise the peasant origins of the Bolivian working class, although June Nash has written vividly about the survival of Indian customs within the mines.

Lora (1977) gives a good summary of the foreign connections of the artisan and left-wing community and the impact of imported ideologies.

6. Buechler and Buechler (1977) and Volk (1975a).
7. Whitehead (1981). See also Klein (1969).
8. Klein (1969) is the best source on early labour legislation: he and Lora (1977) both cover the early politics of the labour movement.
9. The political history of the Uncia union is summarised in Whitehead (1981); see also Lora (1977) pp. 120–8. A permanent union was not established at Siglo XX until 1940, under the influence of a PIR deputy.
10. Klein (1969), however, sees the involvement of the oil companies as less important than popular myth subsequently assumed.
11. Alexander (1958) gives a good account of the framework's operation during 1956, when workers were often able to use their political influence to secure a favourable wage settlement, and management's principal demands for changes in the Code centred on an amendment to give them the right to hire and fire at will.
12. Iriarte (1972) provides a history of Maria Barzola's death: Barrios (1978) a vivid account of the subsequent use to which barzolas were put to attack protesting miners' wives (p. 72). Klein is a good source on the shifting support for the PIR during this period, Lora tending to generalise too quickly from events in the mines to the working-class as a whole. Whitehead (1981) provides a useful summary of the electoral history of the PIR and the MNR in the mining districts during this period.
13. 'Pongueaje' was the *colono's* obligation to provide personal services to the landlord, over and above a share of his own harvest and the labour services he owed to the landlord's home farm.
14. Klein (1969) pp. 374–82. A view of this period from the MNR's point of view is provided by Augustin Cespedes in *El Dictador Colgado*. The USA's antipathy to Villarroel is well summarised in Blasier's article in Malloy and Thorn (1972).
15. Volk (1975b) is an excellent source on this period.
16. The POR had its origins in a united front of Marxists exiled from Bolivia for their anti-war stance during the Chaco War, formed in 1935. Lora (1977) traces the Chilean connection, which arose through the POR's principal founder, earlier a member of the Chilean Communist Party, and then of the Chilean Trotskyist group, *Izquierda Communista* –

although Lora is disdainful of the latter's 'petty burgeois traits' (it later joined the Chilean Socialist Party). Labour movement exiles maintained close contacts with Chilean parties throughout this period, perhaps because political connection were traditionally close: many activists joined Chilean parties as migrant workers in the Chilean nitrate mines, others through railway contacts (workers on the Arica-La Paz line being part of the Chilean FOCH). Arze, founder of the PIR, was deeply influenced by the contemporary Chilean Communist Party's experiment with the Popular Front.

17. Besides Lora, Volk (1975b), Dunkerley (1984) and Mitchell (1977) all provide good accounts of these confused years.
18. Magill (1974) p. 54. In Chapter 8, Magill gives a vivid account of political competition within the mines, oil, and factory unions, and provides a description of the pamphlets and periodicals published by the different groups. Barrios (1978) rarely comments on political divisions within Siglo XX, but she makes a revealing comment on the lack of political education shown by a middle-class right-wing woman trying to use her influence with the miners' wives – who did not even know that China and the USSR were at daggers drawn!
19. Tin prices were to be dogged by the existence of a huge stockpile amassed by the USA during the Second World War, throughout the post-war years, always available to be sold on world markets. Similar stockpiles in the Soviet bloc countries were also dumped on world markets during the 1950s: see Fox (1974).

    Thorn (1971) gives a good summary of the economic problems of COMIBOL in its early years, and the tendency of the MNR to sacrifice tin to oil, investing, in his estimate, US$ 140 million 'in exchange for tax privileges' in YPFB, which drilled over 200 wells. The search for further tin deposits and the pace of modernisation of equipment (already neglected during the last years of private ownership as a result of the collapse of the tin market during the Great Depression) was hampered by the emigration of 170 foreign engineers out of the 200 who had originally run the mining industry at nationalisation, leaving the rest to spread their energies around the 17 different companies out of which COMIBOL was formed. Investment in local smelting capacity and a degree of local rather than foreign private control over marketing were not to be established until the 1970s (Knakal, 1981); the lack of the latter enabled the displaced Patiño to impose a surcharge of 10 per cent of the 50 per cent of COMIBOL production annually smelted at his English plant in Liverpool, in addition to the compensation paid by the MNR.
20. *Latin American Regional Reports*, Andean Region, 9 November 1984. The investment of US$ 27.6 million was self-financed, and included exploration of gold deposits at San Antonio del Rio, lead, silver and zinc at Chicas in Potosi, and poopo in Oruro, and exploration of tin deposits in Chorolque.
21. Cf. Iriarte (1972) p. 52. Iriarte was a priest at Siglo XX. The figures are from a government report in 1967 which found that miners contracted silicosis within an average period ranging from 3 years 3 months in the

worst-affected sections to 7, 9, 10 and 12 years elsewhere. A contemporary survey of 27 000 miners found 45 per cent suffering from lung disease.

22. Llobet Tabolara (1984) p. 324.
23. Whitehead (1976): he points out that legally, union leaders were not supposed to be re-elected, though this provision was rarely honoured. Whitehead (1976, 1981) and June Nash (1979, 1982) both give excellent descriptions of the relationship between Trotskyists and rank and file in Siglo XX, while Whitehead (1976) discusses the varying political traditions of the different mining camps, with Huanuni being the most right-wing.
24. Whitehead (1976) reviews other cases.
25. See Whitehead (1976, 1980) for a discussion of this point, and for quotes from the US Army Handbook on Bolivia on the 'inability' of miners' leaders to control their rank and file: see also Barrios (1978) p.
26. Cf. the comments of Zabaleta (1972).
27. Mitchell (1977) p. 44, citing the MNR's *Estatuto organico*.
28. Mitchell, op.cit. Dunkerley (1984) suggests that the new *central* was based on contacts made during prior efforts by the FSTMB to establish a rival to the CSTB in the 1940s (p. 44).
29. Mitchell provides the clearest account of the organic relationships between MNR and labour movement during this period, but see rather Dunkerley (1984) and Lora (1977) on those between MNR, PCB and POR. Lora comments that the COB's MNR leadership, swelled by the representative weight accorded shadow organisations of public employees, 'set up shop in the Presidential Palace' attempting to purge POR members from plant executive committees. His brother, César Lora, a miner in Siglo XX, was arrested on a trumped-up charge of trying to blow up industrial plant (pp. 289–90).
30. Lora (1977) pp. 291–7 and Dunkerley (1984) p. 77.
31. Mitchell, p. 45. See also Dunkerley (1984) pp. 48–9.
32. Dunkerley (1984) pp. 81, 99.
33. June Nash (1977) reports a retrospective comment of one miner on the prosperity of the pre-1964 years which would tend to contradict the picture presented in Table 5.6, though this may represent no more than the 'after-glow' cast by the slashing of wages post-1964. Barrios (1978) remembers these as years when she and her younger sisters, living on the wage of her young husband, were forced to share a single pair of shoes.

    Calculations of 'real wages' over time are made extraordinarily difficult during this period by hyperinflation (the consumer price index rose 2, between 1952 and 1958) and the absence of a realistic exchange rate, with the official rate grossly undervaluing the dollar and the 'real' black market quoted in Table 5.6 surely over-valuing it as those most badly affected by the Revolution attempted to smuggle their money out of Bolivia. However, studies by Ruiz González (1980) and Walter Gómez quoted in Dunkerley (1984, p. 60) suggests that COMIBOL originally experienced a decline in the proportionate importance of wage costs in spite of rising employment levels, a decline only reversed after 1956 as the deterioration of ore content forced further manning within the mines; and this fact tends to support the view of the Ford, Bacon and Curtis Report.

34. Cf. Barrios (1978) p. 65. Quoted figures rarely break down 'overground' workers into clerical and manual employees, so Whiteheads's (1976) figures for 1967, when face workers, manual workers overground and clerical staff each accounted for roughly a third of COMIBOL's labour force, are invaluable. In view of the disastrous figures for lung disease quoted in Iriarte and above, the comments of successive American observers that Bolivians did not seem to WANT to work underground seem supercilious in the extreme.
35. Nash (1977) gives a vivid picture of pre- and post-Revolutionary housing conditions: see also Alexander's (1958) comments on Huanuni.
36. Whitehead (1976). The national Federation, the executive of 38 plant unions and 29 individual control *obrero* officials together accounted for the 447 trade union officers paid by COMIBOL, receiving on average 20–30 per cent more than their members. Vandyke (1969) has suggested that these paid union officials constituted an in-built layer of 'bureaucrats', and Nash (1982) is sympathetic, but in Whitehead's view their continued election by democratic local and national union assemblies provided a ready means by which the rank and file could assert control: and on the whole, the history of the failure of the MNR's efforts detailed below would seem to bear him out. Distrust of union officers and any possible 'sell-out' seems to have been institutionalised within some mines, notably Siglo XX, thanks perhaps to the combination of post-1952 failures to ameliorate local conditions, as well as the work of the POR.
37. Good descriptions of the real impact of *control obrero* during this period can be found in Whitehead (1976) and Nash (1977, 1979, 1982). Alexander (1958) concurs in the theme of its rapid decline into a form of local union leverage over social and working conditions, as the union lost any ability to influence the direction of the company: Whitehead reports the centrality of verbal attacks on technicians and white-collar workers as 'parasites' to the good name of Escobar, *control obrero* in Siglo XX, among rank and file miners.
38. Malloy (1972) p. 140.
39. The Eder Plan is extensively discussed from the US point of view in Alexander (1958), Zondag (1966), Blasier, Thorn and Wilkie in Malloy and Thorn (1972), and finally Mitchell (1977), where it seems to have provided the decisive input into what Mitchell calls the politics of 'divisive populism'. Eder's conclusion that

    > Factory wages were reported to have been 15% lower in purchasing power in 1955 than in 1951, and the loss was attributed to gains of workers in other sectors of the economy (notably the miners), and not to increased profits of employers. . . .

    (quoted in Mitchell p. 54) sets the tone for all these discussions as it did for local politics, in spite of the evidence of deteriorating conditions within the mines themselves outlined above.

40. See Alexander (1958) and Zondag (1966). Besides experiencing an increase in employment, Zondag claims, the factory sector had also seen a wave of worker takeovers.
41. Dunkerley (1984) p. 91; Mitchell, pp. 64–75.
42. Mitchell is perhaps the best source (though see also Dunkerley pp. 82–92 and 98). Factory workers were not the only ones to suffer from the MNR's drive for greater control over its supporters in the face of deteriorating economic conditions. An attempt to use force to suppress an FSTMB Congress at Colquiri (one of Siles's bases within the mines) in July 1958 was only defeated when delegates escaped under gunfire to San José and reconvened. In 1959, Siles also mobilised a peasant militia in readlines to attack the mines. Control of the MNR's own *comandos especiales*, the force used at Colquiri, was increased during this era by the suppression of all internal democracy within the party.
43. Lora (1977) provides the best source on the strike's success in tapping urban sympathy, Iriarte (1972, p. 46) on the final package negotiated, which represented a defeat for the unofficial strike committee.
44. *Estrategia Socio-economica del Desarrollo Nacional*, quoted in Iriarte (1972) p. 88.
45. Barrios (1978) provides the best account of the hunger strike and its urban links.
46. Lechin had effectively been marginalised from the MNR as Vice-President through a carefully staged 'scandal' and sent into polite exile as Ambassador to Rome. Returning in the 1963 crisis, he led a delegation of strikers to the President, without success, thus further incurring American wrath at the 'scandal' of union power over the MNR. During the subsequent 1963 MNR party convention, the left was denied any voice, and at this point Lechin formed the PRIN.
47. Mitchell, p. 95 and Barrios (1978).
48. Iriarte (1972) cites the Cornell University Report on 406 workers surveyed at Colquiri, of whom 30% were eating less than 2000 calories a day, 57% less than 2500.
49. Cf. Magill (1974). Oil workers had a reputation within the labour movement of being dominated by employees, and relatively docile. Magill's figures for strikes between 1952 and 1967, compiled from press reports, show strikes occurring in the industry only 14 times compared to a total of 139 strikes in the mines, and 72 in factories, though a small labour force would account for much of this difference; more to the point, they participated in only four of the era's general strikes compared to 16 in which miners were involved (although factory workers participated only in two).
50. Dunkerley (1984) p. 226: under Banzer, the private mining sector increased its labour force by 80 per cent and accounted for a fifth of national mineral production.
51. Dunkerley, private comment.
52. Cf. Almaraz Paz, *El poder y la caida*.

53. Lora (1977) gives a full account of the massacre, as of early attempts to organise a clandestine union movement in the mines. See also Barrios (1978) p. 115, and Dunkerley (1984) p. 148.
54. Dunkerley (1984) p. 127: Barrientos conceded mineral rights to such US companies as IMPC and Philips Bros., encouraged the expansion of Gulf Oil's production to the point where by 1967 it accounted for 82 per cent of Bolivia's oil production; and the influx of foreign banks, who controlled 58 per cent of local deposits by 1969. Capital was also leaving the country under Barrientos, with net foreign direct investment of US $27.7 million counterbalanced by repatriated profits of US$320 million.
55. Lora (1972) gives a full account of the Assembly's debates, summarised in English in (1977). Cf. also Dunkerley (1984), Mayorga (1985), and Zabaleta (1974). The reaction of business interests and the right is well-described in Dunkerley (1984) pp. 196–7.

    Dunkerley also gives a summary of the Assembly's composition, dominated by the FSTMB with 38 delegates out of 218: the labour movement as a whole had 123, peasant confederations, chosen from those independent of government control, 23. Klein (1982) complains about the disproportionality of peasant representation.
56. The MNR was given four seats in the first Banzer Cabinet, though Paz himself preferred not to be included: he nonetheless supported the regime.
57. Klaus Alfmann, for instance, a notorious German Nazi whose services to the Banzer and subsequent regimes basically related to repression, was on COMIBOL's books as a 'supplier' (*Latin American Weekly Report*, 28 January 1983).
58. Dunkerley (1984) p. 72.
59. *Propuesto de la politica economica de la COB*, Nov. 1979, pp. 12–13.
60. *Bolivia: 1971-1976, Pueblo, Estado y Iglesia, Testimonios de cristianos* (Lima: CEP, 1976) pp. 104–5.
61. It was a demonstration of striking workers at the nearby Manaco (Bata) factory which triggered the Cochabamba peasant protests. Dunkerley (1984) pp. 211–15 gives a good account of the emergence of independent peasant organisations.
62. Strikes were also prohibited, unauthorised meetings were subject to sanction under martial law, the parties were officially 'in recess' and public administration was placed exclusively in the hands of the armed forces.
63. *Presencia*, 7 May 1976. A survey of miners' wages and conditions in the wake of the strike can be found in the Report of the National Union of Mineworkers' Delegates, *Trade Union and Human Rights in Chile and Bolivia* (London: 1977).
64. Dunkerley (1984) pp. 257–8, gives a full account of the disputes.
65. Dunkerley (1984) pp. 295–6. Garcia Meza wiped out the entire labour force of two small mines.
66. Roberto Laserna, R., 'Movimiento sindical crisis y democracia' in *Elsindicalismo latinamericano en los ochenta* (Santiago: CLACSO, 1985).
67. Idem. 8 July 1983; 16 Sept. 1983; 11 Nov. 1983.
68. Idem.

69. *Financial Times*, 17 May 1984.
70. LAWR, 13 July 1984.
71. The PCB retained three main posts out of its original seven (two vital). LAWR, 14 Sept. 1984 and 28 Sept. 1984.
72. LAWR, 15 Feb. 1985.
73. *Latin American Weekly Report*, 1 May 1985, Idem., 15 Mar. and 29 Mar.

BIBLIOGRAPHY

Alexander, Robert, *The Bolivian National Revolution* (New Brunswick: Rutgers University Press, 1958).

Alexander, Robert, 'Organized Labor and the Bolivian National Revolution', in E.M. Kassalow (ed.), *National Labor Movements in the Post-War World* (Evanston, Illinois: Northwestern University Press, 1963).

Alexander, Robert, *Trotskyism in Latin America* (Stanford: Hoover Institute, 1973).

Almaraz Paz, Sergio, *Bolivia, Requiem para la República* (Montevideo: Biblioteca Marcha, 1980).

Anonymous, *Bolivia: 1971–1976, Pueblo, Estado, y Iglesia, Testimonios de cristianos* (Lima: CEP, 1976).

Barrios de Chungara, Domitila (London: Monthly Review Press, 1978).

Blasier, Cole, 'The United States and the Revolution', in Malloy (1971).

Buechler, H. and Buechler, J-M. 'Conduct and Code: An Analysis of Market Syndicates and Social Revolution in La Paz, Bolivia' (1977), pp. 174–84 of Nash, Corradi and Spalding (see Nash).

Calderón, Fernando, *La politica en las calles* (Cochabamba: CERES, 1983).

Calderón, Fernando and Laserna, Roberto, 'Estado, nacion y movimientos sociales regionales en Bolivia' (Cochabamba: CERES-UNU, 1983).

Calla, Ricardo, 'La encrucijada de la COB, temas del movimiento obrero boliviano, 1982–' (La Paz: CERES-CLACSO-UNU, 1985).

Dunkerley, James, *Bolivia, coup d'etat* (London: Latin American Bureau, 1980).

Dunkerley, James, *Rebellion in the Veins, Political Struggle in Bolivia 1952–82* (London: Verso, 1984).

Escóbar, Filomeno, *Testimonio de un militante obrero* (La Paz: Hisbol, 1984).

Fox, David, *Tin and the Bolivian Economy* (London: Latin American Publications Fund, 1970).

Fox, David, *The Bolivian Tin Mining Industry: Some Geographical and Economic Problems* (London: International Tin Council, 1967).

Inter-American Development Bank, *Economic and Social Progress in Latin America* (Washington: IADB, 1984).

Iriarte, Gregorio, *Galerias de muerte, Vida de los mineros bolivianos* (Montevideo: Tierra Nueva, 1972).

Klein, Herbert, *Bolivia, The Evolution of a Multi-Ethnic Society* (Oxford: Oxford University Press).

Klein Herbert, *Parties and Political Change in Bolivia 1880–1952* (Cambridge: Cambridge University Press, 1969).

Laserna, Roberto, 'Movimiento sindical, crisis y democracia', in CLACSO, *El sindicalismo latinoamericano en los ochenta* (Santiago: CLACSO, 1985).

Lebot, Ivon, L'expérience de cogestion à mayorité ouvrière (1983–84), entre l'utopie et le déclin ouvrier', *Problèmes d' Amérique Latine*, No. 73, 1984.

Llobet Tabolara, Cayetano, 'Apuntes para una historia del movimiento obrero en Bolivia', in P. Gonzalez Casanova (ed.), *Historia del Movimiento Obrero en America Latina* (Mexico: Siglo Veintiuno, 1984).

Lora, Guillermo, *Historia del movimiento obrero boliviano*, 3 vols. (La Paz: Los Amigos del Libro, 1967).

Lora, Guillermo, *Bolivia de la Asamblea Popular al golpe fascista*, (El Yunque, 1972).

Lora, Guillermo, *A History of the Bolivian Labour Movement*, trans. and abridged by Christine and Laurence Whitehead (Cambridge: Cambridge University Press, 1977).

Lora, Guillermo, *Movimiento obrero contemporaneo (1952–1979)* (La Paz: Masas, 1979).

Magill, John, *Labor Unions and Political Socialization: A Study of Bolivian Workers* (New York: Praeger, 1974).

Malloy James, *Beyond the Revolution, Bolivia since 1952* (Pittsburgh: University of Pittsburgh Press, 1971).

Mayorga, René Antonio, 'La crisis del sistema democratico y la central obrera boliviano (COB)', in CLACSO, *El sindicalismo latinoamericano en los ochenta* (Santiago: CLACSO, 1985).

Mitchell, Christopher, *The Legacy of Populism in Bolivia from the MNR to Military Rule* (New York: Praeger, 1977).

Nash, June, 'Worker Participation in the Nationalized Mines of Bolivia, 1952–1972', in idem. (ed), *Popular Participation in Social Change, Collectives and Nationalized Industry* (The Hague: Mouton, 1976).

Nash, June, 'Myth and Ideology in the Andean Highlands' in June Nash, Juan Corradi and Hobart Spalding, *Ideology and Social Change in Latin America* (New York: Gordon & Breach, 1977).

Nash, June, 'Culture, Community and Class Consciousness in Bolivian Tin Mines', *Wilson Centre Working Papers* No. 56 (Washington: 1979).

Nash, June, *We Eat the Mines and the Mines Eat Us* (New York: Columbia University Press, 1979).

Reyes, Simon, *La masacre de San Juan* (Oruro: 1967).

Rojas, Juan and Nash, June, *He agotado mi vida en la mina* (Argentina: Nueva Vision, 1976).

Spalding, Hobart, *Organized Labor in Latin America* (New York: New York University Press, 1977).

Vandyck, Robert, 'Le Mouvement Ouvrier Bolivien et la Révolution Nationale', *Sociologie du Travail*, 1969.

Thorn, R.S., 'The Economic Transition', in Malloy (1971).

Whitehead, Laurence, 'Los trabajadores mineros de Bolivia: Sus tradiciones y perspectivas politicas', *mimeo*, presented to the Bolivia Symposium, Lima, Instituto de Estudios Peruanos, 4–10 July 1976.

Whitehead, Laurence, 'Sobre el radicalismo de los trabajadores mineros de Bolivia', *Revista Mexicana de Sociologia*, Vol. 42, 1 (1980) pp. 1465–96.

Whitehead, Laurence, 'El estado y los intereses seccionales: el caso boliviano', *Estudios Andinos*, Vol. 10 (1974–75) pp. 85–118.

Whitehead, Laurence, 'Miners as Voters: The Electoral Process in Bolivia's Mining Camps', *Journal of Latin American Studies*, 13, 2 (November 1981).

Zavaleta, Mercado, René, *El poder dual en America Latina* (Mexico: Siglo XXI, 1974).

Zavaleta, Mercado, René, 'El proletariado minero en Bolivia', *Revista Mexicana de Sociologia*, Vol. 40, 1 (1978) pp. 517–59.

Zavaleta, Mercado, René, (ed.), *Bolivia, Hoy* (Mexico: Siglo XXI, 1983 including 'Las masas en Noviembre' and 'Forma clase y forma multitud en el proletariado minero' . . .

Zondag, C., *The Bolivian Economy, 1952–1965, the Revolution and its Aftermath* (New York: Praeger, 1966).

6 Chile
Jacqueline Roddick

Chile's is one of the oldest labour movements in Latin America, the Chilean and Mexican labour movements being the first to organise on a nationwide basis, and the first to achieve legal concessions from the State. The Chilean movement harbours the only Communist Party with significant mass support on the continent, formed when the indigeneous Socialist Workers' Party (POS) joined the Third International in 1922 – and also a much broader Marxist tradition expressed in the Communist Party's historical rival, the Socialist Party (now fragmented), and a number of smaller groups. Labour's support played a critical role in the 1970 election of a Marxist President to power, Salvador Allende, and trade unions have been the principal focus of opposition to the military dictatorship which overthrew his government in 1973. But labour's impact on Chilean politics goes much deeper: not only through communists and socialists, but also through their centrist rivals, Radical and Christian Democrat (always concerned to preserve a union base), Chilean labour played a pivotal role in national politics between 1939 and 1973.

Paradoxically, such indications of a strong labour movement coincide with others normally associated with weakness: fundamental political divisions and riotous general strikes. General strikes play an episodic role in the history of many labour movements, but experts usually associate them with the early, 'primitive', stages of trade union formation and perhaps nowhere else in Latin America have they reached the level of predictability visible in Table 6.1. Party domination over the day-to-day activities of the labour movement has been widely recognised;[1] but where elsewhere political divisions have allowed governments to weaken and control labour organisation, in Chile, a multiplicity of parties seems to have preserved labour's role in politics while providing it with a successful defence against government manipulation, from the 1920s to the present day. These two peculiar institutions reinforce one another, with general strikes playing a crucial role whenever sectarianism poses a major threat to working-class unity, bringing mass pressure to bear on the parties to co-operate and providing an occasion for the reforging of

TABLE 6.1 *National* General Strikes and Protest Movements, 1890–1967*
* Regional protests and general strikes, particularly important in the early years, are not listed: see Roddick (1981).

Date	*Organisers*	*Motive*	*Participants*
July 1890	Docks	Anti-inflation: demand pay, pay in sterling, not tokens.	Norte Grande and Valparaíso: docks, railways, Tarapaca nitrates, local industry, bakers. Riots.
May 1907	State railway	Solidarity with striking railmen, own grievances.	Valparaíso-Valdivia railway network, Santiago/Valparaíso foundries, textiles, shoe factories, construction, docks, (Valparaíso), shipyards, ships.
Dec. 1907	Nitrate mines	Erosion of wages and pay in tokens.	Port, urban workers of Iquique 600–2000 miners and families killed.
Apr. 1918 to Aug. 1919	*Asamblea Obrera de Alimentación Nacional*: FOCH, IWW, Democrats Catholic unions	Anti-inflation: demand for lower tax on meat imports, halt to cereal exports, city markets to stop profiteering.	Mass demos in Santiago (60–100 000 in Nov. 1918), Valparaíso (50 000 in Jan. 1919), simultaneously nationwide in August 1919.
Sept. 1919	FOCH, AOAN	Solidarity with striking FOCH brewery workers: protest at attacks on union offices.	Breweries, trams, railways, and shoe workers, bakers, construction, Valparaíso docks, sugar refinery.
Feb. 1926	IWW, anarchists	Against first social security tax.	Print, bakers, shoe and metal workers, tailors, construction.
Mar. 1926	FOCH, UECH, CP	As above.	Tram drivers, white-collar workers.
Jan. 1927	FOCH, IWW,	Solidarity with rail strike.	Failed: some railmen, San Antonio docks.

TABLE 6.1 *continued*

Date	*Organisers*	*Motive*	*Participants*
June 1932		Protest at overthrow of Socialist Republic.	Railmen, Santiago *sindicatos industriales*.
Feb. 1936	FOCH, rail unions	Defence of railmen against mass dismissals, protest at Opposition arrests.	Railmen, Santiago *sindicatos industriales*.
Jan. 1946	CTCH	Protest at police shooting at CTCH demo leaving two dead.	Mining, transport and industry CTCH.
Aug. 1949	University students	Rise in public transport fares.	Civil servants, private sector *empleados*. Riots.
Jan. 1950	CEPCH (union of private sector white-collar workers).	Solidarity with telephone, electricity workers, against Law for Defence of Democracy, further legal curbs on unions.	Telephone, electricity workers: one-day solidarity strikes in banks, insurance and social security offices, hotels, pharmaceuticals, copper mines.
May 1954	CUT	Arrest of CUT President for May day insult to President	Public and private transport, mining, industry, civil service.
July 1955	CUT	Solidarity with State transport strikers, protest turn to dictatorship.	Most CUT members, public and private sectors, many small shops.
Jan. 1956	CUT	Solidarity with copper strike and attack on anti-inflation programme and wage cuts.	Failure: manual workers but few white-collar workers, public or private. Arrests.
Apr. 1957	University students	Campaign against price rises.	Demo, riots in Santiago. CUT arrests.
May 1960	CUT	Defence of Cuba.	Santiago public transport, manual workers.
Mar. 1964	'Gremialismo'	Against Government anti-inflation drive affecting State employees.	State workers, some central civil service, schools, hospitals, municipal workers.

TABLE 6.1 *continued*

Date	*Organisers*	*Motive*	*Participants*
Mar. 1966	CUT	Protest seven deaths when troops fired on striking copper miners at El Salvador.	All copper but Chuqui: nitrate, coal miners, shoe and leather, textile, municipal, some rail, construction.
Nov. 1967	CUT, CEPCH	Against forced savings plan.	96 036 manual workers and 47 247 *empleados*.

SOURCES: Jobet (1955), Barria (1960, 1963, 1970), Barrera (1971), De Shazo (1982).

the fragile political alliances out of which labour history is made. Together they have created an original and durable pattern of organisation, based on competing, cross-sectoral political ties which no government has yet successfully eliminated through repression, capable of a surprising degree of unity in action when it is a question of bringing pressure to bear on the government to adust an unfavourable labour market to workers' advantage, or, more frequently, of holding at bay yet another attempt to resolve the conjunctural crises of underdevelopment at labour's expense.

CLASS IN ACTION: THE 1983–84 PROTEST MOVEMENT

In 1973 the Chilean labour movement sustained the worst massacre in its history: 11 000 killed, according to official figures (and perhaps many more), the creation of several concentration camps, the introduction of mass torture and 'disappearances', a purge of existing unions and a savage cut in wages and living standards. Unemployment trebled, and Chile's consumer price index rose from 235 per cent in the first eight months of 1973 to 500 per cent (officially) or 800 per cent (extra-officially) by the end of the year. The coup was followed by a six-year period when all union life at factory level was frozen and wages were dictated by government decree.

The re-emergence of mass protest in 1983–84 thus provides a fascinating example of the durability of working-class institutions in extreme economic and political conditions; and *ipso facto*, an excellent guide to the labour movement in action.

From liberalisation to crisis

Chile's dictatorship attracted world-wide attention, not only for its ruthlessness but also because of Chile's international role as an experiment in free market policies, pioneering the application of the new anti-interventionist economic ideas associated with Friedman and Hayek, and the associated process of de-industrialisation whose effects are summarised in Table 6.2.

TABLE 6.2 *Manufacturing as a Percentage of Gross Domestic Product*

	(%)		*(%)*
1950	21.7	1970	26.0
1955	21.7	1975	21.5
1960	23.2	1980	22.1
1965	25.8	1982	19.1

SOURCE: ECLA, *Statistical Yearbook for Latin America*, 1983.

The free market experiment had some initial successes in driving down labour costs and increasing productivity (Table 6.3): successes which, in 1979, led the government to try its hand at a drastic reshaping of the existing labour movement, in preparation for which it allowed a degree of local activity and the election of new union officers.[2] In late 1979 the government reintroduced wage bargaining under strict controls, for the first time since the coup.

By 1982, in the face of a world slump, the disappearance of international financial confidence in Chile, and the model's own tendency to promote luxury consumption and speculation at the expense of productive investment, the economy was facing new problems. The result was a second and even more drastic squeeze, perhaps most acute in manufacturing, which by 1983 accounted for only 12.6 per cent of the employed population compared to a historic level nearer 20 per cent (Appendix 2). By 1983 unemployment had reached 22 per cent of the labour force, if one includes those on the government's Minimum Employment Programme, which paid starvation wages; and it was still rising (Appendix 1).

In line with the model's assumption that Chile's unemployment problems could be solved by encouraging a flexible response in the labour market, Chile's Ministry of Labour decreed a new reduction in workers' wages to follow the drastic cuts of 1973–76 and the partial recovery of 1977–81.

TABLE 6.3 *Employment, Salaries and Productivity in Manufacturing 1974–81*

Year	*Employment in Greater Santiago*	*Wages in Manufacturing*	*Labour Cost Per Unit of Production*
1970	254 700*	100.0	100.0
1971	295 200*	109.8@	—
1972	290 800*	143.0@	—
1973	341 000*	143.0@	—
1974	310 700#	49.2^	48.¯
1975	273 100#	40.5^	51.¯
1976	294 400#	48.4^	52.¯
1977	327 800#	63.5^	61.¯
1978	325 900#	69.8^	64.¯
1979	322 900#	69.0^	61.¯
1980	290 000#	73.0^	60.¯
1981	315 800**	———	—
1982	223 500**		
1983	224 400**		

* Ecomanager yearly averages # PREALC figures (Second quarter)
@ Stallings (1978): National level INE figures for wages and salaries in industry, excluding firms with less than 20 workers, deflated by official price index.
^ PREALC version of above, deflated by wholesale price index as an insurance against government misrepresentation.
¯ PREALC calculation.

SOURCES: Ecomanager, *Empleo y salarios*, (Santiago: PREALC, ILO, 1983); Stallings (1978).

Organising the protests

Copper miners reacted dramatically to this threat, coming as it did on top of a cumulative erosion in their own real wages and the loss of many of their confederation's special legal privileges. In spite of a history of conflicts with the pro-Allende labour movement during the early 1970s,[3] they began to explore the possibilities of an alliance with urban workers. Denied access to the national media by censorship laws, they made contact with union organisations in urban factories and construction sites, using contacts in the *Coordinadora Nacional Sindical*, a loose trade union federation tapping the political networks of communists, socialists, and left-wing Christian Democrats, which itself had long-standing links with one of the unions in the El Teniente mine. These links had already been activated well before the protests. Trade union officers in many Santiago factories had been expressing frustration over their inability to use the government's new labour laws as a satisfactory basis for negotiation since 1981 when textile workers made the first call for a national general strike. During 1982, the calls had been repeated by other plants: as a step in this direction, union activists in Santiago were pleased to accept copper miners' solidarity, and the *Confederación de Trabajadores de Cobre* formally joined a committee organised to support striking metal workers.

In practice, the CNS was also able to offer significant middle-class support, particularly among university students and labour lawyers, and even more vital support in the mushrooming shanty-towns among the unemployed.

The government's response was to send troops into the mining areas. This and other pressures led to the general strike orginally planned for 11 May 1983, being 'redesignated' the first in a series of national days of protest. The 11 May mobilisation was a success, with partial stoppages of bus transport in Santiago, Valparaiso and Concepción, token stoppages, meetings or canteen boycotts in factories, mines and banks, protests by university students and sit-ins by law students and Opposition lawyers in Chile's courts. Forty per cent of those employed on the government's Minimum Employment Programme failed to show up for work. Barricades were set up by the young unemployed in poorer neighbourhoods, not only in the three major cities, but also in smaller towns such as Arica, La Serena and San Antonio, and in the evening women in all classes of neighbourhood beat their empty pots in a deliberate echo of a tactic which had played its part in the overthrow of Allende.

The successes of May were repeated in June, with protests in copper and coal mines, print shops, engineering and metalwork, a few textile factories (one of the sectors hardest hit by the free market era) and some pharmaceutical laboratories. Barricades multiplied in the poorer areas of Santiago and protests spread to Antofagasta, Los Andes, Rancagua, Chillan, Temuco, Osorno, Valdivia and Punta Arenas – small towns where the risks to protesters were much greater.

The protests were originally organised by an *ad hoc* co-ordinating front of copper miners, Santiago factories, construction sites, and service workers, called the *Comando Nacional de Trabajo*. The CNT was created in March 1983 as an organisation 'without hegemonic pretensions' or 'global doctrine', that is, deliberately distanced from political disputes between rival networks, although the movement had the co-operation of the left-wing CNS.[4] By the second national protest, the extent of mass support had forced the four major political groupings then dividing the contemporary labour movement to join forces formally as constituents of the CNT: the CNS, the CEPCH (representing white-collar workers), the radical Christian FUT, and even the bitterly anti-communist, AFL-CIO-financed *Union Democratica de Trabajadores*. Independent trade unionists representing factories not affiliated to any of these competing factions now formed the *Movimiento Sindical Unitario*, in an attempt to force the larger organisations to recognise their right to participate, and perhaps also to create a political network of their own.

The protests thus saw an eclipse of calls for a 'less political' labour movement such as had become increasingly powerful over the long years without mass mobilisation, and a reassertion of the primacy of traditional political networks with their traditional ability to co-operate across political boundaries – partially lost during the early post-coup years, when union élites saw their ties to rank and file workers severed, and were relying basically on international contacts to provide them with protection against arrest or 'disappearance'.

The climax of the monthly protests came with a real general strike in October 1984, when police reports estimated that 45 per cent of manufacturing industry was affected, and public transport virtually stopped in Chile's major towns. The government's response was a return to policies of mass repression, particularly in the shanty towns, with systematic round-ups of all males between 16 and 60 and the creation of new concentration camps in the bleak northern desert for political activists. Instances of assassination of the regime's political and trade union opponents increased.

The outcome

Temporarily, the protests came to an end. They had revealed the weaknesses of the contemporary labour movement as well as its strengths. Copper miners' militancy subsided quickly, after a premature general strike of the mines triggered by the arrest of their President, Rodolfo Seguel, was broken by a government programme of mass dismissals which the unions were too weak to counter. Workers in urban industry were reluctant to commit themselves to strike action in the face of rates of unemployment which, for this sector, had risen from 11 per cent in the last three months of 1981 to

25 per cent in the first three months of 1983: so that other forms of protest were popular, such as canteen boycotts, a march round the firm's perimeter, or leaving work collectively an hour early to join the protest. Had the strike of copper miners in June 1983 coincided with the general strike of urban areas in October 1984, the protests might have been more successful. Failure in turn eased the pressure on anti-communist factions to preserve working-class unity at the cost of political principles and US economic support: the UDT took the final step of transforming itself from a political grouping to a self-styled 'union central', the *Central Democratica de Trabajadores*, in 1984, thus formalising labour's existing divisions.

Nevertheless, ten years after a coup which had deliberately set out to eliminate left-wing activists, socialists, communists, MIRistas, or even Christian Democrats, the protests were a demonstration of the continued life in these political networks, remarkable most of all for their success in mobilising those sectors with least economic muscle: workers in the MEP, housewives, and the young unemployed.

The protests did achieve a repeal of further wage cuts, minor modifications to the new Labour Code, and minor modifications in tariff policy. They did not achieve their organisers' aim, the removal of the Pinochet regime, though they did succeed in forcing it into some temporary and illusory concessions towards democratisation. Nor did they eliminate free market economists from government (perhaps because Chile's contemporary dependence on the IMF, itself committed to similar ideas, set limits to the government's own freedom of action here). Nonetheless, they were a defeat for the free market philosophy behind the government's labour policy. By 1984, its most immediate outcome had been, not the predicted depoliticisation of labour projected by Hayek himself, but a reassertion of working-class politics and a clear indication of growing support, particularly in the shanty towns, for the Communist Party and the MIR.

One result was thus a government retreat from some of its labour laws' more extreme propositions, an indication of waning government faith in purely free market techniques of labour control. Nevertheless, the government retained its legal prohibition of sectoral bargaining, union rights to negotiate conditions of work or management donations to union organisation – all elements in the 1979 Labour Code.

The protests' longer-term impact is more problematic. It is worth remembering that the leading proponent of a revolutionary general strike in the 1950s – a Catholic trade unionist by the name of Clotario Blest – traces his own formative experience back to childhood memories of the Santiago Meat Riot of 1906, itself a failure. Given a similar time scale, the dual lessons of the urban crowd's potential power and the repressive role of the State, embodied in the 1983–84 protests, as in so many of their predecessors, will finally bear fruit only when the younger siblings of the young unemployed take up positions of power within the labour movement in 2030.

THE FORMATION OF A MOVEMENT

The history of Chilean labour as a nationally effective movement begins with a general strike, introducing a pattern of action and reaction which has changed only marginally in the succeeding century. In July 1890, faced with a threatened cut in real wages, dockers in the northern port of Iquique went on strike. They made contact with miners in the nitrate camp in the hinterland, some of whom marched down to the port to join in mass demonstrations which quickly became riots. Other local workers joined in: from railways, bakeries, a local foundry. Miners in the surrounding desert began to attack company property.

The strike spread quickly to other ports: Arica, Antofagasta, southern Valparaíso, each repeating the same pattern of mass demonstrations and riots, and a blossoming of local strikes outside the port. Antofagasta's railway maintenance yard came out, triggering a local strike wave involving 3000 workers, and 15–20 000 joined the dock strike in Valparaíso and Viña del Mar. The government felt compelled to intervene. Troops killed 24 in Antofagasta and 70 in Valparaíso. Further army units were brought north to subdue the nitrate fields and south to patrol the coal fields in Lota and Coronel, as well as Central Valley railway construction camps. In spite of them, the strike spread southwards in small eddies, taken up by rail and gas workers in Santiago and the perennially militant bakers in Quillota, Talca and Concepción. In Iquique, Valparaiso and Antofagasta, provincial Intendentes were persuaded to chair negotiations between workers and anti-union employers.[5]

The 1890 strike was a spontaneous movement, since union organisation, whether in the nitrate north or the urban south, was still embryonic.[6] What made it possible?

Origins: 1800–90

'Proletarianisation' is an awkward term in the Chilean context. Constant frontier wars against the Araucanian Indians created a 'free labour' force of sorts here as early as the seventeenth century, of discarded soldiers condemned to vagabondage while the local ruling class imported Indian captives to fill the role of *inquilinos*, tied labour, on their *latifundia*. In vivid contrast to the relatively self-contained rural societies from which labour had to be prised elsewhere, Chile thus had a mobile labour force available for early experiments in mining silver and copper for the world economy – whether employed as self-employed prospectors or their salaried hands. Chile's first 'labour rebellion' broke out in the mining village of Chanarcillos in 1834, and labour's first political involvements date from the regional rebellions of the 1850s, forerunners of the middle-class Radical Party, when miners and artisans were mustered to support the bid for power of a regional bourgeoisie.

By mid-century, these cohorts of floating male labour were being swollen by the expulsion of *inquilinos* as agriculture was rationalised, while they were simultaneously being driven out of the traditional mining areas by government policies of military-style coercion. Emigrants left for Argentina, Australia and California, returning with new ideas of trade unionism and a nationalised version of prevailing international political ideologies. Mobile 'rotos', 'broken men', as they were known to the élite, provided the labour needed for the pioneering development of natural nitrate exports in neighbouring Peru and Bolivia in the 1870s, together with a core of international experience and a tradition of easy migration into which new peasant recruits from the Central Valley could be grafted, a proto-proletarian culture spreading news and ideas the length of the country, which by 1890 was quite capable of keeping miners in touch with dock-workers and seamen and both in touch with the Central Valley.

Labour relations slowly began to emerge from their traditional semi-feudal and militarised patterns around the middle of the nineteenth century, as local and foreign entrepreneurs took advantage of this flexible labour supply to service a boom in agricultural and mineral exports. The transition was slow, and marked with ruling class experiments with tied labour: however, by the 1870s, alongside its already lively artisan tradition, Chile was developing a modern small industrial sector.[8] Scattered relatively large establishments (50–200 workers in the case of factories, several hundred in the ports and railways) coexisted with much smaller firms still rooted in the colonial artisanate. Women were the most immediate victims of this process, as a predominantly rural, female artisan labour force was displaced by one which was predominantly urban and male (Appendix 4).[9] But urban artisans were also slowly losing their traditional colonial prerogatives as they faced competition from foreign 'masters' imported by the élite, and gradually declined into mere employees. In the face of such threats, in the 1860s, they took the first steps towards the creation of a labour movement: political clubs, mutual insurance and friendly societies, night schools and choral and theatre groups.[10] By the late 1870s the movement was well-established enough to trigger imitative organisations among white-collar workers and Catholics. Chile's first trade unions were born under this mutualist umbrella in the last two decades of the nineteenth century, and mutualist societies continued to provide the backbone of the Democratic Party until the 1930s, taking an active role in the 1950 white-collar workers' strike.

The heroic age: 1880–20

A decline in mineral and agricultural exports in the 1870s and consequent economic crisis was solved at the expense of Peru and Bolivia, as Chile capitalised on its expatriates' dominance of the Peruvian and Bolivian nitrate fields to justify a war of annexation of the nitrate territories in 1879, mobilising the remains of its migrant population to give it an easy victory. In spite of its lost exports, the country thus preserved its relationship with the world economy, at the cost of losing any indigenous control over its new principal export to foreign entrepreneurs.

The new nitrate mining enclave injected a degree of renewed prosperity into the old economy, without dramatic changes: the population of the newly annexed Norte Grande never represented more than 8 per cent of Chile's total, while the abysmally low wages paid to its workers (combined with foreign companies' preferences for imports) made it a poor market for Chilean manufactures.[11]

For the labour movement, these were crucial years. The first secular and revolutionary political organisations began appearing in the 1880s.[12] The 1890 strike movement was repeated in 1906–07, with more localised region-wide general strikes becoming a recognised tactic in labour struggles in the intervening years (Table 6.1). The first successes in collective bargaining were achieved in the docks, print, shoe and leather industries and metalworking, where unions emerged with sufficient rank and file support to organise on a city-wide basis and call and win a strike. By the end of the second decade of the twentieth century, the docks had briefly achieved a national organisation, thanks to the anarcho-syndicalist IWW; the plight of nitrate miners in the Norte Grande and their massacre by troops at Iquique in 1907, where 600–3000 died, had become a nationally-recognised symbol of workers' oppression; and the meat-producing region in Chile's furthest southern province, Magellanes, was so well-integrated into the national movement as to be among the best-unionised sectors in the country. White-collar workers such as clerks and teachers had also begun to organise, an indication of the impact which labour struggles were having on the national imagination.[13]

However, employers were convinced proponents of *laissez-faire* and bitterly anti-union. Nitrate employers had a reputation for never honouring a strike settlement, an attitude made possible by the absence of alternative work in the nitrate areas and the semi-military discipline of the camps.[14] In urban areas, union efforts to negotiate were met with attempted lock-outs: by 1906, the union threat was serious enough for employers in the semi-artisan trades (baking, printing, shoemaking, tanning and metalwork) to form counter organisations. As the fourth great wave of unionisation reached its peak at the end of the First World War, Valparaíso merchants and foreign shipping companies joined forces to organise a successful lock-out of the IWW in the ports, a victory which laid the basis for a new national union of employers including the coal mines, bakers, shoe and leather factories, copper mines and others.[15]

Union gains during this period were fragile, extraordinarily dependent on cyclical booms and depressions in the nitrate economy, with waves of organisation and successful strikes followed by periods when unions virtually disappeared, thanks to renewed government repression or the re-emergence of urban unemployment as mines closed and miners were deported south. This underlying cyclical pattern was repeated in the upsurges of 1880–90, 1906–07, 1911–14, and 1917–19, each followed by a partial collapse. Political parties, not unions, provided the basic continuity within the labour movement, suffering at worst only a slow process of ideological evolution, as Catholic syndicalism replaced Catholic mutualism, anarchosyndicalism and the IWW the more primitive anarchism of the 1890s, and the Democratic Party split to provide Chile with its first mass socialist and Marxist party, the POS (*Partido Obrero Socialista*) founded by a prominent Democrat printer and journalist, Luis Emilio Recabarren, in the traumatic aftermath of the 1906–07 defeats, and accepted as a member of the Third International in 1922. It was the Democratic Party, rather than any single union organisation, which first provided the labour movement with a national framework of debate in the early years of the century, as Recabarren founded a network of party newspapers: a tradition continued by the POS, which took over and adapted a Catholic federation of railway workers, the FOCH, in 1914, opening it up to other trades and successfully creating Chile's first national trade union confederation, with support among railway workers, nitrate miners, and factory operatives in Santiago and Valparaiso. By the end of the First World War, Chile's labour movement boasted two national trade union confederations, each with convincing support in many different sectors extending throughout the country, the basis for adhesion to one or the other being political loyalty: support for the Democrats or the POS in the case of the FOCH, and for anarcho-syndicalism in the case of the IWW.

The era of institutionalisation: 1914–27

Just as parties and political activists provided the core of Chile's labour movement, so too its behaviour has to be understood in terms of the central issue in their debates: the extent to which workers could trust their employers and the existing State. Catholic unionism stood for mutual trust and harmony between employer and worker: Democrats and Catholics alike were convinced that the best tactic was to elect sympathetic representatives to parliament, given Chile's formally democratic political system.[16] But the Democratic Party was quickly swallowed up by the temptations of élite politics, since the shifting political alliances which underlay governments in this era had no objection to including even a formally populist party in the spoils of government. Democratic Party connivance in the resolution of the 1906 Central Valley general strike to the government's advantage, showed that influence with government could quite easily become merely a new channel for government control.

Anarchists held out for revolution, the elimination of a political system which was clearly corrupt, and workers' management of production. Employer hostility and the willingness of both employers and governments to resort to violence gave them the better of the argument, and they were the first to institutionalise commemoration of the Iquique massacre, throwing a bomb over the wall of a Santiago convent on 21 December 1911. But anarchism failed to solve labour's underlying economic weaknesses, as the dock lock-out of 1921 clearly showed: work-place and sectoral organisation were inherently too fragile during this period to meet the anarchists' demands.

The credit for successfully resolving this dilemma belongs to Recabarren, partly because, although a Democrat, his integrity was a by-word, and in part because he was the inventor of a middle way. The POS, a reformed parliamentary party, was committed to a revolutionary ideology and thus to preserving its political independence once elected. But it was nonetheless equally committed to using mass mobilisation as a device for pressuring governments to intervene in labour disputes in favour of the workers, and even had some success. Governments were easing their way towards a belief that some intervention in the labour market was desirable: a Labour Office created to centralise information on the new organisations, created in 1907, had begun to investigate work accidents by 1916. By 1917, an executive decree had given provincial *Intendentes* the formal right to chair a 'conciliation committee' overseeing negotiations between employers and striking workers, acting as mediator and as co-signatory to the eventual agreement. By 1918–19, through participating in such 'conciliation committees', the POS-dominated *Federación Obrera de Chile* (FOCH) had achieved recognition for textile workers, State telegraph workers, the *Compañía Chilena de Tabacos* and the sugar refinery of Vina del Mar: about half of all mediation cases in the 1918–19 period involved FOCH members, marking a deliberate difference in outlook between this organisation and its rival, the anarcho-syndicalist IWW, still strongly committed to workers' organising and negotiating with employers independent of any assistance from the State.

Simultaneously, Recabarren carefully preserved the POS's commitment to revolutionary ideals. While anarchists concentrated on the stronger skilled trades, it was the POS which took on the difficult task of organising the poorest and most powerless sectors of the Chilean working-class: nitrate miners in the north, brewery workers, some of the trades dominated by women, and finally peasants in the Central Valley. Many Chilean workers throughout the country had experience of the appalling conditions in the nitrate north, given existing patterns of migration: but employer control over the camp sites, the absence of alternative forms of employment, and the savagery of government repression, made the camps extremely difficult to organise successfully. The POS's dedication to the nitrate workers' cause enshrined its status as the touchstone of true revolutionary traditions for decades to come.

More to the point, Recabarren laid the basis for a resolution of Chile's political schisms by formalising the political alliances which had already begun to underpin labour's May Day celebrations and general strikes, and extending their range beyond the tacit tolerance of anarchists and Democrats for one anothers activists in the manual trades, to include the much more conservative Catholics and middle-class sectors such as clerks and primary school teachers. A man who disliked sectarianism,[17] he had after all built the 'revolutionary' FOCH on the foundations of a conservative federation of railway workers originally created in 1909, encouraging his own activists to join the organisation as Catholic supporters became disillusioned: and as late as 1920, Democrats remained a strong element within its membership, particularly in the south. The FOCH's greatest political success was the *Asamblea de Alimentación Nacional* and its 'Hunger Marches' of 1918–19: a series of simultaneous mass demonstrations in all Chile's major cities, organised by a committee which included POS members, Democrats, anarchists, members of the youth wing of the Radical Party and Catholic trade unionists, the first comprehensive political alliance in the labour movement's history. The 1918–19 demonstrations transformed Chile's traditional pattern of strike-plus-riot into a peaceful mass protest, reducing the risks of massive bloodshed while still containing the threat of revolution. Practically, they forced the Chilean élite into a final abandonment of its *laissez-faire* position and the acceptance of the principle of State regulation of labour disputes. When Arturo Alessandri promised legalised trade unionism under close government control in the course of a markedly demagogic campaign for the Presidency in 1920, he and his conservative rival were already in agreement as to the basic principle.

By the 1920s, the fundamental character of Chile's labour movement was formed. Still fragile at the point of production, its great strength was its ability to compensate for this vulnerability through a series of criss-crossing social and political networks which existed outside the factory, geared to mutual insurance schemes at one extreme (colonised by the Democrats) and at the other, general strikes pillaged from the anarchist CUT philosophy by socialists to bring pressure on the State to alter conditions in the labour market, but drawing on the participation of all tendencies. Political activists provided a core of organisers able to survive the impact of successive waves of repression and recession, and regroup forces when the economy provided a new upturn. The movement's practical cohesion at national level was secured by temporary united fronts of its different political tendencies, spontaneous in the general strikes of the early years, formalised on the initiative of Recabarren and the FOCH after 1918. Each of these fronts had its own rationale and each was relatively short-lived, but the pattern of a union movement held together by constantly recreated alliances was nonetheless set by 1920.

The introduction of legal unions and government-administered medical and pension schemes was bound to have an impact on the character of the movement, but in practice, the transition to a new order had little real impact for a long period on the factory floor. Not until the 1940s was something akin to a stable industrial relations system in place, and not until the 1950s can this be said to have won total acceptance from government and employers – if indeed it ever did.

The slowness with which promised concessions materialised does much to explain the most remarkable feature of Chile's experience: the stubborn refusal of organised labour to make permanent concessions of political loyalty in return for its institutional gains: a state of affairs with parallels in Peru and Bolivia (both much poorer countries) but which stands in sharp contrast to the experience of other industrialising economies in Latin America, like Argentina, Brazil and Mexico. Legal unions were promised in 1920 by both Alessandri and his conservative rival for the Presidency, delivered as legislation only with the aid of a military coup in 1924, and implemented only with the intervention of an outright military dictatorship under Colonel Ibáñez del Campo in 1928–29. Recabarren's heirs, the Communist Party, and anarcho-syndicalists alike opposed legal unionism during the crucial post-dictatorship era. The new legal unions turned instead to the Socialist Party, a Marxist rival to the communists equally formed in Recabarren's image: they met a hostile government, though one still determined to preserve a legal framework for industrial relations alongside its network of police informers, in the administration of the returning President Alessandri between 1932 and 1939.

The proper institutionalisation of labour relations under conditions relatively free from repression thus had to wait for the *Frente Popular* of 1939, a government in which both Communist and Socialist Parties were junior partners, dedicated to the creation of a modern industrial economy: the only possible means of co-opting the political matrix (given its proven ability to survive all attempts to replace it in the intervening two decades) and the result of an initiative stemming from the Communist Party through the medium of an alliance with the Radicals, in true Recabarren tradition.

CHANGING GOVERNMENT POLICIES TOWARDS LABOUR: THE CYCLE OF STATE CONTROL, *LAISSEZ-FAIRE*, STATE CONTROL AND *LAISSEZ-FAIRE*

Over the century of Chilean labour's effective organisation, government and employer attitudes towards labour have altered more than once, as both attempted to reassert managerial control over the rebellious *rotos* and their revolutionary ideas – though repression has been a permanent theme. Government failures to dominate labour ideologically and politically have given Chilean labour history a marked tendency towards *deja vu*: four great waves of repression (1906–07, 1925–29, 1948–50, 1973–76), three of them specifically intended to eliminate revolutionary unionism; five successive attempts to create a populist or corporatist basis for concensus between 1920 and 1940, coinciding with the introduction of legal unionism; four attempts after the outbreak of the Cold War to contain the 'communist virus' by splitting the labour movement into competing central federations, divided along ideological lines;[18] a kaleidoscope of different varieties of State and societal corporatism, as State intervention in the economy became fashionable, from the neo-fascist project which accompanied the introduction of legal unionism in 1927–29 to two distinct post-coup corporatist projects which were finally displaced by a 'free market' takeover of the Ministry of Labour in January 1979.[19] Perhaps the most ironic instance is the present cycle, in which the post-coup regime of General Pinochet has returned once again to the *laissez-faire* ethos within which the political matrix was born.

From State control to *laissez faire*: 1890

In 1890, at the time of the first general strike, Chile was a typical Latin American 'outward-looking' economy and had been so since the beginning of the century. Now dependent on world markets for a single export, natural nitrates (earlier mineral exports having failed for lack of competitive local technology) its ruling class was notionally at least committed to free trade. A free market ideology thus provided the government's first point of reference as it sought for a means of combating the newly emerging threat of revolutionary trade unionism. Casting a sharp eye on the extent to which post-colonial governments had reproduced the old guild system in their attempts to regulate the dock labour force, which was of strategic economic significance, a contemporary economist commented,

> the strikes have been promoted by workers who have been administratively organised by the State . . . The authorities have secured these workers a monopoly . . .[20]

suggesting that the simplest solution was to end government regulation of employment in the docks. Congress dutifully passed a law abolishing all guilds in September 1890.

Three decades of a strictly 'free', unregulated, labour market followed, backed up by the use of secret agents to spy on unions and of troops to break strikes. This first *laissez-faire* era saw an average of one regional general strike a year, and the consolidation of a radical labour movement dependent on combined political and trade union forms of action, whose most important historical reference point would hereafter be the massacre of hundreds (in popular memory, thousands) of passively protesting nitrate miners, wives and children by government troops at Santa Maria de Iquique in 1907: an event first commemorated by an anarchist bomb in Santiago in 1911, subsequently remembered by FOCH and anarchist supporters alike in separate or combined anniversary demonstrations, and one which played its part in confirming the hold of the POS and its Marxist heritage on labour's imagination. As a strategy for containing Chilean labour, *laissez-faire* had demonstrably failed.

The abandonment of *laissez-faire*: 1916–30

Thus, following the third successive wave of mass mobilisation and union organisation between 1916–19, culminating in the *Asamblea de Alimentación Nacional* and its series of mass 'Hunger Marches' in all Chile's major towns, Chilean governments took their first steps towards legalised unions and the introduction of State mediation in labour disputes, the first legal framework for industrial relations of this kind on the continent.[21] The delays which accompanied this process provide the best explanation for the consolidation of the political matrix, and the failure of successive efforts to build a populist movement to strike any local roots.

The 1920–39 period was one of constant economic and political upheaval, triggered by the collapse of the world market for nitrates in the years after 1919, compounded ten years later by the Great Depression itself. Economic crisis led to demands for broad reforms. In 1920 Alessandri was elected to the Presidency after a campaign chiefly notably for its demagogic quality: in 1924, following his failure to push reforms through parliament, he was replaced by a military junta, which in turn suffered an internal coup in early 1925, leading to the exiled President's return. In 1927 his successor as President was replaced by a military dictator, Colonel Ibáñez del Campo. In 1931 Ibáñez himself fell victim to the Great Depression, to be replaced by a new junta, which finally called free elections, returning Alessandri to power. Economic experiments with protectionism and State intervention in the economy went hand in hand with experiments in new labour legislation, falling victim likewise to the prevailing instability until the Popular Front of 1939. Ibáñez himself flirted with import-substitution and State investment in industry: tariff protection was a central plank in the programme of recovery from the Great Depression instituted by Alessandri during his second term.[22] The election of a new Radical President in 1939 and the creation of a State Investment Corporation designed to channel funds into Chilean industry marked a watershed in economic terms, as well as in industrial relations.

Throughout this period, labour's now evident political muscle was constantly appealed to by successive reformist governments, looking for a make-weight to help them introduce reforms in the face of the profound conservatism of the existing ruling élite. There were to be five separate such bids, in 1920, 1924–25, 1928–29, and 1932, ending with the *Frente Popular* in 1939. On three occasions the major political tendencies of the old matrix seemed momentarily to lose control of their supporters to one of these populist initiatives: and had any of them been successful, the history of the matrix might have come to an abrupt end in the formation of new political loyalties such as those which coalesced in Argentina around Peron.

The first was Alessandri's electoral campaign, backed by an alliance of anti-Catholic Liberals, Radicals and Democrats – thus including one labour party prominent in the FOCH, the Democrats, who virtually controlled that era's mutualist societies. An able orator,

Alessandri set out to mobilise the urban crowd on his own behalf in a fashion which terrified the ruling class. Though Recabarren stood against him as a candidate, there is evidence of FOCH support for his campaign in the south, and his electoral alliance produced a credible general strike in Santiago when faced with the prospect of being cheated of its victory due to conservative electoral fraud.[23]

The second occasion was provided by the successive coups of September 1924 and January 1925, when junior officers forced the long-promised labour laws through Congress (combining Alessandri's draft bill with that of his conservative opponent in the process) and toured the country promising workers participation in a Constituent Assembly to draw up a new Constitution. The anarcho-syndicalist IWW remained hostile, though as a result it was to lose some of its own supporters to the umbrella *Unión de Asalariados de Chile* (USRACH) during the heady days of 1925. The FOCH and Communist Party were divided. A joint demonstration against militarism in 1924 organised by Recabarren and Alessandri's supporters attracted only a handful of people. Following Recabarren's subsequent suicide, the FOCH gave total support to the 1925 coup, only to see the Constituent Assembly re-emerge as a committee of representatives of the traditional élite parties, with a few FOCH members for form's sake. The FOCH and the communists subsequently supported the Presidential campaign of a young army surgeon close to Ibáñez in 1925, under the banner of the USRACH.[24]

The third occasion was the Socialist Republic of 1932, when Marmaduke Grove, one of the original junior officers of 1924–25, with a record of opposition to the intervening military dictatorship of Ibáñez, briefly took power in the depths of the Depression and offered workers such basic populist measures as temporary employment in relief works and the release of sewing machines pawned to the *Caja de Credito Popular* – and mobilised working-class support throughout the country for the ten-day duration of his regime, which ended with yet another general strike.[25]

In all cases but the Socialist Republic, governments' limited real concessions and the early reappearance of repression tended to push workers back into the arms of their traditional parties. Alessandri's first Presidency was compromised by the massacre of striking nitrate miners at San Gregorio and his connivance in employers' lock-outs in the docks and in the coal region in 1921; his second, by the massacre of demonstrating peasants at Ranquil, the murder of a communist primary school teacher by the secret police, and attacks on striking railway workers which ultimately triggered the 1936 general strike. The rule of 'progressive' junior officers was marred by the massacre of 6–800 striking nitrate miners at La Coruña in 1925, although the southern labour movement carried on for a time as though nothing had happened: long-term prospects of a labour-military alliance were finally torpedoed by mass dismissals in the State sector, which precipitated a final severing of the FOCH's ties with the military in 1926. Ibanez's dictatorship began with a wave of arrests of labour activists, and his attempts to use government backing of the new legal unions in 1929–31 as a device to consolidate political support had little success, in spite of a wave of official enthusiasm for Mussolini-style corporatism: only two of the new plant-based unions or *sindicatos industriales* supported his short-lived *Confederación Republicana de Acción Civica*.[26] In Chile, attempts to organise a Brazilian or Argentinian-style State corporatist model were doomed by the prior existence of strong traditions of organisation among workers as well as employers, not easily displaced by new governmental forms – particularly as the State was unable to offer substantial and durable economic concessions, in the face of continued employer hostility and its own resources, necessarily limited on the cusp between the end of the nitrate economy and the post-1929 collapse of world trade.

Labour's experience of political involvement during the 1920–40 period underlined the need for a specifically political dimension to labour organisation, while vividly confirming the old anarchist argument that above all, labour must preserve its political independence. Thus the initial impact of these political events was to harden ideological divisions within the labour movement, as anarcho-syndicalists and communists alike, during the heady revolutionary days of the 1920s, fell back upon doctrine to provide a guide to political strategy in a rapidly shifting situation: and the first consequence of government flirtation with a new legal industrial relations system was to generate an era of non-co-operation within the matrix, reaching its nadir in the determination of the IWW and the FOCH to hold separate protest strikes against the renewed threat of a military dictatorship in 1926. The early 1930s saw a period of reaction on the part of the FOCH and the Communist Party to any alignment with bourgeois politicians, which took the form of dedicated submission to the Third International, and open adherence to its rejection of any political alliance. Whatever the importance of external influences here, the new policy drew much of its local relevance from the bitter experience of the FOCH in earlier alliances with progressive junior officers. Both anarcho-syndicalists and communists opposed the fledgling legal unions established in Chile's mining and manufacturing industries after 1929. The 1926–35 period was thus a period when labour's traditional parties went out of their way to distance themselves from the temptation of the new legal system.

Paradoxically the government with the longest impact on working-class politics was to be the one with the shortest life-span. The mobilisation of teachers, railway workers, legal *sindicatos industriales* and others in a self-styled Revolutionary Trade Union Alliance to support the Socialist Republic laid the basis for the creation of Chile's second Marxist party, the Socialist Party, in 1933. The space left vacant by the refusal of communists and anarcho-syndicalists to come to terms with legal unionism before 1936, preserving independence at the cost of sacrificing the advantages of State protection, was thus filled by a typical political tendency of the old matrix, revolutionary in its pronouncements, geared to ideology rather than to any cult of the charismatic populist leader, drawing together a loose alliance of workers from many different social layers, and finding them frequently among those who already had substantial political experience.[27]

The interventionist Labour Code

The seven bills passed on the insistence of the armed forces in 1924 were an amalgam of Conservative (progressive Catholic) and Liberal (*Alessandrista*) solutions to labour militancy drawn up for the 1920 Presidential election. One, drawing on *Res Novarum*,[28] aimed to mobilise employers' paternalist instincts while strengthening their personal control over their unionised labour force. The other aimed to subject unions to the supervision of the State. Both envisaged a role for legal strikes, strictly circumscribed, but no strike fund, and no union right to contract its own employees. One could argue that their coincidence in general aims if not means demonstrates the existence of a substantial, authoritarian concensus within the Chilean ruling élite, the basic parameters of which did not change for 50 years.

The amalgam gave pride of place to that hope of fragmenting an already nationally-united labour movement which was the bedrock of the Catholic project: instituting plant unions (*sindicatos industriales*) financed out of employers' profits, which enjoyed an automatic closed shop, but were forbidden to form sectoral federations with any bargaining power. Voluntary organisations representing not entire factories, but only workers in the same or similar trades (*sindicatos profesionales*) were also allowed: the Liberal and *Alessandrista* solution, these would now inevitably appeal only to the very strong or the very weak, and the combination of the two projects effectively institutionalised the plant union and fragmented bargaining as the norm in Chile's new legal industrial relations system.

Employers' authority was further reinforced by the creation of a deliberate split between manual workers and *empleados* (clerks), the latter forbidden to join the *sindicato industrial*, though they could form *sindicatos profesionales* and enjoyed a rather better individual contract of employment (the right to 30 days notice of dismissal instead of six, a retirement or redundancy bonus, and an annual personal bonus out of employers' profits). All State employees, manual or *empleado*, were simply forbidden to form unions.

This deliberately atomised industrial relations scheme was reinforced by the creation of separate social security schemes for different categories of workers, each with different benefits.[29] Its counterpart – the Liberal solution – was a heavy handed State intervention in collective bargaining centralised through the Ministry of Labour from which unions had to secure permission before they could legally register or negotiate, which supervised their finances and elections, and ran the obligatory conciliation service which now replaced the purely voluntary mediation schema of 1917: tripartite committees chaired by the local Inspector and peopled with Ministry-determined representatives of unions and employers' organisations. Only the Ministry's *Junta de Conciliación* could give permission for a 'legal' strike, which now guaranteed the strikers immunity from dismissal for its duration. No strike funds were allowed.

However, since the new laws failed to recognise that workers might sometimes have to strike a second time to enforce a settlement already signed by the employer, illegal strikes persisted under the new regime (Table 6.4). In 1934 there were 11 illegal to two legal strikes: the heavily repressed years of 1947–50 saw an average of 82 illegal strikes to 39 legal, and when union activity became less restricted in 1950–53, the rate rose from twice to more than three times the legal numbers, 176 to 55.[30]

Penetration of the new Code

In practice, Alessandri's post-1925 return to power failed to secure anything more than an experiment in implementing the new Code

TABLE 6.4 *Legal and Illegal Strikes, 1961–73 (1000 workers)*

	1961	*1963*	*1967*	*1970*	*1973*
TOTAL LEGAL AND ILLEGAL					
No./strikes	973	676	2464	1623	2230
No./workers	257.2	356.4	460.9	502.5	920.7
PRIVATE SECTOR ONLY					
Legal strikes	430	64	1240	203	21
No./workers	32.5	19.4	71.8	75.5	1.4
Illegal strikes	405	369	894	1066	1230
No./workers	119.0	95.0	177.0	256.8	193.8
PUBLIC SECTOR (ALL ILLEGAL)!					
No./strikes	128	236	286	345	880
No./workers	41.7	154.0	145.9	147.1	214.3
OTHER ILLEGAL, INCLUDING INTER-SECTORAL AND GENERAL STRIKES#					
No./strikes	10	*7	*44	*9	*99
No./workers	64.0	88.1	66.1	23.0	511.2

* years of general strikes
! 1970 figures include jointly-owned firms
\# literally 'paros', a residual category including also strikes of unknown source.

SOURCE: Figures collected by Albert Armstrong for DERTO, University of Chile, in *Chilean Socio-economic Review*, 1979.

within Santiago. After the military coup of 1927, revolutionary trade unionism was driven underground in a wave of arrests, but trade unionists supported by the Labour Inspectorate were given security of employment, a vital step in the consolidation of unions, given continued employer intransigence.[31] By 1929, a transitional pattern had begun to emerge: strong independent or anarcho-syndicalist unions either boycotted the system, or transformed their existing free unions into *sindicatos profesionales*, like the 1081 port workers in Magallanes who created a (technically illegal) union of Gente del Mar. The old artisan trades, bakers, carpenters, and their new equivalents, such as drivers of motor vehicles, also formed *sindicatos profesionales*, most of these with less than 100 members. Something of Chile's pre-1924 pattern of union organisation thus remained preserved within the new legal framework as well as outside it, particularly among dockers, seamen, bakers, construction workers, wood and furniture makers, shoe and leather workers, printers. It is striking that where ultimately sectoral bargaining or a near equivalent was achieved under the new Labour Code, the sectors involved were those which had been strongholds of the old free unionism.[32]

Manufacturing industry outside these sectors, and mining without exception, were to be dominated by the new *sindicatos industriales* for the duration of the new Labour Code. Copper miners were to achieve minor modifications to it in the 1950s (such as the right to pay their union officers a half-week's wages, forbidden to other unions by law). Many manual workers attempted to raise the over-all level of benefits by renegotiating for themselves a new legal status as *empleados* through the Labour Courts created by Ibanez in 1931: thus turning *empleado* into the single most misleading category among Chilean statistics (see Appendix 2).

The 1931 Labour Code ultimately forced most of Chile's labour movement into legally differentiated boxes, bargaining under different preconditions and with different institutional horizons. The final result of the system, after its submission to the test of 40 years of working-class pressure, is summarised in Table 6.5: although the figures here are complicated by the introduction of new peasants' unions, sectorally based rather than tied to their individual farms, by a reforming Christian Democrat government in the late 1960s.

State employees were excluded from any bargaining rights under

TABLE 6.5 *The Final Form of Legal Unionism Pre-Coup (100s of workers)*

Type of Union	*No./Members*	*Percentage All Affiliated Union Members*
Total (Legal and Illegal)	1051.3	100.0
State Associations (Illegal)	340.0	32.3
Sindicatos industriales	208.3	19.8
*Sindicatos professionales**	78.7	7.5
Private sector *empleados@*	128.1	23.5
Agricultural unions#	247.5	23.5
Miscellaneous and mixed	48.8	4.6
Labour Force (1970)	2607.4	100.0
TOTAL UNION MEMBERSHIP	1051.3	40.3

* Manual workers only # Created after 1967.
@ about 30 per cent of which were manual workers (see Appendix 2).

SOURCE: Barria (1978) p. 106. The figures do not include 64 600 independent operators and small employers (truck drivers, small farmers, shopkeepers) also organised in 'unions'.

the new Labour Code: a paradox, since this sector was already strongly organised by the 1920s, as contemporary strikes by tram drivers, primary school teachers and telegraph workers all testify. The economic weight of the State sector was also growing with the expansion of State activity during the 1940s and 1950s, a by-product in large part of the State's new responsibilities for social security and medicine introduced after 1927. The bitter conflicts resulting from governments' refusal to negotiate provided a focus of protest throughout the 1930s, 1940s and 1950s around which unions in the fragmented and sometimes politically divided legal system could regroup, finding solidarity for their own conflicts with still hostile employers and an alternative, nationally organised core of free trade unionism less dependent on the goodwill of the State.

The institutionalisation of old and new

In the 1920s Chilean employers blamed labour relations problems on a small band of international agitators. By the 1960s and 1970s, it was almost as popular to blame them on the 1931 Labour Code, either because its deliberate fragmentation and encouragement of 'amateur', unpaid union officials encouraged politicisation (the Christian Democrat view) or because its creation of a closed shop in the *sindicato industrial* gave labour an unfair advantage and the involvement of the State itself encouraged 'politicisation' (the view of the economic Right).

One should be clear that political networks were preserved above all because organised labour had a stake in the ongoing debate over the Chilean economy and what should be done with it: in spite of the fact that all sectors of the labour movement supported industrialisation, particularly after the Popular Front, its cost took the form of a secular rise in inflation (Table 6.7), which played a major part in preserving working-class militancy. Chilean industry, targetted on local markets, depended on revenue from sales of copper to finance the costs of industrial investment in hard currency: and as the copper price fluctuated on international markets, so too did the money available to run the local economy, both its private sector and its increasingly important State sector, also dependent on copper revenues. Balance of payments crises were the result, triggering periodic government-imposed wage freezes which themselves became a powerful trigger for renewed protest movements and repressive reactions on the part of the government.

Economic tensions of this kind lay behind the crises of 1946–48,

TABLE 6.6 *Rising Prices, 1880–1970*

	Percentage Average rate of inflation p.a.
1880–1890	5
1890–1900	5
1900–1910	8
1910–1920	6
1920–1930	3
1930–1940	7
1940–1950	18
1950–1960	36
1960–1970	26

SOURCE: A. Hirschman, *Journeys Towards Progress* (1963) and ODEPLAN (1971).

when copper prices fell due to the collapse of war-time demand. The threat of hyperinflation explains the 'stabilisation' programmes, general strikes and arrests of the 1950s; and rising inflation, the breakdown of the Christian Democrat reform programme in 1968, also sealed by a general strike.[33]

Whether or not governments intended the original Labour Code as a lever with which to force employers to offer workers better wages and working conditions (and there is some evidence that they did, if only in the hopes of pre-empting revolutionary unionism), by the 1950s governments were also using the resources of the Labour Code and their own extra-ordinary legal powers to keep wages under control, with the effective connivance of government and employer to deny local strikes legal status playing its own part in the burgeoning 'problem' of illegal strikes.[34]

Political networks survived easily in the new *sindicatos industriales*, as these now turned to the political parties for free legal assistance in a labour relations system beset with legal trip-wires, for information about pay and conditions and some degree of collaboration with plant unions elsewhere, as an antidote to fragmentation (sectoral federations were often constructed around party and alliance networks) and perhaps most of all for basic solidarity, a network of loyal supporters to finance the *olla commun* (common soup pot) during strikes, as a substitute for the now illegal strike funds. Repression continued under the new legal regime, though its victims now came in fours and fives rather than in hundreds. Its persistence points up the instability of the Chilean economy; but it also reflected an underlying authoritarianism in ruling class attitudes, as well as ruling class failure to secure its own cultural and political hegemony over the labour movement. Extraordinary powers giving the government the right to suppress strikes 'damaging to the national interest' were included in the 1931 Labour Code, amplified in the face of the 1936 rail strike (when Alessandri made the first modern use of a State of Siege, imprisoning left-wing political leaders with no immediate connection with the railway workers), incorporated into new emergency legislation during the 1946 coal strike as the first wave of industrial development hit its post-war depression, and preserved in the Law for the Defence of Democracy, as communists, respectable allies in war time, suddenly became pariahs in every economy dependent on American good will.[35] When this infamous Law was abolished in 1958, it was replaced by the barely less draconian Law for the Internal Security of State, one of the principal legal buttresses for the military regime of 1973, to be incorporated into the first draft of its new law governing the contract of employment itself, in 1978 – giving employers the right to dismiss workers for their political views.

General strikes quickly re-emerged after the collapse of the 1927–31 dictatorship, in spite of the new legal bargaining framework. Initially their focus was railway workers, striking in 1932, 1933, 1934 and 1936 despite government determination to suppress unionisation among State employees. Railmen mobilised support from the new legal *sindicatos industriales* in Santiago's growing manufacturing sector, and there were regional general strikes involving both groups in 1932 and 1936, though the 1932 strike was also a protest at the fall of the Socialist Republic.[36] The 1936 strike – which tapped very widespread support – was a protest at mass dismissals of striking railway workers and also at Alessandri's State of Siege legislation: it brought together a sufficiently wide nucleus of free and legal unions to provide the basis for a new successor to the FOCH, a national trade union confederation covering all but a small rump of independent anarcho-syndicalists, the *Confederación de Trabajadores de Chile* – and this in turn played a critical role in the creation and support of the Popular Front, elected in 1939 on a programme of expanded industrialisation.

Throughout the 1930s and 1940s, governments spearheaded the attempt to institutionalise industrial relations, with employers continuing to show a marked reluctance, if one is to judge by SOFOFA bulletins. President Alessandri's second administration took what steps it could to encourage individual employers to set up welfare departments within their firms during the 1930s; but not until the early 1950s, after the still more positive support given unions by the Popular Front, would key sectors of private industry begin to set up social funds to provide retirement bonuses for manual workers and other benefits – shoe and leather after a strike in 1951, metalwork and engineering in 1953. Long afterwards, the Popular Front's encouragement of unionisation would show up in the relatively high rates of unionisation in the intermediate industries which it played such an important role in establishing: with 59.6 per cent of the labour force in this category unionised in 1972, compared to 36.1 per cent in traditional industries and a comparatively low 22.0 per cent in the 'dynamic', technologically sophisticated firms established later with the help of American investors.[37]

By 1960, within larger factories, plant unions had begun to administer a range of social benefits, provided by the employer under successive negotiated agreements – a union social centre, holiday camp, a day's seaside holiday – while another range of benefits, such as school scholarships, retirement bonuses and special holiday bonuses, were provided by the employer in addition to the basic wage. The extent to which this employer paternalism, such as it was, was concentrated within Chile's monopoly sector is vividly shown by a *Dirección de Estadistica* survey in 1960, when 10 per cent of the firms surveyed accounted for two-thirds of all such payments, and one factory alone for 20 per cent. Whether such benefits had any effect in, for instance, persuading workers not to participate in general strikes is a moot point. They certainly were not used as an alternative to unionisation: Sader's study suggests very similar rates of unionisation between 'monopoly' firms and those of 'medium concentration'.[38]

In some sense, the model for employer paternalism was the treatment of private sector *empleados* laid down by the original Labour Code, with its guaranteed retirement and redundancy benefits. This paternalist model did have some effect in reducing *empleado* strikes, especially after 1937, when President Alessandri added a provision for a guaranteed minimum wage (*sueldo vital*) and family allowance, adjusted in line with inflation by national-level negotiations, though only for those *empleados* who surrendered their right to individual collective bargaining. Only white-collar workers in the copper mines refused this offer.

Nevertheless, too much credit should not be given to employer paternalism or the assistance of governments even here. The *Caja de Empleados Particulares* seems superficially to be a typical example of such paternalist concerns, insulating one category of workers from the problems of the majority: ultimately, it offered the best-financed social security board in Chile, early retirement benefits, mortgages, cheap Caja-owned housing, cheap Caja-owned hotels, and subsidised consumption through a Caja-owned co-operative, living proof of the superior status of *empleados*. But in fact, these benefits were won only after a massive eruption of *empleado* grievances in the 1950 white-collar workers' strike – perhaps the single most important strike in the 1920–73 era, since its generalisation to other sectors in the traditional general strike pattern, won for all Chilean workers a degree of freedom from the Law for the Defence of Democracy itself.

The end of interventionism

By the 1960s, there was widespread concensus among both employers and politicians that the old Labour Code was not effective. Most strikes were now 'illegal', indicating in employers' eyes, an unacceptable level of union indiscipline. 'Political strikes' were not uncommon – employers remembered vividly the one-day strike of protest called in support of the Cuban Revolution, in 1960, forgetting the long sequence of others triggered by purely local repression: the 1936 strike against a State of Siege, the 1946 strike protesting the death of demonstrators at the hands of the police, the 1950 solidarity movement with white-collar workers against the *Ley Maldita*, the 1960 strike protesting more deaths by demonstrators, the 1967 strike triggered by the death of seven miners and their wives when troops opened fire on strikers at El Salvador.

The Christian Democrat reform programme of 1964–70 included a reform of the 1931 Labour Code. The intention was to replace plant unionism with sectoral bargaining, operating in a fashion more akin to the Mexican or Brazilian labour union, allowing the labour movement to employ professionals for the first time in its history,[39] but institutionalising the possibility of up to three competing unions. The new legal framework would thus have eliminated the *sindicatos industriales*' bargaining rights altogether, and jettisoned with it the trade union movement's *de jure* political unity (recognition as bargaining agent would have gone to the largest union, organised presumably around political loyalties). It would also have given governments the power to order back to work any group of strikers demanding a pay increase larger than that authorised by the government, thus institutionalising State wage controls and compulsory arbitration, with the threat of military or police action in reserve.

The model worked in agriculture (Table 6.10) where it provided perhaps the only possible alternative to the domination of the rural *patron* over his own farm. But opposition from within the Christian Democrats own union ranks prevented its extension to any other sector.

Following the coup, the new military government briefly experimented with a somewhat similar project for reform from 1974 to 1976, with the apparent support of employers in textiles, metalwork and engineering.[40] But the era of 'inward-looking development' was coming to an end. The dynamism of manufacturing as a source of new employment had begun to wane during the 1960s, and Chile, with its tiny local market, became a text-book example of the problems of development through import-substitution. Government enthusiasm for State intervention as a general principle came to an abrupt end with the overthrow of President Allende's Popular Unity government on 11 September 1973. The new military regime was easily convinced by supporters of modern free market theories then enjoying a renewed international vogue, that interventionist philosophies had contributed to the dangerous growth of political conflict over economic affairs, giving workers an undesirable degree of economic power, and fostering broad tolerance on the part of all classes of a Hayek-style 'road to serfdom',[41] that is, a slow evolution towards a Communist State.

From 1975 onwards, steps were taken to reduce all forms of overt government intervention in the economy, denationalising State-controlled industries and decontrolling local prices. Thus, in 1979 Chilean labour relations began a new *laissez-faire* cycle, with the government once again attempting to restrain unions' ability to bring non-market pressures to bear on wages and working conditions, resorting as before to unemployment and repression as key levers of control. The old Labour Code, developed in the interventionist 1920s, 1930s and 1940s, was replaced with a new one closely modelled on Hayek's views, emphasising the need to control labour 'monopolies' and to eliminate State or union-inspired 'rigidities in the labour market'.

Even tighter limits were set on the operation of a 'legal' strike: it could only take place within a time-scale originally laid down by the Ministry of Labour, and then only within a negotiating cycle fixed at two-yearly intervals; and once called, it could only last 59 days before all workers involved laid themselves open to dismissal. Union pressure could only be brought to bear on wages – not on working conditions in any form – and then only providing that bargaining confined itself to increases in the individual wage: collective agreements which drew on management funds to support union-run holidays, holiday camps or social centres were made illegal. The plant union was preserved as the essential centre of union activity, but now considerably weakened: its rights to a guaranteed income out of employer profits were withdrawn, and so was its erstwhile power to offer members a closed shop. The new Labour Code looked favourably on the prospect of rival unions competing for the right to negotiate within each plant, and, even more favourably, on the prospect that individuals might prefer not to pay the costs of keeping a union together out of their slim wage packets, and choose to bargain with their employers on an individual basis.

Economists in charge of the Ministry of Labour saw the new system as a model for other countries to imitate, and predicted that it would eventually eliminate the politicisation of Chilean labour. They also saw the new reforms as reinforcing changes which the broader re-orientation of the Chilean economy away from protectionism towards open competition, had already begun. Employers exposed to foreign competition could no longer pass on excessive wage costs to consumers, they claimed; and with the economy importing many of its goods from non-Chilean workers, the possibilities of local unionists exercising 'economic blackmail' through their control over production must necessarily be on the wane.[42]

This was the framework which Chilean unions combined to attack in 1983–84: succeeding, if nothing else, in regaining the right of unions to bargain a wage rate for all workers in the plant, eliminating the possibility of individual negotiations destroying collective bargaining altogether. Even before the outbreak of mass protest, it was already clear that workers, faced with the legal possibility of choosing between competing unions at plant level, would simply preserve the old pre-1979 pattern: one *sindicato industrial* covering manual workers and one or two *sindicatos profesionales* covering white-collar workers and technicians. The idea of competition between local union organisations triggered a deeply-rooted awareness of the dangers of sectarianism.

The protests of 1983–84 proved something more. For all the determination of governments and economists to root out politicisation of the labour force, with every resource afforded by the law, Chilean workers remained members of a set of political networks, organised at national level, and capable of mounting a general strike. The abolition of their pre-1973 trade union confederation, the CUT, might temporarily disorganise this pattern – though the CUT's disappearance was perhaps due as much to the enormous sectarian tensions generated within it during the Allende regime as to any government decree – but no decree could abolish the social institution of the matrix itself.

A better knowledge of labour history might have led the regime to adopt a more cynical view of Hayek's labour philosophy.

THE STRUGGLE FOR UNITY

Organised labour in Chile is sometimes compared with other 'politicised' labour movements such as those of France and Italy. But in spite of its competing political parties, Chile's movement has preserved a unity of action at local and even national level with remarkable consistency, as comparable European movements have not. Rival bargaining agents within the same sector, linked to different political views, made a brief appearance in the free unions of the 1930s: by the 1950s, they had disappeared in favour of a unified local union organisation, with different political tendencies competing for places on its executive committee – the pattern already characteristic of the *sindicatos industriales* and reproduced in the modern *Confederación de Trabajadores de Cobre* today, the voting results of whose local union elections (determining the distribution of seats on its executive committee) are reproduced in Table 6.7.[43]

Attempts to introduce a new legal framework which would have made it possible for competing federations, organised on a political basis, to bargain at sectoral level were fiercely resisted by the entire labour movement when the idea was first raised by the Christian Democrats in the late 1960s, and again when it was mooted by relatively progressive corporatists within the post-1973 military regime. Right and left within the labour movement regarded any step which consecrated different political tendencies as bargaining agents, as a hidden assault on labour's real bargaining power, regardless of the apparent extra economic clout which was promised them under both projected plans of reform.[44]

Nationally, the struggle for unity has always been more difficult,

TABLE 6.7 *The Political Matrix in the CTC, 1986*
Political affiliations of executive committee members, all unions, totalled by zone

Acuerdo Nacional Alliance
CD = Christian Democrat
S(AC) = Socialist supporters of the *Acuerdo Nacional*
MAPU = Marxist party, split from CD in 1969
CL = Christian Left, split from CD in 1970

*Movimiento Democratico Popular**
CP = Communist
S(MDP) = Socialist supporters of the MDP

Other
IND = Independent
GOV = Government supporters

	Chuqui Zone	*El Salvador Zone*	*Andina Zone*	*El Teniente Zone*	*Santiago Zone**	*TOTAL*
CP	3	8	2	8	–	21
S(MDP)	4	1	–	2	–	7
ALL MDP	*7*	*9*	*2*	*10*	–	*28*
CD	12	15	2	4	1	34
S(AC)	–	–	–	2	–	2
MAPU	–	–	–	1	–	1
CL	–	–	–	1	–	1
RP	1	–	–	–	–	1
ALL AC	*13*	*15*	*2*	*8*	*1*	*39*
IND	5	1	3	3	4	16
GOV	–	3	3	18	–	24
TOTAL EXEC	25	28	10	39	5	107
TOTAL MEMBERS	8700	3540	1424	8020	325	22 009

NOTE: Compare Barria's data on the political matrix in copper during the early 1960s, in Appendix 4.

SOURCE: *Solidaridad*, 226, 27 June to 17 July 1986.

since national confederations have a more direct bearing on politics. The most serious threat of a permanently divided movement probably came in the 1920s and 1930s, when labour was polarised between free and legal unions, and 'free' anarchist unions could maintain the

Confederación General de Trabajo as a rival to the CTCH with perhaps 25 000 members, a scale of organisation which later schisms have not been able to match.[45] The danger was avoided. Throughout most of their history, the majority of Chilean workers have been affiliated to a single trade union federation: successively, the CTCH (*Confederación de Trabajadores de Chile*, 1936–46), the CUT (*Central Unica de Trabajadores*, 1953–73) and the *Comando Nacional de Trabajadores* created in 1983. However, the struggle to preserve a precarious unity in the face of the intense competitive tensions of the matrix has dominated the modern history of the labour movement; as it has done since 1983, with Christian Democrats determined to construct a nation-wide Opposition to the dictatorship while excluding the Communist Party from anything other than participation on the Christian Democrats' terms.

After the coup, unity was problematic, as it was during the seven years when rival CTCH's competed with one another during the late 1940s, while their grassroots support slowly drifted away. These two periods of disunity (1946–53 and 1973–83) have much in common. Both coincided with periods of heavy repression, which limited rank and file pressures towards unity and allowed federations to claim representativity they may or may not have had. Both followed periods when the participation of workers' parties in government had maximised sectarian divisions. In both cases, a nation-wide mobilisation visibly brought pressures on the leadership to pool forces in broader labour interests: we have followed the impact of the 1983–84 mass mobilisations on the CNS, CEPCH, FUT, and UDT, and much the same could be said of the 1950 general strike of white-collar workers.

From the CTCH to a divided labour movement, 1939–50

The *Frente Popular*'s appeal rested on the belief that industrialisation would provide a panacea for problems of poverty and underdevelopment (a belief dear to trade unionists of all parties in 1957, after ten years of periodic economic crisis and renewed recession). The CTCH shared the illusion, taking its place on the board of management of CORFO, the new State Investment Corporation, in 1940. So too did the Socialist and Communist Parties, which renounced strike action in favour of obligatory arbitration – their contribution to industrialisation and the world-wide anti-fascist struggle – with the result that over-all, the numbers of strikes fell during the period, and perhaps also of encouraging a temporary revival in support for anarcho-syndicalism, which briefly flourished even in Chuquicamata.[46]

The *Frente Popular* and the Radical Presidencies which followed were a time when old gains were consolidated, and the transition to legal unionism in the urban areas completed, with all its paradoxical preservation of the spirit of a political movement in the new anti-political form, testified to by employer complaints that workers were in the habit of leaving early for demonstrations.[47] But the period saw no major legislative initiative on behalf of union members, and one major disappointment, the blocking of unionisation in the rural areas with the complaisance of Socialist and Communist Parties.[48] Nor did labour parties play any part in the contemporary campaign to win women the vote. However, unions, legal and illegal, expanded their membership dramatically, and the era saw a spurt in the growth of federations of the plant-level *sindicatos industriales*. Both manual workers and *empleados* made real gains in wages during the 1940–45 period, though the relative position of manual workers was to suffer badly during the years of repression which followed.[49]

The era also saw a determined and successful drive by the Communist Party to recover its support among the new legal unions, lost during its commitment to 'free unionism': and its consequent re-emergence as the leading force behind new union campaigns for higher wages in the 1940s, the best known example being the 1947 coal strike. Sectarian rivalry between communists and socialists flourished as socialists gradually lost their control of the new *sindicatos industriales* and found being in government a disadvantage.

These tensions were at the root of the CTCH's failure to anticipate and defend the labour movement against the growing anti-union mood of governments after economic conditions worsened in 1945 – in spite of the CTCH's one general strike (a success) in 1945. Both parties were determined to secure a place in government, lost by the communists as a result of Cold War manoeuvring in 1942. Communists sought to prolong the strike to better their electoral chances in the 1946 Presidential elections: socialists, who were joining the Cabinet of the pre-election government, to end it as soon as possible. The outcome was the division of the labour movement into two warring CTCHs, named after their leaders: the broadly communist CTCH-Araya, with support in mining, metal-working, construction and some textile sectors, and the CTCH-Ibáñez,[50] with other textile firms, the copper mines, bakers, flour mill workers, chemical and pharmaceutical workers, and social security clerks. Government and international forces moved quickly to take advantage of these divisions. Following Bernardo Ibáñez's contacts with the AFL-CIO on behalf of the Socialist Party earlier in the decade (themselves part of a contemporary effort to give the Socialist Party international contacts to match those of the communists) the CTCH-Ibáñez now received financial aid from the AFL-CIO. The Radical government of Gonzalez Videla (once an ally of the communists) used socialists as strike-breakers, alongside troops, to suppress the communist-organised coal strike of 1947.

In 1948, the government brought in the Law for the Defence of Democracy, banning the Communist Party and forbidding its members to participate in union affairs. Though it was introduced as a result of American pressure on the government to declare itself anti-communist, and one of its immediate consequences was the establishment of a concentration camp for communists at Pisagua, the new Law was, as we have said above, simultaneously an attempt to reinforce government control over all unions. Government employees were forbidden to strike, and compulsory arbitration was introduced in the State sector: all illegal strikes of any kind now became a criminal offence, and where legal strikes could be said to affect vital industries or public services, or simply threaten disorder, they too were now banned.

Following its promulgation, the Radical government attempted to co-operate with the Americans in boosting the CTCH-Ibáñez. Ibáñez and his supporters within the Socialist Party were offered seats in Cabinet as labour representatives: the idea was to swing socialist and radical trade unionists behind him, thus providing the core of an 'official' labour movement which could be split off from the 'unofficial', and now heavily persecuted, movement dominated by the communists.

This second effort to divide labour into respectables and revolutionaries suffered a similar fate to that of Ibáñez del Campo's 20 years before it, wrecked on the solidarity of the matrix. The Socialist Party split. Bernardo Ibáñez was expelled, and although he managed to use his government support to found a new faction with the old party name – Socialist Party of Chile – the majority of the party's Congressmen and supporters, including trade unionists in the copper mines, supported the newly christened socialist alternative, the *Partido Socialista Popular*.

White-collar workers were also hostile. State-sector workers were themselves a target of the new legislation, having enjoyed a boom in unionisation during the 1940s which the government regarded as threatening. Politically, their associations had already distanced themselves formally from both wings of the CTCH while the ANEF, the National Association of Civil Servants, led by Clotario Blest, attempted to bring about a reconciliation. By 1947 *empleados* in both State and private sectors were participating in a mass campaign of street demonstrations against rising prices, organised by the CTCH Araya in yet another successful imitation of the 1918–19 *Asamblea de Alimentación Nacional*, and private sector *empleados* were enjoying an upsurge in their organisational strength as a result: a new united federation of white-collar workers, the CEPCH, was formed in 1948 to replace the divided and factional movements characteristic of this sector since the fall of the Ibáñez dictatorship of 1927–31.[51]

The event which triggered the general strike of 1950 was government imposition of price controls, which froze the wages in two US-owned public utilities, whose workers promptly went on strike. The strike was generalised to all white-collar workers by the CEPCH, very aware that new anti-inflation legislation was on the way which would set further limits to trade union rights. Banks, social security offices, chemicals and pharmaceuticals, theatres and the National Transport Company all answered the CEPCH's call for a series of one-day strikes, as did clerks in the copper mines. By the end of the strike's 12-day duration it had spread to manual workers in printing, bakeries and the copper mines. It ended abruptly when miners struck in Chuquicamata, the largest copper mine.

Ironically, then, the 1950 mobilisation brought into action much the same sectors of the labour movement on which the AFL-CIO and Gonzalez Videla had laid their hopes for an anti-communist CTCH. It brought the government's anti-inflation drive to a halt, ended systematic persecution of the communists and laid the basis for the *Caja de Empleados Particulares*. Indirectly, it contributed to the unification of the scattered *sindicatos industriales* in copper, whose contacts during the strike led to the organisation of the *Confederación de Trabajadores de Cobre* in 1951:[52] not the first nor the last time that individual sectors made organisation gains through their contributions to a nation-wide mobilisational in defence of the general interests of the working-class.

The struggle to create the CUT: 1950–53

Despite the success of the 1950 strike, the road to unity was tortuous, the more so because it had to embrace both sides of the divided

CTCH. By 1951 there were two separate unity campaigns, one set up by the rump of Chile's old anarcho-syndicalist movement in alliance with the CTCH-Araya, the other by ANEF and the CEPCH, this time joining forces with the CTCH-Ibáñez. University students convened a timely series of hunger marches which successfully brought both campaigns together on one platform, but the chance to turn this alliance into a more permanent organisation was lost when the President of the CEPCH chose to use it to make his own bid for political power, organising his own kidnapping in the hopes, Blest claims, of provoking a 'Marxist military coup' – reflecting perhaps old socialist contacts with the military which dated back to the Socialist Republic of Grove. Mass support evaporated in the face of this proof of ulterior political designs.[53]

When it was finally constituted in February 1953, shortly after the old dictator Ibáñez was re-elected as President, the new *Central* was formally committed to independence from all governments and all international connections, accessibility to workers of all political and religious creeds, and internal democracy (avoiding the control of any single political party). It was also committed to the class struggle. The AFL-CIO was disappointed:

> Chilean delegates to the ORIT convention which took place in Brazil in December 1952 were warned not to fall into the Communist 'unity' trap. But pressure at home was stronger than pressure from abroad . . .[54]

The CUT was a voluntary organisation, technically illegal under the 1931 Code, operating in a union environment where workers' participation even in legal unions showed a tendency to wax and wane with the political climate (Table 6.8). Its representativity was thus variable. Zapata estimates that in 1967, 49 out of 69 trade union federations were affiliates. Notoriously, workers in large plants or those with real bargaining power often ignored it (the copper mines, the steel plant at Huachipato, State electricity plants and the State oil company are all cited), though copper miners and steel workers nonetheless often supported general strikes. Certainly the CUT was never a key institution in collective bargaining, in spite of its early dreams of reorganising the scattered *sindicatos industriales* into industry-wide unions. During the early years involvement of the country's manual workers, who dominated its founding conference, fell by comparison with that of State sector employees.[55]

Nevertheless, as Table 6.1 demonstrates, the CUT had a very real

TABLE 6.8 *Legal* Unions and Legal Union Members as a Percentage of the Labour Force, 1953–72*
* Private sector only: State sector unions being 'illegal'.

	No./unions	*No./Members*	*Average size*	*% Labour Force*
1953	2067	298 274	144 members	12.2
1954	2068	299 364	145 members	11.9
1955	2177	305 192	140 members	12.1
1956	2382	317 352	133 members	13.9
1957	2121	300 040	141 members	13.0
1958	2382	266 346	112 members	11.9
1959	1752	282 498	161 members	10.3
1960	1770	282 417	160 members	10.1
1961	1764	257 563	146 members	10.6
1962	1774	247 007	139 members	10.0
1963	1852	262 498	142 members	10.3
1964	1863	270 542	145 members	10.3
1965	2038	292 653	144 members	10.9
1966	2870	350 516	122 members	12.8
1967	3336	406 186	122 members	14.6
1968	3854	499 761	130 members	17.5
1969	4195	530 984	127 members	18.2
1970	4519	551 086	122 members	19.4
1971	5118	586 600	115 members	20.6
1972	6001	632 485	105 members	22.2

SOURCE: 1970–72, Baraona (1974), quoting figures from President Allende's Third Message to Congress. Delays in registration during booms and in eliminating inactive unions from the register in downturns explain some of the variation in figures: compare statistics for 1970–2 reproduced in Table 6.13.

function as the first line of defence against an intrusive State. The years of the CUT's hegemony were years of wage controls which now began to affect private sector workers as well as public (1956–57, 1959–62, 1965–69) and of government attempts to change the nature of industrial relations through legal amendments to the 1931 Code (1956, 1965–66). Of some ten general strikes during its lifetime, the CUT called all but two – and one of these was the Bosses' Strike of 1972, supported by employers, shopkeepers, technicians and professionals opposed to the Allende regime.

The CUT thus co-ordinated union bargaining with the government in an economic context dominated by periodic crises, where governments often attempted to intervene in normal bargaining processes, and an easy reversion to authoritarian controls remained a permanent threat. The ups and downs of this 'trade unionism of opposition' could have a major impact on membership levels. Demoralisation after the failure of the 1956 general strike, for example, led to a dramatic drop in support. Barria estimates that the CUT's founding convention drew representatives of 40 per cent of the country's total union membership, its 1957 Congress from a mere 19 per cent, and its 1962 Congress from nearly 60 per cent.[56]

The CUT's early years were dramatic, as it confronted a President with a personal stake in the history of fascist and corporatist ideas in Chile, now presenting himself as labour's loyal ally, perhaps with an eye to the success of Peron in neighbouring Argentina. Ibáñez began his second period in power promising the abolition of the Law for the Defence of Democracy and the introduction of minimum wage laws and family allowances, ultimately keeping all three promises after a fashion.[57] However, a year when inflation reached 72 per cent, together with the CUT's refusal to let any of its executive join the Cabinet, led to a dramatic breach. In 1954–55 Ibáñez allowed his Cabinet to be taken over by the *estanqueros*, right-wing corporatists with military and business connections[58] who proposed a two-year abolition of the right to strike, universally obligatory arbitration, central government control of wages, social security reforms to release capital for investment in construction and agriculture, and a forced savings scheme to pull new investment capital out of workers' wages: a more radical version of the programme promised by the Radical government in 1950 and jettisoned after the 1950 general strike.

With the proposals came a massive attack on the 'illegal' CUT, and the arrest of its President, Blest, and other officers – released after a general strike in May 1954, which in Blest's words, tapped sectors of the population which the labour movement had never seen.[59] The declaration of a State of Siege prevented the organisation of a second general strike in October: but the labour movement mobilised popular and Congressional support for mass demonstrations against this threatened attack on civil liberties, and forced the *estanqueros* to resign. A further one-day strike in July 1955, popularly supposed to be aimed at bringing down the government, attracted mass support and the participation of small shopkeepers.

Ibáñez abandoned hopes of a new authoritarian revolution and turned to more traditional forms of political manoeuvre, conceding many of the CUT's demands in principle, in return for a promise to control further strikes. It was a promise the CUT, as a voluntary organisation, could not keep, and was broken almost immediately by sectors of Blest's civil service. With this broken pledge, and persistently high inflation (84 per cent) Ibáñez won Congressional support for new emergency powers and introduced an alternative anti-inflation programme prepared by American economists. Formal government controls over wages in the private sector were introduced for the first time, together with typically *'laissez-faire'* provisions such as contraction of the money supply and reduced tariff barriers and State expenditure. Workers themselves were worried about inflation, and the general strike called by the CUT in response in January 1956, the seventh or eighth such strike plotted in a two-year period, was a failure. Blest and other CUT officers were arrested, with no mass response.

The failure of the 1956 general strike inaugurated an era of working-class passivity from which the movement recovered only slowly. As Table 6.8 shows, the number of legal unions in the private sector stagnated. The CUT itself was now demoralised. In 1957 riots broke out in Santiago's growing shanty towns in response to the death of a demonstrating student at the hands of the police. Ibáñez had leading figures in the CUT's executive arrested, though they had offered the demonstrators only 'moral support'; and although the CUT was holding a national Congress at the time, no general strike was organised, the movement being more concerned in preventing a complete withdrawal by the Christian Democrats.

The defeat paved the way for an immersion of socialists and communists in electoral politics (Allende having come within a hair's breadth of winning the 1958 Presidential election) and in the local collective bargaining which, the mobilisation of the 1950s had done so much to preserve – thus encouraging a new generation of impatient young activists inspired by the Cuban Revolution, to abandon the existing labour parties and found their own revolutionary alternative, the MIR, in 1956.

In his final six months in power, Ibáñez repealed the Law for the Defence of Democracy, replacing it with the almost equally authoritarian Law for the Internal Security of State.[60]

Failure of a decade of distributive reforms: 1964–73

Following the end of this mini-cycle of *laissez-faire*, which continued throughout the subsequent Presidency of Jorge Alessandri, Chilean politics rapidly became more radical, the beneficiary of Catholic and

TABLE 6.9 *Increases in Rate of Unionisation by Sector, 1967–72*
UNION Members as Percentage of Labour Force

	*May 1967**	*May 1968**	*Dec. 1971@*	*June 1972@*
Agriculture	3.0	3.3	20.9	35.4
Mining	59.3	61.9	61.3	62.1
Manufacturing	30.5	31.9	37.3	38.4
Construction	9.4	10.0	11.6	12.3
Electricity	79.1	83.6	100.0	100.0
Commerce	11.4	11.9	12.7	13.5
Transport	24.2	24.7	32.2	33.8
Services	3.1	3.3	5.6	6.1

* Labour force calculated by ODEPTRA of each year.
@ Labour force as of 1970 Census.

SOURCE: Sader (1973), quoting ODEPLAN, ODEPTRA and *Direccion de Trabajo* figures.

finally American perceptions that the alternative to a Marxist electoral victory must be greater social justice. A Catholic drive to organise rural unions, neglected by socialists and communists since the *Frente Popular*, began in earnest in Molina in 1953 (though as late as 1962, the floor of a CUT Congress refused to recognise their delegates).[61]

Christian Democracy: 1964–70

A Christian Democrat President, Eduardo Frei, was elected in 1964. His administration promised a 'Revolution in Liberty': agrarian reform and rural unions, the 'Chileanisation' of US-owned copper mines through an elaborate buy-out, the creation of new dynamic industries and the enlargement of local markets through Chile's entry into the Andean Pact. A drive to organise the urban poor quickly followed, through neighbourhood committees and Mothers' Unions.

Trade union membership expanded in this climate (Table 6.9), and although the political competition inherent in the matrix restricted Christian Democracy's ability to expand much beyond the watermark of 23 per cent of all union officers already enjoyed party members in 1957, it stimulated a wave of new unionisation which Popular Unity would not be able to match.[62] The challenge posed by the Christian Democrats resulted in a major cross-party organisational drive among 'marginal' sectors hitherto touched, if at all, during general

TABLE 6.10 *Rural Unions and Political Competition*

Confederation	*1968* *No./members*	*% Total*	*1969* *No./members*	*% Total*
'Libertad'*	17 421	23.2	22 542	23.1
'Triunfo Campesino'**	39 388	52.4	45 654	46.8
'Ranquil'@	18 253	24.4	29 329	30.1

* anti-communist Catholic ** Christian Democrat @ socialist and communist

SOURCE: Baraona (1974) p. 147. See also Angell (1972) p. 250–9.

strikes. Rural unions were organised on a significant scale for the first time, and Socialists and Communists began a new drive to win their support (Table 6.10). The drive to organise the urban poor had similar results, as socialists, communists and the newly emergent MIR challenged the Christian Democrats for control of neighbourhood committees.

These were positive developments. More negative was the new government's heavy reliance on American funding, which left the party leadership with long-standing political debts. However, efforts by ORIT to promote a Christian Democrat alternative to the CUT were blocked by the party's trade union department. Anti-communism found little echo within a labour relations system based in practice on the co-operation of communists and other parties in the five-member executive of the *sindicato industrial*. In 1966 the Christian Democrat Party congress formally banned membership or active collaboration with the ICFTU, the ORIT, or the US-inspired AIFLD. (The party's union department also vetoed the government's plans to reform the old labour code along lines already experimented with in agriculture, thus permanently dividing all workers' bargaining agents along party lines.)

Nevertheless, the aid made any long-term political alliance between Christian Democrats and communists inconceivable, thus contributing to the overthrow of Popular Unity in 1973, the end of distributive reforms, and the difficulties of organising a united trade union movement after the coup. Under the changed conditions of 1973, with Marxist tendencies in the labour movement reduced by repression to a fraction of their original strength, some Christian Democrat union leaders were willing to repeat the experiments of 1957, 1962 and 1968, and divide the movement. Others were not. The result was the splitting of Christian Democrat union support between the CNS and the UDT/CDT visible in the 1983/84 protests, a development whose long-term impact is still unclear.

The Christian Democrat 'Revolution in Liberty' had some impact on income distribution: the proportion of the national income going to wages and salaries rose slightly, and the position of the poorest manual workers had improved by the end of the 1960s, while there may have been some squeezing of the relative differentials between manual workers and *empleados*.[63] Otherwise it was a failure, in spite of American finance. Efforts at agrarian reform ground to a premature halt in the face of right-wing opposition in the rural areas, while rising inflation coupled with pressures from businessmen forced the government to implement wage controls in 1967. Over-all, these years saw further steps towards an involuntary tertiarisation of the Chilean economy, and rising rates of unemployment, as investment in modern technology provided fewer and fewer jobs.

Like the first Alessandri administration 40 years earlier, the Frei government broke labour's most significant taboos. Open conflict between the government and labour first emerged in 1966, when a solidarity strike at the El Salvador copper mine was suppressed by troops at the cost of eight lives. The general strike which followed was supported by 20 of the CUT's 49 federations. Another a year later, called to prevent the government introducing a forced savings scheme much like that first proposed by the *estanqueros*, saw Christian Democrats' trade unionists rebelling alongside those of the Left, with 96 036 manual workers and 47 257 *empleados* participating. Barricades were set up in some shanty-towns, and five demonstrators died in confrontations with police, including a child.[64] The forced savings scheme had to be withdrawn. The government made a major concession by signing an agreement over wages with the CUT in 1969, but the gesture came too late to save the unity of the Christian Democrat labour movement, now suffering from the withdrawal of some activists to new parties such as the MAPU and the Christian Left, which were to join forces with the Marxist parties to elect Allende as President in 1970.

The upsurge in general strikes seems to have had some impact on the numbers of workers in small firms and perhaps also *empleados* and technicians, who now became involved in strike activity on their own account, judging by the coincident fall in the number of workers involved in each individual strike (Table 6.11) – echoing patterns in industrial relations dating as far back as the 1890 general strike.

TABLE 6.11 *Inflation, Strikes (Private Sector Only) and Workers Involved, 1961–73*

	INFLATION (%)	NO./STRIKES Legal and Illegal	TOTAL STRIKERS	AVERAGE PER STRIKE
1961	7.7	835	151 453	181
1962	13.9	482	124 391	258
1963	44.3	533	124 334	233
1964	46.0	433	114 342	264
1965	28.8	772	210 397	273
1966	22.9	713	88 498	124
1967	18.1	2134	248 841	116
1968	26.6	913	203 378	223
1969	30.7	1013	242 234	235
1970	32.5	1269	332 325	261
1971	20.1	2116	229 227	108
1972	77.8	2030	203 522	100
1973	235.2*	1251	195 183	156

* official figure, first 8 months only.

SOURCE: Inflation, Stallings (1978), p. 247. Strike data, Armstrong, cited in Mendez (1980).

Popular Unity: 1970–73

By 1970, in spite of the efforts of the Christian Democrats to revive industrialisation, Chile's employment figures were revealing an over-all secular rise in open unemployment and a drift in the labour force towards the service sector (Appendix 2), facing Popular Unity and its trade union allies with difficult issues of tactics as well as economic policy, and a need to build institutional bridges going beyond the riotous general strikes which traditionally linked the labour movement and the shanty towns. The success of unionisation over the decade meant that unionisation was penetrating smaller firms and more marginal sectors (Table 6.8), a phenomena visible in an abrupt fall between 1971–72 in the average number of workers involved in strikes (Table 6.11) comparable with that of the general strike years of the Christian Democrat era, and one which posed delicate problems for government economists, as workers in smaller firms of negligible economic significance demanded nationalisation as a remedy for their problems of industrial relations. Ironically, unionisation continued to lag behind in the technologically sophisticated industries fostered by the Christian Democrats.[65]

The internal life of the movement was marked by intense sectarian activity, within the Popular Unity coalition as well as between its activists and their rivals the Christian Democrats on the right, and the MIR on the left. Attempts initiated by the CUT on a voluntary basis, to realise a long-standing dream of creating sector-wide unions embracing all categories of worker (*empleado* and manual) were regarded by the Christian Democrats as an essay in pro-government parallel unionism, perhaps because Christian Democrats were relatively strongly organised among *empleados*. The new unions collapsed, except in State education, where teachers of all grades combined with manual workers to create the *Sindicato Unico de Trabajadores de la Educación*, the only State-sector union to be given legal recognition before the coup, and an immediate target of military repression in 1973.

The legalisation of the CUT itself was not opposed by the Christian Democrats, but its incorporation into the government's National Development Agency (like the CTCH before it) and involvement in formal consultations over such critical issues as wages policy and the administration of the nationalised sector, was a source of bitter conflict. Christian Democrat members of the CUT executive claimed that they were excluded from these negotiations, even after direct elections for the CUT's national executive (the first universal ballot of ordinary union members in the CUT's history) gave the Christian Democrats the Vice-Presidency.

Management of the nationalised sector became a focus of conflict, generating a fierce debate on participation. Christian Democrats argued that worker control could only exist where workers managed industry directly, and not in co-partnership with the State. Communists, who held a majority on the pre-1972 CUT executive, attempted to keep CUT policy in line with the government's over-all goals and the 'battle for production'; while socialists and other left-wing tendencies demanded more rank and file involvement, rapidly emerging as Popular Unity's internal opposition, in a paradoxical reversal of the two main parties' relative position during the Popular Front, when it was socialists who defended the administration and communists who provided leadership for the era's strikes.

The debate on participation reflected real tensions, which broke out with a strike in the Chuquicamata copper mine over the sacking of a worker in 1971.[66] However, pressure within the governing coalition did contribute to its resolution, at least within the urban areas, with effective participation emerging in Espinosa and Zimbalist's study as strongly correlated with workers' support for the internal opposition.[67] Outside the mines there were no similar strikes.

For Popular Unity, tensions over this issue were transformed by the experiences of the 'Bosses' Strike' of 1972, which led to an upsurge of mass organisation by rank and file committees now linked together in geographical zones, the *cordones*, as well as new shanty town organisations, the People's Supply Committees (*Juntas de Abastecimiento Popular*). The spread of such organisations suggests that the ferment of enthusiasm which the Allende regime let loose, was capable of inventing new mechanisms to overcome structural differences within the ranks of the poor. However, the *cordones* were to become a point of conflict within the coalition in their own right. The CUT itself did not accept their right to exist until the abortive coup of June 1973, and once recognised, the new workers' organisations were confronted with a major political crisis, as the government ordered the return of all factories nationalised except the 104 on its final list of strategic firms, in a vain attempt to block the onrush of the final coup.

Little detailed research is available on the *cordones*, although we know that their political loyalties lay with the internal opposition rather the communists. As organisations based on a geographical area rather than an industrial sector, they opened up the possibility of local ties between factory workers and shanty town dwellers, a cause which the MIR was vociferous in espousing though perhaps ambiguous in resolving, as it determined efforts to safeguard its own base in the shanty towns. The *cordones* may have involved smaller factories and perhaps even some which were semi-artisan, with which the Socialist Party traditionally had stronger connections in any case.[68]

The irony of the Popular Unity era is that its Opposition drew heavily on the labour movement's own traditions of mass mobilisation against governments,[69] involving sections of the self-employed, *empleados* and technicians, peasants, women, and some manual workers. The context for the new mass protests was partially set by the fears small businessmen had of nationalisation, fanned by a campaign of press hysteria which was financed with American funds.[70] Nonetheless, it also reflected a deteriorating economic situation (Tables 6.11 and 6.12). As inflation rose to 77 per cent in 1972 and 227 per cent in the first eight months of 1973, on official figures, the discontent out of which a mass movement could be created inevitably grew.

TABLE 6.12 *Real Variations in Remunerations Indices, 1958–73*

YEAR	*SUELDO VITAL** (%)	*NATIONAL WAGES and SALARIES INDEX*** (%)	*MANUFACTURING WAGES and SALARIES@* (%)	*AGRICULTURE MINIMUM WAGE* (%)
1958	− 4.6	− 3.7	− 3.4	− 1.7
1959	− 1.3	0.3	− 1.0	8.6
1960	−10.3	3.1	− 2.0	8.9
1961	15.7	6.9	9.0	10.3
1962	2.2	0.0	4.4	1.4
1963	−14.2	− 5.5	− 7.9	− 9.1
1964	− 0.3	− 8.5	2.5	2.1
1965	7.4	14.8	10.9	22.2
1966	2.4	12.6	13.9	10.9
1967	− 1.0	15.1	9.9	4.3
1968	− 3.7	0.6	1.9	− 3.7
1969	− 2.1	8.3	4.6	− 2.1
1970	− 2.4	10.2	8.4	21.0
1971	12.2	25.8	27.0	38.7
1972	−14.2	− 6.2	3.9	8.0
1973	−34.2	−24.2	−21.5	−32.1

* legal minimum wage for *empleados*.
** As compiled by the National Statistics Institute for firms of more than 20 workers, excluding construction, State health and State education.
@ Stallings' own weighted average of the minimum industrial wage, industrial *sueldo vital*, and INE sectoral wages and salaries index covering firms with more than 20 workers.
# These figures probably understate real gains to agricultural workers. According to Heskia (1974), in 1960 the average agricultural wage was only 60 per cent of the minimum, reflecting employers' beliefs that the rest could be paid as benefits in kind (land, and so on). By 1969 average salaries coincided with the minimum, and benefits were negotiated as an addition.

SOURCE: Stallings (1978).

In practice, the flexibility of the political matrix and the provision of space for conflict within Popular Unity itself did much to limit the political damage which the government suffered. Its only serious conflict with manual workers was the strike of copper miners at El Teniente in April 1973, notionally supporters of Popular Unity: a strike which broke out because miners claimed the right to automatic cost-of-living increases in addition to those conceded by the government under the national *reajuste*. The Opposition gleefully adopted El Teniente's cause, and the government replied by mass demonstrations in Santiago, tapping the urban *cordones* and successfully dividing the ranks of the strikers, some of whom withdrew. The cost was a series of solidarity strikes in Chuquicamata and extraordinarily bitter divisions between Popular Unity and Christian Democrat trade unionists thereafter, though the socialists retained a base in one of the El Teniente unions, Caletones, even after the coup.[71]

More remarkable is the extent to which other sectors continued to support the Allende government in spite of deteriorating wages. Even *empleados*, the sector where Christian Democrats had their clearest base outside agriculture, were still offering as much support to the communist and socialist parties as to the Christian Democrats in the CUT elections of 1972.[72] Direct elections in SUTE, the educational union, showed the government parties running neck and neck with Christian Democrats in December 1972. No voting figures are available to gauge Popular Unity's general support within the labour movement during 1973: but the government's ability to increase support in the March 1973 Congressional elections does not suggest that it was being abandoned by the labour movement.

The decade of distributive reforms did not collapse because of any inherent ambiguity on the part of the labour movement – Christian Democracy and Popular Unity shared a gamut of policy commitments from generalised income redistribution to agrarian reform, including the development of a modern industrial sector capable of producing for popular needs and a redistribution of power within the workplace in favour of employees. Without those policy commitments, the Christian Democrats would have been unable to secure any union support. The decade collapsed because of powerful internal resistance from the possessing classes to any loss of their consumer power, their political prerogatives, or their right to control the work place, to the dispossessed. Resistance made itself felt *within* the polyclass coalition which was Christian Democracy, halting active implementation in such key areas as agrarian reform after 1967, and pushing it into a confrontation with its own trade unionists over the attempt to limit working-class bargaining power through labour law reform and the forced savings scheme, a confrontation avoided after the general strike of 1967 only at the cost of paralysing the government's general drive for reform.

Resistance to Popular Unity operated outwith the governing coalition, through capital flight, mass protests and 'strikes' of employers, professionals and the self-employed, and CIA-supported tactics of urban violence intended to provoke a military solution. The fact that the campaign was successful says much about the military and the police, and perhaps about the Christian Democratic Party as a whole: but very little about the labour movement, whose Christian Democrat activists were to suffer alongside those of Popular Unity from the mass purges of agitators by employers in the weeks following the coup, even if their political loyalties usually saved them from a worse fate.

Post-coup

The suspension of almost all local union activity after the coup, including all union elections, and the selective elimination of thousands of union officers and activists who were Marxists or thought to be left-wing (Appendix 4) gave a certain air of unreality to union life from 1973–79. Surviving officials in the various pre-coup federations slowly returned to active life after the ILO visit of 1974, which provided a brief interregnum of relative freedom under Minister of Labour Diaz Estrada which lasted until mid-1975, as well as a doomed attempt to reinvigorate the old Christian Democrat corporatist project of labour reform.[73] Even during this period, the harassment and intimidation of union activists meant that Chilean unions were increasingly dependent on foreign political as well as occasional foreign financial support.

Thus, the early post-coup union movement bore very little resemblance to traditional union structures. It was dominated by federations and confederations, not local unions; and above all, by a set of competing politically-organised '*centrals*': the 'Group of Ten' (later 12), led by dockers' leader and Christian Democrat Senator Eduardo Rios, closely tied to the AFL-CIO; the *Coordinadora Nacional Sindical*, an alliance of Christian Democrats with the old Popular Unity parties, led by Manuel Bustos of the textile workers, with considerable European support; the FUT, closely linked to the Christian Left, a local branch of CLAT; and finally the UNTRACH, a confederation organised by government supporters within the labour movement concerned to prevent the emergence of a formally fascist official labour movement to their Right again. The UNTRACH was led by Bernardo Castillo, President of the copper workers' CTC after government intervention removed Gabriel Santana of the 'Group of Ten' in 1976.

While strict controls on the activity of local unions remained in force, these political *centrals* provided channels through which union grievances could be expressed. Pressure from below for a return to rank and file action built up first within the copper mines, which, for all El Teniente's historical role in the overthrow of Allende, were hardly well represented by the political views of Castillo. There was a strike at El Teniente in 1977: a canteen boycott and threatened strike, only averted by military occupation, in Chuquicamata in 1978. At the end of October 1978, under pressure from local business interests to remove controls on labour activity before they created an explosion, Pinochet suddenly called surprise elections for unions in the private sector. Thereafter the government moved quickly to 'normalise' union activity under the totally new set of rules established by its new Labour Code.

For four years thereafter these measures, and the possibilities of making some gains during Chile's brief 'economic miracle', successfully contained labour protests (though they did not eliminate the older generation of politicised labour leaders whom government sources had predicted would disappear as the new labour movement was born). By 1983, the margin for union gains in wages and conditions was gone. Copper miners and workers in the manufacturing belt of Santiago were sufficiently confident and sufficiently desperate to return to the Chilean labour movement's traditional forms of political bargaining. The re-emergence of general strikes during this period is even more remarkable when one takes into account the butchery of the pre-coup union movement inflicted by a combination of free market contraction of local industry, and the new Labour Code (Table 6.13).

The mobilisations of 1983/84 were not successful as Opposition political initiatives, as union members had hoped. Nonetheless, the labour movement made some very important gains as a result of them – and not only in the form of modifications to the new Labour Code. By 1983, although the political *centrals* of the early post-coup years had not altogether disappeared, they were firmly taking second place to the new *Comando Nacional de Trabajadores*, and an executive committee on which both political *centrals* and the major economic sectors of the labour movement were represented, side by side. Still rife with political divisions and uncertainties, the labour movement was once again moving towards the creation of a national confeder-

TABLE 6.13 *Legal Unionism Before and After the Coup*

	No./unions	*No./Members*	*Average Size*	*Percentage of Labour Force*
1970	4585	535 686	117	20.6
1971	4969	616 926	124	23.2
1972	6112	755 936	124	28.7
1973	6550	780 015	119	27.8
1974	6873	797 360	116	28.2
1975	6904	797 103	115	28.3
1976	6941	796 767	115	26.2
1977	6077	557 755	92	16.1
1979*	5000	581 483	116	18.2
1983*	4401	320 903	73	12.2

SOURCE: Clotario Blest, citing Ministry of Labour data in Entrevista, *Analisis* 4 (Apr.-May 1978); figures for 1979 and 1983 from Campero, 'El sindicalismo Chileno en el Regimen Militar (1973–1984)', *Iberoamerica*, XV (1985) 1–2. Data are affected by delays in registering newly-formed unions and in eliminating inactive ones; thus the persistently high levels of unionisation until 1977 probably reflect pre-coup union activity.

ation of sectoral organisations, accepted as legitimate by all its political tendencies, freely registering its changes of political mood: a *central* possessed of 'no hegemonic doctrine', as the original organisers of the 1983 protests so clearly put it, and able to bargain with governments in power on behalf of the union movement as a whole.

The one complication in this scenario was the *Central Democratica de Trabajadores*. Under the guidance of Rios, and the right-wing of Christian Democracy, this group still sought to preserve a national division between 'undemocratic' labour sectors and those acceptable to the Americans – participating in protest movements and in the CNT (which it could hardly abandon without jeopardising its own support among copper miners) but insisting on its own status as a *central*, symbolised by its determination to hold separate celebrations from the CNT each 1 May. Rios' position received powerful support from outside the labour movement, from the Christian Democrat-dominated *Acuerdo Nacional*, a front of Opposition politicians with hopes of becoming the next government. Here again, perceptions of American interest in splitting the labour movement into 'democratic' and 'non-democratic' wings were vital, with the Opposition having been secretly assured by the US Embassy in early 1986 that Pinochet would fall more quickly if the 'democratic' alternative committed itself to banning 'undemocratic' parties such as the CP.

Nevertheless, the extreme weakness of the labour movement after the coup, which had made rival *centrals* acceptable in 1973–79 (perhaps even preferable to a united movement, given the relative ease with which such *centrals* could secure support from abroad to protect themselves from the dictatorship) was now giving way to a period of slow but steady growth. Levels of unionisation, as measured by Ministry of Labour statistics, reached their nadir in the immediate aftermath of the new Labour Code and then began to climb again. Unionisation began to reach some of the sectors which the Code and government had envisaged as a permanent source of cheap labour, given Chile's high rates of unemployment: contract workers employed in the copper mines, for instance, began forming local unions and finally created a sectoral federation of their own in 1985.

The impact the government's strategic move to *laissez-faire* was being felt in the old bases of the union Right. Copper miners, always a peculiarly ambiguous sector (where Left and Right competed in the era of the CUT) continued to move slowly towards the left, matching political loyalties to the still uncertain position as a vanguard which they had chosen in the protests of 1983/84. Government attempts to remove the 'unrepresentative' Seguel, a left-wing Christian Democrat, from his job in El Teniente and thus from his post as President of the CTC, produced mass protests throughout the mining sector, extending as far as Chuquicamata in the north. Chuqui's miners, an old base of the Christian Democrat Right (and notorious for their geographical and political isolation from the national labour movement) staged a mass march to the port of Calama on the coast in Seguel's defence in November 1985, echoing the traditions of militant nitrate miners 78 years before. They capped this surprising demonstration of militancy by choosing half of the minehead union executive from the MDP slate in the union elections of June 1986,[74] thus jeopardising the *Central Democratica de Trabajadores*' most secure source of support. As a result of over-all shifts in loyalty within the copper mines, communists doubled their direct representation on the CTC's executive from two out of 15 to four.

Docks, once the most privileged sector of the pre-coup labour force and a by-word for their support of American-style business unionism, emerged from the massive deterioration of salaries and working conditions imposed by the new Labour Code with a classic general strike in November 1985, which spread through the 20 unions of the port of Valparaiso, north to Vina, Antofagasta and Arica, south to San Antonio and Talcahuano. The strikers seized the opportunity to destroy existing sectional barriers between sectors of the labour force and to echo the demands, now common among Santiago trade unions, for a shelving of political differences at national level. They also joined the CNT's executive.[75]

These changes were slow, and certainly insufficient to produce the kind of solid general strike which could decisively halt national production and international supplies, of the kind at which the labour movement was aiming during these years. Workers' militancy at rank and file level was severely restricted by the very credible threat of unemployment and the fact that unlawful stoppages rendered workers liable for instant dismissal, coupled with a referral of their names to the security services if politics was suspected to be involved. Not all sectors had recovered from the coup. Activity in the State sector, crucial to the 1950 recovery, remained virtually frozen during this one, with government unions forbidden to engage in collective negotiations and employees too chastened by the successive waves of mass dismissals which followed the coup, to do much about it. (Primary schoolteachers managed to preserve their 90-year-long history of aggressive unionism, notwithstanding, and also contributed to the Opposition yet another Secretary of the Communist Party, whose disappearance and murder in early 1985 was to provide a rallying point for the Opposition as a whole in the wake of the failure of the 1984 general strike).

But for all the surges and reverses of the political struggle, and its undoubted frustrations, the mobilisations and general strikes of 1983–86 did labour no harm and perhaps much good. By early 1986, the CNT represented 90 federations, and was popularly reputed to speak for 75 per cent of the labour movement. In spite of Rios's prediction at the christening of the *Central Democratica de Trabajadores* in November 1984, that 'there will never again be only one *central*', by 1986 unionists in Santiago were beginning to say with some confidence that 'the CNT is going to be the *central*.[76]

CONCLUSIONS

Chilean labour has evolved a complicated and tangled pattern of organisation. Perhaps for that very reason, it attracts half-truths like a magnet.

The most costly to the labour movement itself has surely been the AFL-CIO conviction that the movement is 'communist-dominated', and its correlate, which the AFL-CIO has frequently helped out with political support and finance: *non-communist elements should split away from the rest of the movement and form their own organisations, and governments should suppress communists within the labour movement where possible*. This kind of intervention has consistently failed to change the face of Chilean unionism, for good reasons. The fact is that no party dominates labour. Quick to register every conceivable shift in support for existing rival patterns at shop-floor, the matrix is virtually unusable as an instrument of ideological control, and always at its most comfortable, as Barria perceived, with a 'trade unionism of opposition'. The labour movement shows least tolerance for parties which identify themselves with the burdens of government – a reaction which caused Marxist parties to lose some of their support to anarchists, in the early years of the Popular Front: socialists to lose out to communists, as these moved into opposition during the years of Radical governments: Christian Democrats to lose out to Marxists, during the later years of the Frei regime: communists to lose out to socialists and even Christian Democrats, during Popular Unity: and all the other parties to lose in the face of communist gains, during the post-1980 years of opposition to the military regime, as American opposition to their inclusion in any form of broad alliance against the military gave them the unsought cachet of providing the only 'real' opposition to the regime. There is no possibility of an 'official trade unionism' ever enjoying any popular success.

A second half-truth is the suggestion that economic weakness has forced labour into a dependent role on the State, and thus encouraged its politisation and a certain 'legalism' in labour's attitude towards industrial relations, a misrepresentation of some of the conclusions of Alan Angell's comprehensive study of 1972, coloured inevitably by the rosy vision of pre-coup labour relations which has emerged post-coup.[77] The Chilean working-class as a whole certainly suffers from economic disadvantages, given the highly competitive labour markets which face unskilled manual or clerical workers in an underdeveloped economy. Nevertheless, the collapse of one government effort after another at corporatist or populist systems of control hardly indicates a movement which is 'dependent on the State', nor do the details of the pre-coup industrial relations system, with its consistently strong organisation of State employees (legally forbidden to negotiate), consistent ability to mount illegal strikes, and manipulation of political networks to fill the vacuum left by government prohibitions on the employment of professional union officers or on unions holding strike funds.

The fact is that the Chilean State cannot be treated as the provider of an impersonal legal framework, rather than as a set of governments subject to conflicting pressures from different sectors of the ruling class. The relationship between labour and the State is certainly critical to the labour movement: but it has always been a very ambiguous one, as the consistent mistrust of the matrix for its own parties in government would lead one to expect. The governments of the 1920s originally offered an industrial relations system with the expressed intention of controlling labour and eliminating revolutionary unionism. They failed: but if organised labour continued to make use of their industrial relations framework for the succeeding 50-year period, it was at the cost of defending a clearly inadequate system against periodic threats of new authoritarian 'reforms' which proposed a recentralisation of controls over collective bargaining in government hands. More simply, the State was the centre of new efforts at repressing working-class mobilisations and strikes, and occasionally of new ruling class assaults on 'revolutionary unionism', as in the Law for the Defence of Democracy.

Why the State should perpetually have sought a revision of its existing dicta on labour relations, is an interesting question – whether the reasons are economic, or rooted in ruling class fears of the dangerous classes. But whatever the underlying causes, it is difficult to resist the conclusion that if at no time in the history of the labour movement could government and employers be said to have secured a hegemony over their employees, much of the responsibility for that state of affairs lies squarely in their own hands.

The final half-truth which has dominated studies of Chilean labour is the prevailing belief that because so small a proportion of the labour force was legally organised under the old Code, organised labour was a privileged sector with no social or political ties to the real dispossessed. In the 1960s, belief in the labour aristocracy was a hallmark of the Chilean far Left, but also of some foreign social scientists – as for instance James Petras:

> As part of the bargaining framework, the parties of the Left have generally kept labour struggles within manageable proportions by not articulating the demands of the non-industrial poor and rural proletariat, who compose most of the working class. In its role as

> defender of the unionised industrial workers, the Left has raised the standard of living of that group, preserved its electoral base and access to office, and WIDENED THE GAPS between different strata of the working class.[78]

This argument sat rather awkwardly with the small size of most unions in Chile (Table 6.9), but in statistical terms it was true, for reasons deeply rooted in the intentions of the old Labour Code. Rural workers were at a disadvantage under the provisions of the code from 1940 to 1966 (largely because of a threatened revolt against the Popular Front government and the industrialisation programme by Chile's ruling class, for whom the rural areas were a vital political fiefdom). Workers in semi-artisan factories were at a disadvantage in that it took ten manual workers to form a legal plant committee for bargaining purposes, and 25 to form a *sindicato industrial*. Although Sader's 1973 study showed remarkably little difference in rates of unionisation between monopoly and competitive sectors of Chilean industry, workers in the larger firms (50 workers or more) did benefit from a measure of employer paternalism in the form of sector-linked social security provisions and a range of other special benefits linked to the firm itself.

Whatever the evidence, the labour aristocracy thesis was a poor predictive guide either to the behaviour of the labour movement or that of Chile's old Left parties. Political competition within the matrix made it a question of time before individual parties would try to organise the neglected sectors to steal a march on their rivals – as Christian Democrats, socialists, communists and the MIR all did in the 1960s and 1970s. Rural workers were unionised very quickly. New forms of community organisation blossomed in the shanty towns. Under Popular Unity, an effort was made to integrate the self-employed and petty entrepreneurs into the social security system.[79] Workers in small factories played a role in the creation of the cordons.

The experience of the decade of distributive reforms thus suggests that the institutional framework underpinning Chilean working-class politics could partially overcome tendencies towards internal stratification. The 'labour aristocracy thesis' subsequently dwindled into an explanation of the opposition to Popular Unity by some dockers and copper miners (though not all of these sectors) – until, ironically, it was revived as a vital plank in the campaign by the new post-coup military dictatorship to justify its own anti-union labour reforms.

However, the dramatic impact of free market policies on traditional employment patterns has recently stimulated a new version in Martinez and Tironi's work, modelled this time on Gorz's *Farewell to the Proletariat*[80] . . . once again, relying on a core of factual truth. As Appendix 2 shows, 'proletarianisation' in Chile, in the sense of an ever-growing weight of wage-earners within the economy and of large-scale as opposed to small-scale shops, does show signs of running into reverse, perhaps even in manufacturing. Employment in the goods-producing sector of the economy has been declining compared to that in the broadly defined and supposedly 'unproductive'[81] service sector (transport, commerce and services) which now accounts for more than 60 per cent of the entire labour force.

Yet the evidence is ambiguous. Manufacturing's decline within the labour force may go back to 1970, though the policies of Popular Unity induced a temporary expansion; certainly by 1970 there was a clear trend towards increasing informal sector employment in transport, construction, services and mines. Small employers and the self-employed in transport played a critical role in the Opposition campaign against Popular Unity in 1972–73 . . . just as they did in the general strike against President Ibáñez in 1955 . . . and before that in the general strike which enforced President Arturo Alessandri's election, in 1920.

One can readily construct a counter-thesis to the rather arid structuralism behind these arguments. Since it first began to make an impact on national politics in 1890, the Chilean working-class has always lived and organised within an environment in which the classic, goods-producing proletariat was a minority, though an important one. Transport, commerce, services and a polymorphous 'other' have accounted for a fairly uniform 40 per cent of the active population since 1900, while the non-agricultural, goods-producing sectors have never yet reached 30 per cent. Even in the heyday of industrialisation, one in five of those at work nationally was either self-employed or an unpaid family worker. If one includes 'housewives' – many of them hidden members of the informal sector – the figures would be much larger. By 1952, Chile boasted very nearly three 'housewives' for every adult woman 'at work'.[82]

It is this underlying continuity in social structure which enables us to explain what would otherwise be a mystery: the twentieth century attraction of general strikes and mass demonstrations, the mobilisation of an urban crowd, as significant in 1984 as in 1955 and in 1905, which, as this article has attempted to demonstrate, play a vital role in strengthening the over-all bargaining power of a multi-sectoral labour movement, by facilitating political bargaining with the government, by encouraging the spread of formal unionisation and strike activity to new sectors and smaller firms, and by confirming the Chilean working-class's sense of its own identity and unity as the victim of government repression.

But behind the general strikes lies the political matrix, whose organisation along political rather than sectoral lines is what makes possible the contacts between different sectors with widely different economic roots on which general strikes and much broader political initiatives depend. The existence of the matrix explains why the labour aristocracy thesis works so poorly in Chile, and why, whatever the significance of sectoral conflicts of interest at any given moment – and in spite of the efforts of successive governments to exploit sectoral tensions and rigidify sectoral divisions – sectoral analysis is such a very poor predictor of the labour movements' fate.

Consider again the evidence of Table 6.1. The 1890–1920 movement was constructed around the transport sector (docks, railways, trams), core of the era's general strikes and rival national confederations: 'proletarian' coal and nitrate miners were geographically too isolated to provide bargaining power, though a collective awareness of their sufferings is part of the ideological cement binding the labour movement together even today. As the new legal unions began to function in the 1930s, legal *sindicatos industriales* in the Santiago factories and illegal organisations of railway workers joined hands in the new era's first general strikes. During the era of repression between 1947 and 1955, their place was taken by white-collar workers in the State and private sectors (the latter the subject of the most carefully established legal sectoralism in the Labour Code) and these were briefly the centre of the labour movement's most nearly revolutionary mobilisations against a government during the entire pre-coup era. When the Ibáñez era passed, the torch passed with it to the traditional coal mining and manufacturing proletariat, the backbone of Popular Unity. Like white-collar workers, copper miners have been widely regarded by Chile's Marxist trade unionists (structuralists to a man) as politically unreliable: though their intervention decided the 1950 strike of white-collar workers in labour's favour, and it was to provide the trigger for the anti-coup protests of 1983–84.

The success of the Chilean labour movement has always resided in its ability to weave an inter-sectoral web of political loyalties, stretching from docks to factories to government offices, binding into a single party individual workers with apparently different economic interests, and often in a political minority within their own sector. The web is dense, because it is built up of the individual networks of competing parties. Its capacity to mobilise the working-class as a whole is as solid as the ability of its competing networks to co-operate; and over the past hundred years of labour history, their co-operation has often faltered, but it has never disappeared.

NOTES

1. Cf. Alan Angell, *Politics and the Labour Movement in Chile* (London: Oxford University Press, 1972). Much existing writing on Chilean labour history is dominated by the history and disputes of the political parties – the writings of Jorge Barria S. and Gabriel Salazar being significant exceptions.
2. 1060 unions and 97 962 members voted in the 1978 elections, the last to be held under Chile's 1932 Labour Code; 799 of these and 76 414 members were in manufacturing. See Manuel Barrera, *Politica Laboral y Movimiento Sindical Chileno Durante el Regimen Militar*, Washington (Wilson Centre Working Paper, No. 66) 1980.

   This section owes a great deal to research funded by the Economic and Social Research Council and carried out jointly by the author and Nigel Haworth in Chile in 1979–80. For details see N. Haworth and J. Roddick, 'Labour and Monetarism in Chile', *Bulletin of Latin American Studies*, vol. 1 (Oct. 1981) no. 1, and N. Haworth and J. Roddick, 'Tres Cambios de Rumbo en la Political Laboral del Gobierno Militar en Chile', in Gallitelli and Thompson (eds.), *Sindicalismo y regimenes autoritarios en Argentina y Chile* (Amsterdam: (CEDLA), 1982).

   Details on the Pinochet regime's economic policy and the role of 'free market' theory within it can be found in A. Foxley, *Experimentos neoliberales en America Latina* (Santiago: Coleccion Estudios CIEPLAN, No. 7, Mar. 1982); P. O'Brien, 'Authoritarianism and Monetarism in Chile', *Socialist Review* XIV, 5, (September/October 1984) no. 77, and O'Brien and Roddick, *Chile: The Pinochet Decade* (London: Latin American Bureau, 1983).
3. The relationship between copper miners and the Allende government is reviewed in Zapata, 'Trade Union Action and Political Behaviour of the Chilean Miners of Chuquicamata' in Cohen, Gutkind and Brazier (eds.), *Peasants and Proletarians* (London: Hutchinson, 1979). Wage data cited by Campero and Valenzuela show that – leaving aside their large nominal gains under the Allende regime – by 1975 miners' real income had declined 50 per cent compared with 1970 levels and by 1979 was still 25 per cent below them (G. Campero and J.A. Valenzuela, *El movimiento sindical en el regimen militar chileno 1973–1981*, Santiago: Estudios ILET, 1984). Other grievances included the introduction of contract

labour as a substitute for union members in cleaning and maintenance duties, and the suspension of the *Confederación de Trabajadores del Cobre*'s rights to administer hospitals and other treatment centres for the mining community.

4. Quotations from *Solidaridad* report on the CNT's formation, no. 152, March 1983. No comprehensive study of the 1983/84 protest movement has yet been written. Thus, the above relies heavily on *Solidaridad*, the bi-weekly journal of the Catholic Church's local human and social rights organisation; on *Paginas Sindicales*, a bulletin produced by the independent institute, Vector; on the full account of the July protests produced by another independent institute, SUR; and on A. Quiroga's article in *Arauco*, 'El movimiento social en Chile. Balance de un año (1983–84)', Santiago, I, 1, June/July 1984.
5. Details are taken from M. Monteon, 'The Enganche in the Chilean Nitrate Sector 1880–1939', *Latin American Perspectives*, Issue 22, Summer 1982; and H. Ramírez Necochea, *Historia del movimiento obrero en Chile, Antecedentes, Siglo XIX* (Santiago: Editora Austral, 1956).
6. Chile's first union, a 'resistance society' modelled on the old mutualist pattern but with strike action as its primary aim, emerged in 1987 in Santiago's railway engineering shop and quickly acquired imitators throughout the Santiago-Valparaiso area. Northern unions began to be organised in 1900, but on a different pattern, the *mancomunal*: a federation of different trades based on the docks but deliberately extended to include nitrate workers, offering social insurance, a newspaper, and an executive to negotiate on members' behalf during the era's still spontaneous strikes (cf. Alan Angell, 'The Origins of the Chilean Labour Movement' in *Peasants and Proletarians*, op. cit., 1979.
7. I am enormously indebted to Gabriel Salazar for this argument and for the wealth of empirical material now available on pre-1890 labour relations. Salazar estimates that during the 19th century, 40 000 Chileans migrated to California, near 50 000 to Argentina, 25 000 to Peru, and 10 000 to the Peruvian and Bolivian nitrate provinces (later the Norte Grande) as well as 3–400 to Australia. Chilean railway workers carried traditions of unionisation with them into Bolivia and Peru. See Entrepreneurs and Peons in the Transition to Industrial Capitalism: Chile 1820–1878, Ph.D. thesis, U. of Hull, U.K., and *Labradores, Peones y Proletarios*, Santiago (Ediciones Sur) 1985.

   The local roots of labour ideologues, printers, carpenters, and other representatives of the skilled trades, are well reviewed by Peter De Shazo in *Urban Workers and Labor Unions in Chile 1902–1927*, Madison (U. of Wisconsin Press) 1983.
8. This early spurt of industrialisation –'manufacture rather than machinofacture' – is now better understood thanks to the work of Gabriel Palma and Salazar. For details of the technological structure and employment patterns of the new industries, see Salazar [English version], pp. 13–65 and Palma, *Growth and Structure of Chilean Manufacturing Industry from 1830 to 1935* (Ph.D. thesis, Oxford University, 1979) pp. 302–63.
9. Women were also once the backbone of Chile's urban informal sector: but legal restrictions were being placed on their traditional role as petty

traders, bakers, and tavern keepers by the middle of the nineteenth century, favouring larger, male-dominated enterprises. Neither as artisans nor as market-women did they make any impact on the artisan-dominated mutual benefit and insurance societies out of which the modern labour movement was forged. See Salazar, 'The Women's Peonage'.

10. The mutualist societies in turn traced their origins back to the introduction of Jacobin ideas in Chile in 1848, through the *Sociedad de Igualidad*. On artisan involvement in regional uprisings during the pre-mutualist period, see M. Zeitlin, *The Civil Wars in Chile* (Princeton, N.J.: Princeton University Press, 1984) p. 56. On mutualist organisations and their relationship to the *Sociedad de Igualidad*, Salazar, op. cit.; Ramírez Necochea, 1956, op. cit.; or Tulio Lagos, *Bosquejo historico de la historia del Movimiento Obrero en Chile* (Santiago: Imprenta 'El Esfuerzo', 1941).
11. Cf. Manuel Fernández, 'British Nitrate Companies and the Emergence of Chile's Proletariat', in B. Munslow and H. Finch (eds), *Proletarianisation in the Third World* (London: Croom Helm, 1984); and *The Development of the Chilean Economy and its British Nitrate Connections, 1895–1914* (Ph.D., University of Glasgow, 1979). Fifty per cent of the nitrate mines were British, 25 per cent Chilean, the rest belonging to an assortment of European and Peruvian interests.
12. The Democratic Party was founded as a more radical alternative to the Radicals in 1897. The first Marxist grouping, the *Centro Social Obrero*, was founded in Santiago in 1896, giving rise to the first Socialist party, the Union Socialista, in 1897.
13. De Shazo (1983) is the best source on the labour movement's gains in negotiations. For accounts of the unionisation of teachers and white-collar workers, see, however, Ramírez Necochea, *Origen y formación del partido Comunista de Chile* (Santiago: Editora Austral, 1961) and J. Roddick, *The Radical Teachers* (PhD, University of Sussex, 1979).
14. The comment is Barria's (*Los movimientos sociales en Chile desde 1910 hasta 1926* (Santiago: Editorial Universitaria, 1960), the explanation drawn from Monteon, op. cit. Attempts to control labour by imposing military discipline were consistent with the government's philosophy of labour control in the Norte Chico, and may have been imported from there. Salazar provides the only adequate information on this earlier period.
15. De Shazo, op. cit., provides the best source for this period.
16. Cf. Roddick, 'The failure of Populism in Chile: labour movement and politics before World War II', Amsterdam, *Boletín de estudios latinoamericanos y del caribe* (1981) no. 31.
17. Witker cites a vigorous attack by Recabarren on the sectarianism of Argentinian anarchists in 1907 (*Los trabajos y los dias de Recabarren* (Mexico: Editorial Nuestro Tiempo, 1977), p. 54. My own doctoral study of primary school teachers (not only 'middle-class' workers, but allies of the IWW) shows the FOCH and the POS as determined and valuable allies in all their campaigns. See Roddick (1977) op. cit.
18. All financed by the AFL-CIO or ORIT. For details on the first three, see

S. Romualdi, *Presidents and Peons* (New York: Funk and Wagnalls, 1967). Romualdi was the AFL's Latin American representative from 1946–65.

19. On pre-coup corporatist projects, see Paul Drake, 'Corporatism and Functionalism in Modern Chilean Politics', London, *Journal of Latin American Studies*, II (1979) 1; and G. Catalan, 'Notas sobre proyectos autoritarios corporativos en Chile' (Santiago: *Escritos de Teoria*, III/IV, December/January 1978–79). Ibáñez's flirtation with Mussolini's ideas in the late 1920s is very clear in the *Boletín* published by the Ministry of Health, Social Security and Labour, as well as in the *Boletín* of the *Asociacion del Trabajo*: see Roddick and Haworth, *Chile 1924 and 1979: Labour Policy and Industrial Relations through Two Revolutions* (Glasgow: Institute of Latin American Studies, Occasional Paper No. 42, 1984). On the two post-coup corporatist projects, see Haworth and Roddick (1983), op. cit.
20. Salazar (1985): details of the abolition of the guilds are from Monteon, *Chile in the Nitrate Era: The Evolution of Economic Dependence, 1880–1930* (Madison: University of Wisconsin Press, 1982).
21. Mexico had earlier guaranteed the right to strike, without establishing a full industrial relations system.
22. On Ibáñez's experiments with import-substitution and State finance for industry, see H. Kirsch, *Industrial Development in a Traditional Society* (Gainesville: University of Florida Press, 1977).
23. Cf. the memoirs of Alessandri's private secretary, A. Olavarría Bravo, *Chile entre dos Alessandri* (Santiago: Editorial Nascimiento, 1962) p. 73ff., and of a contemporary labour lawyer, Carlos Vicuña Fuentes, *La tiranía en Chile* (Santiago: Imprenta y Encuadernacion O'Higgins, 1945) vol.1, p. 110. R. Donoso's classic *Alessandri, agitador y demoledor* (Mexico: Fondo de Cultura Economica, 1952) ably conveys the ruling élite's reaction to his candidacy.
24. The story of Recabarren's last demonstration is told in Olavarría Bravo, op. cit., p. 158, and confirmed by Clotario Blest, interview and *Clotario Blest, Testigos del Siglo XX* (Santiago: Ediciones Aconcagua, 1980); that of FOCH and CP involvement in the January 1925 coup in the memoirs of Marmaduke Grove's coconspirator, lieutenant Charlin (*Del avion rojo a la Republica Socialista*, Santiago: Quimantu, 1972). Ramirez Necochea (*Origen y formación del partido comunista*, op. cit.) provides a hostile and misleading account of the USRACH, which conveniently ignores CP involvement with the military. See rather De Shazo (1983) p. 233, and Roddick (1977) and (1981).
25. Barria, *El movimiento obrero en Chile, Sintesis historico-social* (Santiago: Prensa Latinoamericana, 1971) p. 74, gives the best account of the Socialist Republic, Charlin and Drake, *Socialism and Populism in Chile (1932–1952)* (Urbana: University of Illinois Press, 1978), being disappointingly little interested in the labour movement, although Drake gives a good account of the regime's benefits for workers (pp. 79–80).
26. *Legislacion social y sindicatos legales en Chile* (Santiago: Editorial Ginebra, 1937), published for a regional meeting of the ILO, gives the Labour Inspectors' view of union history to date, which suggests that one

sindicato industrial at the El Teniente copper mine and another in Santiago's electric company supported the CRAC. Others mentioned include newsboys, hairdressers, grocers, and traders in Santiago's Central Market. Contemporary labour ministry bulletins claim involvement by shoe and leather workers, but, given Ibáñez's policy of setting up new 'offical' organisations on the basis of the old name and a handful of corruptable members (as was the case with the Union of White-Collar Workers and that of primary school teachers), further research would be needed to confirm the claim. On UECH 'involvement', see Hinojosa Robles's account in *El libro de oro de los empleados particulares* (Santiago: Editorial Nascimento, 1967): on that of the teachers, Roddick (1977) op. cit.

27. Barria (1970) and Roddick (1977) op. cit. give an account of the Revolutionary Trade Union Alliance.
28. J.O. Morris *Elites, Intellectuals and the Concensus* (Ithaca NY: Cornell University Press, 1967) provides the best guide to the early history of these competing élite projects and the details of the process whereby they were amalgamated, though it is also worth checking Labour Ministry Bulletins. *Rerum Novarum*, the Papal Bull on labour and labour protest promulgated in 1893 marked a watershed in Catholic thinking about labour organisation and did much to inspire the *sindicatos blancos*: but in Chile, Church efforts to provide Catholic mutualist organisations to counter the growing revolutionary threat predated it; see Ramírez Necochea (1956) op. cit., and the description of the 'Sociedad Obreros de San José' founded in 1883 given by Alejandro Magnet in *El Padre Hurtado* (Santiago: Editorial del Pacifico, 1977).
29. *Legislación* is the best source of details on the early differences, much complicated by later legislation. In terms of medical treatment, manual workers originally had a better deal than *empleados*. State workers had a separate scheme. But all these pensions and health insurance schemes were used as sources of funds for Ibáñez's Industrial Investment Bank.
30. *Legislación* gives details of legal and illegal strikes in 1945, the University of Chile (*Desarrollo Economico de Chile, 1940–56* (Santiago: Editorial Universitaria, 1957), p. 7, the later figures.
31. *Legislacion*. Details are also given in the *Boletin* of the Ministry of Labour. The decree establishing immunity seems to have followed shortly after Ibáñez's coup, and was motivated by continuing employer hostility to any form of unionism. Labour courts were established to enforce it.
32. Details of early legal unions are taken from the Ministry of Labour *Boletín*. Barria (*Las relaciones colectivas del trabajo* (Santiago: INSORA, 1967) lists FONACC (shoe and leather), the *Confederación de Molineros* (flour mill workers), *Confederación Maritima de Chile* (docks), *Central de Obreros Graficos de Obras* (print) and *Federación de Panificadores* (bakers) as having achieved some degree of sectoral bargaining.
33. Details of the 1946–48 crisis can be found in Manuel Barrera, 'Desarrollo economico y sindicalismo en Chile' (Mexico, *Revista Mexicana de Sociologia*, XLII (July-September 1978) no. 3; while those of the 1950s

are well covered by Enrique Sierra, *Tres ensayos de estabilization* (Santiago: Editorial Universitaria, 1970). Government attempts to control wages are reviewed in Barrera, above, and in greater depth in Barria, *Trayectoria y estructura del movimiento obrero en Chile, 1946–1962* (Santiago: INSORA, 1963). See also Joseph Ramos's *Politica de remuneraciones en inflaciones persistentes* (Santiago: University of Chile, 1970), for information about the legal basis of post-1950 attempts to control wages. Ramos argues that in practice, private sector salaries remained unaffected while public sector workers were badly hit.

Barbara Stallings provides a review of post-1958 tensions in *Class Conflict and Economic Development in Chile, 1958–1973* (Stanford, California: Stanford University Press, 1978).

34. See Camu Veloso, *Estudio critico de la huelga en Chile* (Santiago: Editorial Universitaria, 1964).
35. There were threats of a US blockade on investment. See Barria, *Historia de la CUT* (Santiago: Prensa Latinoamericana, 1971); and Andrew Barnard, 'Chilean Communists, Radical Presidents, and Chilean Relations with the United States, 1940–1947' (London: *Journal of Latin American Studies*, vol. 13 (Nov. 1981) Part 2. Camu Veloso gives a good summary of the Law, Angell (1972, op. cit.) of the concentration camp.
36. Dates of rail strikes taken from Escobar Zentemo, *Compendio de la legislacion social y desarrollo del movimiento obrero en Chile* (Santiago: 1940). Barria (1970, p. 76) refers to a pro-Grove general strike on 16 and 17 June 1932 by railway workers and trade unions in the capital; *Legislacion* comments on one by *sindicatos industriales* 'at the end of June' regarded by the new government as 'political'; as well as another in solidarity with the mutiny of naval vessels in 1931.
37. See Emir Sader, *Movilización de masas y sindicalización en el gobierno UP* (Santiago: Documento de Trabajo, DESO, Universidad de Chile, 1973). Sader found unionisation concentrated in certain industrial subsectors, particularly textiles (83 per cent), food processing (48 per cent), printing and publishing (60 per cent), paper and cellulose (63 per cent), tobacco (75 per cent), basic metals (100 per cent), non-metallic minerals (58 per cent), and electrical equipment and accessories (51 per cent), figures in each case giving percentage of labour force unionised. These sectors together accounted for 62 per cent of all workers unionised, but only 32 per cent of the labour force in manufacturing.
38. Sader, op. cit.: 42.4 per cent and 41.9 per cent compared to 28.6 per cent for 'low concentration' sectors. Figures on monopoly firms and benefits from (OLD 86) Cf. Peter Gregory, *Sueldos y salarios en la industria manufacturera* (Santiago: INSORA, 1966) p. 53.
39. These experiments are covered in depth in Alan Angell's *Politics and the Labour Movement in Chile*, op. cit.
40. Cf. Haworth and Roddick (1982) op. cit.. Among the changes introduced by General Diaz in the Christian Democrat project was provision to allow all competing unions to bargain jointly with employers.
41. Cf. F. Hayek, *The Road to Serfdom* (London: Routledge, 1946), written in anticipation of the post-war British Labour government.
42. Haworth and Roddick, 'Labour and Monetarism in Chile 1975–80'

(London: *Bulletin of Latin American Research* I (October 1981) 1, based on preparatory Ministry of Labour documents and interviews with participants. Compare the ideas put forward by F. Hayek on Britain in *The 1980's: Unemployment and the Unions* (London: IEA, 1981).

43. Cf. J.S. Valenzuela, *Labour Movement Formation and Politics: the Chilean and French Cases in Comparative Perspective* (PhD, Columbia University, 1979). Federations at sectoral level, which could not bargain under the old Labour Code, were another matter entirely: cases of rival organisations existed in commerce and metalwork.
44. On the Christian Democrat project, see Angell (1972), op. cit., p. 99; on General Diaz's very similar plans, Haworth and Roddick (1982). Diaz met fierce opposition from neo-fascists (who would have preferred a united labour movement with its representatives imposed by the government, and dissident unionists in jail). But he also confronted vocal opposition from union leaders who had retained their public position as, for example, the heads of Federations after the coup.
45. The *Confederación Nacional de Trabajadores*, established with ORIT support in 1957, had 8000 members to the CUT's 300 000, while ASICH, a right-wing Catholic alternative, had 2000. See Barria (1963), op. cit., p. 196.
46. Figures for the survey are cited in Landsberger, Barrera and Toro (1964). On the revival of anarchism, see T. Lagos, *Bosquejo historico del movimiento sindical en Chile* (Santiago: Imprenta El Esfuerzo, 1941).
47. Cf. the SOFOFA *Boletín*.
48. The CTCH formed a *Federación Nacional Campesino* in the early years, with 5000 members among *inquilinos* and small proprietors. Worried about a possible right-wing coup, the more so as landowners' profits were being squeezed by the new price controls intended to benefit urban consumers, the 1940 administration ordered its Inspectors to accept no further requests for legal registration from rural unions, and socialists and communists accepted the decision. In 1947, the last Radical President, Gonzalez Videla, passed special legislation for rural unions so restrictive that its clauses were incorporated into the CHANGE post-1973 dictatorship's new Labour Code. The best account is Barria (1970) op. cit.
49. Statistics covering the whole 1940–52 era are usually cited to show that *empleados* benefited at manual workers' expense (cf. Barrera, 1980, op. cit.) but this ignores the impact of recession and repression after 1947, which touched *empleados* relatively lightly, and the success of *empleados* in holding back a government assault on their wages in the 1950 strike. For a more detailed breakdown, see A. Gunder Frank, 'La politica economica en Chile – Del Frente Popular a la Unidad Popular', (Santiago: *Punto Final* (March 1972) no. 153).
50. Bernardo Ibáñez, ex-primary school teacher, no relation to the dictator Carlos Ibáñez del Campo. On the Socialists AFL-CIO connections, see Drake (1978); on their history as strike-breakers, and the schism, see Angell (1972). Barria (1963) is also valuable.
51. Blest (1963) provides the only really detailed account of this important period.

52. Standard Electric and the *Cia. de Telephonos* were the utilities. Angell (1972) is the best source available on the 1950 strike, which Chilean historians have neglected (compare Barrera, 1980). I have used contemporary memoirs to supplement Angell's account, including Blest's (op. cit.), Vidal and Barria, *Doce dias que estremecieron al pais* (Santiago: 1950), and E. Pizarro, *Victoria al amanecer* (Santiago: 1950), who makes the claim on the *Confederacion de Trabajadores de Cobre*. Barrera's study of copper workers does not mention the 1950 contacts, but the dates are consistent ('El conflicto obrero en el enclave cuprifero chileno', *Revista Mexicana de Sociologia*, XL (Apr.–June 1978) 2.
53. C. Blest, 'La escalada hacia la unidad de la clase trabajadora', *Punto Final* (1971) no. 143. Cf. also Barria (1963), who gives a very full account of this period.
54. Romualdi (1969), op. cit., p. 332. Far from being under communist control, the executive elected at the 1953 convention faithfully reflected all hues of the matrix: five CP, four PSP, three Socialist Party of Chile, three independent Socialists, three anarchists, ten Christian Democrats, two independent supporters of President Ibáñez and Clotario Blest, an independent Catholic socialist and the CUT's first President.
55. Zapata, *Las relaciones entre el movimiento obrero y el gobierno de Salvador Allende* (Mexico: Cuadernos del CES, No. 4, 1974) p. 31. Barria (1963, op. cit., and *El sindicalismo, fuerza social chilena* (Santiago: DERTO, 1976) provides the best survey. His 1963 study shows that manual workers in mining and manufacturing provided 67 per cent of the union membership represented at the CUT's founding convention, declining to 51 per cent by 1962, while the proportion of State employees rose from 27 per cent to 41 per cent (p. 192). But these were years when State workers were deeply involved in the fight against wage cuts and were critical to the era's general strikes.

    Federations with a strong right-wing tradition within their matrix (the docks, print) also varied their participation in the CUT according to the pressures of popular mobilisation, their own current internal balance of forces and the dictates of relationships with ORIT.
56. Barria (1963), p. 192. 'Trade unionism of opposition' is his concept (Barria, 1976).
57. A minimum wage for manual workers in agriculture was established in 1953, along with family allowances: a minimum wage for urban manual workers in 1956. Cf. Ramos, op. cit., pp. 17, 103.
58. Barria (1963) gives a good summary of the programme. For a broader background on Ibanez's relationship with fascist and corporatist tendencies, see Drake (1979, op. cit.) and H. Bicheno, 'Anti-parliamentary Themes in Chilean History: 1920–70' (London: *Government and Opposition*, VII (Summer 1972) 3.
59. Interview, 1980. Other participants confirm this impression. See also Barria (1963).
60. Barria (1963) p. 115. The new Law legalised the Communist Party, but defined as subversive any attempt to change Chile's republican Constitution or undermine its currency, and any contact with a foreign power.

61. Barria, p. 139. Angell (1972) provides a summary of the background to rural unionism, p. 250.
62. See Landsberger, Barrera and Toro on comparative levels of political support for the different parties, 'The Chilean Labor Union Leader: a Preliminary Report on his Background and Attitudes', *Industrial and Labor Relations Review XVII* (April 1964) 3. For the history of unionisation during this period, the best source is Emir Sader (1973), op. cit. The over-all numbers unionised increased by 53 000 between 1967 and 1972, but only 14 000 of these formed unions during Popular Unity. Political competition between Marxists and Christian Democrats in the earlier period presumably explains this discrepancy, plus the limited applicability of union forms to very small firms under the old Labour Code.
63. Cf. A. Foxley: 'The participation of salaried workers in national income rose [between 1960 and 1970] from 51.6 per cent to 53.7 per cent. Secondly, the differences between manual workers' average income and that of *empleados* seems to have dropped: in 1960, the average income of an *empleado* was 397 per cent the average of a manual worker, while in 1969 it was 205 per cent. Meanwhile, the proportion of manual workers earning less than a *sueldo vital* [the *empleado*'s minimum salary] fell from 81.7 per cent to 58.5 per cent'. In J.M. Baraona (ed.), *Los actores de la realidad chilena* (Santiago: Talleres Graficos Corporacion, 1974) pp. 16–17.

    One explanation for the squeeze on differentials, as Heskia points out in the same volume, is the success of some manual workers in legally redefining themselves as *empleados*.
64. For details see Barria (1971), Angell (1972) and Barrera (1971).
65. Sader (1973). Only 22.0 per cent of the labour force in the new 'dynamic' industries was unionised, compared to 36.1 per cent of that in 'traditional' and 59.6 per cent in 'intermediate'. On strikes he comments that 44 per cent in the first six months of 1971 involved *empleados*, but the percentage later fell. There were 98 strikes in construction in the first six months of 1971, 137 in the second six months, and 200 in the first six months of 1972, with the numbers of workers involved rising as larger construction sites struck.

    So far as the pressure of small and medium firms for nationalisation is concerned, the relative weight of textile firms within the nationalised sector is an index of these pressures, though similarly treated cement factories and the Ford plant may have been more crucial to the government's economic plans. Angell, *Political Mobilization and Class Alliances in Chile 1970–1973* (Rotterdam: Institute for New Chile, n.d.), comments on the existence of 100 'people's enterprises' taken over but excluded from the nationalised sector, employing a total of 5000 workers (p. 79), and a further 'Social Area of the Poor' consisting of 80 firms abandoned by employers, employing 10 000.
66. The strike was led by USOPO, a faction of the Socialist Party not part of Popular Unity. Cf. Zapata (1974).
67. For a detailed account of the participation debate, see Santa Lucia, 'The Industrial Working Class and the Struggle for Power in Chile', in P.

O'Brien (ed.), *Allende's Chile* (New York: Praeger, 1976), Angell (n.d.), op. cit., and Espinosa and Zimbalist, *Economic Democracy, Workers' Participation in Chilean Industry 1970–73* (New York: Academic Press, 1981). The latter study was based on a sample of 35 firms in the State sector. Its authors looked for a measure of the negative impact of sectarian conflict on participation, but failed to find any significant correlations.

68. A history of the *cordones* is given in Santa Lucia, op. cit., in Roxborough, O'Brien and Roddick, *Chile: The State and Revolution* (London: Macmillan, 1977) and in Angell, n.d. Angell's data and mine relate to Cordon Cerrillos-Maipu, an early and thus exceptional initiative, which started with conflicts in a semi-artisan factory in the food-processing sector (where unionisation was growing) and in a relatively rural area. Santa Lucia's data unfortunately include no information on the make-up of the *cordones* by types of firms or sectors of industry, but they do include programmes for Cordon Vicuna Mackenna as well as Cerrilos-Maipu, and a list of other *cordons*.

    G. Falabella, *Labour under Authoritarian Regimes: the Chilean Union Movement, 1973–1979* (PhD thesis, University of Sussex, 1980) comments on the Socialist Party's historic ties to smaller firms. On the mobilisation of shanty town dwellers during this period, see 'Shantytown Dwellers and People's Power' by Monica Threlfall in O'Brien (1976) op. cit.

69. How far the imitation was conscious is an interesting point. See Armando Mattelart's comments on 'the mass line of the bourgeoisie' in *Politique Aujourd'hui* (Paris: January 1974).

70. See O'Brien and Roddick, *Chile: The Pinochet Decade*, op. cit., for details of local contacts: the Senate Committee on External Relations for details of over-all funding levels.

71. I have relied here on the account of a left-wing Catholic observer writing for *Mensaje* during the strike. The striking miners were skilled manual workers who had renegotiated themselves a new legal status as *empleados*: the foundry seems to have remained a bastion of support for Popular Unity throughout. Ruiz Tagle points out that Popular Unity held all posts on the five member zonal council when the strike broke.

    After the coup, El Teniente appeared to be a bastion of support for the dictatorship's own favoured union leader, Guillermo Medina, with the foundry once again remaining sympathetic to the left.

72. Baraona (1974), op. cit., provides the figures.

73. For details on changes in government policy before the introduction of the new Labour Code, see Haworth and Roddick (1982) op. cit.

74. Table 6.7 only partially reflects this shift in political balance because of other unions included the Chuqui Zone. Chuqui's *sindicato industrial* with 2600 members elected two communists, two MDP socialists, two Christian Democrats and an Independent; its *sindicato profesional* with 5000 members elected one communist, two MDP socialists, two Christian Democrats, one Radical and an Independent. *Solidaridad* 226, 1986.

75. *Solidaridad* 213, Nov. 1985, gives details of the dockers strike. They joined the CNT executive in April 1986.

76. Rios' quotation, Nov. 30 1984, in *Solidaridad* 189. 'El Comando va por Central', *Solidaridad* 225, June 1986. See programme of CONAGRA, *Solidaridad* 176, May 1984: 'CONAGRA trabajara por la constitucion de una Central de Trabajadores amplia, pluralista y democratica'.
77. Angell's point was that the State's own legal framework encouraged and perpetuated economic weakness. Cf. Angell (1972). For other views of the inherent legalism of Chilean unionism see G. Campero, 'Las nuevas condiciones en las relaciones del trabajo y la accion politica en Chile', Mexico, *Revista Mexicana de Sociologia* XLI (May–June 1979) 2; Cristina Hurtado-Beca, 'Chile 1973–1981: Desarticulación y reestructuración autoritaria del movimiento sindical', Amsterdam, *Boletín de Estudios Latinoamericanos y del Caribe*, no. 31, December; and Alicia Garriazu, *The Chilean and Argentinian Labour Movements: A Comparative Study, 1880–1930* (M. Phil thesis, Birkbeck College, University of London, 1980).
78. James Petras, *Politics and Social Forces in Chilean Development* (Berkeeley: University of California Press, 1969) pp. 164–5.
79. Carmen Mesa-Lago, *Social Security in Latin America* (Pittsburgh: University of Pittsburgh Press, 1978) p. 57.
80. The debate originated with Martinez and Tironi, 'La clase obrera en el nuevo estilo de desarrollo: un enfoque estructural', Mexico, *Revista Mexicana de Sociologia*, XLIV (Apr.–June 1982) 2; and *Clase Obrera y Modelo Economico, Un estudio del peso y la estructura del proletariado en Chile, 1973–1980* (Santiago: SUR Documento de Trabajo No. 21, January 1983): for their debt to Gorz, see (1983). The evidence is reviewed in Lagos and Tokman, [Monetarism, Employment and Social Stratification', *World Development*, XII (1984) 1, who look specifically at the comparable free market administrations in Chile and Argentina, but whose background lies in PREALC's concern for the informal sector (see 'Introduction' to this volume).
81. After Poulantzas? See Campero and Valenzuela (1974), op. cit.
82. The 1952 Census gives 1 272 018 'housewives' to 539 140 female members of the active labour force. According to the Census, 21.6 per cent of Chile's labour force was self-employed. In 1960, the figure was 21.6 per cent and in 1970, 19.6 per cent. Using quarterly survey data taken in December each year, one can estimate that 17.9 per cent of Santiago's total labour force was self-employed in 1963 and 1968, 17.2 per cent in 1970, 18.5 per cent in 1972, 22.1 per cent in 1973, 18.3 per cent in 1977. Tokman ('Informal-formal sector relationships', *CEPAL Review*, 1978) suggests that in 1967, the informal sector accounted for nearly a third of urban employment.

APPENDICES

Appendix 1 The Modern Era of Laissez-Faire, 1974–82

TABLE 6A.I *Macroeconomic Results of the Free Market Experiment: Unemployment and Real Wages, 1974–82*

NOTE: Wage series published after the coup are problematic. All figures which involve a recalculation of 'real' benefits after 1973 are based on a consumer price index which many argue was falsified under Allende (as compared with black market prices – the contrary argument is that many workers got goods through their Neighbourhood Distribution Committees at the official price). Almost everyone accepts that the consumer price index was falsified during the period of hyperinflation which immediately followed the coup. CIEPLAN economists argue that the figures were falsified again after 1976, as the government attempted to bring down 'inflationary expectations'. For further details, see Haworth and Roddick, 'Labour and Monetarism in Chile, 1973–1980', London, *Bulletin of Latin American Research*, I (October 1981) 1.

Furthermore, the official wage index published by the INE ignores such vital sectors as manufacturing firms with less than 20 workers, construction, commerce, and public-sector education and health. For a broader view, cf. Ruiz Tagle's periodic reports on the 'Consumer Price Index of the Poor' in *Mensaje*.

	*Unemployment as a Percentage National Labour Force**	*Government Minimum Employment Programme (1000 workers)*	*National Index of Wages and Salaries*
1970	5.7	—	100.0#
1971	3.8	—	—
1973	4.8	—	83.0@
1974	9.2	—	64.5@@
1975	15.3	60.6	60.4
1976	21.1	157.8	63.0
1977	20.0	187.7	71.7
1978	18.6	145.8	75.1
1979	17.7	133.9	82.2
1980	17.9	190.7	89.1
1981	15.7	185.6	94.5
1982	22.6	245.6<	103.1
1983	34.6	491.6<>	—

* Includes minimum employment workers after introduction of this programme in 1975

Yearly average

@ First eight months only
@@ Second quarter figure
< Includes new employment programme for heads of families
<> Average of first four months

SOURCES: A. Foxley, *Experimentos neoliberales en America Latina* (Santiago: Colección Estudios CIEPLAN No. 7 1982) pp. 45 and 69; Mario Marcel, *Ciclo Economico e Indicadores: Chile, 1974–1982* (Santiago: CIEPLAN Notas Tecnicas No. 59, 1983) p. 91; and Programa de Economia de Trabajo, *Situación Economica de los trabajadores*, Informe No. 8, *La crisis economica 1982–3*, August 1983.

Appendix 2 Labour Force and Social Structure 1875–1982

TABLE 6A.II *Manufacturing Employment in Small Firms as a Percentage of Total Sectoral Employment, 1925–60 and 1960–77*

SERIES 'a'			*SERIES 'b'*		
Firms with four workers or fewer			*Firms with nine workers or fewer*		
Year	*Employment*	*Percentage Total Employed*	*Year*	*Employment*	*Percentage Total Employed*
1925	198 000	70.7	1960	196 000	48.8
1930	161 000	62.6	1961	211 000	50.2
1935	150 000	60.0	1962	234 000	52.4
1940	140 000	50.4	1963	235 000	51.5
1945	170 000	51.4	1964	235 000	50.4
1950	194 000	50.7	1965	250 000	50.6
1955	203 000	48.0	1966*	273 000	52.1
1960	207 000	46.3	1977	329 000	57.1

* No data on manufacturing firms with less than 50 workers were collected between 1967 and 1977.

SOURCES: Series 'a': ECLA (1966) figures quoted in David Landes, *Import-substitution, Industrialization and the Demand for Labor in Urban Chile, 1930–1970* (PhD Ann Arbor, Michigan).
Series 'b': PREALC figures quoted in Lagos and Tokman, 'Monetarism, Employment and Social Stratification *World Development* XII (1984) 1.

The inconsistencies vividly illustrate the inherent difficulty of collecting reliable data on this sector.

TABLE 6A.III *Distribution of the Chilean Labour Force by Sector, 1875–1930*

	1875	*1907*	*1920*	*1930*
Total Labour Force (1000)	865.7	1240.7	1370.2	1460.5
	(%)	(%)	(%)	(%)
	100.0	100.0	100.0	100.0
NON-AGRICULTURAL, GOODS-PRODUCING SECTORS	29.5	22.2	22.6	25.9
Mining	3.4	2.9	3.9	5.7
Manufacturing*	23.4	16.2	15.7	15.9
Construction	2.8	3.1	3.0	4.3
AGRICULTURE#	44.5	36.9	36.3	37.5
SERVICES AND OTHERS	25.9	40.9	41.4	36.6

* including artisan
# The low percentage of the labour force directly employed in agriculture reflects the importance of rural handicrafts; see Salazar (1984).

SOURCE: Gabriel Palma, *Growth and Structure of Chilean Manufacturing Industry from 1820–1935* (PhD, Oxford, 1979). Chilean Censuses provide valuable material on population and the economy from the 1850s, although employment data were classified by profession, not sector, until 1920 and inconsistently thereafter until 1940. The above are thus estimates based on Palma's own reclassification.

TABLE 6A.IV *Distribution of the Labour Force by Sector, 1930–82 (1000 workers and percentage)*

	1930	*1940*	*1952*	*1960*	*1970*	*1982**
** Data for 1982 do not include the unemployed, distributed previously by sector.*						
TOTAL	1460.5	1810.3	2155.3	2388.7	2607.4	3191.4
%	*100.0*	*100.0*	*100.0*	*100.0*	*100.0*	*100.0*
AGRICULTURE	583.9	716.6	749.5	753.5	627.6	537.1
%	*40.0*	*39.6*	*34.8*	*31.5*	*24.1*	*16.8*
MINING	77.6	96.1	101.4	91.1	75.3	59.0
%	*5.3*	*5.3*	*4.7*	*3.8*	*2.8*	*1.8*
MANUFACTURING	206.5	287.9	408.7	428.9	415.4	502.7
%	*14.1*	*15.9*	*19.0*	*18.0*	*15.9*	*15.6*
ELECTRICITY and	20.0@	20.0@	20.5	18.9	21.3	27.3
%	*1.4@*	*1.1@*	*1.0*	*0.8*	*0.8*	*0.9*
CONSTRUCTION	56.8	58.1	102.3	135.8	148.5	161.5
%	*3.9*	*3.2*	*4.7*	*5.7*	*5.7*	*5.1*
SUBTOTAL: NON-AGRICULTURAL GOODS PRODUCING SECTORS						
%	*24.7*	*25.5*	*29.4*	*28.2*	*25.3*	*23.5*
TRANSPORT	65.3@	64.8@	95.3	117.9	155.5	207.7
%	*4.5@*	*3.6@*	*4.9*	*4.9*	*4.9*	*6.0*
COMMERCE	113.3	147.7	222.9	241.0	303.1	614.1
%	*7.8*	*8.2*	*10.3*	*10.1*	*11.6*	*19.2*
FINANCE	9.4	11.2	@@	@@	42.0	115.6
%	*0.6*	*0.6*	@@	@@	*1.6*	*3.6*
OTHER SERVICES	256.8	433.9	478.9	544.3	667.5	1023.1
%	*17.5*	*24.0*	*22.0*	*22.7*	*25.6*	*32.1*
SUBTOTAL: TERTIARY SECTOR						
%	*30.4@*	*36.3*	*36.9*	*37.8*	*44.8*	*61.4*
UNSPECIFIED	148.6	70.1	77.3	148.5	226.4	2.3
%	*10.2*	*3.8*	*3.6*	*6.2*	*8.7*	*0.1*

@ CORFO figures for these years fused Transport with Electricity and Gas into a single sector. 20 000 workers have therefore been deducted from 'transport' to provide an estimate for electricity and other public utilities, and percentage weights calculated on this basis.
@@ Financial services were not disaggregated from other services in these years.

SOURCES: 1930 and 1940 figures from CORFO data: 1951, 1960 and 1970 Census data, 1982 from the INE *Compendio Estadistica* based on Nov. 1981 survey data.

TABLE 6A.V *Wage-Earners and Others as a Percentage of The Labour Force by Sector, 1952–79*

SECTOR	*YEAR*	*WAGE-EARNERS*	*EMPLOYERS*	*OTHERS**	*TOTAL*
Agriculture	1952	67.7	2.5	29.8	100
	1960	67.0	1.9	31.1	100
	1970	61.8	3.3	34.9	100
	1979	44.4	2.3	53.3	100
Mining	1952	95.7	0.6	3.7	100
	1960	96.2	0.3	3.5	100
	1970	93.1	0.9	6.0	100
	1979	90.3	0.7	9.0	100
Manufacturing	1952	69.0	2.6	28.4	100
	1960	76.1	1.9	22.0	100
	1970	80.5	2.3	17.2	100
	1979	76.2	2.7	21.1	100
Construction	1952	85.6	1.4	13.0	100
	1960	88.7	0.7	10.6	100
	1970	87.9	1.1	11.0	100
	1979	75.0	2.7	22.3	100
Transport	1952	83.4	1.0	15.6	100
	1960	81.2	0.7	18.1	100
	1970	76.4	3.2	20.4	100
	1979	70.6	3.3	26.1	100
Commerce	1952	47.1	4.2	48.7	100
	1960	45.7	2.8	51.5	100
	1970	44.8	7.4	47.8	100
Services	1952	86.7	0.9	12.4	100
	1960	91.4	0.6	8.0	100
	1970	82.4	1.6	16.0	100

* Self-employed, paid and unpaid family workers, unknown. Only paid family workers were counted in the 1960 Census.

SOURCES: 1952–70 figures calculated from Census data: 1979 figures based on INE Employment Survey data, from Martinez and Tironi (1983), who do not give data for Commerce and Service: using different categories and 1980 data, Lagos and Tokman (1984) reach similar conclusions.

TABLE 6A.VI *The Class Significance of 'Empleado', 1952 and 1970 (100s of workers)*

	1952	*(%)*	*1970*	*(%)*
TOTAL	417 300	100	735 200	100
Professionals and technicians	70 700	17	151 000	21
Managers and administrators	12 000	3	15 400	2
Office workers	148 300	35	223 900	31
Salespeople	21 565	5	53 200	7
Farmers, hunters, woodcutters	15 600	4	17 100	2
Miners	500	–	–	–
Drivers, chauffeurs, and so forth	26 200	6	52 100	7
Skilled workers and artisans	27 800	7	89 400	12
Unskilled workers	500	–	16 700	2
Domestic and service workers	36 300	9	60 600	8
Unknown, unspecified, unemployed	57 600	14	55 800	8

SOURCE: Censuses, 1952, 1970.

Appendix 3 Women in the Labour Force

TABLE 6A.VII *Women in the Labour Force, 1907–70 (1000s)*

YEAR	*1907**	*1920**	*1930**	*1940**	*1952*	*1960*	*1970*
% TOTAL LABOUR FORCE BY SECTOR**							
Manufacturing (with artisan)	167.3	149.2	69.0	93.1	131.9	101.8	108.6
%	56.0@	45.7@	33.4	32.3	32.3	23.7	26.1
Commerce	17.9	24.1	21.3	37.7	56.0	58.7	88.9
	16.7	17.4	18.9	25.5	25.1	24.4	29.3
Services	159.1	133.0	140.0	247.0	286.2	312.1	326.6
	62.1	47.0	52.5	55.4	59.8	57.3	47.5
Finance	——	——	0.9	1.4	——	——	9.2
			9.6	12.5			21.9
TOTAL ACTIVE	361.0	356.1	259.3	423.2	539.1	534.3	601.5
% women over 12	30.7	26.6+	21.7+	31.5	25.5	20.9	19.1
% Labour Force	28.7	26.0	17.7	23.4	25.0	22.4	23.1
DOMESTICS	67.7	102.5	——	——	——	181.4	157.4
% f. labour force	18.8	29.2				33.6	26.2

*SOURCE: 1907 and 1920 figures reclassified from existing Census data 1930

and 1940, CORFO reclassifications. Other material is taken directly from Census data.
** Only sectors where women account for more than 10 per cent of the labour force have been included.
@ These extremely high figures are consistent with Salazar's findings (1984): female artisans concentrated in the rural areas accounted for nearly 80 per cent of Chile's artisan sector in the nineteenth century.
@@ Here included to provide a measure of the importance of female white-collar workers.
+ Covarrubias (1978) attributes the 1907–30 drop in female participation rates to the expansion of secondary school education for girls. However, if female (but not male) secondary school students were included in the labour force, and assuming a rise from 11 000 in 1915 to 40 000, the proportion of women in the labour force would still only reach 20.5 per cent in 1930.

Appendix 4 Labour Movement and Politics

TABLE 6A.VIII *Political Competition in the CUT: Party voting patterns of Congress delegates 1953–68, and mass vote for CUT direct election of Executive, 1972.*

(Figures have been rounded to the nearest percentage and may not sum to 100)

	1953 (%)	*1957* (%)	*1959* (%)	*1962* (%)	*1965* (%)	*1968* (%)	*1972* (%)	*1972** (%)	*1972@* (%)
Christian Democrat	6	15	15	18	12	10	25	16	42
Radical	6	9	4	6	5	8	4	2	8
Communist	21	40	45	31	42	46	33	39	23
Socialist		23	28	28	33	22	28	33	20
(PSP	13								
S de Chile	4								
Independent	8	3							
USOPO)							1	1	
Anarchist	8	2	2	2					
MAPU							6	8	2
MIR/FTR**							3	2	4
Trotskyist	1	1	1	1	1				
Independent	7			1					
Other	27	9	5	13	7	9	1		

*manual workers only @ *empleados* only ** probably includes the Christian Left, which presented a joint list with the MIR. FTR (Federation of Revolutionary Workers) was a MIR front.

SOURCE: Delegates' affiliations. Angell (1972), p. 224, after Barria's calculations and 'inspired guesses' (1963): 1972 CUT figures. Lira in O'Brien (1976), which seem to be identical with those of Angell(n.d.), though clearer on the MIR/FTR.

All figures are rough approximations. Figures for the 1972 CUT elections were bitterly contested, and not published for several months. Baraona (1974), with different political sympathies, gives slightly different global percentages on a larger total vote: 31 per cent rather than 33 per cent for the Communist Party, 26 per cent rather than 24 per cent for the CD. His more complete summary of smaller parties gives the FTR 1.8 per cent, the Christian Left 0.6 per cent, the MIR itself only 0.1 per cent and USOPO 0.9 per cent. Other Popular Unity fractions such as API and the Social Democrats took almost 0.6 per cent, as did the PIR, a right-wing fraction of the Radicals, and Independents. Null and blank votes accounted for 2.4 per cent.

TABLE 6A.IX *Union Losses from the 1973 Coup*

STATE SECTOR	
Sindicato Unico de Trabajadores de la Educación (SUTE)	1200 of 2000 local association officers
Asociación Nacional de Empleados de Servicio de la Educación	10 of 13 federation officers
Asociación de Profesionales y Empleados de la U. de Chile	9 of 15 federation officers
Federación Nacional de Trabajadores de la Salud	1560 of 2350 local association officers
Federación de Profesionales y Técnicos del S.N. de la Salud	All federation officers
Asociación Nacional de Empleados Fiscales (ANEF)	10 out of 13 federation officers
MANUFACTURING	
Federación Metalurgica	320 of 740 plant-level officers All 32 federation officers
Federación Nacional Textil	28 out of 32 federation officers
MINING	
Confederación de Trabajadores	7 out of 13 federation officers
Federación Industrial Minera	335 out of 400 plant-level officers
DOCKS (INCLUDING CUSTOMS)	
Sindicatos de la Empresa Portuaria de Chile	51 out of 100 plant-level officers
Federación Nacional de Trabajadores	7 out of 15 federation officers
Associación de Empleados de Aduanas	7 out of 14 federation officers

SOURCE: Campero and Valenzuela (1984) p. 175, using ILO Report (1974) data.

BIBLIOGRAPHY

Books and articles have been classified by the period for which they are most important: those covering a broader period are starred.

Supplementary sources are cited in full in the text; however, I have used primary sources such as the *Boletín de la Asociación de Trabajo*, the *Boletín del Ministerio de Higiene e Seguridad*, and the *Boletín de la SOFOFA* freely to supplement information on the crucial but still under-researched period between 1925 and 1945.

1. The era of self-creation and laissez-faire

ANGELL, A. (1979), 'The origins of the Chilean Labour Movement', in R. Cohen, P. Gutkind and P. Brazier (eds), *Peasants and Proletarians* (London: Hutchinson).

BARRIA, S.J. (1953), *Los movimientos sociales de principios del siglo, 1900–1910* (Santiago: Editorial Universitaria).

BARRIA, S.J. (1960), *Los movimientos sociales en Chile desde 1910 hasta 1926* (Santiago: Editorial Universitaria).

BERGQUIST, C. (1981), *Exports, Labor and the Left: An Essay on Twentieth-Century Chilean History*, Washington, Wilson Centre, Working Paper No. 97, May.

DE SHAZO, P. (1979), 'The Valparaiso Maritime Strike of 1903 and the Development of a Revolutionary Labor Movement in Chile', *Journal of Latin American Studies*, II, 1, May, London.

*DE SHAZO, P. (1983), *Urban Workers and Labor Unions in Chile 1902–1927* (Madison: University of Wisconsin Press).

JOBET, B.J. (1955), *Luis Emilio Recabarren, Los origenes del movimiento obrero y del socialismo chileno*.

FERNANDEZ, M. (1984), 'British Nitrate Companies and the Emergence of Chile's Proletariat', in B. Munslow and H. Finch (eds), *Proletarianisation in the Third World* (London: Croom Helm).

GARIAZZU, A. (1980), *The Chilean and Argentinian Labour Movements: A Comparative Study, 1880–1930*, M. Phil. thesis, Birkbeck College, University of London.

KAEMPFFER, V.G. (1962), *Así sucedió. Sangrientos episodios de la lucha obrera en Chile* (Santiago).

MONTEON, M. (1979), 'The Enganche in the Chilean Nitrate Sector 1880–1930', *Latin American Perspectives*, Issue 22, Summer.

MONTEON, M. (1982), *Chile in the Nitrate Era: The Evolution of Economic Dependence, 1880–1930* (Madison: University of Wisconsin Press).

RAMÍREZ Necochea, H. (1956), *Historia del movimiento obrero en Chile, Antecedentes, Siglo XIX* (Santiago: Editora Austral).

SALAZAR, G. (1984), *Entrepreneurs and Peons in the Transition to Industrial Capitalism: Chile, 1820–1878*, Ph.D. thesis, University of Hull.

SEGALL, M. (1953), *Desarrollo del capitalismo en Chile* (Santiago: Editorial del Pacifico).

STICKELL, A. (1979), *Migration and Mining: Labor in Northern Chile in the Nitrate Era, 1880–1930*, Ph.D. thesis, University of Indiana.

WITKER, A. (1977), *Los trabajos y los dias de Recabarren* (Mexico: Editorial Nuestro Tiempo).

2. The era of the first form of legal unionism, 1920–73

ALEXANDER, R. (1962), *Labor Relations in Argentina, Brazil and Chile* (New York: McGraw-Hill).

ANGELL, A. (1972), *Politics and the Labour Movement in Chile* (London: Oxford University Press).

BARAONA, S.J.M. (1974), 'La evolucion del movimiento laboral', *Los actores de la realidad chilena* (Santiago: Talleres Graficos Corporación).

BARRERA, M. (1971a), 'Perspectiva historica de la huelga obrera en Chile', *Cuadernos de la Realidad Nacional*, No. 9, September, Santiago.

BARRERA, M. (1971b), 'El sindicato como instrumento de lucha de la clase obrera chilena' (Santiago: Instituto de Economía).

BARRERA, M. (1978), 'El conflicto obrero en el enclave cuprifero chileno', *Revista Mexicana de Sociología*, XL, 2, April-June, Mexico.

BARRERA, M. (1980a), *Politica Laboral y Movimiento Sindical Chileno Durante el Regimen Militar*, Washington, Wilson Centre Working Paper No. 66, May.

BARRERA, M. (1980b), 'Desarrollo economico y sindicalismo en Chile', *Revista Mexicana de Sociología*, XLII No. 3, July-September, Mexico.

BARRIA, J. (1963), *Trayectoria y estructura del movimiento obrero en Chile 1946–1962* (Santiago: INSORA).

BARRIA, J. (1967), *Las relaciones colectivas del trabajo* (Santiago: INSORA).

BARRIA, J. (1970), *El movimiento obrero en Chile, Sintesis historico-social* (Santiago: Prensa Latinoamericana).

BARRIA, J. (1971), *Historica de la CUT* (Santiago: Prensa Latinoamericana).

BARRIA, J. (1976), *El sindicalismo, fuerza social chileno* (Santiago: DERTO).

BLEST, CLOTARIO (1971), 'La escalada hacia la unidad de la clase trabajadora', *Punto Final*, No. 143, November, Santiago.

BLEST, CLOTARIO (1980), *Clotario Blest, Testigos del Siglo XX* (Santiago: Ediciones Aconcagua).

CATALAN, G. (1978/79), 'Notas sobre proyectos autoritarios corporativos en Chile', *Escritos de Teoria III–IV*, December–January, Santiago.

CHILE, HOY (1970) (Santiago: Siglo XX).

COVARRUBIAS, PAZ, and FRANCO, R. (1978) (eds), *Chile, Mujer y Sociedad* (Santiago: UNICEF).

DI TELLA, T., *et al.* (1967), *Sindicato y comunidad: dos tipos de estructura sindical latinoamericana, Huachipato y Lota* (Buenos Aires: Editorial del Instituto di Tella).

DRAKE, P. (1978), *Socialism and Populism in Chile, 1932–1952* (Urbana: University of Illinois Press).

DRAKE, P. (1979), 'Corporatism and Functionalism in Modern Chilean Politics', *Journal of Latin American Studies*, II, 1, London.

ESCOBAR, Z.A. (1940), *Compendio de la legislación social y desarrollo del movimiento obrero en Chile* (Santiago).

ESPINOSA, J.G., and ZIMBALIST, A.S. (1981), *Economic Democracy, Workers' Participation in Chilean Industry 1970–73* (New York: Academic Press).

FALETTO, E. and RUIZ, E. (1970), 'Conflicto politico y estructura social', in *CHILE, HOY*, op. cit.

FRANK, A. Gunder (1972), 'La politica economica en Chile – Del Frente Popular a la Unidad Popular', *Punto Final*, No. 153, March, Santiago.

GUERRIERI, A. and ZAPATA, F. (1967), *Sectores obreros y desarrolo en Chile* (Santiago: ILPES).

HINOJOSA ROBLES, F. (1967), *El libro de oro de los empleados particulares* (Santiago: Editorial Nascimiento).

LANDSBERGER, H., BARRERA, M. and TORO, A. (1964), 'The Chilean Labor Union Leader: A preliminary Report on His Background and Attitudes', *Industrial and Labor Relations Review*, XVII, 3, April.

LEGISLACIÓN SOCIAL SINDICATOS LEGALES EN CHILE (1937) (Santiago: Editorial Ginebra).

MAGNET, ALEJANDRO (1954), *El Padre Hurtado* (Santiago: Editorial del Pacifico).

MORRIS, J.O. (1967), *Elites, Intellectuals and the Concensus: A Study of the Social Question and the Industrial Relations System in Chile* (Ithaca, New York: Cornell University Press).

PEPPE, P., *Working Class Politics in Chile*, Ph.D. thesis, Columbia University.

PETRAS, J. (1969), *Politics and Social Forces in Chilean Development* (Berkeley: University of California Press).

PETRAS, J. and ZEITLIN, M. (1967), 'Miners and Agrarian Radicalism', *American Sociological Review*, XXXIII, 4, August.

PETRAS, J. and ZEITLIN, M. (1973), 'En torno a la situacion politica Chilena: huelga en El Tenniente', *El Trimestre Economico*, No. 160, Mexico.

RAMÍREZ NECOCHEA, H. (1965), *Orígen y formación del Partido Comunista de Chile* (Santiago: Editorial Austral).

*RODDICK, J. (1977), *The Radical Teachers, The Ideology and Political Behaviour of a Salaried 'Middle Class' Sector in Chile*, 1920–1935, Ph.D. Thesis, University of Sussex.

*RODDICK, J. (1981), 'The failure of populism in Chile: Labour movement and politics before World War II', *Boletín de Estudios Latinoamericanos y del Caribe*, No. 31, December, Amsterdam.

ROMUALDI, S. (1967), *Presidents and Peons* (New York: Funk & Wagnall).

SADER, E. (1973), *Movilización de masas y sindicalización en el gobierno U.P.* (Santiago: DESO, U. de Chile, Documento de Trabajo).

SANTA LUCIA, P. (1976), 'The Industrial Working Class and the Struggle for Power in Chile', in P. O'Brien (ed.), *Allende's Chile* (New York: Praeger).

STALLINGS, B. (1978), *Class Conflict and Economic Development in Chile*, 1958–1973 (Stanford, California: Stanford University Press).

VALENZUELA, JULIO S. (1976), 'The Chilean Labor Movement: The

Institutionalization of Conflict' in A. Valenzuela and J. Samuel Valenzuela (eds), *Chile: Politics and Society* (New Brunswick, New Jersey: Transaction Books).

VILLABLANCA, Z.H. and PORCELL, G.N. (1972), *Conflictos sociales y propaganda del Estado* (Santiago: Quimantu).

*WITKER, A. (1984), 'El movimiento obrero chileno' in P. Gonzalez Casanova (co-ord.), *Historia del movimiento obrero en America Latina*, IV (Mexico: Siglo XXI).

ZAPATA, F. (1974), *Las relaciones entre el movimiento obrero y el gobierno de Salvador Allende*, Mexico, Cuadernos del CES, No. 4.

ZAPATA, F. (1976), 'The Chilean Labor Movement and the Problems of the Transition to Socialism', *Latin American Perspectives*, Issue No. 3, Winter.

ZAPATA, F. (1979), 'Trade Union Action and Political Behaviour of the Chilean Miners of Chuquicamata' in Cohen, Gutkind and Brazier, *Peasants and Proletarians* (London: Hutchinson Library).

3. The era of military rule, 1973–84

CAMPERO, G. (1979), 'Las nuevas condiciones en las relaciones del tranajo y la accion politica en Chile', *Revista Mexicana de Sociología* XLI, 2, May-June, Mexico.

CAMPERO, G. (1981), 'Syndicalisme: evolution depuis 1973', *Amerique Latine*, No. 6, Summer, Paris.

CAMPERO, G. (1982), 'Los cambios en la estructura social', *Revista Margen*, March, Santiago.

CAMPERO, G. and VALENZUELA, J.A. (1984), *El movimiento sindical en el regimen militar chileno 1973–1981* (Santiago: Estudios ILET).

CORTAZAR, RENÉ (1980), 'Distribucion del ingreso, empleo y remuneraciones reales en Chile, 1970–1978', *Colección Estudios CIEPLAN*, June, Santiago.

CORTAZAR, RENÉ (1983), *Chile, resultados distributivos 1973–82*, CIEPLAN Notas Tecnicas No. 57, June.

*FALABELLA, G. (1980), *Labour under Authoritarian Regimes: the Chilean Union Movement, 1973–79*, Ph.D. thesis, University of Sussex.

*FALABELLA, G. (1982?), *Labour in Chile under the Junta 1973–1979*, London, University of London Institute of Latin American Studies, Working Paper No. 4.

FOXLEY, A. (1982), *Experimentos neoliberales en America Latina*, Colección Estudios CIEPLAN, Mar. 1982, No. 7, Santiago.

HAWORTH, N. and RODDICK, J. (1981), Labour and Monetarism in Chile 1975–80', *Bulletin of Latin American Research*, I, 1, October.

HAWORTH, N. and RODDICK, J. (1982), 'Tres Cambios de Rumbo en la Politica Laboral del Gobierno Militar en Chile', in B. Gallitelli and A. Thompson (eds), *Sindicalismo y regimenes autoritarios en Argentina y Chile* (Amsterdam: CEDLA).

HAWORTH, N. and RODDICK, J. (1983), *Chile, 1924 and 1979: Labour policy and industrial relations through two revolutions*, Glasgow, University of Glasgow Institute of Latin American Studies, Occasional Papers No. 42.

HURTADO-BECA, C. (1981), 'Chile 1973–1981: Desarticulación y reestructuración autoritaria del movimiento sindical,' *Boletín de Estudios Latinoamericanos y del Caribe*, No. 31, December, Amsterdam.

LAGOS, R. and TOKMAN, V.E. (1984), 'Monetarism, Employment and Social Stratification,' *World Development*, XII, 1.

MARTINEZ, J. and TIRONI, E. (1982), 'La clase obrera en el nuevo estilo de desarrollo: un enfoque estructural', *Revista Mexicana de Sociología*, XLIV, 2, April–June.

MARTINEZ, J. and TIRONI, E. (1983), *Clase Obrera y Modelo Economico, Un estudio del peso y la estructura del proletariado en Chile, 1973–1980*, Santiago, SUR Documento de Trabajo, No. 21, January.

MELLER, P., CORTAZAR, R. and MARSHALL, J. (1979), 'La evolución del empleo en Chile: 1974–1978', *Colección Estudios CIEPLAN*, No. 2., December, Santiago.

MENDEZ, J.C. (1980), *Chilean Socioeconomic Overview* (Santiago: Banco Central de Chile).

O'BRIEN, P. (1984), 'Authoritarianism and Monetarism in Chile, 1973–1983', *Socialist Review XIV*, 5, No. 77, September/October.

O'BRIEN, P. and RODDICK, J. (1983) *Chile: the Pinochet Decade* (London: Latin American Bureau).

QUIROGA, A. (1984), 'El movimiento social en Chile. Balance de un ano (1983–1984)', *Arauco*, I, 1, June/July, Santiago.

RUIZ-TAGLE, J. (1980), *Antecedentes para el estudio de los salarios y sueldos en una perspectiva historica: 1959–1979*, Academia de Humanismo Cristiano Programa de Economia del Trabajo, March, Santiago.

7 Colombia

Daniel Pécaut

HISTORICAL OVERVIEW

The rise of the working-class: 1905–30

Economic development came late to Colombia. To be sure, coffee exports had reached a fairly high level by the years 1880–95, but it was not until the beginning of the twentieth century that their full impact became visible. They tripled in volume between 1895 and 1918 and tripled again during the next 12 years. Whereas coffee accounted for 39 per cent of total exports during the period 1905–09, that figure had risen to 69 per cent by 1925–29.[1] Coffee cultivation, which had been mainly concentrated in the west of the country, spread eastwards at a rapid rate as a result of colonisation from Antiocha towards Caldas and the northern Cauca valley. While this colonisation did not end the pre-eminent role of large property it did lead to the emergence of an important stratum of small and medium producers whose contribution to production was by no means negligible[2] and whose expansion was especially noteworthy on the eve of the Great Depression.[3] The coffee bourgeoisie was thus not affected because its most powerful fraction derived a large part of its profits from purely commercial activities.[4] By setting up the National Federation of Coffee Growers in 1927, it took an important step towards asserting its economic and political authority.

Industry began to develop as exports expanded. The case of Medellín, cradle of the large textile industry, demonstrates the interconnections between the commercial and the industrial bourgeoisies. Industrial take-off, which started during the years 1905–10, accelerated after 1920 with the arrival on a large scale of American capital which triggered a rapid growth of industrial as well as of infrastructural investments, particularly in roads and railways.

Paradoxically, these transformations took place at a time when political structures in Colombia remained unchanged. During the 1880s, the Conservative Party became the most influential political force in the country at the expense of the Liberal Party, whose federalist vision and free-trade policies had failed. Having come out of various civil wars and of the disastrous Thousand-Day War, which shook the country from 1899 to 1902, as the victorious party, it held on to power through electoral manipulation and through the support it received from the Church as the guardian of order. To be sure, the party had a solid base of political support among the Antiochian bourgeoisie and it was able to adapt the apparatus of the State to the requirements of its new economic functions. However, after 1926, it lost the confidence of large sectors of the bourgeoisie by failing to control the 'dance of the millions' which resulted from a series of foreign loans and, more significantly, to face up to a sharp rise in the level of social conflict. These conflicts were primarily agrarian in nature, involving salary demands put forward by *peones*, demands by sharecroppers for a readjustment of the charges they had to pay and by colonists wanting legal title to their land. For ten years, from the mid-1920s to 1935, these struggles shook the great coffee estates of Cundinamarca. However, there were also other kinds of conflicts, other kinds of struggles which foreshadowed the emergence of the working-class.

The working-class as such was still not very large in 1925–30; the greatest number of workers were artisans. 'Large industry' involved in the production of textiles, beverages and tobacco, employed at the most 30 000 workers. Another 20 000 worked in transportation, including the railways, as well as inland and maritime shipping. Public works employed a highly fluctuating labour force which rose to almost 40 000 at the height of the boom in 1928.

Two things should be noted at this stage. First, foreign immigration made no significant contribution to the formation of the working-class; the reserves of rural labour were sufficient to supply the requirements of the dynamic sectors. Secondly, the workers were spread among several regional centres – Bogota, Medellín, Cali and Barranguilla – each with its own specific cultural features. Except in Barranguilla which was a major maritime port, contacts with representatives of the various currents of the international labour movement were very limited. Because of its geographical fragmentation, the Colombian labour movement was not influenced by the debates and theoretical divisions of the period to the same extent as many other countries of the sub-continent.

Industrial workers and artisans did not play a predominant role in the social conflicts of the 1918–30 period. Some strikes did take place in factories in Bogota, Cali and even Medellín. There were even some spectacular actions taken by groups of artisans, either to press for certain specific objectives – as in the case of the demonstrations of 1919 protesting against the importation of military uniforms[5] – or in defence of certain political objectives. However, the greatest struggles involved workers in the service sector and in foreign enclaves.

The most combative sectors – and the least isolated one from the other – were the railway workers who were distributed throughout the various parts of the rail network, and the dockers and seamen who worked in the maritime ports as well as on the Magdalena river through which most of Colombia's international trade was routed. In January 1918 a powerful movement of dockers and railway workers shook Cartagena, Barranquilla and Santa Marta. In 1919, 1920, 1924 and again in 1926, strikes were held on certain railway lines, sometimes in sympathy or solidarity with work stoppages in the ports of the Magdalena river. More often than not, attempts to co-ordinate these various actions were unsuccessful, but in spite of these difficulties, discontent soon spread to Girardot, Honda, La Dorada and Barranquilla, all places where the Magdalena river comes into contact with the railway system.[6]

The foreign enclaves were mainly the oil fields and the plantations of the United Fruit Company. Major strikes took place in 1924 and 1927 at the major oil field of Barrancabermeja operated by the Tropical Oil Company, a subsidiary of Standard Oil of New Jersey. In both cases, the strikes were ill prepared; they were dealt with by the government and the company as acts of insurrection. The strikes failed and resulted in large scale dismissals and heavy prison sentences. The events which took place in the plantations of the United Fruit Company at about the same time were even more tragic. After many years of accumulated grievances about the living and working conditions suffered by a work force of 25 000 people, a major strike erupted in January 1928. At the company's request, the army was called in to crush the strike at a cost of several hundred lives. The Colombian public was only told of the massacre several months later through the interventions in the Chamber of a young parliamentarian called Jorge Eliecer Gaitan. As a result, the conservative regime suffered even greater discredit.

These various actions were only rarely carried out by trade unions as such; there were, in fact, very few properly constituted unions and those that existed were mainly made up of artisans. They had little regard for legal regulations. Two pieces of legislation regulated the right to strike. The first, adopted in 1919, asserted that the right to strike could not be exercised at the expense of the right to work.

Another, adopted a year later, set up a compulsory procedure to be followed before any strike could take place, involving an initial stage of direct negotiations followed where necessary by third-party arbitration. A third feature of the 1920 legislation made strikes illegal in strategic sectors of the economy, including the transport sector. These provisions were ignored by workers, employers and government alike.[7] Conflicts often took the form of working-to-rule and were used to compel employers to negotiate. Beyond this, there was also the expression of a diffuse solidarity which was gradually spreading among the workers – not only in the transport sector – and of a generalised hostility towards the conservative regime, which went deeper than the adversarial attitudes associated with the formulation of economic demands.

Certainly these groups of workers also showed divergent political tendencies. During the years 1918–22 many of them identified themselves with 'socialism', but it was a 'socialism' largely associated with the Liberal Party; in 1922 these groups supported the liberal leader Benjamin Herrera in the presidential election. Simultaneously, anarcho-syndicalist elements began to crystallise, in Bogota around a group called *Antorcha libertaria*, and in the Atlantic region, particularly in Barranquilla, around the newspaper *Via Libre* and the Workers' Federation of the Atlantic Coast (*Federación Obrera del Litoral Atlantico*). A communist current also became noticeable from 1924–25. Competition among these tendencies produced a division within the workers' congress which met in Bogota in 1924 with the intention of setting up a trade union confederation. At a second congress held a year later, the communists succeeded in placing Ignacio Torres Giraldo on the secretariat of the new National Workers' Confederation (*Confederación Obrera Nacional* – CON) and in ensuring that the CON would join the *Internationale Syndicale Rouge*. The Revolutionary Socialist Party (*Partido Socialista Revolucionario* – PSR) created in 1926, was also under strong communist influence; later, in 1930, it was to provide the raw material out of which the Communist Party was created.

It is easy to give an exaggerated impression of the importance and coherence of these divisions. A man such as Eduardo Raul Mahecha who stood behind a series of actions up and down the Magdalena river does not fit any category or label. The Marxism of someone like Ignacio Torres Girando, even more so of a Maria Cano – the voice of the oppressed in 1926–30 – cannot be assimilated to Bolshevism. The PSR was severely criticised by the International in 1930 for its 'weaknesses' and its 'deviations'. Not only was it still heavily influenced by artisan elements; it also remained under the spell of liberalism. This led the party to become identified with a number of political initiatives: attempted putschs in 1928–29 involving 'revolutionary-socialists' and veterans of the civil wars, which led to the insurrections of Tolima and Santander in July 1929; reformist projects which brought together representatives of the popular movement and a liberal intellectual aristocracy[8] in response to the agrarian conflicts of Cundinamarca; finally, a modernisation spirit promoted by Alfonso López Pumarejo, a representative of the upper liberal bourgeoisie, to which urban popular sectors responded with favour.

It is therefore not surprising that the success of the liberal candidate at the 1930 presidential elections – an achievement made possible by a division within the Conservative Party – brought about important changes in the relationship between the working-class and State institutions.

Trade unionism during the liberal period: 1930–45

Because of the traditional links between the Liberal Party and the popular sectors, the new relationship became visible as early as 1930. In 1935–36, however, the change acquired a spectacular character. Having been elected president in 1934, Alfonso López Pumarejo announced a series of reforms to the cry of 'the revolution marches on'. Among these, a reform of land tenure was put forward as a means of bringing to an end the struggle over land which had sharpened in Cundinamarca and Tolima. Other aspects of the reformist programme dealt with taxation, the status of the National Federation of Coffee Growers and the trade unions themselves. While no new measures were adopted in the area of labour relations, there was clear evidence that a new attitude now prevailed: López Pumarejo began to intervene in labour disputes, to promote the setting up of trade unions and, in 1936, of a trade union confederation to be called the Confederation of Colombian Workers (*Confederación de Trabajadores de Colombia* – CTC). He was rewarded by enthusiastic labour support. The *rapprochement* reached its peak on 1 May 1936 when political leaders associated with the labour movement, including some communists, were invited to address the crowd from the balcony of the presidential palace. Communists and socialists considered then that they were part of a genuine Popular Front. Later on, the level of enthusiasm was to subside from time to time, but the alliance with the Liberal Party was never broken. Indeed, Liberals and trade unionists moved even closer together in 1944–45 during the second presidency of Alfonso López Pumarejo, when the need to form a front against the 'fascist threat' and the Conservative Party became a matter of high priority, and when social legislation being promulgated seemed to be the harbinger of a new reformist era.

Political alliances and the liberal model of economic development
There is no basis for arguing that this relationship between the liberal regime and the trade unions developed as a result of a 'crisis of hegemony' or a 'compromise state' that might have emerged following the supposed collapse of 'oligarchical rule'. The agro-export sector did suffer the effects of the crisis, at least for a while. However, because a large number of small producers absorbed much of the shock of the crisis and Brazil's coffee policy made it possible for Colombia to avoid taking strong interventionary measures, the agro-export sector was able to maintain – indeed to consolidate – its power. While the Coffee Producers Federation had to make room for a representative of the State, it continued to function as a private organisation. In fact, it became the institution which allowed other interest groups to demonstrate an obstinate commitment to 'economic liberalism'.[9] To be sure, examples of State intervention became numerous, but they did not challenge any of the privileges and prerogatives of the various fractions of the bourgeoisie. Thanks to an average annual industrial growth rate of 10.8 per cent between 1933 and 1938, and of 6 per cent from 1939 to 1945, the industrial bourgeoisie began to consolidate itself. However, it did not surrender its close ties with the coffee and the import bourgeoisies, and it continued to maintain an unremittingly hostile attitude towards an expanding trade union movement and the recognition of new social rights.

There is no basis for believing in the emergence of the so-called 'middle sectors' in Colombia. López Pumarejo and his family had been heavily involved in financial activities linked with the coffee sector; the country was governed by a bourgeois aristocracy which left to the middle sectors certain subordinate powers in local politics.

Concessions made to the trade unions did not threaten the liberal model of economic development which was by then becoming stabilised. Until 1944–45 no labour legislation of any significance was adopted. Real wages dropped significantly to the point where they were probably lower in 1944–45 than they had been in 1933.[10] At no point was government policy presented in populist terms. There were two objectives behind government overtures towards the trade unions. The first was to provide the State with a social base which would substantiate its claims to represent the unity of the nation over and above the partial and short-term interest of the bourgeoisie. The second objective, by far the most important, was specifically political in nature. With the suffrage effectively becoming universal, and with a rate of urbanisation that had risen from 23.2 per cent to 34 per cent between 1925 and 1945, the search for a secure electoral majority had assumed great importance for the Liberal Party. The second objective was thus to ensure that the party would be in a position to mobilise the support of the new urban masses.

Political unity by proxy

How can the unions' sudden allegiance to the Liberal Party best be interpreted? In terms of the workers' rural origins? Even if we suppose that this factor has played the role which certain sociologists have assigned to it, it is doubtful that it had a significant influence. In 1938 the working-class was made up of no more than 80 000 to 100 000 persons (in comparison with 350 000 artisans);[11] it is unlikely that this slow growth in working-class numbers should have been achieved through 'rural' migration. Could the unions' Liberal allegiance be explained in terms of the Communist Party's change of political direction at the end of 1935? In fact, the communists were the first to realise as early as 1933–34, at a time when they were still claiming to maintain a policy of total opposition to liberalism, that the base of the party, including the population living along the Magdalen River, were being seduced by liberal promises. The fact remains that the support later offered to various Liberal governments by the Communist Party – in search of a democratic-bourgeois revolution and seeking allies in the struggle against the fascist threat – certainly contributed to the consolidation of this political alliance. A third explanation of the unions' support for liberalism might focus on concessions offered by the regime, but these were few and far between.

Going back to the points made earlier, at no time had the urban popular sectors completely escaped the hold of the Liberal Party. Between 1928 and 1933 the workers' movement was losing ground in spite of having staged a number of spectacular actions. The economic crisis was associated with a reduction both in workers' strikes and inter-regional solidarity. For different reasons, industrial workers, service sector workers and artisans came to respond favourably to the stated intentions of the Liberal governments. Spread over many small factories, faced with employers who refused to countenance the formation of unions and lacking a trade tradition, the industrial workers put their faith in legislation and intervention 'from above'. Service sector workers either worked for the State or depended on it indirectly. As for artisans, more than ever they called from some sort of protective apparatus to help them survive. Thus, those three sub-sectors could only subscribe to the 'developmental' language put forward by Alfonso López and directed against the 'archaic' forces as well as the 'egoism' of the industrialists.

Moreover, it was not a difficult task to gain the workers' support by putting forward a vision of national unity over and above class divisions, which the State was now fostering. Fragmented as they were, both by regions and by economic sectors, they found in this new relationship with the State and the Liberal Party the means of achieving their own unity. To be sure, it was a political unity by proxy, but nevertheless one whose representation exercised a certain fascination, even though it was a vision which could not escape being partisan, one which was entirely compatible with traditional political practices. The State had only achieved a most precarious kind of cohesion based on a thriving liberal model of development, and alignment with the Liberal Party had spawned a political identity directed much more against the Conservative Party than against the archaic 'classes'.

Nevertheless, it was on the basis of this political unity by proxy that the working-class became organised into trade unions.

The setting up of trade unions

A new law governing trade union organisation was adopted in 1931. Among its provisions was a distinction between trade-based (*gremiales*) and company-based (*industriales*) unions; it also allowed unions to form federations, established compulsory legal recognition and required that strikes could only take place if supported by a two-thirds majority vote of union members.[12]

However, López Pumarejo's role was probably more decisive than this legislation in relation to the setting up of trade unions. It is difficult to know exactly how many unions were active at the time of the *revolución en marcha*. An official survey done in 1937 gave a figure of 558 unions set up between 1909 and 1937, though it pointed out that only 187 unions with a total of 34 436 members were really operating.[13] Another study also done in 1937 suggests the existence of 437 unions with a total of 41 800 members.[14] In 1936, the CTC confederation was formed; its executive committee included only four communists while eight posts went to the Liberals, three to the socialists and one to the anarcho-syndicalists. Regional and sectoral federations also emerged. Among the latter the most important were the Fedemal, which brought together the workers of the Magdalen River area, and Ferrovías, the federation of railway workers' unions. In fact, within the CTC, which was the sole confederation, service sector workers and artisans continued to contribute the bulk of the membership. Trade unions were just beginning in the industrial sector. So much so that out of 446 organisations represented at the CTC Congress in Cali in 1938, there were no industrial unions from Medellin, only one from Cali, none from Barranguilla and 15 from Bogota.

In general, trade unions were extremely fragile organisations. Many unions born in the period 1936–37 went into a kind of hibernation when subsequent liberal governments became more circumspect towards them. In 1940–41 the number of unions sending delegates to the CTC congress was only 200 with a total membership of 20 000. The federations were also relatively weak. The Antioquia and the Cundinamarca federations had only a limited influence on their member unions. Ferrovías, which was dominated by moderate liberals suspicious of the CTC, found it difficult to ensure that its directives would be followed throughout the country. Fedemal was the exception. In July 1937, it won a hiring monopoly throughout the Magdalen River region and succeeded in negotiating several favourable agreements, albeit at the cost of several strikes. As for the CTC, it started out living from hand to mouth, then it accepted government subsidies[15] and suffered internal divisions.

Trade unionism 'from the base' gradually became predominant. It gave rise to an atomisation of trade union demands and seemed to be the correlate of the liberal style of development. As negotiations became increasingly institutionalised, the trade unions made greater use of intermediaries such as lawyers and political figures. As a result, both the solidarity and the autonomy of the working-class were threatened.

There were few strikes during this period, almost none between 1930 and 1933. During the government of Alfonso López employers were denouncing the rapid spread of strikes; in fact the Labour

Department counted 23 in 1935, 21 in 1936, and about 20 in 1937. Towards the end of Alfonso López' first presidency and during the Second World War strikes were even rarer: nine between 1 August 1938 and 31 May 1939; not a single one 'is worth mentioning between May 1941 and April 1942'.[16] They were still rare throughout 1943 and 1944. In general, while strikes did sometime affect the industrial sector, they were much more frequent among artisans and in transportation.

The low level of strike action is even more remarkable if we remember that real wages had dropped significantly in relation to 1933, as mentioned already. The reasons for this apparent lack of militancy were essentially political. A moderate stance on the part of the unions was required by the alliance with the Liberal Party. In 1938 the CTC leadership, including the communists, condemned the 'abuse' of strikes and referred to them as 'crazy' measures. The war only reinforced this attitude.

The gap began to widen between the widely dispersed unions at the base faced with a group of employers determined to block their progress, and the political strategy of supporting the Liberal Party. At certain times, it became a veritable precipice.

The strategy of alliance with liberalism

We have already mentioned that populism was not relevant in this case. What we have, rather, is a system of restricted democracy which consolidated itself as part of the liberal model of development. The idea of corporatism is even less appropriate. In fact, trade unions retained a degree of independence demonstrated by the influence which the communists were able to exercise.

The Communist Party had considerable strength in many federations, beginning with Fedenal, which was largely under its control.[17] It also occupied key positions in the Executive Committee of the CTC, especially towards the end of this period: in 1945 it controlled eight of the 30 positions including those of general secretary, organisation secretary and treasurer.

This significant degree of influence was not incompatible with the alliance with the Liberal Party, except during the period 1940–41.[18] Indeed the Communist Party wanted to maintain this commitment, and it presented it in 1936 as a prerequisite for moving towards a popular front. Later, in 1938, the alliance was put forward as a coalition with the progressive bourgeoisie, in 1941 as an expression of the anti-fascist front, in 1945 as the implementation of the policy of 'worker-employer collaboration'. The Communist Party pushed its policy of conciliation even further where, in August 1944, it abandoned its 'communist' label and adopted the name Democratic Socialist Party, thus bringing to a close what it referred to as its 'stone age'.[19]

It seems that the strategy of alliance with the Liberal Party was an obvious choice for everyone. But it was not without danger. After 1937, the liberal regions refrained from promoting reforms that would have alienated the bourgeoisie. In 1942, with the re-election of Lopez Pumarejo, the regime entered into a deep crisis. It was, all at once, an economic crisis caused by a climate of speculation, a moral crisis provoked by the increasing interpenetration between the State and private interests, and a political crisis based, to begin with, on aggressive conservative attempts to regain power and, from 1944, on the rise of the *gaitanista* movement. An attempted military coup in 1944 was a direct result of this malaise. Alfonso López was forced to resign in 1945.

In spite of the increasingly discredited liberal institutions and anti-union measures then being considered by López himself, the CTC's support for liberalism continued unabated. The CTC justified its attitude by referring to social measures adopted in 1944–45 by an exhausted regime. Decree no. 2350 of 1944 and 1945 legislation created a more stable basis for trade unions and provided for a limit to the working day, paid leave and various other benefits, as well as the *fuero sindical*, a measure designed to protect the trade union leadership against arbitrary action by management. These measures were to give rise to a large number of new unions at precisely the time when the bourgeoisie as a whole was seeking to eliminate the forces that threatened to check its power.

The crisis of the regime had repercussions for the trade union movement. The underlying tension between the communists and the liberals remained in spite of the latter's conciliatory attitudes. Moreover, a new challenge, that of *gaitanista* populism, punctured the myth of a social citizenship, associated with the figure of Pumarejo, which provided the working class with a political identity.

The years of violence: 1954–57

Like many other countries, Colombia was at a crossroad in 1945. The bourgeois block came out of the war years more self-confident than ever, while the *gaitanista* movement was sweeping everything along its path. In the face of these two phenomena, the trade unionism of the CTC was bound to be the loser. Its decline and ultimate defeat ushered in a period known in Colombia as the years of *La Violencia*.

Bourgeois hegemony and political crisis

The resources that had been accumulated during the war combined with rising revenue from coffee exports, which was particularly significant from 1949 to 1954, created the conditions necessary for a period of rapid development. Industry was the first to benefit and industrial production doubled between 1945 and 1953 without the liberal model of development being put into question. The industrial bourgeoisie, dominated by the *antioquenos* and organised under ANDI (the National Association of Industrialists) chose to neglect the basic and intermediary goods sector rather than to abandon the model. The coffee bourgeoisie, the import bourgeoisie and the large landowners continued to hold on to their share of power.

After the 1946 elections which the Liberals lost as a result of internal divisions over *gaitanismo*, the Conservative Party returned to power; this did not, however, disturb the equilibrium within the bourgeois block. Neither socially nor economically were the liberal and conservative bourgeoisies differentiated. The attack on the popular sectors was launched in 1944–45 even before the political change had taken place. It continued afterwards without the old *lopista* bourgeoisie raising a voice of protest.

On the other hand, it became clear that the latent political crisis was deepening. After the assassination of Gaitan and the Bogota riots of April 1948, the *violencia* spread throughout the rural areas, masquerading as a product of the rivalry between the two parties. By 1953 it had reached such disquieting proportions that the bourgeoisie appealed to General Rojas Pinilla. This convenient manner of dealing with a serious political crisis carried no risk of the bourgeoisie losing any of its prerogatives. General Rojas Pinilla was to find that out at his own expense in 1957 when the same bourgeoisie that had carried him to power decided to overthrow him.

The war between the two parties led to a near dislocation of the State apparatus and to a shift in the locus of politics towards the rural areas. These two developments helped give a new and unexpected lease of life both to the liberal model of development and to the system of restricted civilian democracy.[20] This could probably not have taken place without the destruction of the old trade unionism.

The rise of trade unions up to 1947

At the beginning, however, the social measures of 1944–45 allowed a sharp rise in the number of trade unions. A trade union census prepared in 1947 placed the number of unions at 892, of which 172 had been set up in 1944, 441 in 1945 and 116 in 1946. Thus some 80 per cent of all unions which existed in 1947 were created during the three previous years.

The census also shows that these same years witnessed the spread of trade unions into the private industrial sector. The following table shows the number of unions in the industrial sector for the three largest Colombian cities.

TABLE 7.1 *Industrial Sector Unions in Three Largest Cities*

	BOGOTA		*MEDELLIN*		*CALI*	
	No. of unions	No. of members	No. of unions	No. of members	No. of unions	No. of members
Set up before 1944	23	2518	1	220	1	129
between 1944–47	30	2055	19	5977	11	1476
TOTAL	53	4573	20	6197	12	1605

These figures show that trade unions were not yet well established in the industrial sector. It should also be stressed that a majority of those unions were not affiliated to the CTC but to a new confederation called the Union of Colombian Workers (*Unión de Trabajadores de Colombia-UTC*) which was linked with the Church and the Conservative Party.

The next table, also compiled from the 1947 trade union census, shows the degree to which CTC unions were concentrated in the public sector.

We can see that in spite of the political crisis, the CTC retained its ties to the Liberal Party. Recruitment for the public sector was based on party affiliation and the Liberal Party, which was involved in government until 1949, controlled most public sector jobs. However in the eyes of the *gaitanistas* and of the bourgeoisie, this pattern of recruitment identified the CTC as the representative of a 'privileged' sector.

TABLE 7.2 *Participation of Public-Sector Workers in the Three Major CTC Federations*

	ALL UNIONS		PUBLIC SECTOR		
	No. of unions	*No. of members*	*No. of unions*	*No. of members*	*Percentage of public sector members*
Workers' Federation of Cundinamarca	134	31 174	26	12 742	40
Workers' Federation of Antioquia	31	8 564	8	4 912	57.3
Workers' Federation of the Cauca Valley	40	15 305	7	9 781	63.9

NOTE: The category 'public sector workers' includes government employees, municipal employees and employees of decentralised public services. One thousand workers have been added to the figures to take account of the Antioquia railway workers' union who were not included in the census.

Resistance against gaitanismo and conservatism

In the conflict between *gaitanismo* and traditional liberalism which erupted in 1944, the CTC stood firmly on the side of the latter. It supported Gaitan's liberal opponent during the 1946 presidential elections in spite of the fact that he was identified with the 'oligarchy', and at its 1945 congress, the CTC condemned the *gaitanista* movement as 'divisionist, fascist, anarchist and dangerous'. Most of the CTC liberals held that view. But the most extreme anti-*gaitanistas* were undoubtedly the communists, who had always viewed the *gaitanista* phenomenon as 'the sharp end of fascism'[21] and were pressing the CTC to take a clear cut position.

Meanwhile, Gaitan was hostile to both the CTC and the communists. He saw the Confederation both as an object of manipulation by the communists and as a tool used by the oligarchy for electoral purposes. In December 1945 he even tried to establish a new trade union confederation with the support of the conservatives. The support he enjoyed among the urban masses and the response that he provoked among many unions – notably the Federation of Railway

Workers – led him to present the CTC as an apparatus cut off from its working-class base.

There is no doubt that the strikes called by the CTC between 1945 and 1947 were aimed at restoring salary levels. At the same time, they were designed to stop the rise of *gaitanismo* by ensuring that both the mood of militancy spreading throughout the country, and the confusion which followed the election of a conservative president after 1946, would turn to the CTC's advantage. This was also true of the December 1945 launched by Communist elements within Fedenal which ended in defeat and caused the downfall of this powerful CTC federation; of the October 1946 strike by the oil workers of Barrancabermeja which was accompanied by a high degree of social agitation in many cities; and it is especially true of the general strike of 13 May 1947 which followed, which the CTC leadership wanted to use in order to upstage *gaitanismo* and arrest the consolidation of conservatism in the government.

In fact, these tactics failed and *gaitanismo* continued to move forward at the expense of the CTC. By witholding support of these actions including the general strike which he had originally advocated, and by protesting hardly at all against the dismissals which the strike provoked, Gaitan helped to weaken the Confederation and the Communist Party and emerged as the unchallenged leader of the resistance to conservatism. This *gaitanista* success was taking place at a time when the social goals he had been pursuing were taking second place to the need for the federal party to return to power.

The CTC had become no more than a supportive actor in a political battle; on 9 April, when the assassination of Gaitan gave rise to a veritable social explosion in Bogota and in other cities, its role was minimal. Later, on 24 November 1949, it co-operated with the Liberal Party by launching an abortive strike encouraged by the party leadership in order to stem the rise of the most violent elements among the conservatives.

In reality, the syndicalist credentials of the CTC were lost as soon as 1947, a victim of its weaknesses, of its stubborn hostility to *gaitanismo* and of the bourgeois offensive which the CTC leadership had failed to properly understand.

Trade unionism contained

The bourgeois offensive designed to prevent the rise of an independent trade unionism began, as already mentioned, in 1945. It took different forms at different times. In the years 1945–49 the liberal and conservative bourgeoisies came together in an effort to neutralise both the CTC and the *gaitanistas*. First, the liberal government of Lleras Camargo mobilised public opinion against the 'privileged sectors' of the working-class and against Fedenal at the time of the strike of December 1945. Then, liberal labour ministers allowed the firings that took place after the strikes of 1946–47. The liberal bourgeoisie was explicit about its opposition to all new social reform measures.

From 1949 the emergency measures decreed by the government of Rojas Pinilla suppressed all autonomous working-class initiatives. The State of siege, the imprisonment of ex-trade union leaders, the expulsion of 'communists' from many enterprises removed all possibilities of action. Not only did strikes disappear but real wages began to stagnate after 1949, until by 1954 they were almost down to 1938 levels, which means that for many sectors they were inferior to those of 1933.

The most important innovation was the creation, in 1946, of a new trade union confederation, the UTC (*Unión de Trabajadores de Colombia*), under the guidance of the Catholic Church and with the support of the Conservative Party. The UTC, which spread rapidly throughout the country, was the outcome of an idea born in the 1930s that Catholic workers' organisations should be set up. In 1946 the Liberals had issued a decree designed to place the CTC in a monopoly position by outlawing 'parallel' unions as a way of stopping the growth of the UTC. This decree was abrogated in 1949 and the same year the UTC set up local federations in the principal departments. In fact, UTC unions often replaced those of the CTC thanks to management complicity and the support of the political authorities. Even the CTC's most solid areas were not immune to UTC inroads, as in the case of the oil industry where the UTC succeeded in setting up a federation in 1953. A 1955 union census demonstrated that the new confederation now enjoyed a quasi monopoly: of a total of 350 unions, 288 were affiliated to the UTC while the CTC was down to 27.

However, in spite of its rapid growth, the UTC did not have the impact of the old CTC. It rejected strikes which it saw as a 'last resort', it encouraged its member unions to put forward diffident demands rather than the traditional *pliegos de peticiones*, it promoted co-operation with employers and indeed in Antioquia it was represented by a federation controlled by employers. On the other hand, when it tried to act, it faced a series of obstacles associated with the socio-political climate. Yet, at the same time, it induced changes which were to become visible only much later. To begin with, UTC unions, albeit passive ones, moved into private industry. Local unions, which had been favoured by the Labour Code's insistence that there should be a single union per firm,[22] received a new impulse. Then, the scene was set for the appearance of a 'liberal' unionism, willing to play the game of negotiation with employers who were themselves committed to 'economic liberalism'. The emphasis on apoliticism is part of that logic. Further, the UTC joined the fight against General Rojas Pinilla's attempt to set up a trade union organisation controlled by the State, along Peronist lines. That struggle having been won, the UTC again found itself working hand in glove with employers to precipitate the general's fall from power in June 1957. This liberal unionism, which was quite foreign to populism, was to become a significant element in the system of restricted civilian democracy that was soon to emerge. Finally, in spite of its surface apoliticism, the UTC's close relation with the Conservative Party, at least during this period, was a new element connecting trade unionism with the political environment.

The years of violence, this surrogate for an authoritarian State designed to break the popular movement, can be summed up in terms of four processes affecting the working-class. First, workers lived through a period of almost complete disorganisation. With the failure of corporatist schemes,[23] they found themselves trapped in a system of direct, decentralised negotiations with employers. At the same time, the working-class was pulled into the orbit of traditional political cleavages. Finally, it lost part of its strategic political significance as a result of a shift of major sources of political power to the rural areas.

Under the banner of restricted civilian democracy: 1958–80

In 1958, after a brief military interlude, restricted civilian democracy was restored. There were many doubts about the viability of a National Front. It confirmed the political monopoly of the two traditional political parties,[24] their alternate control of the presidency, equal shares of government offices and a two-thirds majority requirement for important legislation, all seemingly designed to bring about a paralysis of the regime. However, it must be said that, with a few alterations, the model survived for the full 16 year period for which it had been planned and it has remained since 1974 – albeit with a few attenuations – the institutional keystone of the entire system.[25] The fact that it was supported by a near permanent state of seige and that it allowed the military an increasing share of power takes nothing away from the originality of the system.

This stability is especially surprising if we consider that the Colombian economy has undergone the kinds of changes usually associated with authoritarian regimes.[26] Industrialisation has shifted towards the production of consumer durables as well as intermediate and capital goods.[27] A policy of export diversification including industrial exports was launched in 1967: in 1968, non-traditional exports (as opposed to coffee and oil) accounted for less than one-third of the value of total exports. By 1974 that figure had risen to 50 per cent, a quarter of which was made up of new industrial exports.[28] Foreign investment, not very significant until 1960, rose quickly: by 1974 industrial firms with some direct foreign participation accounted for 43 per cent of industrial production and 28.3 per cent of the industrial labour force.[29] The State also increased its role with public investment climbing from 16.2 to 27.1 per cent of total investment between 1957 and 1973.

That these transformations did not bring down the system of restricted civilian democracy is probably due to the fact that the bourgeoisie did not feel threatened by the popular sectors who were still suffering the effects of the years of violence. However, this period is not a homogeneous one. Trade unionism was reconstructed from 1957 in a way which allowed the bourgeoisie and traditional political leaders to exercise considerable control over it until the years 1966–68, albeit at the cost of some concessions. This was much less true during the years that followed as the economic changes became more profound and the traditional political parties gradually lost their overall domination.

Trade union reconstruction under the National Front

Unions became active very quickly at the beginning of this period. Between 1959 and 1962 several important strikes, some of them very militant and very long, lasting up to two months, testified to the workers' combative spirit. They were now hitting the private sector, both the more traditional type of firm and the more modern ones often linked with foreign capital. Other sectors, such as banking, commerce and administration, were also affected. Strikes were especially rife around Cali where foreign investment was significant and where refugees from the *violencia* were concentrated. The dramatic strikes of 1959 in the nearby sugar *ingenios* cannot be understood without reference to the decade of violence which shook this area of the country. Bogota and Medellín were not spared. Between 1962 and 1965, as the figures shown further on indicate, the same kinds of long and difficult strikes were widespread.

To be sure, there were demands of a specific character behind these strikes, including better salaries and social benefits as well as a negotiated introduction of the so-called 'scientific organisation of work'. However, in a labour market heavily biased against workers, security of employment through the elimination of clauses which allowed employers to fire workers at will became a major goal.[30] More generally also, workers had to fight for their unions to be accepted by employers who had successfully avoided this during the years of violence and who continued to sidestep such recognition in a variety of ways.

Several of these conflicts were the expression of the resurgence of radical political tendencies among certain groups of workers. The experience of violence, the attitudes of the employers and the influence of the Cuban revolution, all these factors played a role. Many unions, especially in Cali and Bogota, were under the influence of the Communist Party. Other groups, such as banking employees, oil workers, workers in municipal enterprises and certain factories were closer to Castroist currents associated with such organisations as the MOEC and the FUAR.[31]

Thus a substantial proportion of the new reconstituted unions were able to avoid being dominated by the bourgeoisie and the traditional parties. The UTC did not lose its monopoly position simply because unions that had joined it as a result of the special circumstances prevailing before 1957 were now leaving it; it was also shaken by dissidents who took over such important departmental federations as that of the Valle. As for the CTC, it showed signs of recovering its former importance as a major confederation but not, as previously, under liberal tutelage since left-wing unions, particularly those which were close to the Communist Party, seemed to be in a position to gain control.

This takeover was not, after all, to take place. After a series of initial reversals, and in the tense atmosphere created by the 'struggle against communism', the 'moderate' unions managed to retain their predominant position. Far from being destroyed, the UTC succeeded in retaining its status as the majority confederation. Under the energetic leadership of its president, Tulio Cuevas, who is still in office, the CTC gradually distanced itself from the Church and applied itself to political bargaining within the National Front. However, it continued to give priority to demands of a mainly economic character and to nurture close relations with the two traditional parties. These developments were confirmed in January 1965 when it briefly shook the regime by threatening to call a general strike in protest against the government's economic policy.[32] As for the CTC, it was not taken over by the left. Helped by the police, by the employers and by ORIT, its liberal leadership conducted a systematic purge of all suspect unions, a policy which significantly reduced its membership and its prestige. It remained an important force only in the Atlantic zone, in Bogota and in the Cauca Valley. Nevertheless, it contributed, along with the UTC, to the task of stemming the expansion of class unionism, already handicapped by political divisions. Unable to take over the CTC, the communists decided in 1964 to set up a third confederation, the CSTC (*Confederación Sindical de Trabajadores de Colombia*) whose membership was soon to surpass that of the CTC. Other unions, closer to newly emerging currents on the left, came together in 'independent blocks' in the Valle and in Antioquia. A third group simply stayed away from the blocks and the confederations.

Approximate membership figures for 1967 are as follows: the UTC, 350 000; the CSTC, 130 000; the CTC, 100 000; the independent blocks and autonomous left unions, about 35 000. An official, though imprecise, study of union membership in Bogota conducted the same year estimated that of 62 231 union members, 15 004 belonged to the UTC, 12 496 to the CTC, 3838 to the CSTC, 1700 to a Christian Democratic federation, 16 383 to autonomous unions and 22 805 for whom no membership information was available.[33]

Government intervention, such as the refusal to recognise the CSTC until 1974, or various other repressive measures, do not provide a satisfactory explanation of the dominance of the UTC-CTC axis. Three other factors must be considered.

The first has to do with the popular sectors themselves. Their origins was largely rural: between 1951 and 1964 the rural population was increasing by 1 per cent a year compared to a rate of 5 per cent for the urban population. The figures for Bogota, Cali and Medellín were 6.8 per cent, 6.3 per cent and 6 per cent respectively. In 1964 three-quarters of the economically active population (EAP) of Bogota were born outside the capital, half had arrived within the 11 preceding years. Many had been exposed to violence, which continued, although in an attenuated form, until 1965 in various regions.[34] These various factors contributed to the emergence of an instrumental view of trade unionism and helped perpetuate the effects of political socialisation associated with the two traditional parties[35] of which the UTC and the CTC were the expression.

The second factor was the bias in favour of local trade unionism and of collective bargaining at the level of the individual firm. For the bourgeoisie, this was a means of promoting the fragmentation of the working-class and retarding its politicisation. The UTC and CTC unions found it easier to gain acceptance insofar as they fully accepted these rules of the game.

Third were the concessions that were granted with respect to wage levels and social legislation. Workers' wages, which had started to climb in 1955, were clearly on the rise during this period. Between 1955 and 1965, day labourers' real wages rose by 95 per cent.[36] This figure was far higher than the increases gained by employees, waged artisans and agricultural workers and reflected a temporary trend towards a reduction in the deep inequalities in income distribution prevailing in Colombia.[37] In addition, several measures designed to facilitate collective bargaining were adopted, notably Decree no. 2351 issued after the threatened strike of 1965 which widened the scope of the *fuero sindical*, disallowed work by those who were opposed to a legal strike, provided for the extension of benefits gained under a collective agreement to non-unionised workers and granted new benefits such as tripled hourly rates for Sunday work.[38]

These developments were taking place during a period when a drop in coffee prices on world markets was creating serious economic difficulties.[39] They show that a part of the bourgeoisie was eager to neutralise the working-class by offering short-term concessions in the hope that this might reduce opposition to the National Front and stem the rising tide of uncontrolled social protest.

The trade unions and the new industrial policy: 1967–80

From 1966, and to an even greater degree from 1970, government policy towards the unions was modified. Yet GNP growth was accelerating, reaching an annual rate of 6.2 per cent between 1966 and 1974 compared with 5 per cent during the period 1958 to 1966. Growth of a more irregular kind continued through the years 1970 to 1975. Emphasis throughout was on the need to contain labour costs in order to facilitate industrial redeployment in favour of basic and durable goods as well as goods suitable for export.

Taken globally, labour costs as a proportion of GDP dropped from 41.2 per cent in 1970 to 36.5 per cent in 1975. Real wages were now dropping considerably, especially between 1971 (index of 100) and 1977 (index of 77.4).[40] The slight improvement which took place later on did not affect the broader trend, which also reflected reduced differentials between workers' wages on the one hand, and wages prevailing in the informal and agricultural sectors on the other.[41]

The year 1966 marked a turning point in the area of social legislation. A decree issued that year stipulated that strikes should not go on beyond 43 days; after this period, the dispute would be resolved through a system of compulsory arbitration. This decree, which was approved by the UTC and the CTC, took away much of the unions' power. When collective bargaining takes place at the level of the individual firm, only a very long strike can extract significant concessions from management.[42] Subsequently, several laws and judicial decisions accentuated the trend towards a gradual reduction in trade union rights, notably through the extension of arbitration procedures.[43] Between 1974 and 1976, certain measures adopted by the López Michelsen government seemed to show that new rules of the game providing for national consultation were emerging. These measures included the legal recognition of the CSTC and of a fourth confederation, the CGT, of social democratic orientation; a suspension of the 43-day rule for strike action already mentioned, and certain other developments such as a strengthening of industrial unionism. In the end, however, these initiatives changed very little and had no impact on the fundamental objective of restricting the wages of a working-class still regarded as a privileged sector.[44]

It was also during this phase that the strengthening of the State apparatus and the crisis of the traditional parties became apparent. The State was reinforced by granting greater powers to the Executive Branch,[45] by giving new roles to a technocracy dedicated to economic management,[46] and by the emergence of the military as an increasingly significant factor in political life. The traditional parties, perhaps mainly the Liberal Party, were divided, unable to renew themselves and practised an increasingly cynical type of clientelism which became a method of government after 1978. These two developments also interfered with each other. They may well have been the expressions of a single underlying trend, but they also contradicted each other because the State was affected by the loss of political legitimacy, and the proliferation of political clans, while the two parties avoided dislocation by appropriating parts of the State apparatus.

In any case it was clear that the traditional parties' hold on the urban and even the rural masses was becoming more and more precarious. To be sure, the two parties were more than ever overwhelmingly important in the political process. The MRL (*Movimiento Revolucionario Liberal*), a dissident Liberal faction that had served as a channel of protest for certain social sectors, had returned to the Liberal fold in 1967. The ANAPO (*Alianza Nacional Popular*), led by General Rojas Pinilla, had mobilised the support of the poorest sectors of the population and reached its peak of support in 1970 when it almost won the presidential elections, but it had collapsed soon afterward.[47] However, the two traditional parties were unable to occupy the political space that was now available. Could the disappearance of moderate oppositions have provided opportunities for other, more radical, oppositions? The extreme left did not make use of these opportunities, at least not in the electoral arena: in 1978, for example, in a political climate which seemed favourable, all the extreme left groups together only managed to obtain 4.4 per cent of the vote (1.3 per cent of registered voters) in the elections to the Senate, and 2.5 per cent of the vote (less than 1 per cent of registered voters) in the presidential election. It would appear that internal divisions were a factor in these mediocre results. But the persistence of, and indeed the spectacular increase in, guerrilla activity – including, in the case of M 19 support from many middle-class elements – suggests that opposition can take other forms. Moreover, while electoral abstention is neither new (it varied between 50 and 65 per cent since 1960) nor necessarily a form of protest, it had reached its highest levels since 1976 and made deep inroads in the regime's political base. It was particularly high in the large cities (75 per cent at the 1978 presidential elections against 32 to 42 per cent in the rural areas),[48] showing in effect that a large majority of the urban sectors stood outside the system.

Under these conditions, we may well ask to what extent the protective function of the UTC and the CTC can be maintained. Could it be that unionism has become an opposition political force by taking up the space left by a weak extreme left? Before we can answer this question, we must examine the popular roots as well as the struggles of trade unions during the period under discussion.

Trade unions in Colombian society

Structure of the economically active population

Colombia has become a mainly urban society. The economically active population (EAP) in the agricultural sector has dropped from

TABLE 7.3 *Distribution of the Population Employed in Industry, by Industrial Zone*

		Percentage
Bogotá-Soacha	144 609	29.9
Medellín-Valle Aburra	113 239	23.4
Cali-Yumbo	59 551	12.3
Barranquilla-Soledad	38 426	7.9
Rest	121 116	73.5
TOTAL	483 941	100

SOURCE: *Boletín Mensual de Estadísticas*, February 1979.

54 per cent of the total EAP in 1951 to 30 per cent in 1973. Industry was only able to absorb a limited number of these new potential workers, most of whom ended up in an overcrowded services sector.[49] Waged labour rose to something like 60 per cent of the EAP by the late 1960s. However, during the period 1970 to 1980, it is estimated that the informal sector accounted for nearly half of the total number of jobs.[50] Urban unemployment was very high in 1969–70,[51] declined during the period 1971 to 1978, and has tended to rise again in recent years. In December 1980 it reached 16.2 per cent in Medellin which was badly affected by the problems of the textile and metalurgical industries.

The industrial working-class has experienced a moderate degree of expansion, growing by 21 per cent between 1971 and 1978. In absolute numbers, counting both workers and employees, industry employed 484 000 persons[52] spread over four principal industrial sectors.

The distribution of the population employed in industry by size of firm is shown in Table 7.4. These figures show clearly that large firms account for more than half of industrial employment, and that the traditional sectors still predominate. Moreover, the regional divisions mentioned at the beginning have not entirely disappeared and remain a factor in the fragmentation of the working-class.

TABLE 7.4 *Number of Persons Employed in Industry, by Size of Firm*

Size of firm	*Number of employees*	*Percentage*
1 to 4	322+	1.1
5 to 9	4 859+	
10 to 14	12 790	2.6
15 to 19	13 308	2.7
20 to 24	13 373	2.8
25 to 49	52 149	10.8
50 to 74	36 850	7.6
75 to 99	28 937	6
100 to 199	73 373	15.2
200 and over	247 980	51.2
Total	483 941	100

+The survey covered only firms with more than 10 employees, thus these are residual figures.
SOURCE: Boletín Mensual de Estadísticas, February 1979

TABLE 7.5 *Number of Trade Unionists in Bogota in 1967 and Rate of Unionisation*

	Number of workers	*Number of unionised workers*	*Rate of unionisation*
Mines and quarries	432	621	43.4
Industry	60 272	19 431	32.2
Commerce	14 595	1 147	7.9
Transportation	11 851	10 007	84.4
Communications	480	346	75.2
Electricity, gas and water	1 715	1 277	74.5
Banking, insurance	13 148	6 511	49.5
Personal and social services	8 316	1 540	19.8
Central administration	58 902	26 858	45.6
Domestic service	5 750	2 160	37.6
Construction	2 496	593	23.7

SOURCE: G. Castro, *La realidad de la organización sindical en Bogotá* (Bogota: 1967).

Distribution of union members

Unfortunately no recent survey of trade union members in Colombia is available. In 1967 the Ministry of Labour conducted a survey in Bogota which covered 70 per cent of the employed population and sought to establish the level of unionisation in various areas of economic activity.[53]

The survey shows that the level of unionisation was especially high in the service sector, and that the number of union members in public sector services was significantly higher than in industry.

Using data obtained from the Ministry of Labour, another study gives some indication of more recent developments.[54] The information relating to the number of trade unions is based directly on this data which we should treat with caution because of problems of updating (new unions are always emerging, others disappear) and of overlapping among the various official categories of unions (*gremiales, de base, de industria*). The information concerning the number of union members was worked out on the basis of extrapolations which some would regard as questionable. Thus the figures are probably inflated.

TABLE 7.6 *Number of Trade Unions and Rate of Unionisation by Economic Sector, January 1974*

Sector	*EAP in 1973 ('000)*	*Unionised workers ('000)+*	*Percentage unionised workers in relation to EAP*	
Agriculture	684	2339	184.4	6.7
Mining	67	82.8	17.8	21.5
Industry and artisans	1051	1012.8	466.8	46.1
Electricity, gas and water	64	33.7	13.8	41
Construction	185	311.9	25.3	8.1
Commerce, restaurants, hotels	403	902.7	74.4	8.2
Transport and communications	417	270	15.6	42.8
Financial sectors	195	105.6	49.8	47.2
Communal, personal and social services	695	1424.2	207.6	14.6
Others	159			
Total	3920	6882.7	1155.5	16.8

SOURCE: Jaime Tenjo, op. cit., p. 3.

With the required reservations in mind, we note that industrial workers do not make up a majority of union members. We note also that the level of unionisation goes beyond 40 per cent in industry, banking and transportation. Finally, the data corresponding to 'communal and social services' shows the importance of public sector employees, a trend which has been accentuated in recent years and to which we shall return further on.

Membership base of various confederations and independent organisations

Here again the figures can only be approximate. There are no reliable surveys of the membership base of the confederations and frequent changes in affiliation further complicate matters. On the basis of data available at the Ministry of Labour, one author gives figures for the year 1981.

TABLE 7.7 *Number of Unions and Union Members, by Confederation, 1981*

	Syndicats	*Affiliés*
UTC	1002	450 156
CTC	677	229 734
CSTC	426	153 574
CGT	328	100 466
Indépendants	714	223 339

NOTE: For the CSTC, we have used the figure mentioned in footnote by Herran as it seems more accurate than the figure which appears in the author's table.
SOURCE: M.T. Herran, *El sindicalismo por dentro y por fuera* (Bogota: Editorial La Oveja Negra, 1981) 20–1.

These figures probably overstate the number of CTC affiliates and understate those of the CSTC. However, they reflect a trend that has been visible since 1970: a loss of influence of the two traditional confederations, the UTC and the CTC, and a corresponding gain for the CSTC and the 'independents'.

To be sure, the UTC remains the largest confederation. It has a solid base among small and medium-sized industries. It is also very influential in the metallurgical, chemical and textile industries as well as in the public sector, including the social security administration and the postal service. It also controls a number of powerful federations such as the seamen and hotel personnel federations. However, it is no longer the dominant force, as it was during the 1960–70 period, among workers in large industries.[55] While its president, Tulio Cuevas, has more or less managed to maintain his authority, it has been unable to prevent some regional federations from making a show of dissidence in recent years. Such was the case of the Santander Workers' Union which came under the influence of various left-wing currents, and of the Cundinamarca Workers' Union, part of which left the UTC in 1981 to join the CGT, mainly as a result of personal rivalries.

As for the CTC, it was in the throes of a deepening crisis until 1976. It continues to function by gradually expelling those federations and local unions that still maintain a certain degree of cohesion or by seeing them withdraw. It has lost much support in Cundinamarca and among public sector unions, and while it retained its influence in the departments of the Atlantic coast and in the Cauca Valley, its prestige was at an all time low.[56] In 1976, José Raquel Marcado, its immovable president who was the symbol of a type of unionism often referred to as *entreguista* by his opponents, was assassinated by a group of M 19 guerrillas. Since then the CTC has tried to come out of its isolation, though not without many hesitations and internal conflicts between traditionalist and more left-wing currents. In 1982 the left seemed in a dominant position and conversations were taking place with the CSTC with a view to a possible merger.

The CGT did not manage to take off at the expense of the UTC and the CTC. It gained official recognition in 1975 and has long been disrupted by divisions between moderate and more radical currents ('socialist', Trotskyists and so on). The more conciliatory faction is now the most influential as evinced by the fusion with the UTC affiliated Federation of Cundinamarca whose president, notorious for his rejection of any class-based vision, was chosen to head the CTC. CGT unions come mainly from the public sector and from small and medium industry.

The CSTC has progressed steadily during the last decade. Its leadership, which has always been closely associated with the Communist Party, has demonstrated great flexibility. It has built up a solid base among the large industrial firms, domestic as well as foreign, traditional as well as modern, particularly in the metallurgical, textile, food processing and automobile sectors; it is even stronger in the cement and construction industry. It is in this industry that, a few years ago, the CSTC managed to build up one of the few effective industrial federations: the Federation of Workers in the Construction and Cement Industry (FENALTRACONCEM) which has demonstrated much dynamism by co-ordinating demands and strike actions in several cement factories and by setting up in 1974 a unified union of workers in the construction and construction materials industry (SUTIMAC). It has also set up, though less successfully, industrial federations in the textile and metallurgical industries. It scored a significant victory when the National Federation of Public Sector Workers (FENALTRASE), an important union in a pivotal sector of Colombian trade unionism, added its 200 000 members to the ranks of the CSTC. However, these achievements are not as significant as one might think as they are highlighted by the relative impotence of the traditional confederations. In fact the CSTC has not been able to prevent other no less strategic organisations (teachers, oil workers, bank employees) from joining the large group of the 'independents'.

This group is fairly heterogeneous. It includes unions that have withdrawn from the confederations, but it also comprises other left-wing unions who are hostile to the 'pro-Soviet' stance of the CSTC. At the same time, a significant minority of the independents often take a CSTC line. The Teachers' Federation (FECODE) for example, which has more than 100 000 members, left the CSTC a few years ago under the influence of pro-Chinese and Trotskyite currents. The oil workers Federation (FEDEPETROL) has been proclaiming its independence since the 1960s under the influence of radical currents who have called several very militant strikes, often of a political character, that were severely repressed. Many large industrial unions, notably from Cali and Medellin, also belong to the group of independents. As a growing force playing a pivotal role in debates about unity, the independents have a strategic role to play in the evolution of trade unionism in Colombia. However, the electoral reverses suffered by the extreme left as well as the confused state of the 'Chinese' currents could alter this picture.

As the statistics tend to show, there is no doubt that trade union divisions contributed significantly to the working class's weak capacity for action, especially after 1977.

The strikes

The tables which follow show that the use of the strike weapon was relatively limited. We see a significant increase between 1962 and 1965 followed by a decline during the years 1967–70. The number of strikes is again on the increase in 1972, 1973 and especially in 1977. Given the drop in real wages from 1970 onward, the trade union response is neither militant nor continuing.[57]

To be sure, both the use of State repression and labour legislation constituted significant obstacles. The near permanent state of siege and, in 1978, the new security regulations meant that trade unions were under constant surveillance. The decision to ban strikes in the public sector was a powerful weapon as the notion of public sector was broadened to suit the requirements of each situation. It en-

TABLE 7.8 *Number of Strikes, of Persons on Strike and of Lost Working Days, 1962–81*

Strikes Year	*Strikes*	*Persons on strike*	*Lost working days*
1962	36	48 000	464 000+
1963	59	110 000	1 151 000
1964	75	118 000	1 925 000
1965	84	172 000	2 300 000
1966	73	100 500	–
1967	45	–	–
1968	44	41 500	494 000
1969	59	58 000	400 000
1970	64	143 000	1 200 000
1971	37	152 000	2 500 000
1972	67	162 000	3 880 000
1973	54	105 000	3 150 000
1974	75	82 800	940 000
1975	109	197 500	1 700 000
1976	58	117 110	2 128 720
1977	93	210 200	4 697 164++
1978	68	366 000	2 088 937
1979	60	90 200	2 202 400
1980	49	303 380	1 758 850
1981	94	786 580	3 084 250

+*Incomplete data*
++*Does not include the general strike of 14 September 1977*

SOURCE: Alvaro Delgado, 'Doce anos de luchas obreras', in *Estudios Marxistas*, no. 7, 1974–75, pp. 3–58, and from 1974 onward, statistics published in various issues of *Voz Proletaria*.

compassed all activities deemed to be 'essential to the life of the nation', including the public service, the oil industry, electricity and the production of certain foodstuffs. Trade union leaders and even individual strikers who ignored the strike ban were liable to be dismissed and indeed, a large number of them were. In addition, a 1966 decree significantly reduced the amount of pressure which

TABLE 7.9 *Strikes and Strikers, by Economic Sector, 1962–68 and 1975–81*

(1) Number of strikes *(2) Number of strikers*

	INDUSTRY		CONSTRUCTION		TRANSPORT		AGRICULTURE		MINING		EDUCATION*		OTHER* SERVICES		COMMERCE	
	(1)	(2)	(1)	(2)	(1)	(2)	(1)	(2)	(1)	(2)	(1)	(2)	(1)	(2)	(1)	(2)
1962	13	11 580	1	400	2	3 800	0	0	1	800	19		31 240			
1963	19	17 230	9	4 870	3	6 070	2	10 640	5	8 300	18		35 570			
1964	19	8 100	5	850	3	53 760	1	285	0	0	47		55 000			
1965	43	21 720	3	1 020	0	700	0	0	4	1 400	34		147 160			
1968	22	5 500	3	80	0	–	0	0	1	80	20		35 840			
1975	34	20 409	1	80	9	9 403	7	9 070	0	0	31	109 300	27	39 286		
1976	33	17 000	0	0	1	300	1	120	3	580	5	36 850	15	62 260		
1977	44	24 320	1	280	6	4 320	2	2 700	3	1 200	7	69 840	29	107 150	1	400
1978	25	11 517	3	1 160	3	19 800	1	80	1	100	5	165 200	30	168 113	0	0
1980	21	23 980	0	0	4	5 380	1	80	0	0	11	253 100	12	20 840	–	–
1981	31	22 560	4	3 365	13	63 412	1	37	1	150	11	622 940	33	74 115	–	–

SOURCE: Alvaro Delgado, Ibid. Data on 1979 not available.

*Between 1962 and 1968, data for Education and other Services are amalgamated.

unions could apply through using strike action by imposing compulsory arbitration after 43 days. The government has refrained from making systematic use of this procedure since 1975, but the threat of it is still there.

However, these measures do not explain everything. They did not prevent the frequent use of strike action by public sector workers whose unions accounted for a large majority of strikes. Every single year, more teachers than industrial workers were involved in strike action. In the late 1970s, other public sector employees – from the ministries, autonomous institutions and the social security administration – became involved, including doctors who staged a spectacular strike lasting 52 days in 1976. There are several factors which explain why these groups are so militant in spite of the threat of dismissal and other sanctions: low salaries, even the late payment of salaries in the case of teachers, the uncertain statutory position of these employees, disorganised administration and so on. Faced with a State in full crisis since 1975–76, 'official workers' and 'public employees' found themselves in the vanguard of trade union action.[58]

At the same time, the existence of such restrictive measures is not a sufficient explanation of the low level of strike action in the industrial sector. As we can see, the number of workers involved in strike actions in the late 1970s is barely higher than in 1965. The level of unemployment is part of the explanation during certain periods including the years 1967–70 and again after 1979. However, we must also take into account the trade union divisions which resulted from a preponderance of base unions. Strikes were often very difficult trials and went on for a long time: in 1976 they lasted on the average more than 40 days and some went on for three or four months. Often the support that could be obtained from the Federations was purely formal. Wage supplements of some 30 per cent or more, illegally added on to the basic wage by employers, helped to preserve a system of collective bargaining marked by many divisions. Co-ordinated action by several unions became impossible when, as was sometimes the case, individual plants belonging to a single industrial group were given independent legal status.[59] Moreover, local unions were not in a position successfully to confront subsidiaries of large multinationals which could easily absorb the costs of a local strike. Also, because of their monopolistic position in the domestic market, they were able to avoid having to pay the costs of prolonged conflicts. For all these reasons, industrial workers' capacity to act was generally restricted.

It should also be said that while the UTC and the CTC no longer rejected strike action, they tended to rely on negotiations. Indeed there is evidence that the CSTC and independent unions used the strike weapon much more often than the UTC and the CTC.[60]

This correlation between a 'left' orientation and the use of strikes should be seen in the context of a kind of trade unionism moving towards a class identity. A liberal approach to development had, for a long period, favoured trade union fragmentation, especially in industry, but it also meant that the unions would become used to confront employers face to face. On the other hand, the weakness of the State and the climate of repression meant that they were not vulnerable to the government's appeals for 'consultation' with the unions, appeals which never led anywhere in any case.

Towards co-ordination of trade union action

Since 1970, union struggles have gone beyond the fight against the decline in workers' purchasing power. They have also had to struggle against attempts to restrict their rights and to withdraw the fruits of previous victories.[61] They have also had to take into account the radicalisation of the popular sectors who have been without political representation since the collapse of Anapo in 1972.

The year 1977 was a crucial one. The sudden increase in strike action, and most of all the general strike launched on 14 September, as the expression of years of accumulated social tensions. It was also at that time that the National Trade Union Council (*Consejo Nacional Sindical* – CNS) was set up by the four confederations as a first step towards trade union unity. Other steps would follow, by the CSTC, by independent unions but also by certain local unions. However, none of this really means that the problem of trade union divisions had been resolved.

(a) The general strike of 14 September 1977. The possibility of calling a general strike supported by all of the existing confederations had been discussed on several occasions during the National Front period; however, disagreement among the confederations was such that these plans either led nowhere or were only partially carried out as had been the case in January 1965, January 1969 and March 1971. In fact, the problem was that the UTC and the CTC were finding it extremely difficult to go down the same road as the CSTC.

That is why the general strike of 14 September 1977 was so important. For the first time, the four confederations together took the initiative to protest declining living standards and the restrictions on political and trade union rights. Public protest went beyond trade union action and, in the periphery neighbourhoods of Bogota, grew into full-scale riots which were repressed at the cost of dozens of casualties. In the knowledge that the extreme left had only a limited capacity for mobilisation, the unions showed that they could themselves become a broad social force.

*(b) The National Trade Union Council (*CSN*).* The CNS was set up at the time of the general strike. The four confederations gave their support to a declaration stating that the activities of the CNS should be 'guided by a class orientation' and move towards 'organic and programmatic unity of the organised working class'. In fact the function of the CNS turned out to be more modest: it was to provide the means of institutionalising the dialogue among the confederations. However, the differences among them remained and in 1980–81, without leaving the CNS, the UTC and the CGT tended to give low priority to consultation with the CSTC and the CTC.

c) The unity discussions of 1981. In 1981 the independent currents as well as the CSTC took new initiatives designed to achieve a degree of unity of action. In February the Oil Workers' Federation (Fedopetrol), the Federation of Public Sector Employees (Fenaltrase) and the Teachers' Federation (Fecode), plus representatives of other federations and of 400 unions met for the first time in Zipaguira: the various extreme left groups who attended agreed in principle to set up a United Trade Union Co-ordination Committee, more dynamic than the CNS. In August, these organisations met with the CSTC, the CTC and delegates from a large number of unions. The UTC and the CGT refused to attend. In spite of this, three UTC federations and several UTC and CGT unions decided to participate.

It was at this meeting that a decision was made to call another general strike to protest against the decline in purchasing power and to attack the 'Statute of Security' which had been decreed in 1978 at a time when the regime was moving towards increasing militarisation. The UTC and the CGT withdrew their support, followed shortly thereafter by the CTC. In spite of this the strike, supported by the CSTC and the independents took place on 21 October 1981 and had a considerable impact.

(d) Other forms of co-ordination. There are indications that the loss of influence experienced by both the old confederations and the

extreme left created a need for new patterns of re-grouping. For example, the Federation of Public Sector Workers (Fenaltrase) brought together workers of different tendencies, even though it had been affiliated to the CSTC for some time. In the Department of Santander, a committee was set up at the initiative of the Oil Workers' Federation and the old – now dissident – UTC federation, to co-ordinate the activities of local unions. Finally, there is a tendency for industrial federations to come together.

(e) The limits of the evolution towards unity. It has become quite clear that more than ever before, the trade union movement can lay claim to a certain degree of independence in relation to more specifically political organisations. By doing this, labour was becoming a more autonomous social and political force.

However, this trend will not necessarily continue in the same form. The drop in the number of strikes in 1980 and the unwillingness of the UTC, the CGT and even the CTC to take part in the general strike of October 1981 demonstrates that the capacity for trade union action and co-ordination remains uncertain. In industry, local unions continue to play an essential role.

Both the UTC and the CTC have maintained close links with the traditional parties. However, the political crisis and the need not to be cut off from the grass roots have led to some slackening of these ties. There is no guarantee that in other circumstances, a new, even closer relationship with the parties might not be favoured with the UTC, the CGT and the CTC advocating 'political bargaining' to help them stand up to a potential challenge from more radical organisations.

On the other hand, the left's modest electoral successes show that the radical orientation of many unions does not attract significant support if it seeks to express something other than a certain sense of workers' identity or certain kinds of demands. Recent developments can be explained perhaps not primarily in terms of workers' revolutionary objectives but rather in terms of the need to achieve a greater degree of unity to confront employers who are increasingly associated with foreign capital and with an archaic State sliding towards authoritarianism.

Editors' note. Major developments which took place since the above contribution was written are worth signalling. First, the search for unity of the trade union movement suffered a serious setback in 1984 when two large blocks of confederations were set up along ideological lines. One was the Democratic Trade Union Front (*Frente Sindical Democratico* – FSD) which brought together the UTC, the CTC and the CGT, the three so-called 'moderate' confederations. The formation of the FSD seems to have been a response to an appeal to all local unions, which the CSTC had made some months previously, to initiate discussions on the need for a single unified labour movement. The left and the independent movement came together under the banner of the National Trade Union Co-ordinating Committee (*Coordinadora Nacional Sindical* – CNS). There were now two well-defined blocks, each with its own political orientation, one prepared to collaborate with the government (see below) and another demonstrating a greater degree of militancy in its response to the economic crisis.

The FSD demonstrated its willingness to co-operate with the government and the traditional parties by negotiating a 'social pact' with the government. By signing this agreement, which they did in 1985, the unions accepted the policies of structural adjustment which the 1980s recession was said to require, in return for concessions on wages and price controls. In view of the very harsh economic conditions created by both the recession and the government's response to it, the social pact was opposed by the rest of the trade union movement and by large sectors of the three confederations which had signed it.

NOTES

1. On the coffee economy, see J. McGreevey, *An Economic History of Colombia* (Cambridge: Cambridge University Press, 1971) and M. Palacios, *Coffee in Colombia, 1850–1970* (Cambridge: Cambridge University Press, 1980).
2. Estimates vary. According to S. Kalmanovitz, *Desarrollo de la agricultura en Colombia* (Bogota: Editorial La Carreta), in 1932 farms of less than three hectares accounted for 86.8 per cent of the total number of farms and 49 per cent of production.
3. J.A. Bejarano, 'Origenes del problema agrario', in M. Arrubla (ed.), *La agricultura colombiana en el siglo XX* (Bogota: Instituto Colombiano de Cultura, 1976) pp. 17–82.
4. M. Palacios, op. cit.
5. M. Urrutia, *Historia del sindicalismo* (Bogota: Ediciones Universidad de los Andes, 1969).

6. The reader is referred to the works of I. Torres Giraldo who was a prominent revolutionary trade unionist at the time.
7. See the memoirs of Torres Giraldo.
8. D. Montana Cuellar, *Colombia pais formal y pais real* (Buenos Aires: Editorial Platina, 1963).
9. This topic is discussed in greater depth in the author's doctoral thesis, *Sindicalisme et système politique*, Thèse de Doctorat d'Etat (Paris: Université de Paris V, 1979).
10. M. Urrutia and M. Arrubla, *Compendio de Estadísticas históricas de Colombia* (Bogota: Universidad Nacional, 1970).
11. A. Berry, 'The relevance and prospect of small scale industry in Colombia' (Bogota: 1971, mimeo).
12. On the evolution of labour legislation, see V.M. Moncayo and F. Rojas, *Luchas obreras y politica laboral en Colombia* (Bogota: Editorial La Carreta, 1978).
13. Ministerio de Gobierno, *Reseña del movimiento sindical* (Bogota: Imprenta Nacional, 1937).
14. A. Garcia, 'La economia colombiana y el movimiento sindical', in *Acción Liberal*, Nos. 43–6, February 1937, pp. 49–73.
15. These subsidies were conditioned on the public authorities having the right to inspect the books.
16. According to various reports by the Ministry of Labour and Hygiene.
17. Augusto Duran headed the federation before becoming general secretary of the party.
18. As a result of the temporary break at the beginning of the First World War.
19. See V.M. Moncayo and F. Rojas, op. cit.
20. D. Pécaut, 'Politique du café et démocratie civile restreinte: le cas de la Colombie', in *Cultures et Développement*, Vol. XII, no. 3–4, 1980.
21. See the Communist paper of the time, *El Diario Popular*.
22. Except where craft unions are also being organised.
23. Corporatism, which the government of Laureano Gómez advocated, never made any inroads. A majority of the ruling classes, including conservative elements, opposed it.
24. Other political currents had to put forward candidates under the umbrella of one or other of the two parties. Thus Communist candidates often ran under the label of the MRL, a dissident group of the Liberal Party.
25. Since 1974, all of the parties may run under their own name and the rule of alternation no longer applies. Nevertheless, the two traditional parties must still have 'equitable' representation in the government.
26. See D. Collier (ed.), *The New Authoritarianism in Latin America* (Princeton: Princeton University Press, 1979).
27. A. Berry, R. Hellman and M. Solaun (eds), *Politics of Compromise, Coalition Government in Colombia* (New Brunswick, N.J.: Transaction Books, 1980) p. 308.
28. A. Berry and R. Soligo (eds), *Economic Policy and Income Distribution in Colombia* (Boulder: Westview, 1980) p. 155ff.
29. See J.I. Arango, 'Inversion extranjera en la industria manufacturera

colombiana', in *Boletín Mensual de Estadisticas*, DANE, No. 302, September 1976, pp. 111–223.

30. Under the government of Rojas Pinilla, a 'reserve clause' had been added to the labour legislation making it easier to dismiss workers. This was used as a weapon against trade unionists.
31. The 'Worker-Peasant-Student' movement was set up in 1959 and tried to link up with armed groups who survived on the basis of violence. The United Revolutionary Action Front attempted to revive old *gaitanista* ideas by relating them to the question of solidarity with the Cuban revolution.
32. This threat of strike came at a time when the government's inability to reverse the economic downturn, as well as its low political credibility, made a military coup seem possible. Tulio Cuevas was suspected of contemplating such a possibility.
33. See details of this study in Gustavo Castro, 'La realidad de la organización sindical en Bogota', in *Documentos Politicos*, No. 78, January-February 1969, pp. 19–32.
34. F.P. Schultz, 'Internal Migration: quantitative study of rural urban migration in Colombia', in R. Nelson, P. Schultz and R. Slighton, *Structural Change in a Developing Economy* (Princeton: Princeton University Press, 1971) pp. 45–76. However, we should also say that migration to the cities was already significant during the years 1938–51. On the question of violence and its casualties, there were 174 056 casualties between 1946 and 1957, and 17 487 from 1958 to 1966. See P. Oquist, *Violencia, Conflicto y Politica en Colombia* (Bogota: IEC, 1978) pp. 18–20.
35. On the migrants' instrumental conception of trade unionism and on their political orientations, see our survey: D. Pécaut and M. Pécaut, 'La classe ouvrière en Colombie' (Paris: CEMS, 1971, mimeo).
36. See M. Urrutia, 'El desarrollo del movimiento sindical y la situacion de la clase obrera' in various authors, *Manual de Historia de Colombia* (Bogota: Biblioteca colombiana de Cultura, 1980) p. 199.
37. M. Urrutia and A. Berry, *La distribución del ingreso en Colombia* (Medellín: La Carreta, 1975). These authors show that income distribution in Colombia at that time was more unequal than in most of the large countries of Latin America. See p. 57.
38. For details on these measures, see V.M. Moncayo and F. Royas, *Luchas obreras y politica laboral en Colombia* (Bogota: La Carreta, 1978) p. 206.
39. The growth of industrial employment between 1962 and 1968 was 2.5 per cent per year, and between 1953 and 1962, 3.7 per cent. See F. Thoumi, 'Industrial Development Policies during the National Front Years', in Barry, Hellman and Solaun, op. cit., pp. 327–40.
40. See H. Gomez Buendia, 'La encrucijada laboral', in *Coyuntura Economica*, November 1977, pp. 59–79.
41. See Berry and Soligo, op.cit.
42. Certain strikes went on for as long as six months. This had brought the UTC to advocate compulsory arbitration in view of the few resources available to the unions. See *Mas allá de la huelga* (Cali: UTRAVAL, 1966).

43. Worthy of mention is Law 48 of 1968 which authorised the President to impose compulsory arbitration at any time during a conflict which threatened public order (a measure not applied so far) or allowing the workers to call for arbitration at any time; legal recognition of employers counter proposals (which in practice, prevented workers from refusing arbitration after 40 days); and 1974 legal decisions which established that arbitration tribunals should not create new benefits. See V.M. Moncayo and F. Rojas, op. cit., pp. 219–599.
44. Among the provisions of the proposed amendments to the labour legislation presented by the government appears the concept of 'integral salary' which refers to salaries plus benefits. Yet benefits were a means used by workers to defend their living conditions.
45. Through constitutional reform, as mentioned earlier.
46. See F. Cepeda and C. Mitchell, 'The trend toward technocracy', in A. Berry, R. Hellman and M. Solaun, *Politics of Compromise*, op.cit., pp. 237–56.
47. Anapo appeared as a coalition of liberals and conservatives who presented candidates under these two labels. It was only in 1971 that it became transformed into a third party, but with total lack of success.
48. R. Losada, 'El significado politico de las elecciones de 1978 en Colombia', in *Coyuntura Economica*, Vol 18, August 1978, No. 3.
49. CIE-DANE, *Contrubución al estudio del desempleo* (Bogota: DANE, 1971).
50. *Coyuntura Economica*, April 1981.
51. The International Labour Organisation had published an alarmist report which estimated open unemployment at 14 per cent of the urban population. See *Hacia el pleno empleo* (Geneva: ILO, 1970).
52. DANE, *Boletín Mensual de Estadisticas*, No. 331, February 1979, p. 99 ff.
53. G. Castro, 'La realidad de la sindicalizacion en Bogota', in *Documentos Politicos*, No. 79, January–February 1969, pp. 19–33.
54. J. Tenjo, 'Aspectos cuantitativos del movimiento sindical', in *Cuadernos Colombianos*, 2nd year, 1st trimester, 1975, pp. 1–40.
55. See A. Delgado, 'En torno al la crisis de la UTC', in *Estudios Marxistas*, No. 5, 1975, pp. 33–68.
56. Many of the key figures of the regime were worried about this because the CTC had served to keep the unions within the orbit of the traditional parties.
57. In addition to the studies by Delgado which provide the basis for the statistics in this area, see the article by H. Gomez Buendia and R. Losada, 'La actividad huelguistica en Colombia', in *Coyuntura Economica*, Vol 7, May 1977, No. 1, pp. 120–33.
58. The right to work distinguishes between these two categories. Public employees do not enjoy the right to collective bargaining and, of course, are not allowed to strike. Official workers have the right to present sets of demands and to engage in collective bargaining even if they do not have the right to strike. Many strikes were called in response to government attempts to change the status of groups of workers from official workers to public employees.

59. I.D. Osorio Ochoa, in *Tendencias y carquistas sindicales en la gran industria colombiana* (Medellín: Centro de Investigaciones EAFIT, 1981), discusses the case of the industrial group Coltejer (itself part of a large financial group) whose nine major factories were legally independent. In two of these factories there were no unions. The unions operating in the other seven belonged to different tendencies, making it impossible to co-ordinate their demands. See also M.T. Herran, *El sindicalismo por dentro y por fuera*, op. cit.
60. See the analyses by A. Delgado in *Voz Proletaria*.
61. In particular, the government tried to end the system of illegal benefits by putting forward the notion of 'integral salary' which would have allowed the State and the employers greater control over salaries. Until now, the unions have succeeded in preventing this.

BIBLIOGRAPHY

ARANJO, J.I. (1976), 'Inversión Extranjera en la Industria Manufacturera Colombiana', in *Boletín Mensual de Estadísticas*, DANE, No. 302, pp. 111–223.

BEJARANO, J.A. (1976), 'Orígenes del Problema Agrario', in M. Arrubla (ed.), *La Agricultura Colombiana en el Siglo XX* (Bogota: Instituto Colombiano de Cultura).

BERRY, A. (1971), 'The Relevance and Prospect of Small-scale Industry in Colombia', mimeo.

BERRY, A., R. HELLMAN and M. SOLAUN (eds) (1980), *Politics of Compromise – Coalition Government in Colombia* (New Brunswick, N.J.: Transaction Books).

BERRY, A. and R. SOLIGO (eds) (1980), *Economic Policy and Income Distribution in Colombia* (Boulder: Westview Books).

CASTRO, G. (1969), 'La Realidad de la Organización Sindical en Colombia', in *Documentos Politicos*, No. 78, January/February, pp. 19–32.

CIE/DANE (1971), *Contribución al Estudio del Desempleo* (Bogota: DANE).

COLLIER, D. (ed.) (1979), *The New Authoritarianism in Latin America* (Princeton: Princeton University Press).

DANE (1979), *Boletín Mensual de Estadísticas*, No. 331, February.

DELGADO, A. (1975);, 'En Torno a la Crisis de la UTC', in *Estudios Marxistas*, No. 9, pp. 33–68.

GARCIA, A. (1937), 'La Economia Colombiana y el Movimiento Sindical', in *Acción Liberal*, Nos. 43/46, February, pp. 49–73.

GOMEZ B., H. (1977), 'La Encrucijada Laboral', in *Coyuntura Economica*, November, pp. 59–79.

GOMEZ B., H. and R. LOSADA (1977), 'La Actividad Huelguística en Colombia', in *Coyuntura Economica*, Vol. VII, No. 1, May, pp. 120–33.

KALMANOVITZ, S. (1932), *Desarrollo de la Agricultura en Colombia* (Bogota: Editorial La Carrete).

LOSADA, R. (1978), 'El Significado Politico de las Elecciones de 1978 en Colombia', in *Coyuntura Economica*, Vol.. 18, No. 3, August.

MCGREEVEY, M. (1971), *An Economic History of Colombia* (Cambridge: Cambridge University Press).
MINISTERIO DE GOBIERNO (1937), *Reseña del Movimiento Sindical* (Bogota: Imprenta Nacional).
MONCAYO, V.M. and F. ROJAS (1978), *Luchas Obreras y Politica Laboral en Colombia* (Bogota: Editorial La Carreta).
MONTANA, C., D. (1963), *Colombia Pais Formal y Pais Real* (Buenos Aires: Editorial Platina).
OQUIST, P. (1978), *Violencia, Conflicto y Politica en Colombia* (Bogota: IEC).
OSORIO OCHOA, I.D. (1981), *Tendencias Carquistas Sindicales en la Gran Industria Colombiana* (Medellín: Centro de Investigaciones EAFIT).
PALACIOS, M. (1980), *Coffee in Colombia, 1850–1970* (Cambridge: Cambridge University Press).
PECAUT, D. (1980), 'Politique du café et démocratie civile restreinte', in *Cultures et Développement*, Vol. XII, No. 3–4.
PECAUT, D. (1979), *Syndicalisme et système politique*, thèse de Doctorat d'Etat, Université de Paris V.
PECAUT, D. and M. PECAUT (1971), 'La classe ouvrière en Colombie' (Paris: CEMS, mimeo).
SANCHEZ, G. (1976), *Los Bolcheviques del Libano* (Bogota: El Mohan Editores).
SCHULTZ, F.P. (1971), 'Internal Migration: Quantitative Study of Rural Urban Migration in Colombia', in R. Nelson, P. Schultz and R. Slighton, *Structural Change in a Developing Economy* (Princeton: Princeton University Press).
TENJO, J. (1975), 'Aspectos Cuantitativos del Movimiento Sindical', in *Cuadernos Colombianos*, 1st Quarter, pp. 1–40.
URRUTIA, M. (1980), 'El Desarrollo del Movimiento Sindical y la Situación de la Clase Obrera', in *Manual de Historia de Colombia* (Bogota: Biblioteca Colombiana de Cultura).
URRUTIA, H. (1969), *Historia del Sindicalismo* (Bogota: Ediciones Universidad de los Andes).
URRUTIA, M. and M. ARRUBLA (1970), *Compendio de Estadísticas Históricas de Colombia* (Bogota: Universidad Nacional).
URRUTIA, M. and A. BERRY (1975), *La Distribución del Ingreso en Colombia* (Medellín: La Carreta).
UTRAVAL (1966), *Mas Allá de la Huelga* (Cali: Ultraval).

Index

(Figures are in italic, tables in bold)